Celebrate the Day
A Teacher's Calendar of Activities, Internet Sites, and Resources for Grades 1-6

Linda Billman Venekamp
Dakota State University

Boston New York San Francisco
Mexico City Montreal Toronto London Madrid Munich Paris
Hong Kong Singapore Tokyo Cape Town Sydney

ISBN 0-205-34999-4

Printed in the United States of America

10 9 8 7 6 5 4   08 07 06 05 04

Table of Contents

August

"By the sea, by the sea,
By the beautiful sea,
You and me, you and me
Oh! How happy we'll be!"[i]

Special Month

Month of No Holidays
There are no national holidays in August, so invent some of your own. As children's author Byrd Baylor says, *"I'm in charge of celebrations."* [ii] In her award-winning book, Baylor promotes celebrating the natural phenomena we are fortunate to see, if we take time to look. Some of the days she celebrates are Dust Devil Day and Rainbow Celebration Day. I celebrate a day in January when I can see the sunrise and the moon set at the very same time; one on the eastern horizon and one on the western horizon. I call it Perfect Balance Day. What celebrations can your students make up? Of course, what's a holiday without decorations, food, games, entertainment and all of the other trappings that make it special? Have the students plan an outrageous party to celebrate their holiday.

- A Month With No Holidays? Make Up Your Own! http://www.education-world.com/a_lesson/lesson018.shtml
- I'm In Charge of Celebrations http://www.kidstrek.com/1star/celebrate.html
- Teacher Resource File: Byrd Baylor http://falcon.jmu.edu/~ramseyil/baylor.htm

Note: Evidently Canada also did not have a national holiday in August, so they created one called Civic Holiday. Civic Holiday is the first Monday in August. Sometimes it is called by other names depending on the province or territory. It is not celebrated in Quebec, Newfoundland, or Yukon.

Actually, something probably did happen on just about every day in August. Use the following sources to find out what it might be.

- Clickable Calendars http://www.clickablecalendars.com/click.htm
- Those Were The Days http://www.440.com/twtd/today.html
- On This Day http://www.nytimes.com/learning/general/onthisday/

Inventor's Month
With two famous inventor's birthdays (Orville Wright and Willis Carrier) in August, it is a perfect time to recognize those people whose creative genius and knowledge have led to inventions that enrich our lives. You may want to begin with a large group introduction to inventors and inventions by reading together the *Invention Article*. It provides a concise discussion about inventions. Then, tour the *Inventor's Museum*. And finally, see what invention is being featured at the *Inventor's Club*.

- Invention Article http://school.discovery.com/homeworkhelp/worldbook/atozscience/i/280160.html
- Inventor's Museum http://www.inventorsmuseum.com
- The Inventor's Club http://www.dkonline.com/twtw2/private/club/index.html

There are some excellent lesson plans and webquests about inventions and inventors on the Internet.

- Inventions (simple machines) http://www.pbs.org/teachersource/thismonth/may01/index.shtm
- Invention Connection http://www.cecm.winnipeg.mb.ca/resources/tours/Carolyn/invent.htm
- Inventing a New Kind of Pencil http://www.noogenesis.com/inventing/pencil/pencil_page.html
- The Greatest Inventions and Inventors http://tqjunior.thinkquest.org/5847/homepage.htm

- Necessity of the Mother of Invention
  http://curry.edschool.virginia.edu/go/edis771/98webquests/student/scynthiarigsby/home.html
- Inventors and Inventions http://www.stemnet.nf.ca/CITE/inventors.htm

Background Information
- Inventors @ About http://inventors.about.com/science/inventors/mbody.htm?once=true&

Writing Activities

1. Bio-Poem

Have the students choose an inventor to research. Share their information by writing a bio-poem.
- Inventors A – Z http://inventors.about.com/library/bl/bl1_1.htm
- The Invention Dimension http://web.mit.edu/invent/www/archive.html
- Autobiographical Poem
  http://www.geocities.com/EnchantedForest/5165/pages/poetry_samples.html#autobiographical

2. Biographical Report

Ask the students to write a report about an inventor. Have them include the following information: Life, Family, Inventions, Impact on society. They should also include drawings and a time line to make their report appealing. Make sure they have a bibliography.
- National Inventor's Hall of Fame http://www.invent.org/
  - Index of Inventions http://www.invent.org/book/book-index.html
  - Index of Inventors http://www.invent.org/book/book-text/indexbyname.html
- How to Write a Biographical Report http://mustang.coled.umn.edu/inventing/report.html
- Timeline http://www.teach-nology.com/web_tools/materials/timelines/
- How to Compile a Bibliography http://www.intac.com/~aroldi/biblio.html

Note: The same information the students are writing could be used to make a multimedia presentation using a program such as PowerPoint or a web page. Refer to the Interview with the Inventors site.
- Interview with the Inventors http://www.campusschool.dsu.edu/fieldtrips/inventor/default.htm

3. Create a rubric to give guidance to the students and help assess the product.
- Rubrics from the Staff Room http://www.odyssey.on.ca/~elaine.coxon/rubrics.htm
- Rubric Creator http://www.teach-nology.com/web_tools/rubrics/

Additional Resources
- The Great Idea Finder http://www.ideafinder.com/history/timeline.htm
- African American Inventors http://www.ehhs.cmich.edu/~rlandrum/
- Women Inventors http://www.inventorsmuseum.com/women.htm
- Smithsonian Inventors and Innovation http://www.si.edu/resource/faq/nmah/invent.htm
- Forgotten Inventors http://www.pbs.org/wgbh/amex/telephone/sfeature/index.html
- History of Toys and Games http://www.historychannel.com/cgi-bin/frameit.cgi?p=http%3A//www.historychannel.com/exhibits/toys/

Odds and Ends

There are so many cool things on the Internet related to inventions. You'll find games, interactive activities, weird and strange information. Give everyone a site and have him or her review it and then, do a walk-through for the other students.
- Inventor's Games http://www.nationalgeographic.com/features/96/inventions/
- Wacky Patent of the Month http://colitz.com/site/wacky.htm
- Welcome, Time Traveler http://popularmechanics.com/popmech/sci/time/1HOMETIME.html
- US Patent and Trademark Office
  http://www.uspto.gov/web/offices/ac/ahrpa/opa/kids/kidbright.html
- Iz and Auggie and the Invention Snatchers http://www.headbone.com/derby/invent/main.b.html
- Build It Yourself Toy Laboratory http://www1.shore.net/~biy/parade.htm

- Schoolhouse Rock: Mother Necessity
  http://www.apocalypse.org/pub/u/gilly/Schoolhouse_Rock/HTML/history/necessity.html
- Beyond 2000 http://www.nationalgeographic.com/world/9901/beyond-2000/
- Etch-a-Sketch http://www.ideafinder.com/history/inventions/story077.htm

Special Week

1st Week
Clown Week

Clowns have been entertaining us since about 2000 BC! Every culture has their clown or comic character. Read the *History of Clowning* and then learn about some of the famous clowns from our past.
- History of Clowning http://www.shrineclowns.com/educa8.html
- Clown Hall of Fame http://home.earthlink.net/~tfraymond/History/chof.html
- International Shrine Clown Association http://www.shrineclowns.com/

Famous Clowns
These clowns have been making us laugh for over a century. Learn about some famous clowns and try out some of their classic tricks.
- Famous Clowns http://home.earthlink.net/~tfraymond/History/famous-clowns.html

Emmet Kelly was the clown with the sad face who entertained audiences in movies and the circus. Kelly did not speak, which is a characteristic of many clowns. He was famous for a type of comedy technique called mime. One of his famous acts was called 'sweeping the spotlight.' After reading about Emmet Kelly and a little about mime, have your students try it out. Mime is most effective if the clown is doing something we all can relate to. Have the students brainstorm a list of daily activities, such as brushing your teeth, eating breakfast, walking to school. Then, think of something that would put a twist on it, such as having no tooth paste left in the tube, putting salt on the cereal instead of sugar by mistake, having gum on your shoe. Have the students mime that situation. Add another character – the 1st brother uses the last of the tooth paste, no one else at the breakfast table mistakes the salt for the sugar, the other kids don't have gum on their shoe and don't realize the 1st character does.
- Emmet Kelly http://www.biography.com/cgi-bin/biomain.cgi
- What is Mime? http://www.carytrivanovich.com/acad.asp?page=theart
- Marcel Marceau http://www.marceau.org/

Charlie Chaplin was not a circus clown, but played a clown character in silent movies and on stage. He not only used mime, but also developed a type of performance called slapstick. Slapstick is physical comedy; like laughing when someone slips on a banana peal. Cartoon characters often use slapstick when the bad character is outwitted by the good character and usually ends up being flattened by a heavy anvil. After having the students read the steps of classic slapstick, have them try out a couple. Again, brainstorm a list of potential scenes and try them out. WARNING: this can get out of hand, so set limits early. You don't want anyone getting hurt when the chair is pulled out from under him!
- Time 100: Charlie Chaplin http://www.time.com/time/time100/artists/profile/chaplin.html
- Slapstick http://silent-stars.com/Slapstick/home.html
- What is Slapstick? http://www.jacaranda.org/frasca/if/slapstick/SLAPSTICK.htm

Now that you have your act together, you will want to 'take it on the road' to the nearest nursing home. First, you need a little make-up.
- How To Make Face Paint
  http://kidsartscrafts.about.com/c/ht/00/07/How_Face_Paint0962932450.htm?once=true&

Ronald McDonald

Of course every student will recognize Ronald McDonald. The McDonalds Home Page offers games and activities for students to play online. It will also be interesting for your students to learn about the 'golden arches' around the world. On a more serious note, Ronald McDonald House Charities support many services for children with long-term illnesses and their families. The RMHC site will suggest ways your students can get involved.

- Welcome to McDonalds http://www.mcdonalds.com
    - Ronald and Friends http://www.mcdonalds.com/mcdonaldland/index.html
- Ronald McDonald House Charities http://www.rmhc.com/

From Opera to Rodeo

No, not just in the circus, clowns are everywhere. From operas to rodeos, clowns are entertaining audiences. Explore the wide range of clowns.

- Bugs Bunny Sings Italian Clown Opera
  http://www.angelfire.com/ma2/outhouse/Attentionspanradio/clips.html
- Opera: Pagliacci http://www.r-ds.com/opera/resource/pagliacci.htm
    - Listen http://maria_pellegrini.tripod.com/wtchlistn.html
- Chinese Opera: Traditional Clown Character - Chou
  http://www.gergo.com/pauline/china/opera.htm
- Red Sublett – Rodeo Clown http://phillip.l.sublett.com/family/RedSublett.htm
- Pro Rodeo http://www.prorodeohome.com/
    - Dr. Ben Crazy - Rodeo Clown http://www.prorodeohome.com/Duane.html (he's a South Dakota boy, you know!)

Clown and Trickster Characters in Folktales

Here are some tricky characters I think your students will like. I know there is some controversy over the Uncle Remus stories; you choose if they are appropriate for your students. After reading these stories about tricksters, try writing some of your own.

- Uncle Remus Tales http://www.uncleremus.com/selections.html
- Annotated Iktomi and Coyote http://web.utk.edu/~gwhitney/tales/inktomi/Main1.htm
- Anansi the Spider and Old Hag
  http://www.umassd.edu/specialprograms/isn/Newfiles/anansiwitch.html
- Create An Original Folktale http://www.pbs.org/williamsburg/kin/contest.html

Odds and Ends

- Clown Clip Art http://www.rats2u.com/clipart/animation/clipart_kids.htm
- Be a Clown, by Cole Porter Midi http://www.midihaven.com/midi/alpha_b2.html
- Animated Juggle Clown http://www.juggling.org/pics/ascii/stark/
- Slapstick Science http://www.slapstickscience.com/media.htm

2nd Week
National Smile Week

Harvey Ball created the first "smiley" face 1963. His little smiley face has been bringing smiles to people's faces ever since. Learn more about the smiley face, and, learn the *Smiley Face Song*.

- World Smile Cooperation http://www.worldsmile.com/aboutwsc.htm
- World Smile Day http://www.worldsmileday.com/ (October 5)
- The Smiley Face Song http://www.plainfolk.com/Smileysong.html

Create Your Own Smiley Face

Use any drawing program and make your basic circle shape. Use your imagination to go from there! If you need some ideas to get started, the *Smiley Face Place* has some pretty cute ones.

- Smiley Face Place http://www228.pair.com/judygale/

Computer Smiley Faces

Of course you can make smiley faces and other faces on the computer. What can your students think of?

:-) smile	:-D laugh	:-(frown
;-) wink	:-# braces	:-} grin

Need a little help? You can even download a smiley face freeware.
- Elizabeth's Smiley Face Dictionary
  http://www.davidson.edu/academic/economics/martin/smiley.htm
- Smiley Face http://www.angelfire.com/mb/lalim/images/smilefce.htm

Laughter is the Best Medicine

We've all heard the expression, 'laughter is the best medicine' but is it really so? Check it out.
- Is Laughter the Best Medicine? http://www.mdausa.org/publications/Quest/q34laughter.html
- Open Wide and say Ha! Laughter as Medicine http://my.webmd.com/content/article/1700.51330
- A Dose of Laughter Medicine http://www.isma.org.uk/Laughter.htm

Lets put the theory to the test. Have your students try out some of these. You're guaranteed to feel better.

> *Knock, knock.*
> *Who's there?*
> *Little old lady.*
> *Little old lady who?*
> *I didn't know you could yodel.*

- Jokes, Jokes, Jokes http://www.scatty.com/
- Kids Jokes http://www.kids-jokes.com/
- Knock Knock Jokes http://www.azkidsnet.com/JSknockjoke.htm#top
- Kids Are Punny http://www.katscratch.com/aMEWsments/mews28.html

Of course, you can always try writing your own. This site is for grown-ups but I think it is applicable for students as well.
- How to write jokes http://vt.essortment.com/writejokes_rcej.htm

Odds and Ends

Sing a song.
- Smiles http://www.melodylane.net/smiles/ (user name = abc, password = 123)

Oh, that famous Mona Lisa Smile!
- Why is Mona Lisa Smiling?
  http://www.thinkquest.org/library/lib/site_sum_outside.html?tname=13681&url=13681/data/link2.htm
- Mona Lisa Images for a Modern World http://www.studiolo.org/Mona/MONALIST.htm

3rd Week
Air Conditioning Appreciation Week
Ever since early man developed shelters, he wanted to make them more comfortable. We all know about the comfort fire brought, but did you know that as early as 180 AD Chinese inventor Ting Huan developed a water-powered fan to cool the Han Dynasty Palace? But it took an American, Willis Carrier to invent the modern air conditioner. Speaking for myself, thanks!

- Home and House http://members.madasafish.com/~ancienthistory/house&home.htm
- History of Air Conditioning
  http://www.allsands.com/History/Objects/airconditioning_vsb_gn.htm
- Engines of our Ingenuity: Willis Carrier http://www.uh.edu/engines/epi688.htm
- How Air Conditioners Work http://www.howstuffworks.com/ac.htm

Dog Days of Summer
According to mythology, the dog days of summer occur when the great star Sirius, the Dog Star, is at its zenith. Sirius, the brightest star in the summer sky, is part of the Canis Major constellation. Early people thought that Sirius added its heat to that of the sun, making this the hottest period of the year. Can your students find Sirius in the night sky? Learn a little more about modern dog days and take the *Dog Days of Summer Quiz*.

- Sirius http://antwrp.gsfc.nasa.gov/apod/ap960902.html
- Sirius Star Map http://reptile.users2.50megs.com/cart/c102199c.html
- Sirius, the Dog Star http://www.physics.purdue.edu/astr263l/forum/Sirius.html
- Dog Days of Summer: What are they? http://wilstar.com/dogdays.htm
- Dog Days of Summer: Bring On Air Conditioning Appreciation Days
  http://www.ari.org/consumer/articles/1999/990618dogdays.html
- Dog Days of Summer Quiz http://www.familyeducation.com/quiz/0,1399,22-8055,00.html

Summer Temperatures
It seems like every year, these summer days are hotter and more humid than they used to be. It that true? What are the hottest days of summer? How does the temperature in the United States compare with other countries? What is the temperature in outer space? Inquiring minds want to know.

- August Sets Global Temperature Record
  http://itdomino1.icfconsulting.com/ghg/cion.nsf/ls/AugustSetsGlobalTemperatureRec
- NOAA http://www.noaa.gov/
- Weather.gov http://weather.gov
- Interactive Weather Information Network http://iwin.nws.noaa.gov/iwin/main.html
- Australia: Bureau of Meteorology http://www.bom.gov.au/
- World Meteorology Organization http://www.wmo.ch/web-en/member.html
- Surface Temperature Record http://www.vision.net.au/~daly/graytemp/surftemp.htm
- Global Temperature Anomalies http://www.ghcc.msfc.nasa.gov/temperature/ (in space)

Graph the weather in your community
Record the temperature at noon at your school. Enter the data in a spreadsheet. At the end of the month, make a chart. You could also record sunny days, rainfall amount, clouds, fog, etc.

Odds and Ends
Learn the warning signs of being overheated and some first aid treatments.

- Stay Cool and Beat the Heat Safety http://www.acep.org/2,13,0.html
- Dr. Ready: Heat Cramps, Heat Exhaustion and Heat Stroke http://www.drreddy.com/heat.html

These sites have fun activities and lesson plans.

- Beat the Heat http://disney.go.com/educational/cyberlesson_aug99.html

- Dog Days of Summer Unit Plan: Dogs http://www.geocities.com/jpieczko/dog.html

Date Varies

1st Sunday
National Kids Day
National Kids Day is a day set aside to tell kids they are loved and special. The day is sponsored by an alliance of youth organizations. They would like to challenge communities and families nationwide to help share a moment, create a memory, and make a kid's day. To learn more about National Kids Day and to get involved, check out the *National Kids Day* site, sponsored by PBS. In honor of National Kids Day, *Kid Wizard* offer 100 things to do with kids, so you won't be at a loss about what to do and how to celebrate the day.
- National Kids Day http://www.kidsday.net/home.asp
- Kid Wizard http://www.kidwizard.com/newsletters/100thingstodo3.html

Our State Fair

For a number of months, young people, moms and dads, grandmas and grandpas have been busy preparing for the state fair. This is an opportunity to show off their prized livestock, handiwork, jams and pickles, corn, beans, flowers and vegetables. The youngsters in 4H are particularly involved with everything from showing to judging. Not just for farm kids anymore, 4H clubs are for everyone. Learn more about the 4H clubs in your area and the different activities they sponsor.
- National 4H Council http://www.fourhcouncil.edu/
- 4H Headquarters http://www.4h-usa.org/
- Are You Into It? http://www.areyouintoit.com/
CyberCamp – A Virtual 4H Camp is a terrific Internet site for kids. Just like a real camp, there are songs and stories, crafts, science activities, recreations and lots more. You will want to spend the day and then some.
- CyberCamp http://cybercamp.unl.edu/fishindex.html

The Barns
State fairs were originally started as a way for farmers to learn about new farming techniques and machinery and to learn about the advances in raising livestock. Visit these online farms, play some games and check out the livestock, kick the tires. You might even win a ribbon or two.
- Virtual Farm http://www.ext.vt.edu/resources/4h/virtualfarm/
- John Deere Kids http://www.deere.com/deerecom/_Kids/default.htm
- Agriculture for Kids http://www.fsa.usda.gov/ca/agforkids.htm
- The Kids Ag Page http://www.agr.state.il.us/kidspage/index.html
- Animal Science http://www.ars.usda.gov/is/kids/animals/animalintro.htm
- Barnyard Buddies Coloring Book http://www.execpc.com/~byb/paint.html
- Make a Farm http://www.yourchildlearns.com/farm.htm

The Exhibit Hall
In the olden days, while the men folk were looking at the livestock, the women were oohing and aahing over fancy needlework – quilts, embroidery and such. Truly their handiwork is an American craft treasure. Everyone will enjoy making some of these simple crafts. Arrange the completed projects in like groups and place on a long table. Be sure to award ribbons for everyone.
- Kids Domain Crafts http://www.kidsdomain.com/craft/
- The Idea Box http://www.theideabox.com/ideas.nsf/craft

The Food

One old-timer said the best part of going to the fair was that he could *"fill up on fried chicken and wash it all down with cold lemonade."* It doesn't matter if you are showing it or eating it, here are some easy recipes for kids to make and a coloring book thrown in for kicks.

- Kids Kitchen http://www.scoreone.com/kids_kitchen/ (kids around the world submit their favorites)
- Cooking with Kids http://www.weeklyreader.com/features/cookwka.html (yes, it is from Weekly Reader!)
- Jell-o Kids' Cooking Fun http://www.kraftfoods.com/html/features/jello.html
- Farmer's Market Coloring Book http://www.ams.usda.gov/directmarketing/coloringbook.htm

My neighbor's son won a blue ribbon at the county fair with these cookies. They are great!

Blue Ribbon Cookies

_ c. shortening	2 c. flour
_ c. butter	_ tsp. Soda
_ c. white sugar	1 tsp. Cream of tartar
1 egg (beaten)	1 tsp. Vanilla

Cream shortening and sugar. Add egg. Stir in dry ingredients and vanilla. Make into round balls; dip glass into sugar and flatten. Bake at 350* until slightly browned.

The Midway

Of course, the most fun for kids is usually the midway with its rides and games and other amusements. The world's first midway was at the World's Columbian Exposition in Chicago, 1893. The Ferris Wheel was the highlight of the Exposition. It was built by bridge builder, George Ferris. The Ferris Wheel remains the center of attraction at fairs today.

- Midway Plaisance http://users.vnet.net/schulman/Columbian/columbian.html#MIDWAY
- Ferris Wheel http://www.amusementhistory.com/ferris.html
- Trigonometric: Ferris Wheel http://www.ies.co.jp/math/products/trig/applets/kanran/kanran.html
- Amusement Parks http://www.amusementpark.com/ap/home.html (view a video of The Legend)
- Design a Roller Coaster http://www.education-world.com/a_lesson/00-2/lp2033.shtml
- Chills, Thrills and Spills http://www.discovery.com/exp/rollercoasters/thrills/thrills.html
  - Build A Roller Coaster (online) http://www.discovery.com/exp/rollercoasters/build.html

Super Highway to Your State Fair

You might not be able to actually attend your state fair this year, but I encourage you to take the super highway and enjoy some of the famous state fairs across our country. Just go to Google.com and search for (your state)+state fair. Here are some of the oldest and the biggest.

- Iowa State Fair http://www.iowastatefair.com/
- Texas State Fair http://www.texfair.com/
- Minnesota State Fair http://www.mnstatefair.org/
- Google.com http://www.google.com

Odds and Ends

- Listen to the midi from Rogers and Hammerstein's State *Fair* http://www.rnh.com/search/index.html

Take A Vacation

August is a traditional month for families to get away. Child psychologist Haim Ginott's philosophy is "what children can't have in reality, give them in imagination." So, off you go…. Have a large group discussion about vacations. Start with a spreadsheet and make a list of places your class has been on vacation – Grandma's house, cabin at the lake, Disneyland, whatever. Make a graph to show the results of your survey. Then, use PBS's *Road Trip* to talk about different types of vacations and the history of vacations.

- Road Trip http://www.pbs.org/wgbh/amex/kids/index.html
- Who was Haim Ginott? http://www.kingsleyschool.ca/who_was_haim_ginott.htm

Plan a Vacation

Here are two different lesson plans that will help your students plan their dream vacation.

1. Rodgers Robins has developed a very well organized webquest called *Vacations Anyone?* Students work in teams to plan their perfect vacation. Whether you use it as is or modify it, I think you and your students will enjoy getting away.

- Vacation Anyone? http://affton.mints.more.net/robbins/vacation/index.html

2. Disney Lesson Plans also has a nice vacation lesson plan about traveling to National Parks.

- Virtual Trip to a National Park http://disney.go.com/educational/cyberlesson_august.html

3. Education World's vacation lesson plan has students traveling to different Internet sites including museums, historical sites and vacation spots around the United States.

- My Summer Vacation http://www.education-world.com/a_lesson/lesson070.shtml

4. Plan your vacation itinerary with *Trip Advisor*.

- Trip Advisor http://www.tripadvisor.com/

The Cook's Tour

Since 1841, Thomas Cook, or his company, has been planning group tours. His concept of making the arrangement for the transportation, lodging, the sites to see and caring for all of the other details helped make traveling popular for the average tourist. His tours are synonymous with organization and quality. Have the students plan a vacation using the Thomas Cook Tours site. You will want to have a guidebook for your travels. Fodor's has the best online guidebooks. Just identify where you want to go. This site will give you lots and lots of valuable information about what you will be able to see.

- History of Thomas Cook Tours
  http://japan.park.org/Japan/Hitachi/variety/tour_of_tours_e/pro/toumas_p.html
- Thomas Cook Tours http://www.tcholidays.com/
- Fodor's Guides http://www.fodors.com/

Wish You Were Here

Use a publisher program or word processor to have the students design and print postcards. Have the postcard represent the location. They can use the copy/paste feature to include actual pictures. Blue Mountain has postcards from all 50 states. So, if for some reason you don't want to make your own, get them free from Blue Mountain.

- Blue Mountain Postcards http://www.bluemountain.com/cdb/NR/USP/

Games For The Road

Have your students prepare a brochure about games that can be played in the car. Brainstorm a list of games, such as the Alphabet Game. Only using road signs and billboards they see, find each letter of the alphabet – in alphabetical order. Then, divide the class into partners. Have each group write the rules for the game using a word processor. Copy and paste each document into a publishing program so you can include all of the games. Make copies for everyone to keep in their car. Need a little help thinking of games? These sites will help you out.

- Classic Car Games
  http://family.go.com/travel/activities/feature/famf48cargames/famf48cargames.html
- Great Games for Travel
  http://family.go.com/raisingkids/child/dev/feature/kids78games/kids78games.html
- Travel Games http://family.go.com/travel/activities/feature/famf48invent/famf48invent.html
- Travel Games for the Road http://www.familyeducation.com/printables/package/0,2358,22-16239,00.html (you need to print the game board for these games)

Get Your Kicks on Route 66
Route 66, the Mother Road, begins in Chicago and ends in Santa Monica, 2448 miles later. This was the main travel route for people traveling west. In 1926 only 800 miles were paved and wasn't paved end-to-end until 1937. Today, much of the old route is not longer in use as interstate highways have taken its place. But, the old Route 66 has nostalgic and historical value for students today. Follow the old route having students stop to 'see the sights' along the way. Use MapQuest to get the current mileage. Compare the old route with new routes.
- Historic Route 66 http://www.historic66.com/
- Route 66 http://route66.exmachina.net/
- Explore Route 66 http://www.national66.com/
- MapQuest http://www.mapquest.com

Odds and Ends
Have your students take a tour through the United States by reading children's books. Carol Hurst provides book titles for each state plus classroom activities.
- United States Through Children's Literature http://www.carolhurst.com/subjects/uslit.html
Need some help on how to take those vacation pictures? Fodor's will help you out.
- How To Take Travel Photos http://www.fodors.com/focus/
Yes, it's the old What I Did On....., but with a new twist. Students can add their stories to others on the Internet!
- What Did You Do On Your Summer Vacation?
  http://www.aaa.com/scripts/WebObjects.dll/AAAOnline.woa/1005/wo/qO4000BJ100vO7009/0.0.
  AAAHome.9.7.3.1.1.0.1
I don't have a lifetime list of places I'd like to visit, but maybe I should. What would be on your list? Your student's list?
- National Geographic's 50 Places of a Lifetime
  http://www.nationalgeographic.com/traveler/index50.html
Land's End, the catalog people, has some way out vacations we all can dream about.
- Beyond Lands End Adventures http://beyond.landsend.com/index.html
Take a field trip to a science museum – anywhere in the world!
- Field Trip http://www.tryscience.com/fieldtrips/fieldtrip_home.html
Traveling with kids can really be fun, but sometimes we need just a little help getting organized.
- Daddy, are we there yet? http://www.bergen.com/travel/takekid27200105278.htm
Have the students use Norman Rockwell's painting, *Coming and Going*, for a story starter.
- Coming and Going http://www.normanrockwellmuseum.org/pictures-tour/page02.html

Back to School
For many of us, it's New Year's Day! Armed with a new outfit and lots of hope for the future, we're making bulletin boards, firing up the computers and getting ready for the sound of little feet in the halls. *America Goes Back to School* is a nationwide initiative to encourage and support family and community involvement in improving children's learning. Now is the time to get involved.
- America Goes Back to School http://www.ed.gov/Family/agbts/

- ABCs of America Goes Back to School
  http://www.smarterkids.com/rescenter/library/articles/atozschool.asp

School Shopping

Help the students make a list of all of the items they will need for the new school year. Use a spreadsheet to make a budget for expenses. Or, use a spreadsheet to record comparison shopping for something like a backpack.

- Office Max http://www.hasd.org/ges/talltale/talltale.htm
- Office Depot http://www.officedepot.com/
- Wal Mart http://www.walmart.com/
- K-Mart http://www.bluelight.com/
- Lands End http://www.landsend.com/cd/frontdoor/

Make a Class Web Page

If you don't have one already, these sites offer free templates and server space for classroom web pages. This is an excellent way to post student assignments, communicate with parents and showcase student work.

- SchoolCity http://www.schoolcity.com
- Electric Schoolhouse http://www.eschoolhouse.com
- Tripod http://classroom.tripod.com
- Blackboard http://www.blackboard.com
- My School Online http://www.myschoolonline.com/
- Big Chalk http://www.bigchalk.com/cgi-bin/WebObjects/WOPortal
- Scholastic.com http://homepage.scholastic.com/classpages/start_hp.cfm

Classroom Ideas and Themes

Do you need some new ideas for the New Year? Check these out!

- Back to School http://www.knownet.net/users/Ackley/school.html
- Back to School Themes http://www.childfun.com/themes/school.shtml
- It's Time for Back to School http://www.bry-backmanor.org/backtoschool.html
- Back to School Ideas http://members.aol.com/MGoudie/Backtoschoolideas.html
- Back to School Unit http://www.geocities.com/Athens/Troy/5059/9.html
- Back to School http://www.geocities.com/Heartland/Hollow/1213/back.html
- Back to School with ProTeacher http://www.proteacher.com/030005.shtml
- Education World: Back to School http://www.education-world.com/a_special/back_to_school99.shtml
- A – Z Themes: Back to School http://atozteacherstuff.com/themes/backtoschool.shtml
- abcTeach: Back to School http://www.abcteach.com/Backtoschool/backtoschoolTOC.htm
- Debbie's Back to School Theme Unit http://www.themeunits.com/September_bk.html
- Kids Domain: Back to School Printables http://www.kidsdomain.com/holiday/school/print.html

For Parents

Do you have parents who are a little anxious about sending young people back to school? Use you publisher program to make a little brochure to give them that refers them to some excellent Internet sites.

- Essential Back to School Tips
  http://www.smarterkids.com/rescenter/library/articles/back_to_school_tips.asp
- Back to School Family Handbook
  http://www.globalgourmet.com/food/egg/egg0997/backschool.html
- Back to School Guide http://www.homearts.com/depts/family/88prim11.htm
- Back to School Tips for Parents http://www.ncpc.org/10adu1.htm

- Going Back to School http://kidshealth.org/kid/grow/back_to_school.html
- Family Corner: Back to School http://www.thefamilycorner.com/dir/Education/Back_To_School/
- Back to School Safety Checklist http://www.cpsc.gov/cpscpub/pubs/btsimage.html
- Back to School in 6 Easy Steps http://www.familyeducation.com/article/0,1120,20-2384,00.html

But not for everyone....

We are so fortunate in America because we have wonderful schools right around the corner that all children are free to attend. But that is not the case everywhere in the world. Read about the wonderful work the people are doing to support children in need. What could your students do this year to help out?

- Back to school, if you have one http://www.savethechildren.org.uk/backtoschool/
- Stop Gender Apartheid in Afghanistan http://www.feminist.org/afghan/back2school.asp
- Schools Deming Schools http://www0.un.org/cyberschoolbus/banmines/index.asp

Special Days

August 1
Anniversary of the World Wide Web

No doubt about it…the World Wide Web has changed all of our lives! When I began teaching if someone had told me that I would be in daily contact with the parents of my students, that students would submit their homework electronically and that I could receive it anywhere in the world, that my students would work on collaborative projects with other students in Japan or Australia or even the next town down the road, that we would be involved in telecommunication seminars with the Secretary of Education and that I could ask questions from my classroom, I would have said they were crazy. Take my class on a field trip to the Louvre? Watch baby animals live from the San Diego Zoo? How could this be possible? Get information from any library in the world? Impossible! Well it's all here and MORE! As I sit in my kitchen writing this book, knowing that it won't be published for a year, I'm scarred. How can I possibly tell you about how we as teachers can use the Internet in our classrooms, when I haven't a clue what is going to be developed this year that will change our classrooms dramatically? What I do know is that we are just beginning to learn about the most exciting thing that's happened to education since Socrates asked his first question. Hang on! It's an exciting ride!

History of the World Wide Web

Need to know a little bit about how the whole thing got started? Check these sites out. I particularly like timelines. Have the students use the Timeliner to make a timeline for your classroom. If you don't have one, download a demo copy. Add personal tidbits to the timeline, such as, when your school got its first computer, when the lab was last updated, etc.

- The Roads and Crossroads of Internet History http://www.netvalley.com/intval.html
  - History of the Internet Timeline http://www.netvalley.com/archives/mirrors/davemarsh-timeline-1.htm
- A Brief History of the Internet http://www.isoc.org/internet/history/brief.html
- Hobbes' Internet Timeline http://www.zakon.org/robert/internet/timeline/
- Life on the Internet Timeline http://www.pbs.org/internet/timeline/index.html
- History of the Net http://www.sc.edu/bck2skol/fall/lesson2.html
- Tom Snyder Productions: Timeliner http://www.tomsnyder.com/

Learning to Use the Net

One of the things I like best about the Internet is that it teaches you about itself! These are some of my favorite sites for learning how to use the Internet. Whether you are a novice or an expert, there is always something new to learn. And, to help your students understand and use the World Wide Web, I've listed two sites: *WWW Workbook* and *Webmonkey for Kids*.

- Learn the Net http://www.learnthenet.com/english/index.html
- Using the Internet http://www.spa3.k12.sc.us/usinginternet.htm
- Kathy Schrock: Slide Shows for Teaching http://school.discovery.com/schrockguide/shows.html
- World Wide Web Workbook http://www.fi.edu/primer/setup.html
- Webmonkey for Kids http://hotwired.lycos.com/webmonkey/kids/

Teaching Kids About Technology

These are just a sample of the lesson plans that Discovery School has about computers and technology.

- All About Computers
  http://school.discovery.com/lessonplans/programs/allaboutcomputers/index.html
- Invention: Computer Technology
  http://school.discovery.com/lessonplans/programs/inventioncomputertechnology/index.html
- Understanding Computing
  http://school.discovery.com/lessonplans/programs/understandingcomputing/index.html
- Cyberspace http://school.discovery.com/lessonplans/programs/cyberspace/index.html

There is no doubt about it; technology has changed the way we speak. Well, maybe not the words we use, but certainly the meaning we attach to them. Take 'mouse' for instance. Have the students make an ABC Chart or book for your room of 'technology related' terms.

- The Jargon Lexicon http://www.tuxedo.org/~esr/jargon/html/The-Jargon-Lexicon-framed.html

Web-based Projects

You can make all kinds of exciting interactive projects for your classroom. This is a sample of the Internet sites that have interactive web-based tools for teachers to use.

- The WebQuest Page http://edweb.sdsu.edu/webquest/webquest.html
- Everything WebQuest http://www.ozline.com/learning/index.htm
- Teaching Tools http://school.discovery.com/teachingtools/teachingtools.html
- Interactive Exercise Makers http://lang.swarthmore.edu/makers/index.htm
- Puzzlemaker http://puzzlemaker.school.discovery.com/
- Puzzle Center http://puzzles.apte.com/

August 6, 1945
Hiroshima Day

At 8:15 in the morning, U.S. bombers dropped the world's 1st atom bomb on the Japanese city of Hiroshima. Over 200,000 people were killed and most of the city was destroyed. Three days later, a second bomb, killing 120,000 people was dropped on Nagasaki City, Japan. On August 15, 1945, Japan accepted the Potsdam Declaration by the Allied Powers, thereby surrendering unconditionally, and thus ending World War II. Today, ceremonies are held in both of the cities at the Peace Memorial Parks where people gather to remember those who died and to pray for world peace. Have your students read the accounts of the bombings and view some of the pictures. Ask them to write a two journal entries for that day for imaginary students their age – one American, living in your hometown and one Japanese, living in Tokyo.

- Dropping the Atomic Bomb and End of WWII
  http://www.jinjapan.org/kidsweb/calendar/august/kinenbi.html
- Hiroshima http://www.peacewire.org/photoexhibits/Hiroshima/photo1.html

Sadako and the 1000 Paper Cranes

Today, the citizens of Hiroshima invite the world to visit their city and the Peace Memorial Park. We can view past ceremonies of remembrance. At the *Kids Peace Station*, read the story of little two-year-old

Sadako. Sadako survived the bombing of her city, but died ten years later of leukemia. Her story has become a lesson for us all in world peace. Teach your students to make origami cranes to hang in your room as a visual symbol of how precious and fragile peace is.

- Hiroshima Information http://www.hiroshima-cdas.or.jp/hiroshima/e_index.html
- Welcome to Hiroshima http://www.city.hiroshima.jp/
  - Kids Peace Station http://www.pcf.city.hiroshima.jp/kids/KPSH_E/top_e.html
- Cranes for Peace http://www.he.net/~sparker/cranes.html
- How to get the paper crane http://www.csi.ad.jp/suzuhari-es/1000cranes/paperc/index.html
- Hiroshima Peace Site http://www.pcf.city.hiroshima.jp/peacesite/indexE.html
- A Personal Record of Hiroshima A-Bomb Survival http://www.coara.or.jp/~ryoji/abomb/e-index.html
- Eleanor Coerr: Sadako http://members.tripod.com/EleanorCoerr/authorof.htm
- Sadako http://www.sadako.com/
- Thousand Cranes Peace Network http://rosella.apana.org.au/~mlb/cranes/reslink1.htm

August 6, 1917
Barbara Cooney's Birthday

Two-time Caldecott Award winning author/illustrator Barbara Cooney was a self-taught artist. Her mother was a well-known artist who let Barbara use her paints and brushes, but, did not instruct her on how to use them. Barbara began illustrating children's books but was unhappy with her technical ability. She began taking lots of pictures. She said that through photography she was able to paint the mood of the place she was illustrating. It was very important to her to "get it right." After reading her biography, have the students take digital pictures of a place they would like to draw. It could be something on the playground or something inside the school or classroom. After you have printed the pictures, have the student use the picture as a model to draw from.

- Barbara Cooney Teacher Resource File http://falcon.jmu.edu/~ramseyil/bcooney.htm
- Barbara Cooney http://www.penguinputnam.com/Author/AuthorFrame?0000005287
- Beads on a String: the Art of Barbara Cooney http://www.lib.uconn.edu/Exhibits/cooney/conyfpg.htm
- Featured Author: Barbara Cooney http://www.carolhurst.com/newsletters/32dnewsletters.html
- Making Picture Books – The Pictures by Barbara Cooney http://www.hbook.com/cooney.shtml

Women's Army Corps

Ms Cooney joined the Women's Army Corps during the summer of 1942. Learn more about women in the army at these sites:

- Women Come to the Front http://www.loc.gov/exhibits/wcf/wcf0001.html
- Fresh History http://www.discovery.com/area/freshhistory/fresh1.1.html
- Women in WWII http://userpages.aug.com/captbarb/femvets5.html

Selected Books by Barbara Cooney
Chanticleer and the Fox – Caldecott Award
Ox-Cart Man – Caldecott Award
Miss Rumphius
Emily
Roxaboxen
Letting Swift River Go
Basket Moon
Peter and the Wolf
Emma
Hattie and the Wild Waves

Island Boy
Bambi: A Life in the Woods
Seven Little Rabbits
Spirit Child: A Story of the Nativity
Kildee House
The Year of the Perfect Christmas Tree: An Appalachian Story
The Remarkable Christmas of the Cobbler's Sons
The Story of Christmas

August 9
National Polka Day

The polka represents the music of central Europe. Some say polka music is the happiest sound around. So, if you and your students need a little fun, put on your dancing shoes and grab a partner. It's polka time!

- Grandpa Schober's Polka Midis http://www.geocities.com/Nashville/8769/
- Learn to Polka http://www.freewheelers.org/1DancingFool/polka.htm
- Just Plain Silly http://www.yuckles.com/pigpolka.htm

Lawrence Welk's Orchestra has been entertaining people since 1924. This farm boy from North Dakota traveled the world playing his music, but his big break came in 1951 when he brought his show to millions through the magic of television. The Lawrence Welk Show remains the longest running show on television, viewed by loyal follows on PBS.

- Biography http://www.germanheritage.com/biographies/mtoz/welk.html
- Lawrence Welk Opera House http://www.campusschool.dsu.edu/fieldtrips/PV/opera.htm
- Lawrence Welk http://lawrence.welk.com/welk.htm lots of music
- PBS http://www.pbs.org
- Contemporary Polka Bands http://www.itspolkatime.com/bands.html

August 10, 1846
Smithsonian Institute Founded

On this day, President James K. Polk signed the bill that founded the Smithsonian Institute. The Smithsonian Institute was to be a national museum for government collections, a laboratory, an art gallery, and a library. The Smithsonian Institute was funded with a bequest from James Smithson. In his will he left his fortune "to the United States of America, to found at Washington, under the name to [sic] the Smithsonian Institution, an Establishment for the increase & diffusion of knowledge among men."[iii] Today, the Smithsonian is the largest museum complex in the world. If you can't get to Washington D.C. in person, tour the online Smithsonian.

- James Smithson http://www.150.si.edu/chap1/one.htm
- Smithsonian Institute http://www.si.edu/
  - Museums http://www.si.edu/info/museums_research.htm

Make an Online Museum

The Smithsonian is dedicated to documenting American culture. What do you have in your classroom or school or homes that would make an interesting online museum display? Could you make a display of writing tools (pencils, pens, chalk...) or tree leaves or rocks? Collect your artifacts. Document each artifact with as much information as the students can find. *Note: do not use materials that are copyrighted, such as paintings you may have in your school.* Take digital pictures of your artifacts being careful to create a dramatic effect. Import the pictures to your web site with the documentation. New displays are always celebrated with a big opening. So, invite another class and the principal and the parents to your museum opening.

August 11, 1944
Joanna Cole's Birthday
Joanna Cole has written both fiction and non-fiction, but it is her Miss Frizzle and the Magic School Bus series that she is best known for. She says that even when she was in the 5th grade she knew that she enjoyed explaining things. Science and writing were her favorite subjects.
- Joanna Cole http://www.edupaperback.org/authorbios/Cole_Joanna.html
- Visit with the Author http://teacher.scholastic.com/authorsandbooks/authors/cole/bio.htm

"Explain Things"
Ms Cole says that as a child she loved nature and being outdoors. Take your class on a real life field trip to a neighborhood park. Have the students pretend to be the smallest things in the park, such as an ant. Take digital pictures of the park from the ant's point of view. You will have to use the zoom feature of the camera and also think about the point of view from which the ant would see that particular thing – like the leaf or rock. When you get back to the classroom, print the pictures and arrange them in a logical order. Write a story about your ant's field trip. This part can be fictional. Prepare each page with the picture and the story text. Then, write the real or non-fiction explanation of what is in the picture, such as the leaf and put that in a side bar.

Selected Books by Joanna Cole
The Magic School Bus:
- And the Electric Field Trip
- Explores the Senses
- World of Animals
- At the Waterworks
- Inside a Hurricane
- Inside the Human Body
- Lost in the Solar System
- In the Time of the Dinosaurs
- On the Ocean Floor
- Inside a Beehive
- Inside the Earth
- Plants Seeds – A Book About How Living Things Grow
- Plays Ball – A Book About Forces
- In the Artic – A Book About Heat

How You Were Born
Asking About Sex and Growing Up
I'm a Big Sister
I'm a Big Brother

August 13
International Left-hander's Day
What do Presidents James Garfield, Herbert Hoover, Harry S Truman, Gerald Ford, Ronald Regan, George Bush Sr., Bill Clinton and artist Leonardo de Vinci have in common? They are all left-handed. Who else is a member of this select club? Check it out!
- Famous Left Handers http://www.indiana.edu/~primate/left.html
Learn more about left-handers, everything from history to advice for teachers, to brain-teasers.
- Left-Handers's Day http://www.left-handersday.com/
- Left-Handers's Day http://www.holidayinsights.com/other/lefthand.htm
- Lefties http://www.umkc.edu/imc/lefties.htm

Keyboarding

According to Rosemary West, there are 1447 English words typed with the left hand alone and only 187 words typed with the right hand. Challenge your students to see who can think of the most words typed solely with the left hand in 10 minutes.

- Rosemary West's Left-Handed Page http://www.rosemarywest.com/left/

August 17, 1786
Davy Crockett's Birthday

"Be always sure you're right, then go ahead."

Davy Crockett

All twenty verses of the *Ballad of Davy Crockett* tell the legend of this real-life American hero. Yes, he was born in Tennessee and yes, he was known for his hunting ability. But, to learn more about the man behind the legend, read his biography. Compare the biography with the ballad.

- Biography http://etext.lib.virginia.edu/railton/projects/price/acrocket.htm
- Davy Crockett http://www.infoporium.com/heritage/crockett.shtml
- The Ballad of Davy Crockett http://www.geocities.com/TelevisionCity/Set/1486/Ballad.html

Storytelling

Known for his storytelling, Davy Crockett could mesmerize his audience with his adventures. Have your students read *Bear Hunting in Tennessee*. Students should practice retelling the story using as much of the original language and spirit as possible.

- Bear Hunting in Tennessee http://etext.lib.virginia.edu/railton/projects/price/crockett.htm
- Retelling Folktales http://www.storyarts.org/classroom/retelling/
- Story Retelling Rubric http://www.crt.state.la.us/FOLKLIFE/edu_unit5w_story_retelling.html

Remember the Alamo

Yes, Davy Crockett was one of the 180 brave men who died at the Alamo in February and March 1835, fighting for Texas independence. Relive one of the most famous battles in American history.

- Remember the Alamo http://www.pointsouth.com/csanet/greatmen/crockett/alamo.htm
- The Alamo http://school.discovery.com/homeworkhelp/worldbook/atozhistory/a/010520.html
- The Siege and Battle of the Alamo http://www.lsjunction.com/events/alamo.htm

August 18
Gold Rush, Discovery Day – Alaska

"None of the gold-crazed stampeders who struggled over the mountain passes above Skagway to reach the Klondike ever forgot the terrors of the trail. But few took time to record their thoughts as they searched for the end of their personal rainbows."

Jack London, The White Silence

Alaska Gold Rush

Read all about one of America's last great adventures! The Alaska Gold Rush inspired adventurers, men and women, from all over the globe to leave home and family and set out for the Frozen North. Travel with them as they face danger, hardship and for some, glory.

- Depression, Discovery and Klondicitis: A Short History of the Klondike Gold Rush
  http://www.gold-rush.org/ghost-02.htm
  - Gold Rush Timeline http://www.gold-rush.org/ALASKA/time/Ala02.html

- Gold Rush Women http://library.thinkquest.org/11313/Gold_Rush/index.html

Visit Alaska

Take a field trip to our 49th state. Have your students use a publishing program to make brochures about Alaska. Divide the students into groups giving each group a different topic to research. Topics might include: State Symbols, Famous Alaskans, Native Americans, Alaska in the 21 Century, Alaskan Art, etc. These Internet sites are a good place to begin.
- Alaskan State Symbols http://www.dced.state.ak.us/tourism/student.htm
- Visit Alaska http://www.dced.state.ak.us/tourism/
- Alaska Homepage http://www.state.ak.us/

Stories of the Past

"There are strange things done in the midnight sun
By the men who moil for gold;
The Arctic trails have their secret tales
That would make your blood run cold"

- Robert W. Service[iv]

These are the opening lines of Robert Service's famous poem, the *Cremation of Sam McGee*. Service worked for the Canadian Bank of Commerce. He was stationed for eight years in the gold fields at Whitehorse, Yukon Territory. Robert Service recorded in verse the stories of triumph and tragedy of the early gold-rush minors. Other stories, fact and fantasy, have survived to entertain and enlighten us. After reading about Robert Service, have the students practice reading aloud a story of the Alaskan gold rush. Students may work in small groups or individually. You may want to modify the Oral Interpretation Rules for Performance to meet the age and abilities of your students.
- Robert W. Service http://www.ude.net/service/service.html
- Cremation of Sam McGee http://www.hyperborea.org/writing/sammcgee.html
- Stories of the Past http://www.gold-rush.org/ALASKA/stories/Ala03.html
- Ghosts of the Gold Rush http://www.gold-rush.org/
- Oral Interpretation http://spot.pcc.edu/academ/vapa/oralinterp.html
- Oral Interpretation Rules for Performance http://www.nsaahome.org/textfile/speech/drama.htm

Odds and Ends

Use these pictures of the Gold Rush as story-starters.
- Pictures http://www.gold-rush.org/ALASKA/photo/Ala04.html

How far is your school from the capitol of Alaska?
- MapQuest.com http://www.mapquest.com

This is a way cool writing project that takes the students from words to sentences to paragraphs with auditory prompts and pictures.
- The Klondike Gold Rush Writing Project http://www2.actden.com/writ_den/h08/direct.htm

August 18, 1920
19th Amendment

The right of citizens of the United States to vote shall not be denied or
abridged by the United States or by any State on account of sex.

- 19th Amendment

Beginning in the mid-19th Century, women began the lengthy and arduous struggle for the right to vote, a right some women felt should have been included from the very beginning. Jane Adams, wife of then delegate John Adams, wrote in one of her numerous letters to her husband 'remember the ladies.'

- 19th Amendment http://www.nara.gov/exhall/charters/constitution/19th/19th.html

Jane Addams and Susan B. Anthony Dialog
Have students read Jane Addams, *Why Women Should Vote* as a Reader's Theater. Some of this is quite lengthy, so have students edit their parts. Merge selections from Susan B. Anthony's speech, *Women's Right to Vote*. Students take the part of these famous women and read their part from their character's point of view.

- Why Women Should Vote http://douglass.speech.nwu.edu/adda_a03.htm
- Susan B. Anthony: Women's Right to Vote
  http://www.fordham.edu/halsall/mod/1873anthony.html

The Struggle for Women's Suffrage
Read *Women Win the Right to Vote*! Note that the 19th Amendment passed by just one vote. Who was president during the critical periods of women's suffrage? Have the students make a timeline of the Women's Suffrage Movement adding quotes and to give it a true historical perspective, adding other important events in U. S. History.

- Women Win the Right to Vote! http://www.aracnet.com/~histgaz/hgv3n5.htm
- Chronology of Woman Suffrage Movement Events
  http://teacher.scholastic.com/researchtools/articlearchives/womhst/chrono.htm
- Suffrage History From PBS http://www.pbs.org/onewoman/suffrage.html
- Living the Legacy: Women's Rights Movement http://www.legacy98.org/
- From Parlor to Politics http://www.umkc.edu/imc/suffrage.htm
- Women's Suffrage http://gi.grolier.com/presidents/aae/side/wsffrg.html
- Passage of the 19th Amendment: New York Times 1919-1920
  http://www.fordham.edu/halsall/mod/1920womensvote.html
- Votes for Women 1850-1920 http://memory.loc.gov/ammem/vfwhtml/vfwhome.html

Lesson Plans and Activities
- Women's Suffrage Web Quest http://et.sdsu.edu/JDeLaCruz/womensufferage.html
- My Vote Counts http://www.macarthurschool.org/projects/chee/caldera.html

August 19
Aviation Day

"For once you have tasted flight, you will forever walk the earth with your eyes turned skyward, for there you have been, and there you will always long to return."

- Leonardo da Vinci[v]

Aviation Day is celebrated on aviation pioneer Orville Wright's birthday. Take the day to learn about famous aviators. Learn to sing *Come Josephine in Your Flying Machine*.

- Come Josephine http://www.niehs.nih.gov/kids/lyrics/flying.htm

Who Am I?
Have the students develop a Who Am I Game. Use PowerPoint to list clues from the hardest to the easiest. Reveal one clue at a time until the correct person is identified. Write each clue in its own text box. Use animation sequencing to reveal the next clue on a mouse click.

```
┌─────────────────────────────────────────────────────────────┐
│                                                               │
│                      Who Am I?                                │
│   I was born in 1897.                                         │
│                    I lived a life of firsts.                  │
│                                                               │
│                    I was the 1st woman to fly across the      │
│             Atlantic (as a passenger.)                        │
│                                                               │
│       I was the 1st woman to solo across the Atlantic.        │
│                                                               │
│               I was the 1st woman to fly from Hawaii to California. │
│                                                               │
│   I attempted the 1st flight                                  │
│   around the world.              I disappeared over the       │
│                                  Pacific Ocean in 1937        │
│                                                               │
│                                                               │
│                       Amelia Earhart                          │
│                                                               │
└─────────────────────────────────────────────────────────────┘
```

- Flight http://www.pbs.org/wgbh/amex/kids/flight/index.html

The History of Aviation
- National Air and Space Museum http://www.nasm.si.edu/
- Aviation History Online Museum http://www.aviation-history.com/
- Women in Aviation History http://www.ninety-nines.org/bios.html
- Aviation History - Australia http://www.tne.net.au/wil/avhis.html
- Jay Miller Aviation History http://www.cals.lib.ar.us/miller/
- Fly Girls http://www.pbs.org/wgbh/amex/flygirls/

The Science Behind It
The *Science of Aviation* is a great site to help students understand how an airplane works. It offers online experiments about air and flight plus instructions for building a glider.
- Science of Aviation http://www.ag.ohio-state.edu/~flight/
- How Stuff Works: Airplanes http://www.howstuffworks.com/airplane.htm
- Airplane Projects to Make http://www.ptialaska.net/~bundyd/anyday2.html#Flight
- Air Travelers http://www.omsi.edu/explore/physics/air/

August 19, 1871
Orville Wright's Birthday
On December 17, 1903 near Kitty Hawk, North Carolina, Orville and his brother, Wilber, made the world's first flight in a powered, heavier-than-air machine. With Orville at the controls, the plane flew 120 feet in 12 seconds. The brothers became interested in aeronautics at an early age, reading and learning all they could. Little did they know that after that first tentative flight, the world of transportation would never be the same again. Fortunately for us, there are a number of great Internet sites that will help us understand the work of these two important American inventors. Many of these sites have multimedia components such as slide shows and video clips.
- Aviators: Orville and Wilber Wright http://exn.ca/Mini/Flightdeck/Aviators/wright.cfm
- Orville Wright http://www.lucidcafe.com/library/95aug/wright.html
- The American Experience: The Wright Stuff http://www.pbs.org/wgbh/amex/wright/index.html

- Time 100 Scientists and Thinkers: Orville and Wilber Wright
  http://www.time.com/time/time100/scientist/profile/wright.html
- A Science Odyssey: People and Discoveries
  http://www.pbs.org/wgbh/aso/databank/entries/btwrig.html
- The Wright Brother's National Memorial http://www.nps.gov/wrbr/

Odds and Ends
Read Orville Wright's account of that first flight.
- How We Made the First Flight http://www.aero-web.org/history/wright/wriframe.htm
View these early Wright Brother's photographs.
- The Wright Brothers Photographs http://www.outerbanks.com/wrightbrothers/wrightlc.htm
Visit Kitty Hawk, North Carolina, today.
- Kitty Hawk http://www.kitty-hawk.com/
- Pier WebCam http://www.surfchex.com/cameras/kittynew.htm

> *"If the twenty-fourth of August be fair and clear,*
> *Then hope for a prosperous Autumn that year."*
>
> - John Ray *English Proverbs*

August 25, 1959
Lane Smith's Birthday
Lane Smith was born in Oklahoma, but by the age of three, his family had moved to California. He says one of the things that influenced him was the families' annual summer trip back to Oklahoma along Route 66. "Once you've seen a 100-foot cement buffalo on top of a donut-stand in the middle of nowhere, you're never the same."[vi] Lane was introduced to writing partner, Jon Scieszka, by Jon's wife in 1986. They wrote their first book, *The True Story of the Three Little Pigs* in 1989. Although publishers first rejected it, *The True Story* has sold over a million copies and has been translated into 10 different languages.
- ChuckleBait http://www.chucklebait.com/
- Lane Smith http://www.penguinputnam.com/Author/AuthorFrame?0000024178

Point of View
Most of us grew up thinking the Big Bad Wolf was the bad guy. It wasn't until Lane Smith and Jon Scieszka wrote the *True Story of the Three Little Pigs* did we learn that we have been miss judging him all these years. Looking at an event from another person's perspective or point of view often can change the whole thing! Have the students rewrite a familiar folktale taking another character's perspective. For example, how would the story change if Cinderella's sister were telling it?
- List of Sites with Mythology or Folktale Links http://www.storyarts.org/links/folktale/

Knowing When to Stop
Lane Smith says, "The trick is to know when to stop. Sometimes I keep adding more and more layers until I've ruined the piece."[vii] Fortunately, computers come with an undo feature. To practice undoing and more importantly, knowing when to undo, have the students use a paint program and draw a simple picture. Save the picture and open it in a photo program, such as PhotoStudio. Have the students change and manipulate the original drawing until they've gone too far. Print the last picture and then undo and print the second to the last picture. Have the students tell why the last picture was too much and why the second to the last picture was 'just right!' If you don't have a photography program, you can download a demo copy of PhotoStudio.

- PhotoStudio http://www.arcsoft.com/products/software/en/photostudio2000.html

Some Books by Lane Smith
2095
The Good, the Bad and the Goofy
Knights of the Kitchen Table
Math Curse
Squids Will Be Squids
The Stinky Cheese Man
The True Story of the Three Little Pigs
Your Mother Was a Neanderthal

August 28, 1961
Brian Pinkney's Birthday
You could say that Brian Pinkney had no choice as far a choosing a career goes. Both his father (Jerry) and his mother (Gloria) were involved in writing and illustrating children's books and his wife, Andrea Davis Pinkney is a children's book author! From an early age, Brian loved to paint. His father helped him set up an art studio in a closet using his old art supplies.
- Brian Pinkney http://www.eduplace.com/kids/hmr/mtai/bpinkney.html
- Jerry and Brian Pinkney http://www.nccil.org/exhibit/pinkney.html
- Brian Pinkney, My Favorite Illustrator http://dmsreading.tripod.com/brianpinkneytxt.html

Scratchboard Style
Brain Pinkney often uses an artistic technique called scratchboard. You can have the students simulate this style using your paint program. First, fill the page with black. Then, use the eraser and draw your picture. Some photography programs allow the user to build layers. If you have one of these available, you can use a photography for the bottom layer, cover that with a solid black layer and finally, use the eraser tool for the third layer to scratch out (erase) the desired picture. The Electronic Media lesson plan describes this technique in detail. If you want a 'real' paper and paint project, refer to the *Scratchboard Lesson Plan* for directions.
- About Scratchboard http://www.chazart.com/scratchboard.html
- Beginner's Scratchboard http://www.dianalee.com/beginners_scratchboard.htm
- Electronic Media: Scratchboard Lesson Plan
  http://www.northeast.isd.tenet.edu/lee/depart/fineart/art/art1/scratch/scratless.htm
- Scratchboard Lesson Plan http://curry.edschool.virginia.edu/go/wil/MLK.pdf

Note: I was playing around with the demo copy of PhotoStudio and could get a similar effect by opening a photograph and using the fill tool with black, colored portions of the original picture. I don't think I'm going to win any awards with this, but it does show students the technique.

Following in His Father's Footsteps
Brian Pinkney's father Jerry Pinkney is also a Caldecott Award winning illustrator. Although he says his father never gave him art lessons, he does recall watching his at work and trying to imitate what he observed. Have your students identify what their parents do. Ask them to research their parent's or other significant person's occupation. Ask them to complete a matrix. Compare the different occupations.

Occupation	Teacher	Doctor	Lawyer	Merchant Chief
Responsibilities				
Pros				
Cons				
Education Required				
Average Income				
Parent's Comments				

Some Books by Brian Pinkney
Sukey and the Mermaid – Coretta Scott King Honor Book
The Dark-Thirty – Newbery Honor Book
The Faithful Friend – Caldecott Honor and Coretta Scott King Award
Duke Ellington – Caldecott Honor
Where Does the Trail Lead?
A Wave in Her Pocket: Stories from Trinidad
Dream Keeper & Other Poems
Harriet Tubman
Seven Candles for Kwanza
Cut from the Same Cloth
Bill Pickett – Rodeo Ridin' Cowboy
In the Time of the Drums
Max Found Two Sticks
Jojo's Flying Side Kick
The Adventures of Sparrowboy
Cosmo and the Robot

[i] Melody Lane: By the Beautiful Sea http://www.melodylane.net/sea.html August 2, 2001
[ii] Baylor, Byrd I'm In Charge of Celebrations, ill. Peter Parnall, Scribners, 1986.
[iii] A Gift http://www.150.si.edu/chap1/one.htm August 3, 2001
[iv] Robert Service, Cremation of Sam McGee, http://www.wordfocus.com/wordactcremation.html August 5, 2001
[v] BrainyQuote: Leonardo da Vinci http://www.brainyquote.com/quotes/quotes/l/q125723.html October 14, 2001
[vi] About Jon and Lane, Lane Smith http://www.chucklebait.com/bio.htm August 5, 2001
[vii] Penguin Putnam: Lane Smith http://www.penguinputnam.com/Author/AuthorFrame?0000024178 August 5, 2001

5/3/2002

September
Moon of Drying Grass

"Climb the mountains and get their good tidings. Nature's peace will flow into you as sunshine flows into trees. The winds will blow their own freshness into you, and the storms their energy, while cares will drop away from you like the leaves of autumn."

John Muir

Special Month

Library Card Sign-up Month
Library Card Sign-up Month began in 1987 as a response to Secretary of Education Bennett's challenge "Let's have a national campaign…every child should obtain a library card - and use it."[i] The American Library Association, with partners from schools, businesses and concerned citizens, sponsors the events. The ALA says, the most important school supply your child needs is a library card! Visit their site for the most current information and resources to help you plan your celebrations.
- Library Card Sign Up Month http://www.ala.org/pio/librarycard/

One library you can visit that doesn't require a card is the Internet Public Library. Check out their reading room. Use the *Compact for Reading* sponsored by the Department of Education to encourage parents to support reading in the home.
- Internet Public Library http://www.ipl.org/
- A Compact for Reading http://www.ed.gov/pubs/CompactforReading/

Read Any Good Books Lately?
What do you want to do when you've just finished a good book? You want to tell someone about it. So do kids. These are some online book discussion clubs for kids.
- Reading Scene http://www.eduplace.com/readingscene/
- Simon Says http://www.simonsays.com/subs/txtobj.cfm?areaid=183&pagename=resources_materials
- Scholastic Book Central http://www.scholastic.com/titles/index.htm

And, for some motivational programs that encourage children to read, check these out.
- Book Adventure http://www.scholastic.com/titles/index.htm
- Pizza Hut Book It http://www.pizzahut.com./news/pressreleases/1999/092999_bookit_facts.asp

Accelerated Reading
The Accelerated Reading Program validates student's reading comprehension by using computer-assisted assessment. It encourages students to read more, longer, and harder books and provides formative feedback for the teacher. To learn more about Accelerated Reading refer to the following sites.
- What is accelerated reading? http://readingonline.org/critical/topping/rolarD.html
- Accelerated Reader http://www.perma-bound.com/arinfo.htm
- Increase the Joy of Teaching and the Love of Reading http://www.renlearn.com/ar/
- Accelerated Reading http://www.indiana.edu/~eric_rec/ieo/bibs/accl-rdr.html

Reading Resources for Parents and Teachers
There are many organizations that provide resources about reading for parents and teachers. Many of these sites also have interactive activities for children.

- International Reading Association http://www.reading.org/
  - Reading Online http://www.readingonline.org/
- Reading Rainbow http://gpn.unl.edu/rainbow/
- Reading is Fundamental http://www.rif.org/
- Reading Pathfinder http://readingpath.org
- Reading Recovery http://www.readingrecovery.org/
- World of Reading http://www.worldreading.org/

Latin American Month
September 15 – October 15
The Latin American population is the largest growing minority in the United States. Take this month to get to know Hispanic people, culture and some exciting legends. It is important for us, as teachers, to understand the heritage of our students. I recommend the following sites:
- Teaching from a Hispanic Perspective http://www.literacynet.org/lp/hperspectives/contents.html
- Hispanic Culture in Arizona http://www.azcentral.com/culturesaz/hispanic/hispindex.shtml
- Celebrate Hispanic Heritage http://teacher.scholastic.com/hispanic/index.htm
- Latino – Hispanic Heritage Month http://eduscapes.com/42explore/latino.htm

With most of the new immigrants coming from Mexico and Latin America, learn something about their native country. Use the following sites for map study and online tours.
- Mexico for Kids http://www.elbalero.gob.mx/kids/index_kids.html
- Discovering Mexico http://www.nationalgeographic.com/mexico/index.html
- Countries in Latin America http://lanic.utexas.edu/subject/countries.html

Nothing is so reflective of a culture as the language. Add some Spanish words to your 'word wall' and encourage the students to use them in their writing throughout the month. First, go to *Speak Spanish* and copy the alphabet on cards to display with the American alphabet on the front chalkboard. Then, learn some simple phrases such as *yes, no, please and thank you: se, no, por favor y gracias.* Use the *Palabras=words* site to see how similar some Spanish and English words are. Go to the *Little Explorers Dictionary* and turn on the English to Spanish option. Use this resource to make a class ABC book in Spanish. When you're ready for some more, go to the *Latino Lingo* site.
- Speak Spanish http://www.olvera-street.com/spanish.html
- Little Explorers Dictionary http://www.enchantedlearning.com/Dictionary.html
- Palabras = words http://teacher.scholastic.com/hispanic/act11.htm
- Latino Lingo http://www.latinolingo.com/

Listen to some personal stories and oral histories.
- Hispanic Voices http://www.azcentral.com/culturesaz/voices.shtml#hispanic

And, while you're listening, check out the impact Latino music is having on American pop music.
- Hispanic Music and Dance (with clips)
  http://www.azcentral.com/culturesaz/hispanic/hispmusic.shtml
- LaMusica http://www.lamusica.com/main/ (online radio station)
- Pop Latino Music http://www.freezone.com/popculture/latin/cover.html
- Folk music http://www.jps.net/gil98/
- Musica Latina http://www.ondanet.com/latinos/welcome.html

La Llorona
- One of the best-known, and most exciting Hispanic folk tales is "La Llorona," weeping woman. The story tells of a woman who marries a man of a different social background. She bears him several children, but he rejects her, leaving her for another woman. Distraught, the woman drowns her children and in regret, drowns herself. Her ghost, La Llorna walks the earth late at night along river bottoms looking for her lost children. This story is very old, going back several hundred years. It is also told in many different countries and therefore, makes it an excellent tool

to study evolution of folk tales. Modern versions, written for younger children do not have the mother killing the children. For an early, authentic version, go to *La Llorona* (1), but for a chilling interactive version, go to *La Llorona* (2). When you are at this site, be sure to look at the timeline. This will give you some good information for the courtroom or talk show activity.

- La Llorona (1) http://www.literacynet.org/lp/hperspectives/llorona.html
- La Llorona (2) http://www.lallorona.com/

Different Versions of La Llorona

- Texas Version http://thealamo.net/~jeffket/Llorona.html
- German Version http://www.ghosts.org/faq/germanllorona.html

Lesson Plans for Teaching La Llorona

- Folklore of the Southwest: La Llorona
  http://regcol.edb.utexas.edu/online/EASYTECH/readfinl/lalloron/laindex.htm
- La Llorona: Giver of life or taker of life
- http://www2.cwrl.utexas.edu/sheila/314f95/projects/group5/LLORONA.HTM
- Lesson Plan for Teaching La Llorona
  http://memorial.sdcs.k12.ca.us/LESSONS/LaLloronaUnit/ronatg.htm

Even though this story is hundreds of years old, the themes of betrayal, jealousy, envy and revenge are as modern as today. This is a story that could come from the newspaper headlines. Therefore, it lends itself very well to reenactment as either a courtroom drama or a TV talk show; either one of these an exciting classroom activity.

- Texas Mother Charged With Killing Her Five Children
  http://www.cnn.com/2001/US/06/20/children.killed/

Recent Print Versions of La Llorona

- *Maya's Children*, Anaya, R.
- *Prietita and the Ghost*, Anzalua, G.
- *In My Family/En Mi Familia*, Garza, C.L.
- *La Llorona, The Weeping Woman,* Hayes, J.
- *Stories That Must Not Die*, Sauvageau J.

Special Week

Last Week
Banned Book Week

> *"One of the unsung freedoms that go with a free press is the freedom not to read it."*
> - Ferdinand Mount

Banned Book Week celebrates our freedom of speech; a right guaranteed by the 1st Amendment of the Constitution. The American Library Association sponsors the week's activities and maintains a web site to distribute information and resources. Also, refer to the *Loyola University Online Display of Banned Books*. Discuss with your students why some people feel certain books should be banned.

- Banned Book Week http://www.ala.org/bbooks/
- Banned Books and Censorship http://www.luc.edu/libraries/banned/

Banned Books and the 1st Amendment

> *"If there is a bedrock principle underlying the First Amendment, it is that the Government may not prohibit the expression of an idea simply because society finds the idea itself offensive or disagreeable."*

Have your students read a copy of the 1ˢᵗ Amendment of the Constitution. The first site would be good for younger students; the second site is better for an older student. Students can also search for Thomas Jefferson quotes about freedom of speech and censorship.

- 1ˢᵗ Amendment http://gi.grolier.com/presidents/aae/side/amend.html
- 1ˢᵗ Amendment http://caselaw.lp.findlaw.com/data/constitution/amendment01/
- Thomas Jefferson On Politics and Government http://etext.virginia.edu/jefferson/quotations/

Note: For teachers, who want to read more about freedom of speech on the Internet, refer to the Blue Ribbon Campaign http://www.eff.org/br/

Banned Book Display

Proponents of banning books would outlaw such children's books, as *Dr. Dolittle*, *Huckleberry Finn*, and the *Grimm's Fairy Tales*. Read why these and other books have been placed on the banned books list. Make a display of banned books for your library or better yet, a storefront on Main Street!

- Banned Books Online http://digital.library.upenn.edu/books/banned-books.html
- Most Frequently Banned Books http://www.cs.cmu.edu/Web/People/spok/most-banned.html
- 100 Most Frequently Challenged Books http://www.ala.org/alaorg/oif/top100bannedbooks.html

Date Varies

1ˢᵗ Day of Fall
Autumnal Equinox
September 21, 22, or 23

Like the spring equinox, the exact day of Autumnal Equinox can vary. In the case of the Autumnal Equinox, it can vary as much as three days. On the equinox, the sun rises exactly in the east and sets, exactly in the west. It is one of two days during the year that everyone on Earth has exactly 12 hours of daylight. Both of these sites have very nice diagrams showing the movement of the sun. Find an object that is directly west of another a known object. Use your digital camera to take a picture of the object, everyday at the same time at sunset. Start a week before the equinox and continue for a week after the equinox. It is surprising how you can see the sun move.

- The Equinox http://solar.physics.montana.edu/YPOP/Classroom/Lessons/Sundials/equinox.html
- The Autumnal Equinox http://www.stcloudstate.edu/~physcrse/astr106/emapautumn.html

For a cartoon explanation and illustration of fall equinox, refer to Star Man.

- Star Man http://www.arval.org.ve/SmSep97.htm

Native American Day is the 4ᵗʰ Friday of the month. This may be near Autumnal Equinox. *Autumn Equinox* is an article that first appeared in the Bear Tribe Newsletter from Alabama that shows a little of how some Native Americans feel about the equinox.

- Bear Tribe: Autumn Equinox http://www.ewebtribe.com/BearTribe/news-events/autumn/fall.html

This is a collection of original poems by people from all over the world, celebrating a day of world peace, when the world is in perfect balance.

- Project Equinox http://www.el.net/poem/

Fall Color

What causes the leaves to change from green to the beautiful colors of the fall, red, orange and yellow? According to Indian legend, when the hunters in the sky kill the Great Bear (constellation), his blood drips on the forests changing the color from green to red. Or, some believe that Jack Frost paints the leaves with frost causing them to change. To explore a more conventional answer, check out these web sites.

- Why do leaves change colors in the fall? http://www.sciencemadesimple.com/leaves.html

- Separate colors in a green leaf (experiment)
    http://www.sciencemadesimple.com/leaves.html#PROJECTS
- The Chemistry of Autumn Colors http://scifun.chem.wisc.edu/chemweek/fallcolr/fallcolr.html

Make a scrapbook of fall leaves. Have the students collect leaves. Scan them and use them to make a multimedia scrapbook using a publishing program such as PowerPoint. The *Common Trees* site will help you identify the leaves and gives brief information for each tree.

- Common Trees http://www.dcnr.state.pa.us/forestry/commontr/common.htm

Midis

- Dance of the Autumn Leaves http://www.kididdles.com/mouseum/d043.html
- Autumn Leaves http://www.wwa.com/~blewis/MIDI/Swing/Autumn.html
- September Song http://jadierose.com/midicollection.html

For the fall colors near you, go to the USDA web site. They also link to other fall related sites.

- USDA Forest Service Hot Line http://www.fs.fed.us/news/fall.shtml
- GORPs Top Ten Scenic Drives http://www.gorp.com/gorp/activity/byway/topten.htm

Note: Since you have the leaves, make nature t-shirts @ http://family.go.com/crafts/sew/craft/naturetee/?clk=1011356

Odds and Ends

- Kids Domain http://www.kidsdomain.com/holiday/fall/paper.html
- Fall / Autumn Theme http://www.childfun.com/themes/fall.shtml
- Fall Activities and Crafts http://members.nbci.com/luv4kids/fall_activities.html

> ## Sugar Maple
>
> The sugar maple typically reaches
> 60'-80' high. Its hard wood is used
> for furniture, musical instruments,
> and flooring. The
> sap is tapped for maple syrup
> production.

Grandparents Day
1st Sunday after Labor Day
Grandparent's Day was the brainchild of Marian McQuade, a housewife from West Virginia. She wanted to champion the cause of lonely elderly in nursing homes. In 1978, five years after its West Virginia inception, the United States Congress passed legislation proclaiming the first Sunday after Labor Day as National Grandparents Day. September was chosen for the holiday, to signify the "autumn years" of life.[ii] Read more about how Grandparents Day got started and how it is celebrated.

- National Grandparents Day http://www.grandparents-day.com/
- Grandparent's Day http://www.geocities.com/Heartland/Forest/5675/gramindex.html
- Annie's Grandparent's Day Links http://www.annieshomepage.com/grandparentsdaylinks.html

A Couple of Classroom Projects

With families today being so non-traditional, it may be difficult to meet the needs of all of your students with conventional grandparent activities. Depending on your class, students could do these projects for their grandparents or in keeping with Marian McQuade's original intention, for 'grandparents' in the nursing home.

1. Have the students copy and paste one of the pictures into a paint program. Use the computer tools to 'color' the picture. Print the pictures. Glue a picture of the child who colored the picture on the paper before you laminate them. Take them to a local nursing home to use as placemats on their tables.

- Coloring page for Grandma http://www.dltk-kids.com/crafts/grandparents/mgrandmaposter.htm
- Coloring page for Grandpa http://www.dltk-kids.com/crafts/grandparents/mgrandmaposter.htm

2. Use the conversation starters to interview the 'grandparent.' Have the students make a 'This is Your Life' presentation for each person based on the interview.

- Conversation starters http://www.igrandparents.com/grandTopics/articles/Mini-Sites/GrandparentsDay/GPConvStarters.asp

Aging in the United State

What are the problems and concerns of the elderly in our society today? Have the students work in pairs to make a list of 10 things that they find that are on the minds of aging people in our society. With a word processor, make a table. Minimize the table and open each site and minimize that so they have two windows open at the same time. Skim the headlines at each site to see what's being discussed. What conclusions can students draw from this information? If they were a legislator, how would they view this information, an adult with an elderly parent? How does the information from the U. S. Census Bureau impact their thinking?

Top Concerns of the Elderly

	NIA	NCA	AARP	ASA
Health	X		X	X
Insurance		X	X	
Jobs		X		
Housing	X		X	
Income				

- National Institute on Aging http://www.nih.gov/nia/
- National Council on Aging http://www.ncoa.org/
- American Society on Aging http://www.asaging.org/ASA_Home_New5.cfm
- AARP http://www.aarp.org/
- Census Facts About the Elderly http://www.census.gov/Press-Release/fs97-09.html

Grandparents Day Projects

- A Grandparent Letter to Fill In http://www.searsportrait.com/storybook/gp_day_00_form.html
- Billy Bear's Grandparents Day Activities http://www.billybear4kids.com/holidays/grandparents/day.html
- Projects http://www.geocities.com/Heartland/Forest/5675/gramprojects.html

- Web Quest: Grandparent's Day http://www.grandparents-day.net/
- Family Tree Template http://www.grandparents-day.com/family_tree.htm

Labor Day
1st Monday

"Human history is work history. The heroes of the people are work heroes."

-- Meridel le Sueur

"Labor is man's greatest function.
He is nothing, he can do nothing,
he can achieve nothing,
he can fulfill nothing, without working."

-- Orville Dewey

President Cleveland signed the United State's Labor Day observance into law in the late 1894. Labor Day is dedicated to the social and economic achievements of American workers. It is a yearly national tribute to the contributions workers have made to the strength, prosperity and well being of our country.[iii] After having the students read the history and origins of Labor Day, have the students use the information to write a play.   The following scenario might be appropriate: The Pullman Strike, Labor Reformers, or Contemporary Celebrations.
- History of Labor Day http://www.dol.gov/dol/opa/public/aboutdol/laborday.htm
- Labor History http://home.earthlink.net/~scheppg/lab_hist.html
- Labor Day http://www.geocities.com/~cybergrandma/labor.htm
- Labor Day - Honoring Working Women
  http://www.geocities.com/TheTropics/Bay/5177/laborday.htm
- Origins of Labor Day http://www.pbs.org/newshour/bb/business/september96/labor_day_9-2.html
- Spotlight Biography: Labor Reformers http://educate.si.edu/spotlight/labor.html

Note: Patricia and Fredrick McKissack's A Long Hard Journey: The Story of the Pullman Porter, is an
excellent book to read to your students.

These sites have many ideas to help you celebrate Labor Day.
- Labor and Labor Day http://tlc.ai.org/laborday.htm
- Labor Day Funology http://members.aol.com/_ht_a/funology1/laborday.htm
- Celebrating Labor Day http://www.geocities.com/holidayzone/labor/index.html
- Labor Unions in the 21 Century http://idahoptv.org/ntti/nttilessons/lessons2000/yopp.html

What do you want to be when you grow up?
The answer was a lot easier for me than for my daughters because I had so few choices - teacher, nurse, waitress, beautician. My daughters, fortunately, had so many more choices. But, what will be the options for all workers in the new millennium? Have your students do some brainstorming – tour guide on Mars, robot repairperson. I'm sure your students will be much more creative. Have the students choose one job from the list and write a Help Wanted ad for the Millennium Press, Labor Day 2100.

Native American Day
4th Friday

"Even the seasons form a great circle in their changing,
and always come back again to where they were.
The life of a man is a circle from childhood to childhood,
and so it is in everything where power moves."

- Black Elk, Oglala Sioux Holy Man

Native American Day has been set aside to recognize the contributions the first Americans have made to the establishment and growth of our Nation. Take this opportunity to learn more about the great Native American chiefs. Ask small groups of students to prepare a report about one of these great leaders. Display a map of the United States on a bulletin board. When the students make their presentation, ask them to hang up a picture of their chief on the map in the area where the chief lived. Play Native American music in the background while the students give their report.

- Biography Research Paper http://www.abcteach.com/Writing/biography.htm
- Pictures of Great Chiefs http://www.geocities.com/RainForest/7694/chiefs.html
- Indian History http://www.indian-history.com/
- Pre-Contact Housing http://www.kstrom.net/isk/maps/houses/housingmap.html
- Quotes from Our Past http://www.ilhawaii.net/~stony/quotes.html
- Native American Navigator http://www.ilt.columbia.edu/k12/naha/nanav.html
- Native American Music http://www.geocities.com/RainForest/7694/music.html
- Native American Icons and Clip Art http://members.aol.com/poison64/nagifs/gifs.html

Native American Calendar
The first Americans have very descriptive names for the months (moons) of the year. Make titles for the months and fasten them to your classroom calendar. Choose the names used by the tribe indigenous to your state.

- Names of the Indian Moons http://members.tripod.com/~PHILKON/moons.html

Odds and Ends
This site has music, stories, songs, information about different tribes and lots more that is easy to use for younger students.

- Marilee's Native American Links
  http://www.ameritech.net/users/macler/nativeamericans.html#ClipArt

Looking for some general information about Native American Day? This is it!

- Native American Day http://www.holidayinsights.com/other/native.htm

These links are a sample from the book of the same title.

- On This Day In North American Indian History http://members.tripod.com/~PHILKON/

This is another site with lots of links.

- Native American Sites http://www.nativeculture.com/lisamitten/indians.html

Native Americans are well known for their storytelling. This is a great introduction to Native American Legends.

- Cyberhunt: Native American Legends
  http://teacher.scholastic.com/lessonrepro/reproducibles/instructor/crossword/0104/index.htm

And, *Education World* offers lots of well-prepared lesson plans related to a variety of Native American issues.

- Education World: Native Americans http://www.education-world.com/a_special/native_americans_2000.shtml

Note: Native American Month is celebrated in November. Refer to November for many more resources and suggestions for honoring the indigenous peoples of the Americas.

Rosh Hashanah

In September or October, Jews believe that God opens the Book of Life for ten days, starting with Rosh Hashanah (the Jewish New Year) and ending with Yom Kippur (the Day of Atonement). Rosh Hashanah is observed on the first and second day of the month of Tishrei. Rosh Hashanah means, literally, "head of the year" or "first of the year." [iv] It is a time to look back on the past and plan for the future. *Torah Tots* has a very easy to understand explanation of this most important holiday of the Jewish year, plus many stories and activities for children.

- Torah Tots http://www.torahtots.com/holidays/rosh/roshstr.htm
  - Tishrei http://www.torahtots.com/holidays/rosh/tishrei.htm
- Listen to a shofar http://www.holidays.net/highholydays/shofar.htm
- Listen to Yiddish Radio http://www.soundportraits.org/on-air/yiddish_radio_project/

Yom Kippur

Yom Kippur falls on the eve of the tenth day of Tishrei. It begins with a fast that lasts for 25+ hours. It is the most solemn day of the year, a day of fasting and prayers. It is also the happiest day of the year, as people feel closer to G-d because all of their sins have been forgiven and they have resolved to be better in the coming year. Again, the *Torah Tots* site offers and excellent description of the holiday.

- Torah Tots http://www.torahtots.com/holidays/yomkipur/yomk.htm
- Yom Kippur http://www.jewfaq.org/holiday4.htm
- Akhlah http://www.akhlah.com/holidays/roshhashana/RoshHashannah.asp
- Yom Kippur http://www.joi.org/celebrate/yomkipp/

Special Days

September 3, 1766

Uncle Sam's Birthday

Although no one is certain how and who created Uncle Sam, the consensus is he was named for Samuel Wilson of New York. Read the legend of Uncle Sam, a symbol who has come to stand for the United States.

- Biography of Uncle Sam http://home.nycap.rr.com/content/us_bio.html
  - Uncle Sam Image Gallery http://home.nycap.rr.com/content/us_contents.html
- Uncle Sam http://bensguide.gpo.gov/3-5/symbols/unclesam.html
- Who2: Uncle Sam http://www.who2.com/unclesam.html
- Uncle Sam Coloring Page http://www.statefarm.com/kidstuf/politcolor/polcolor.htm

I Want You

Although Uncle Sam's image has appeared on everything form soup to nuts, the most famous is the *I Want You* poster painted by James Montgomery Flagg during WWI. See the original poster at the Library of Congress. Make a poster of Uncle Sam and use it for the bulletin board where you list the classroom helpers for the week. Use sayings such as, "I want you for the line leader," or "I want you to water the plants."

- I Want You Poster http://lcweb.loc.gov/exhibits/treasures/trm015.html

The Library of Congress is also hosting a joint exhibition of John Bull (the English symbol) and Uncle Sam British American Relations. You can view the exhibit online.

- John Bull and Uncle Sam http://www.loc.gov/exhibits/british/

Mascots

Uncle Sam is a symbol that represents the United States. Whenever people see his image, they think of the United States. Mascots are symbols that represent schools and athletic teams. What is your school mascot? Have your students design a mascot for your classroom. Discuss the controversial use of Native American symbols for mascots.

- Indian Mascots and Logos http://pages.prodigy.net/munson/
- I Who's Honor? http://www.inwhosehonor.com/
- American Indian Sports Team Mascots http://earnestman.tripod.com/1indexpage.htm

Odds and Ends

- Make an Uncle Sam Folk Art Figure http://www.holidays.net/independence/craft.htm
- Symbols of the United States http://www.mcm.edu/~williamm/ussymbols/
- Symbols of the United States http://www.kn.pacbell.com/wired/fil/pages/listussymj.html
- Symbols of the United States http://bensguide.gpo.gov/k-2/symbols/index.html
- Simple WebQuest: Symbols of the United States
  http://www.nashville.k12.tn.us/webquests/united_states_symbols.htm

September 7, 1860
Grandma Moses' Birthday

"Life is what we make it, always has been, always will be."

- Grandma Moses

Anna Mary Robertson Moses, Grandma Moses, began painting in her seventies when the responsibilities she had, as a busy farm wife, no longer occupied her time. She became one of America's most noted folk artists, creating over 1500 paintings, (well, she did live to be 101 years old!) Read more about the life of this inspirational woman.

- Grandma Moses' Art http://www.jsonline.com/onwisconsin/arts/apr01/moses16_s041301.asp
- Memory is a Painter http://www.tfaoi.com/newsm1/n1m45.htm

The Story of the Painting

Have the students choose one of their favorite Grandma Moses paintings. Copy and paste it to a word processor. As the students look at the picture, have them make lists of everything they notice, colors, sites, people, animals, etc. Have them identify ten to twenty words related to the picture. Make a glossary of their words using the Glossary Maker. This will give them other forms of the word plus definitions and synonyms. Have the students write a story about what's happening in the painting, using their word list.

- The Bennington Museum http://www.benningtonmuseum.com/grandmagallery.html
- Glossary Maker http://school.discovery.com/teachingtools/glossarybuilder/index.html

Odds and Ends

- Artist of the Week Lesson Plan http://hometown.aol.com/powers8696/page11.html
- Grandma Moses Quotes http://www.bemorecreative.com/one/18.htm
- Ask Art http://askart.com/artist/M/anna_robertson_moses.asp

September 8
International Literacy Day

"A room without books is like a body without a soul."
-- Cicero
"The man who does not read good books has no advantage over the man who can't read them."
-- Mark Twain

What a great way to start the new school year – promoting literacy! The purpose of this day is to focus attention on the worldwide literacy issues and needs. It is estimated that more than 880 million of the world's adults do not know how to read or write. More than 120 million children lack access to education. The International Reading Association and the United Nations sponsor International Literacy Day. Refer to their sites for more information about worldwide literacy concerns and suggestions for celebrating Literacy Day in your community. PBS also has a great lesson plan for International Literacy Day.

- IRA http://www.reading.org
  - International Literacy Day http://www.reading.org/meetings/ild/index.html
  - Campaign for World Literacy http://www.reading.org/advocacy/campaign.html
- United Nations http://www.un.org
- Literacy Day http://www.pbs.org/teachersource/prek2/issues/index.shtm

Folktales From Around the World

Storytelling is a great form of entertainment found all over the world. It is truly 'international.' These sites have wonderful folktales. Make it a goal to read a story from every continent. Have the students download and print a world map. After the students have read a story, have them write in the title of the story on the appropriate continent.

- World Map http://www.abcteach.com/Maps/world.htm
- World Folktales http://www.catawba.k12.nc.us/webquest/johnson/storywebsites.htm
- Folktales http://www.peacecorps.gov/wws/folktales/index.html
- Tales of Wonder http://members.nbci.com/darsie/tales/
- Absolutely Whootie - Stories to Grow By http://hazel.forest.net/whootie/default.html

For the Teacher

- Researching the Folktale http://www.aaronshep.com/storytelling/A65.html
- Legends in Their Times
  http://www.nytimes.com/learning/teachers/lessons/001018wednesday.html

Keypals and Books

Locate a school in a Spanish speaking country to be your keypals for the year. Save your points from your books orders and throughout the year, use your extra points to buy books in Spanish. Send them to your keypal partners. Students can read the same books and 'discuss' the books with their keypal. Tradin' Places is a neat lesson plan about exchanging slide shows or photo albums with keypals.

- Internet Keypal Exchanges http://www.cln.org/int_keypals.html
- Tradin' Places
  http://www.kodak.com/global/en/consumer/education/lessonPlans/lessonPlan069.shtml
- Scholastic Book Club http://teacher.scholastic.com/clubs/
- Trumpet Book Club http://www.trumpetclub.com/

September 8, 1900
Galveston Hurricane

For people in Galveston, Texas, 'the storm' always refers to the hurricane that tore across Galveston on September 8, 1900, and left the city in ruins with more than 6000 men, women and children dead. That is twice as many people than who died in the San Francisco Earthquake, and four times as many people who died on the Titanic. It is the deadliest natural disaster that ever happened in the United States. To get a historical perspective on the great storm, read these accounts. You can watch a video of the Galveston Hurricane at the Discovery site.

- Remembering the Great Hurricane: 1900 Storm http://www.1900storm.com/
- Isaac Cline's Account of the Storm http://www.history.noaa.gov/stories/cline2.html
- The Galveston Hurricane
  http://www.kidscastle.si.edu/channels/history/articles/historyarticle14.html
- The History of Galveston http://www.galvestonhistory.org/history.htm
- The Dallas Morning News http://www.dallasnews.com/tsw/galveston/
- CNN: The Galveston Hurricane http://www.cnn.com/SPECIALS/2000/galveston/
- Galveston History http://www.galvestonhistory.org/history.htm
- Super Storms: Galveston Hurricane http://www.discovery.com/stories/science/hurricanes/see.html
- This Century's Greatest Hurricanes http://www.stormsignals.com/greatest.htm

Hurricanes

At the time of the Galveston hurricane, there was little known about predicting hurricanes. Isaac Cline was the chief of the U.S. Weather Service bureau in Galveston during the 1900 storm. After the storm, his study and research about tropical storms gave guidance to weather forecasters until WWII. What is a hurricane? How can we predict when they will happen? How can we prepare for them?

- Storm of the Century http://www.weather.com/newscenter/specialreports/sotc/storm4/page1.html
- FEMA Hurricanes http://www.fema.gov/kids/hurr.htm
- National Hurricane Center http://www.nhc.noaa.gov/
- Hurricanes http://eduscapes.com/42explore/hurricane.htm
- Disaster Safety: Hurricane
  http://www.redcross.org/services/disaster/keepsafe/readyhurricane.html

Weather Forecast

In the early 1900's there were no nightly weather forecasts. We are fortunate today that we not only have forecasts but storm warnings and alerts to help us prepare for hazardous weather. Have your students work in teams to prepare a weather forecast. Use the charts and maps, including live Doppler, to prepare their forecast. Have them copy and paste the pictures they need to PowerPoint or another presentation tool. In addition to these national sites, look at your local television station's weather site.

- Weather http://www.weather.com
- NOAA http://www.noaa.gov/wx.html

Journal Writing

At the time of the Galveston hurricane, there was no such thing as support groups or counseling. But, everyone knew tragedy; they had lost a loved one, seen their home destroyed or had been hurt themselves. The way many of the people dealt with their feelings was to write about them. Many of these journals, including Isaac Cline's Weather Report are now in the Rosenberg Library in Galveston. Have your students write about a sad or scary or disappointing time in their life. Have them describe how they felt at the time and now.

- Rosenberg Library http://rosenberg-library.org/gthc/1900storm.htm

September 11
9-1-1 Emergency Number Day
President Ronald Reagan signed a proclamation in 1987 making September 11th "9-1-1 Emergency Number Day." September 11th was chosen for the annual celebration for obvious reasons (9/11.) What a great way to kick off the new school year. Help children learn when and how to make emergency calls. Have them make a list of information they will need to know. Print the list on magnetic paper so they can keep it on the refrigerator.
- National Emergency Number Association http://www.nena9-1-1.org/
- 911 Emergency http://911-emergency.com/
- Dial 911 Practice Phone http://www.statefarm.com/jscript/phone.htm
- Magnetic Computer Paper http://www.avery.com/

September 11, 2001
Terrorists Attack The United States
On this bright fall day, the unimaginable happened. Four commercial American airlines were hijacked and used as flying bombs to destroy the World Trade Center in New York City, part of the Pentagon in northern Virginia and cause the crash of one airline in western Pennsylvania. Over 6,000 innocent men, women and children were killed. Firefighters, police officers, emergency care providers and citizens from around the world came together to help the wounded, find the lost and give comfort to each other and all of us. Helping children understand what happened and feel safe became a top priority. These sites provide guidance.
- The National Mental Health Association: Coping with Disaster http://www.nmha.org/
- Discussing Tragedy with Children http://www.lightspan.com/portal/anationaltragedy.htm
- How to Help Children http://www.abcteach.com/wwcenter.htm
  - USA Pride http://www.abcteach.com/USA/usatoc.htm
- Scholastic http://www.scholastic.com/
- Discussing Terrorism http://school.discovery.com/conversations/attacks1.html
- Information for Children http://www.departments.dsu.edu/library/Kids.htm
- EDUHound http://www.eduhound.com/
- Peace Stories http://www.martinauer.net/KINDER/krieg/

The Tragedy
- Terror Hits Home http://www.time.com/time/photoessays/wtc/
- Photo Essay http://www.time.com/time/photoessays/reaction/
- It Didn't Seem Real http://www.time.com/time/photoessays/firefighter/
- The Flag Is Still There http://www.time.com/time/photoessays/usa/
- The Rescue Continues http://www.time.com/time/photoessays/rescue2/

The World Mourns
- A Heartfelt Thank You http://www.google.com/thankyou/

September 15, 1914
Robert McCloskey's Birthday
Caldecott Awarding winning author and illustrator, Robert McCloskey was born in Ohio, but spent most of his life in New England. As a young person, he loved playing the piano and thought he would be a musician. Read more about his life at the following Internet sites.
- Robert McCloskey http://www.edupaperback.org/authorbios/McCloskey_Robert.html
- Radio Interview http://www.hbook.com/exhibit/mccloskeyradio.html

Write about your area…

Robert McCloskey has written many books about Maine. He loves the fish and the birds of the area. Ask the students what they would write about if they were to write about the wildlife in their state. Have the students write a story outline.

- Books about Maine http://childrensbooks.about.com/library/weekly/aa050100a.htm

Fill in between the pictures….

In his biography, Robert McCloskey said, "I really think up stories in pictures and just fill in between the pictures with a sentence or a paragraph or a few pages of words."[v] Have your students explore this way of writing. Use a story grammar chart. Have the students choose three clip art pictures at random. Have the students use the first picture for the beginning of the story, the second picture for the middle of the story, and the third picture for the end of the story. The trick is, all of the pictures must fit in and the story must make sense.

- Story Grammar http://www.sasked.gov.sk.ca/docs/ela/ela_sgra.html
- Do you know your story grammar? http://www.auburn.edu/~murraba/breakthroughs/burnsrl.html

Odds and Ends

- Make Way for Ducklings
  http://www.mcps.k12.md.us/curriculum/socialstd/grade1/Make_Way.html
- Watch video of Blueberries for Sal http://www.readthebooks.com/pages/blueberriesforsal.html

Selected Books by Robert McCloskey
Make Way For Ducklings – Caldecott Award
Blueberries For Sal – Caldecott Honor
Centerburg Tales
One Morning In Maine
A Time of Wonder
Burt Dow, Deep-Water Man
Lentil
Homer Price

September 15, 1934
Tomie De Paola's Birthday

Tomie De Paola's Irish and Italian background plays an important part in his many stories, as does his affections and interactions with his grandmothers. Tomie has been honored for his work by receiving both the Caldecott Honor Award and the Newbery Honor Award, among others. Learn more about his background at the following Internet sites.

- Tomie DePaola (official homepage) http://www.bingley.com/MyWebPage.html
- Tomie DePaola http://www.edupaperback.org/authorbios/Depaola_Tomie.html
- Tomie DePaola
  http://www.simonsays.com/subs/183/Kids_Author_Bio.cfm?AUTHOR_KEY=706320&areaid=18
  3
- Tomie DePaola http://www.penguinputnam.com/Author/AuthorFrame?0000031532

Grandparents & Kids: A Writing Project

Many of Tomie DePaola's books are about his grandparents. In honor of Grandparents Day, have the students invite a grandparent to school. (Grandparent can be any older person.) Have the grandparent and the student team up to write a story. Ask the grandparent to tell a story from their life to the student. Story ideas might include: first day of school, about bothers and sisters, a pet, etc. Have the student take notes and ask clarifying questions until they fully understand the story. Then, have the student use a word processor to write the story. As Tomie says, "I don't write for children, I write from my own experience as a child, and I feel that as I get older those experiences are becoming more vivid with distance."[vi]

- A Little Advice for Interviewing
  http://www.countyconnections.org/projects/vistadlc/cruces/advice.html

Let's Pretend
Tomie DePaola credits his imagination to listening to the morning radio show, "Let's Pretend" when he was a child. Play a midi and ask the students to imagine the story that is happening. Of course, this is exactly what Walt Disney did when he created the classic Fantasia. These are a couple of my favorites.

- Tchaikovsky's 1812 Overture http://acctweb.tripod.com/music/1812.html
- Rimsky-Korsakov's Flight of the Bumblebee
  http://www.crosswinds.net/~musichistory/hist/romantic7.html
- Strauss's Blue Danube Waltz http://www.classicalarchives.com/midi-n-s.html#s
- Sousa's The Washington Post http://www.classicalarchives.com/midi-n-s.html#s
- Dubussy's The Snow is Dancing http://www.classicalarchives.com/debussy.html
- Copland's Tender Land Stomp Your Feet
  http://www.laurasmidiheaven.com/Classical/cgi/index2.cgi?action=displaycomp&compchoose=Copland,%20Aaron
- Fantasia http://www.dismusic.com/

Odds and Ends
- Teacher Resource File: Tomie DePaola http://falcon.jmu.edu/~ramseyil/depaola.htm

Selected books by Tomie DePaola
Strega Nona – Caldecott Honor
26 Fairmount Avenue – Newberry Honor
Christopher the Holy Giant – Aesop Award
What the Mailman Brought – Golden Kite Award
The Friendly Beast: An Old English Christmas Carol – Horn Book Honor Book
Giorgio's Village – Golden Kite Award

September 16, 1810
Mexican Independence Day

"Mexicanos, Viva México!"

- Miguel Hidalgo y Costilla

On this day in 1810, Miguel Hidalgo y Costilla, a Catholic priest, called the native Indians to retaliate against the hated native Spaniards who had exploited and oppressed Mexicans for ten generations. He urged them to recover the lands that were stolen from their ancestors. Learn more about the Mexican Revolution. *Note: A number of sites about Mexico are written in Spanish. You can translate them with Babel Fish.*

- Independence Day http://www.elbalero.gob.mx/kids/about/html/home.html
- Mexico Online http://www.mexonline.com/grito.htm
- Babel Fish Translator http://world.altavista.com/

Complete the matrix that was started in July.

Flag	
National Anthem	National Anthem of Mexico
Date of Independence	September 16, 1810
Language	Spanish / Español

- National Anthem of Mexico and Flag http://www.copcity.com/anthems/mexico.html
- Mexico http://www.cia.gov/cia/publications/factbook/geos/mx.html
- Mexico Daily http://www.mexicoguide.com/

Field Trip to the capital, Mexico City
Mexico City is the largest city in the world. Tour this historic city. What is the largest city in your state? How much larger is Mexico City?
- Mexico City http://www.cnn.com/TRAVEL/CITY.GUIDES/WTR/north.america.profiles/nap.mexico.html
- The Roots of the City http://www.mexicocity.com.mx/history1.html
- Population of Mexico City http://www.sru.edu/depts/artsci/ges/discover/d-6-45.htm

Fiesta!
Mexico is famous for it's wonderful music and colorful costumes. Celebrate Mexico's Independence Day with a Fiesta! After you have viewed some of these local dances, have the students make a presentation about regional dances of Mexico and other customs.
- Alegria: Regional Dances http://www.alegria.org/rgndance.html
- Mexico for Kids http://www.elbalero.gob.mx/index_kids.html
  - Myths and Stories http://www.elbalero.gob.mx/kids/about/html/myths/home.html

Note: This is the beginning of Hispanic American Month. You will find many more ideas and suggestions in that section.

September 17, 1952
Constitution Day

"We the People of the United States…"

On September 17, 1787, fifty-five delegates to the Constitutional Convention met in Philadelphia to sign the Constitution of the United States. It would be another year before all 13 states would ratify the Constitution. During that year, there was much argument and disagreement among the people, many were opposed; in fact, probably over half of people in the entire country opposed it. But with the promise of the Bill of Rights, it was finally passed. One hundred and seventy one years later, September 17, 1952, congress passed PL 82-261 and made September 17th a national holiday. The National Archives and Records Administration has an excellent site with many original documents, lesson plans and activities to help you celebrate the cornerstone of the United States of America.
- Constitution Day http://www.nara.gov/education/teaching/constitution/home.html

Visit the National Constitution Center for additional information and more lesson plans and activities. At this site you can order free copies of the Constitution for each of your students and a kit to help you plan an "I Signed the Constitution" day complete with copies of the Constitution, buttons and more. *Note: you need to order your kit by June 1, so plan ahead for next year.*

- National Constitution Center http://www.constitutioncenter.org
- Order Kit http://www.constitutioncenter.org/sections/news/events/sign_info_req.asp
- Constitution http://memory.loc.gov/const/abt_const.html

Amendments to the Constitution
Twenty-seven amendments have been added to the Constitution since 1789. The first ten amendments, known as the Bill of Rights, were adopted as a unit in 1791. It is interesting to see what proposals are made for additional amendments. Go to *Thomas* and search for the word *Constitution*.
- Thomas http://thomas.loc.gov/

Field Trip to Philadelphia
Take a field trip to the largest city in the United States; at least it was in 1787.
- Virtual Tour of Historic Philadelphia http://www.ushistory.org/tour/index.html
- US History http://www.ushistory.org/

The Great Compromise
Throughout the summer of 1787, the delegates debated many issues. One of the most hotly contested was about slavery. The delegates from the North wanted to abolish slavery and the delegates from the South wanted to keep it. Read about the Great Compromise. Ask your students how would our history have been different if the northern delegates would have won that debate? Do students think it would have changed race relations in America? We often hear "Hindsight is 20/20." Discuss with your students what they would change if they could know the future. Have them write an essay about either wanting to know the future or not wanting to know the future.
- The Great Compromise http://www.nara.gov/exhall/charters/constitution/conhist.html
- Composition Patterns: Personal Essay
  http://cctc.commnet.edu/grammar/composition/personal.htm

September 21, 1897
New York Sun Editorial "Yes Virginia"
In answer to a little girl's question, newspaperman Francis Church wrote the most famous editorial in history. Ask your students why they think it is still so famous after all of these years? Why to they think the paper published the editorial in September and not December? Choose another mythical figure, such as the tooth fairy, the Great Pumpkin, or Uncle Sam and have them write an editorial either proclaiming its existence or disavowing it. *Only a Matter of Opinion* is an excellent lesson plan about editorials including a great 'how to' section.
- Yes Virginia http://www.geocities.com/cxtine6/poem_02.htm
- Editorials: Only A Matter of Opinion http://library.thinkquest.org/50084/editorials/

September 25, 1932
Shel Silverstein's Birthday
Shel Silverstein is best known in children's literature for his poetry; however, he was also a cartoonist, composer, lyricist and folksinger. One his hit songs was *A Boy Named Sue* recorded by Johnny Cash and he received a nomination for an Academy Award in Music for the song, *I'm Checkin' Out*. Enjoy the day by reading and listening to some of Shel Silverstein's poetry. *Note: Not all of the poetry one these Internet sites is for children.*
- Shel Silverstein
  http://www.poets.org/poets/poets.cfm?prmID=105&CFID=2390819&CFTOKEN=65468122
  (listen to him read The Toy Eater)
- Music and Lyrics of Shel Silverstein http://www.banned-width.com/shel/misc/lyrics.html
- If You're a Dreamer http://www.angelfire.com/anime2/mya2000/shel/index.html

- Teacher Resource File: Shel Silverstein http://falcon.jmu.edu/~ramseyil/silverstein.htm
- Shel Silverstein: A Retrospective
  http://www.nytimes.com/books/99/05/16/specials/silverstein.5a.html February 10, 2002

September 26, 1774
Johnny Appleseed's Birthday

John Chapman, better known as Johnny Appleseed, was born on September 26. The exact year and even place varies in different reports. He spent his life living simply, traveling all over western Pennsylvania, Ohio, Kentucky and Indiana planting apple trees. Some of those trees are still bearing fruit today.

- Johnny Appleseed's Birthday http://exit3.i-55.com/~vickib/johnny.html

Johnny Appleseed has become a folk hero, along with Paul Bunyan and Pecos Bill. The only difference is, unlike the others, he was a real person. But, his adventures and stories read like fiction. Enjoy some Johnny Appleseed stories with your students.

- Harper's 1871 - Johnny Appleseed, A Pioneer Hero
  http://mason.gmu.edu/~drwillia/apple/ja1sm.html
- Johnny Appleseed and Uncle Sam http://www.news-sentinel.com/ns/heartlnd/applseed/index.shtml
- Appleseed Alley http://www.geocities.com/Heartland/Fields/9587/
- Johnny Appleseed History http://www.jappleseed.org/history.html
- The Johnny Appleseed Homepage
  http://www.msc.cornell.edu/~weeds/SchoolPages/Appleseed/welcome.html
- Retelling of Johnny Appleseed's Life Story (2nd grade project)
  http://cnug.clackesd.k12.or.us/cedaroak/Teachers/old%20teachers/McClain/mcclain.html
- The Story of Johnny Appleseed (another 2nd grade project)
  http://www.hipark.austin.isd.tenet.edu/projects/second/ja/ja.html

Johnny Appleseed Story Starters

In the article about Johnny Appleseed and Uncle Sam, the author tells a few more stories about Johnny Appleseed, such as the time he put out the campfire so the mosquito wouldn't get burned. Have your students take one of these one-line stories to use for a story starter. Add their stories and illustrations to your web site and invite the 2nd grade teachers (see above) to share them with their students.

- Johnny Appleseed and Uncle Sam Tie-in http://www.news-sentinel.com/ns/heartlnd/applseed/index.shtml
- Tall Tales http://www.millville.org/Workshops_f/Dich_FOLKLORE/FOLKTEXT/lesson2.htm
- Tall Tales http://www.hasd.org/ges/talltale/talltale.htm

Johnny Appleseed Puzzles, Games and Lesson Plans

- Johnny Appleseed Puzzle http://www.marshall-es.marshall.k12.tn.us/jobe/Appleseed.html
- Johnny Appleseed Hidden Pictures http://www.niehs.nih.gov/kids/apples.htm
- Johnny Appleseed Hunt http://www.kn.pacbell.com/wired/fil/pages/huntjohnnyamr.html
- Primary Unit Plan http://home.att.net/~elteach/appleseed.html
- Johnny Appleseed Unit Plan
  http://www.richmond.edu/~ed344/webunits/khistory/johnnyappleseed2.html
- Johnny Appleseed Web Quest http://www.warren.k12.in.us/student/webquest/johnnyapple/
- Johnny Appleseed Cyber Trek
  http://www.anthonyschool.org/Connect/Johnny%20Appleseed/web/LP2johnny.htm

Apples

Apples were an important food for the people living on the frontier. They provided a nutritious source of food that lasted well into the winter and if the apples were dried, until the next harvest. Today, we know that apples are one of our best sources of vitamins. Learn a little more about how apples are raised, the different types of apples and the uses for apples. Then, host an apple tasting. Slice a variety of apples and place them on paper plates. Have the students describe each apple and vote for their favorite. Record their responses on a spreadsheet. Make a chart of their favorite apples.

- Apples http://www.abcteach.com/MonthtoMonth/September/applesTOC.htm
- Anthony Apple http://www.dole5aday.com/encyclopedia/apple/apple_menu.html
- Apples http://eduscapes.com/42explore/apples.htm
- History of Apples http://www.212.net/apples/apple3.htm
- Apples and More http://www.urbanext.uiuc.edu/apples/index.html

Odds and Ends
- How to Make An Apple Pie and See the World http://atozteacherstuff.com/lessons/apple-pie.shtml
- Apple Center Activities http://atozteacherstuff.com/lessons/apple-exploration.shtml
- Mott's Cyber Orchard http://208.240.91.227/indexp.htm
- Apple Corps http://apple-corps.westnet.com/apple_corps.html
- Apples http://www.geocities.com/Athens/8854/apples.html

September 27
Paul Goble's Birthday
Paul Goble was born and educated in England. He studied at the Central School of Art in London and later worked as a furniture designer, industrial consultant and art instructor. He became fascinated by Native American lore and culture as a young boy and visited South Dakota a number of times before moving to the United States in 1977. He became a citizen in 1984. He is an avid researcher and thoroughly researches the ancient stories before he retells them. Because he is so sympathetic to Native American ways many tribes have adopted him. He has always said that he particularly writes and paints to encourage Indian children to be proud of their culture.[vii] Paul Goble was awarded the Caldecott Award for *The Girl Who Loved Wild Horses* in 1978.

- Paul Goble http://monet.unk.edu/mona/contemp/paulgoble/goble.html
- Canku Ota Newsletter: Paul Goble http://www.turtletrack.org/Issues00/Co02262000/CO_02262000_Goble.htm
- Tipi Legend http://www.imdiversity.com/villages/native/Article_Detail.asp?Article_ID=5707

Ledger Art
The native artists from the Plains Indian Tribes developed a style of painting that represented and recorded their daily life, ceremony and history. Originally, these paintings were done on animal skins, but when the children were forced from their families on the reservations to attend boarding schools, the paintings were done on their ledger books or copybooks. They used colored pencils, crayon, and occasionally watercolor paints. Paul Goble uses an artistic style similar to ledger art. Today, these ledger books are highly prized not only for their history but also for the exquisitely simple artwork. Make a multimedia art display of Native American Ledger Art. Use a presentation tool such as HyperStudio. Copy and paste the artwork on to a slide. Add Native American music for background. Document all resources. *Note: Most Internet sites will allow use of their materials for classroom use only. A presentation made for and view in the classroom would be permissible, but do not attach it to your web page.*

- Ledger Art http://weber.ucsd.edu/Depts/Ethnic/fac/rfrank/Ledger.Project.Web/Ledger.Home.html
- Many Horses – Artwork of the Plains http://www.manyhorses.com/ledger.htm
- Pictograph Robes of the Plains First Nation http://www.glenbow.org/srobe/srobe.htm
- Ledger Drawings Then and Now http://www.collectorsguide.com/fa/fa056.shtml
- Native American Midis http://www.geocities.com/RainForest/7694/music.html

Illustrate a Native American Legend

Paul Goble retells Native American legends and illustrates them. He says that legends change and evolve through time. Have the students find a Native American story and use clip art to illustrate it. Use Flip Album to make their books. You can download a demo copy of Flip Album.

- Flip Album http://www.flipalbum.com

Native American Stories and Legends

- Myths and Legends of the Sioux
  http://etext.lib.virginia.edu/cgibin/toccer?id=MclMyth&tag=public&images=images/modeng&data=/lv1/Archive/eng-parsed&part=0
- Old Indian Legends
  http://etext.lib.virginia.edu/cgibin/toccer?id=ZitLege&tag=public&images=images/modeng&data=/lv1/Archive/eng-parsed&part=0
- Native American Lore http://www.ilhawaii.net/~stony/loreindx.html

Native American Clip Art and Backgrounds

- Native American Clip Art http://members.aol.com/poison64/nagifs/gifs.html
- Clip Art http://school.discovery.com/clipart/index.html

Selected books by Paul Goble
The Girl Who Loved Wild Horses – Caldecott Award
The Great Race
Return of the Buffalo
Her Seven Brothers
Brave Eagle's Account of the Fort Fetterman Fight
Iktomi and the Boulder
Adopted By Eagles
Beyond The Ridge
Death of the Iron Horse
Gift of the Sacred Dog
Iktomi and the Berries
Love Flute
Star Boy

Sept 30, 1927
Babe Ruth – Home Run Record (60)

George Herman "Babe" Ruth was born February 6, 1895; he would become the most famous athlete of all time, baseball's greatest star. Throughout his baseball career he made many baseball records, but the most famous of all was the 1927 single season home run total of 60. Throughout his career, he made 714 home runs. Both records have been broken now, but his remain, at least by some, the most memorable. Read about his amazing career and about three of the players who recently broke his record, Mark McGuire, Sammy Sosa and Barry Bonds.

- Babe Ruth Birthplace and Museum http://www.baberuthmuseum.com/html/client_frames.asp
- Babe Ruth http://www.baberuth.com/
- The Sultan of Swing: Mark McGwire http://www.markmcgwire.8m.com/
- Slammin' Sammy Sosa http://www.latinosportslegends.com/sosa.htm
- Barry Bonds http://sports.espn.go.com/mlb/players/profile?statsId=3918

Be A Record Maker

Ruth's hitting philosophy was, "I swing as hard as I can, and I try to swing right through the ball. I swing big, with everything I've got. I hit big or I miss big."[viii] Have your students think big and write a paper about what record they would like to break. It doesn't have to be in sports, it could be in the arts or in business or exploration or whatever else strikes their fancy. If they can dream it they can do it! Publish their papers in a book called, *We Can Do It*. Make copies for the class and challenge them to get out the book in 30 years to see how things are coming.

---

[i] ALA Fact Sheet http://www.ala.org/pio/factsheets/libcardmonth.html August 19, 2001

[ii] National Grandparent's Day http://www.grandparents-day.com/ August 19, 2001

[iii] U. S. Department of Labor *The History of Labor Day* http://www.dol.gov/dol/opa/public/aboutdol/laborday.htm August 21, 2001

[iv] Torah Tots *Rosh Hashana* http://www.torahtots.com/holidays/rosh/roshstr.htm August 21, 2001

[v] Robert McCloksey http://www.edupaperback.org/authorbios/mccloskey_robert.html August 20, 2001

[vi] Simon Says Kids *Tomie DePaola*
http://www.simonsays.com/subs/183/Kids_Author_Bio.cfm?AUTHOR_KEY=706320&areaid=183 August 21, 2001

[vii] Canku Ota Newsletter: Paul Goble http://www.turtletrack.org/Issues00/Co02262000/CO_02262000_Goble.htm August 21, 2001

[viii] Babe Ruth Birthplace and Museum. Babe's Legacy on the Lists http://www.baberuthmuseum.com/html/client_frames.asp August 23, 2001

5/3/2002

October

"Double, double toil and trouble;
Fire burn, and cauldron bubble."

    Macbeth, William Shakespeare, Act 4, Scene 1[i]

Special Month

International Dinosaur Month

What is it about a dinosaur that captures the imagination of both children and adults? From movies to stories to models, we are fascinated by these ancient creatures. The Internet offers so many things for young children, serious study and/or just browsing. I like to start with the big picture. Go to *What were the dinosaurs and where did they live?* for a great introduction to dinosaurs. For younger children, the Enchanted Learning site, All About Dinosaurs would be a great site to find information for a timeline and to do some classification; it even has suggestions for writing a great dinosaur report. The Dinosaur Interplanetary Gazette is a great resource for the older student. As students research their dinosaur, have them enter the information on a database or spreadsheet. Decide ahead of time on the field names. Use the filter or query feature of your spreadsheet to locate specific dinosaurs. Encourage the students to look for patterns, such as do more herbivores or carnivores have 2 or 4 legs? Which weighted more - herbivores or carnivores?

Dinosaur Database

Name	length (feet)	height (feet)	weight	period	diet	legs	found
Acrocanthosaurus	30-40		2.5 tons	Cretaceous	carnivore	2 legs	USA
Brontosaurus	70-90	10-15	33-38 tons	Jurassic	herbivore	4 legs	USA
Diplodocus	90	16	10-20 tons	Jurassic	herbivore	4 legs	USA
Iguanodon	30	9	4-5 tons	Cretaceous	herbivore	4 legs	All continents
Stegosaurus	26-30	9	3.5 - 4 tons	Jurassic	herbivore	4 legs	USA, England, Asia
Triceratops	30	7	6-12 tons	Cretaceous	herbivore	4 legs	USA
Tyrannosaurus rex	40	15-20	5-7 tons	Cretaceous	carnivore	2 legs	USA, Asia

- What were the dinosaurs and where did they live?
  http://palaeo.gly.bris.ac.uk/communication/dinobiol.html
- All About Dinosaurs
  http://www.enchantedlearning.com/subjects/dinosaurs/allabout/alphadinos.shtml
- The Dinosaur Interplanetary Gazette http://www.dinosaur.org
- When Dinosaur's Roamed America http://dsc.discovery.com/convergence/dinos/dinos.html (get to know your neighbors)

Have students use their database to make a multimedia report using PowerPoint or another presentation tool.

What it ate

- The Albertosaurus ate flesh.
- The Albertosaurus got its food by hunting and by eating already decayed animals.

Field Trips

Continue your study by visiting the Museum of Paleontology and the Dinosaur Art Studio. Then visit South Dakota's own, Sue at the Field Museum. There are also some different activities for children at the Field Museum.

- Museum of Paleontology http://www.ucmp.berkeley.edu/
- Dinosaur Art Studio http://www.dinoart.com/
- Sue at the Field Museum http://www.fmnh.org/sue/

Take your students on a dinosaur dig. You can visit real digs or virtual dinosaur digs.

- Mitchell Prehistoric Indian Village http://www.curriculum.k12.sd.us/ao006/
- I Dig Dinosaurs http://www.can-do.com/uci/ssi2000/dinosaurs.html
- VNMH Dinosaur Dig http://www.vmnh.org/dinodig.htm
- Montana Dinosaur Dig http://www.scimath.musn.edu/dinosaurs/webhome.html

The Dinosaur Field Trip is an online research project for your students. This is an example of the TourMaker tool described in the Computer Month activities.

- Dinosaur Field Trip http://www.field-trips.org/sci/dino/index.htm

Odds and Ends

- Dino Clip Art http://www.isgs.uiuc.edu/dinos/GIFs_path.html
- Dino Cartoons http://www.dinosaurcartoons.com/
- Jurassic Park http://www.jurassicpark.com/maingate_flash.html
- Jurassic Park the Ride Online Adventure http://jurassic.unicity.com/
- Dinosaur Dig http://kidsdomain.funschool.com/current/games/dg1_ds1,1
- Dinosaur Dig http://www.sdnhm.org/kids/dinosaur/
- Dinosaur Eggs http://www.nationalgeographic.com/features/96/dinoeggs/
- Dinosaur Movie http://www.brainpop.com/science/plantsandanimals/dinosaurs/index.weml

Computer Learning Month

Whether you are an old hand at computing or just a novice now is the time to celebrate the technology that is available in our schools. Challenge your students and yourself to learn something new this month. Show off what you've accomplished at a Family Technology Night. Microsoft will help you organize your event.

And, above all, celebrate what you are doing with some ideas from the Computer Learning Month Homepage and invite the community to visit your classroom to see the computer activities you and the students have been doing throughout the month.

- Computer Learning Month Homepage http://www.computerlearning.org/CLMAct.htm
- Family Technology Night http://www.microsoft.com/family/what.asp

National Technology Standards and Checklists

If you are developing a technology plan for your curriculum or school, check out the ISTE and NETS Standards. The two literacy checklists have interesting information for students, parents and teachers.

- ISTE http://www.iste.org/
- NETS National Educational Technology Standards http://cnets.iste.org/
- Computer Literacy Checklist http://www.smarterkids.com/rescenter/library/articles/computer_literacy.asp
- Grade 1-2 Literacy Checklist http://my.athenet.net/~franklin/1-2cklist.html

Internet Guides and Tutorials

If you are a novice or an experienced computer user who just needs some tips, two sites that offer online workshops for teachers are Microsoft Tutorials (for those who use Microsoft products) and Karen Schrock's Guide for Educator. You can never emphasize too much how important it is to be safe when using the Internet. Brainstorm a list of safety tips with your students and make a big poster for you classroom and lab.

- Microsoft Tutorials http://www.microsoft.com/education/?ID=Tutorials
- Karen Schrock's Guide for Educators http://school.discovery.com/schrockguide/shows.html
- Internet Safety http://www.disney.go.com/cybersafety/
- Rules of the Road http://www.usdoj.gov/kidspage/do-dont/kidinternet.htm

Searching the Internet

If you just want to do some surfing, check out 10 Things You Can Do On The Internet This Week. Teachers will enjoy the Roadmap to the Internet and EduHound: Everything for Education K-12. And if you haven't helped your students learn effective searching skills, work through the Seven Steps Toward Better Searching and Search with Savvy. Your students will find Kid's Search Tools a valuable resource.

- Roadmap to the Internet http://www.thejournal.com/features/rdmap/
- 10 Things You Can Do On The Internet This Week
  http://www.learnthenet.com/english/index.html
- EduHound Everything for Education K-12 http://www.eduhound.com/
- Seven Steps Toward Better Searching http://edweb.sdsu.edu/WebQuest/searching/sevensteps.html
- Searching with Savvy http://www.education-world.com/a_tech/tech001.shtml
- Kid's Search Tools http://www.rcls.org/ksearch.htm

Make a Field Trip

Download a demo of TourMaker and develop a tour about a topic you are currently studying. To try one that is already done, refer to Dinosaur Field Trip or the Rainforest Field Trip or check out the other field trips that are available.

- TourMaker http://www.field-trips.org/index.htm
  - Dinosaur Field Trip http://www.field-trips.org/sci/dino/index.htm
  - Rainforest Field Trip http://www.field-trips.org/sci/rainforest/index.htm

Another free tool available for classroom use is KeeBoo. This program allows you to capture web pages and other documents including photos, word documents, scanned drawings, etc. You can create KeeBooks for all of your themes.

- KeeBoo http://www.keeboo.com

Note: I really like using computers and the Internet, but they may not be the best or most effective teaching / learning tool. I always ask myself two questions: what can the students do better or faster because we're using computers and could we do this [activity] if we weren't using computers?

Family History Month

There are so many activities on the Internet that you can do to celebrate family history. For the younger children, I suggest using the Family Tree Maker by Disney. This is a very simple family tree that only goes back to grandparents. The Sesame Street family tree is an off-line version of a family tree that would be great for an open house.

- The Family Tree Maker http://disney.go.com/ads/sponsors/ancestry/treemap.html
- Sesame Street Workshop: Family Tree
  http://www.ctw.org/celebrate/athome/article/0,1439,18111,00.html

For upper elementary and older students, encourage students to learn more about their family history by doing an online search for family records. The ZDNet site offers valuable advice for those who want to trace their family history. Helm's Genealogy Toolbox and Ancestry.com provide interesting databases such as census records, civil war records and immigration directories.

- Tree of Lives: using the net to trace your family tree
  http://www.zdnet.com/zdhelp/stories/main/0,5594,2678390,00.html
- Helm's Genealogy Toolbox http://www.genealogytoolbox.com/

- Ancestry.com http://www.ancestry.com/

Houghton Mifflin's Education Place provides two activities to celebrate family history appropriate for young children.
- Family Celebrations Lesson Plan http://www.eduplace.com/rdg/gen_act/time/cele.html
- Family Pictures: Math Activity http://www.eduplace.com/rdg/gen_act/family/picture.html

Apple Month

After reading Steven Kellogg's *Johnny Appleseed*, you might want to learn more about apples. Try some of the activities from the following list of Internet sites. You will find everything from some great art ideas to some interesting facts about apples to some apple songs and recipes.
- Apple Activities http://www.iup.edu/~njyost/KHI/apleact.html
- A Bushel of Fun
  http://family.go.com/Categories/Activities/Features/family_1998_09/famf/famf98appleactivities/
- Apples and More http://www.urbanext.uiuc.edu/apples/education.html
- Great Apple Activities for Young Children
  http://www.geocities.com/Heartland/Acres/8911/apple.html
- Cool Stuff About Apples http://www.dole5aday.com/encyclopedia/apple/apple_menu.html#menu
- "Picking Apples" http://kididdles.com/mouseum/p017.html

Refer to September 26, Johnny Appleseed's Birthday.

Popcorn Popping Month

What makes popcorn pop? What are some crafts you can make with popcorn? What does car racing have to do with popcorn? If your students have earned a popcorn party, you might want to check out these sites to play popcorn games and learn more about one of our favorite snack foods.
- PopSecret http://www.popsecret.com/pettys_paint/home.html
- Jolly Time Popcorn http://www.jollytime.com/index.html
- Popcorn Screen Saver http://coolsavers.tripod.com/
- Wyandot Popcorn Museum http://www.wyandotpopcornmus.com/
- The Popcorn Board http://www.popcorn.org/mpindex.htm
- Popcorn Science http://www.popweaver.com/scifair.htm
- Popcorn http://www.popcorn.org/index.cfm

Special Weeks

1st Week

Fire Prevention Week

Since 1922, the National Fire Prevention Association has sponsored a Fire Prevention Week – a week to help educate the public about the dangers of fire and how they can protect themselves and others. Refer to the NFPA Internet site for lesson plans and activities. Risk Watch has ideas for parents and teachers as well at students.
- National Fire Prevention Association http://www.nfpa.org
  - Risk Watch http://www.nfpa.org/education/professional_educators/RW/index.html

Say 'Thanks'

Have the students use a publishing program to make a thank you card for your local fire department.
- Daves Fire Department http://www.geocities.com/daves_gallery/index.htm

Lesson Plans

The Internet has many lesson plans and activities already developed that could be appropriate for Fire Prevention Week. For younger students, I recommend

- Smokey the Bear http://www.smokeybear.com/
- Fire Safety Tips http://www.kidsource.com/kidsource/content3/news3/fire.safety.html
- Fire Prevention Children Activities http://firesafety.buffnet.net/children.htm
- Sparky the Fire Dog http://www.sparky.org/index.html

For older students, I recommend

- The Great Chicago Fire Lesson Plan http://www.education-world.com/a_lesson/lesson080.shtml
- The Great Chicago Fire & The Web of Memory http://www.chicagohistory.org/fire/

And you just have to sing, *One Dark Night* and the backwards version also. Rick Rambo's Wood Badge Songbook http://www.geocities.com/rickram.geo/songbook/songbk1c.html#onedarknight

2nd Week
National Wildlife Week

Select a different class (mammal, bird, amphibian, reptile, and fish) of animalia each day. Ask the students to find information about an animal in that class. Decide on the field titles for each record. Enter your data into a data base program. Have the students think of different queries at the end of the week. This can be as simple or as complex as you and your students want to make it. For the very young student, you could simply use the fields: Animal – Class – Home and of course for the most advanced students, you could include all of the subclasses and infraclasses.

- Animal Classification Lesson Plan http://school.discovery.com/lessonplans/programs/animaladaptations/
- Classification of Living Things http://anthro.palomar.edu/animal/default.htm
- Animal Diversity Web http://animaldiversity.ummz.umich.edu/index.html

Odds and Ends
- Wild Life Tour http://www.ajkids.com/tours/wildlifeTour.asp
- Jim Fowler's The Wild Planet http://beyond.landsend.com/fowler/index.html?sid=0994791607234

Visit the Wildlife Conservation Society

This is a marvelous site! There are wildlife current events, visits to online exhibits at the Bronx Zoo, education pages with distance learning exhibitions and a super, very interactive kids page. You may want to use parts of this to introduce this week and then go back to it to have the students explore the site. My favorite part is the sights and sounds with lots of beautiful pictures and videos.

- Wildlife Conservation Society http://wcs.org/educatin/ntmp

3rd Week
World Rainforest Week

Rainforests cover 2% or the earth's surface or 6% of its landmass, yet are home to over have of its plants and animals. The Internet is a wonderful resource for information and activities about the rainforest; it's resources and peoples.

- About Rainforests http://www.ran.org/info_center/about_rainforests.html
- Rainforest Action Network http://www.ran.org/
  - Kids Corner http://www.ran.org/kids_action/
- Rainforest Web http://rainforestweb.org/
- Rainforest Database http://www.gn.apc.org/livingearth/rainforestDB/
- Global Distribution of Current Forests Map http://www.unep-wcmc.org/forest/global_map.htm

Evaluate Web Sites

Have pairs of students choose a site to review and share with the rest of the class. Have the students contribute their information to a class web page of the best Rainforest Web Sites. In evaluating web sites, decide on the criteria the students will use. The Internet Site Evaluation Form and the Blue Web'n site provide suggestions.

- Internet Site Evaluation Form http://www.open.k12.or.us/jitt/evalform.html#UserFriendly
- Blue Web'n Site Evaluation Rubric http://www.kn.pacbell.com/wired/bluewebn/rubric.html

Rainforest Web Sites for Evaluation
- Jungle Trekker http://www.jungletrekker.com
- Wildlife's Last Resort http://www.wildlifeslastresort.com/
- Animals of the Rainforest http://www.animalsoftherainforest.org/
- Children's Tropical Forests http://www.tropical-forests.com/
- Rainforest Live http://www.rainforestlive.org.uk/
- Alex's Earth Patrol http://www.alextheape.com/earthpat.htm
- Amazon Interactive http://www.eduweb.com/amazon.html
- Kid's Planet http://www.kidsplanet.org/
- GreenKeepers http://www.greenkeepers.com/
- The Great Green Forest http://www.jayzeebear.com/
- Journey into Amazonia http://www.pbs.org/journeytoamazonia/
- Passport to the Rainforest http://passporttoknowledge.com/rainforest/intro.html
- Rainforests of the World http://mbgnet.mobot.org/sets/rforest/
- All About Rainforests
  http://www.enchantedlearning.com/subjects/dinosaurs/allabout/alphadinos.shtml
- Just for Kids http://www.rarespecies.org/kids/
- The Children's Rainforest http://childrenrainforest.tripod.com/

Odds and Ends
- Collaborate with other students with Endangered Animals of the World
  http://www.tenan.vuurwerk.nl/indexusa.htm
- Have students write letters in response to Global Response http://www.globalresponse.org/
- Project Rainforest
  http://www.thinkquest.org/library/lib/site_sum_outside.html?tname=26252&url=26252/index1.htm
- Rainforest Field Trip http://www.field-trips.org/sci/rainforest/index.htm

Date Varies

Daylight Saving Time Ends
USA Last Sunday in October

Early to bed and early to rise,
Makes a man healthy, wealthy, and wise.
Benjamin Franklin (1706-1790)

"Remember that time is money."
Advice to a Young Tradesman, 1748 from Benjamin Franklin

Never leave that till to-morrow which you can do to-day.
~Benjamin Franklin~

What is daylight saving time? When did it start and why? Do all countries or for that matter, states have daylight saving time? Learn more about daylight saving time at these sites:
- Daylight Saving Time http://www.webexhibits.org/daylightsaving/
- End Daylight Savings Time http://www.standardtime.com/

Then, reset your clock to the correct time by looking at the official time in the United States.
- Official Time in the United States http://www.time.gov/

And, finally, look at how time moves around the globe.
- The World Clock http://www.timeanddate.com/worldclock/
- Greenwich Time http://greenwichmeantime.com/index.htm
- World Time Zones http://www.hilink.com.au/times/usa.html

Read about what time means to our lives and different ways we have developed for measuring it at the following sites:
- Times of Our Lives http://www.trinity.edu/~mkearl/time.html
- Walk Through Time http://physics.nist.gov/GenInt/Time/time.html

Sukkot
15th day of the Hebrew month of Tishri,

> "'Sukkot' is the Hebrew word for "huts", and refers to the temporary homes that were used by the Jews in the wilderness thousands of years ago, after they were slaves in Egypt. We celebrate Sukkot as a reminder of our people's life in the desert."[ii]

For an excellent site about the meaning and celebration of Sukkot, I suggest Celebrate Sukkot. It has lots of teaching ideas.
- Celebrate Sukkot with Virtual Jerusalem's Jewish Holiday Site http://www.vjholidays.com/sukkot/index.htm
- Sukkot on the Net http://www.holidays.net/sukkot/
- Succoth: The Jewish Harvest Festival http://www.familyculture.com/holidays/succoth.htm

For information about all of the Jewish holidays, plus stories, language and much more, the Akhlah: The Jewish Children's Learning Network is the very best Internet site!
- Akhlah: The Jewish Children's Learning Network http://www.akhlah.com/default.asp

2nd Sunday
National Children's Day

> "As the inventors, artists, teachers, farmers, businessmen and women, decision-makers, and leaders of tomorrow, children are our most important resource."
>
> Ronald Reagan, June 30, 1982

The data may vary from year to year, but the sentiment is the same - our children are our most important asset! Take some time to write a note to each of your students, telling them exactly what you like about them.
- Absolutely Incredible Kid Day http://www.campfire.org/aikd_set.html

Use your favorite search engine to find the current year's Presidential Proclamation. This is a quote from President Clinton's Children's Day Proclamation, October 7, 2000. "I urge all Americans to express their love and appreciation for children on this day and every day throughout the year."

Many other countries honor their children and youth throughout the year. The following is a list of some of them:

- Festivals of Thailand http://www.sriwittayapaknam.ac.th/childday.html
- Nepal http://www.thamel.com/balmandir/htms/eventindex.htm
- Taipei http://www.taipeitimes.com/news/2000/04/04/story/0000030954
- Youthwork Links http://www.youthwork.com/dates.html
- Japan http://www.rice.edu/projects/topics/internatl/holidays/new-years-page1.htm

2nd Monday
Health Sports Day, Japan

Undoukai, (*Taiiku no Hi*) or Health Sports Day is a Japanese holiday that commemorates the 1964 Tokyo Olympiad. Many schools hold track and field events that foster a sound mind and body. Teams often wear either red or white. After having the students read the history of Undoukai, plan a Field Day for their room or school.

- Undoukai http://www.kidlink.org/KIDPROJ/MCC/mcc0288.html
- Health Sports Day http://www.jmission-eu.be/whatnew/picspor.htm
- Sports http://www.jinjapan.org/kidsweb/japan/e.html
- History http://www.jinjapan.org/kidsweb/calendar/october/sports.html

Have the students research Olympic track and field events. Make a poster using a publishing program for each event.

- Track and Field Events: 100 Year Comparison http://www.seorf.ohiou.edu/~af317/ot&f.htm
- USA Track and Field Homepage http://www.usatf.org/

Three Olympic Games have been held in Japan. When were they? Use your search engine to locate the dates and locations: *Answer: Tokyo hosted the Summer Games in 1964, and the Winter Games were hosted by Sapporo in 1972 and Nagano in 1998.*

Read: Miss Nelson Has A Field Day, by Harry Allard, illustrated by James Marshall (see October 10).

2nd Monday
Thanksgiving, Canada

Perhaps one of the most common holiday throughout all countries is Thanksgiving, a day set aside to give thanks for a bountiful harvest. Ancient people honored their gods with bonfires, song and dance. Today, Canadians set aside the 2nd Monday in October for Thanksgiving Day. The 1st Canadian Thanksgiving was celebrated in 1957. Today, the day is a family day that centers on a great feast similar to the way Americans celebrate Thanksgiving on the 4th Thursday in November. Use Web 66 to locate a Canadian school. Send them a virtual Thanksgiving card. Ask the Canadian students to write back giving information about how they celebrate Thanksgiving.

- Web 66 http://web66.coled.umn.edu/schools.html
- Canadian Thanksgiving Cards http://123greetings.com/events/canadian_thanksgiving/

Have the students compare and contrast how Canadians celebrate thanksgiving with how the day is celebrated in America. Use a chart similar to this:

Canada	Both	America

Canadian Thanksgiving gives both the history and traditions of the Canadian Thanksgiving and some fun classroom activities.

- Canadian Thanksgiving
  http://kidexchange.about.com/kids/kidexchange/library/weekly/aa092898.htm

Ask the students to plan their favorite menu. Look at the Canadian Thanksgiving site for ideas.

- Recipes for a Canadian Thanksgiving
  http://www.canadianliving.com/features/food/thanks/thanks-f.html

Refer to November, Thanksgiving

Special Days

October 1
Homemade Cookies Day

What a great way to start out a month of treats! Everyone loves a warm cookie, just out of the oven, so put a pan of cookies in the and enjoy the wonderful aroma as you an your students work on some social studies and math problems. For a special treat, make a Chocolate Cookie Pizza, yum!

- Chocolate Cookie Pizza
  http://www.bettycrocker.com/recipedb/33333.asp?returnURL=recipes%2Frecipe%2Fdesserts%2Findex%2Ehtml

Did you know that the first chocolate chip cookies were made accidentally in 1930, when Ruth Wakefield, an innkeeper in Whitman, Mass.? Mrs. Wakefield was trying to make all-chocolate cookies by breaking a semi-sweet chocolate bar into a buttery batter, thinking the morsels would melt throughout. It didn't produce the all-chocolate cookies she wanted, but the new variety proved very popular with her guests. She named the chocolate chip cookies "Toll House cookies" after her inn, The Toll House Inn (originally on the toll road between Boston and New Bedford, where horses were changed and people ate).

Cookie Math

Copy the recipe for the Original Toll House Chocolate Chip Cookie and have the students double or half the recipe. The site is an attractive, large print recipe.

- The Original Toll House Chocolate Chip Cookie
  http://www.acs.ucalgary.ca/~eahobday/tollhouse.htm

Chocolate Chip Math is a teacher developed lesson plan. It is great for teaching consumer education in the upper grades.

- Chocolate Chip Math http://explorer.scrtec.org/explorer/explorer-db/html/824796003-81ED7D4C.html

Decorate A Cookie is another teacher developed lesson plan designed to reinforce one to one correspondence and addition facts.

- Decorate A Cookie http://www.education-world.com/a_tsl/archives/00-1/lesson0073.shtml

Half the cookies baked in American homes are chocolate chip, with seven billion eaten annually[iii]. On the average, if there are 276,000,000 people living in America, how many chocolate chip cookies does each one eat? Check the Census Bureau for a minute-by-minute update.

- POPClock http://www.census.gov/main/www/popclock.html

Cookies and Social Studies

Mining A Chocolate Chip Cookie is a teacher developed lesson plan that works well with a unit on mining or as a neat way to teach observation, predicting, inference and classifying skills.

- Mining A Chocolate Chip Cookie ftp://ftp.unr.edu/pub/archive/mailing-lists/galileo/cookie.min

Learn a little about medieval recipes, along with diverse facts on food & feasting in the Middle Ages and Renaissance. When was the cookie invented?

- A Boke of Gode Cookery http://www.godecookery.com/godeboke/godeboke.htm

Cookies are also big business in our country, as Mrs. Fields found out! Using a search engine, such as AltaVista or Google, have the students type in "Mrs. Fields Cookies". Have the students read the history of the company. Discuss how they would start a business using their unique talents and skills.

- AltaVista http://www.altavista.com/
- Google http://www.google.com/

October 2
1st Peanuts Comic Strip published
The city of St. Paul, Minnesota honored Charles Schultz by displaying decorated Snoopys all around the town. Go to Snoopy http://www.snoopy.com to get some ideas. Then, give the students a blank snoopy and let them decorate Snoopy. You might want to give them a theme, such as "something about me", "something about our town, school, state, etc." "Halloween" or leave it up to the students.

- A blank Snoopy is at http://www.unitedmedia.com/comics/peanuts/c_fun/html/c4.html
- The Official Peanuts Web Site http://www.unitedmedia.com/comics/peanuts/index.html
- Charlie Brown in St. Paul http://www.ilovesaintpaul.com/ilsp/stpaulattractions/charliebrown/

October 4, 1957
Sputnik I Launched
Make a timeline of early space exploration. You can either use adding machine tape with pictures copied from the Internet or use a demo copy of Tom Snyder's Timeliner. Have each student tell about his or her mission. You could also have the students write a story about Laika's (1st dog in space) adventures.

- Sputnik Satellites and Launch Vehicles http://nauts.com/histpace/vehicles/histsputnik.html
- Timeliner http://www.tomsnyder.com/classroom/timelineronline/

October 4, 1892
Robert Lawson's Birthday
Author and illustrator, Robert Lawson, is the only person to win both the Newbery and Caldecott awards[1]. Read Robert Lawson's biography. Discuss both the author and illustrator's job. Look at books that have been both written and illustrated by Robert Lawson. Have the students write a story and illustrate it. Ask them which they would rather do. Look at the books illustrated by Robert Lawson. Some illustrators use different techniques and / or change their style over a period of time. Ask the students to analyze Lawson's style.

- Biography http://www.bpib.com/illustrat/lawson.htm

Teachers have developed a unit plan based on Ben and Me. Use this or parts of it throughout the month.

- Ben and Me Unit Plan http://www.geocities.com/Athens/Olympus/1804/Mouse/BenandMe.html

Books by Robert Lawson
They Were Strong and Good - Caldecott Award, 1941
Rabbit Hill - Newbery Award, 1945
Ben and Me
Mr. Revere and I
I Discover Columbus
Robert Lawson, Illustrator; A Selection of His Characteristic Illustrations
Adam of the Road, by Elizabeth Janet Gray, illustrated
Mr. Popper's Penguins, by Richard Atwater and Florence Atwater (Newbery Honor Award, 1939)
The Story of Ferdinand, by Munro Leaf

---

[1] Ruth Sawyer won the Newbery for Roller Skates in 1937. Her books The Christmas Anna Angel (1945) and Journey Cake, Ho! (1954) won the Caldecott Honor and Caldecott Award respectively for their illustrators.

October 5
Pablo Picasso's Birthday
Picasso is known for is his use of cubism. Have the students look at some of his work at Online Picasso Project. Take a digital picture of each student. Open it in a paint program. Next, have the students "cut" out squares of their painting and "paste" them on another slide to rearrange them in a "cubism" manner.
- Biography http://www.clubinternet.com/picasso/
- Online Picasso Project http://www.tamu.edu/mocl/picasso/
- Picasso http://www.boston.com/mfa/picasso/

October 9
Leif Erikson Day PL 88-566
Did Leif Erikson and the Vikings really discover American 500 years before Columbus? Read about the early Viking days to see for yourself. Make a map of the route Erikson would have taken. Compare that with Columbus's voyage. (See October 12)
- Leif Erickson Day http://www.geocities.com/NapaValley/3227/vikings.htm
- Leif Ericson http://www.mnc.net/norway/Leif.htm
- Leif Ericson Vikingship http://libertynet.org/~viking/
- The Viking Adventure
  http://beyond.landsend.com/archive/archive_viking_98.html?sid=0994781992234

October 10, 1946
Robert San Souci's Birthday
Read Robert San Souci's biography. Both he and his brother, Daniel, have more in common than just writing children's birth, they were born on the same day! Note that many of his books are retellings of folktales and legends.
- Biography http://www.eduplace.com/kids/hmr/mtai/sansouci.html
- Robert San Souci
  http://www.coe.ufl.edu/faculty/lamme/student/author/SArticles/SanSouciRobert.html

Practice retelling stories with your students. Choose one of the Cinderella variants. Read it to the students and then have the students reread it. Have them retell it to a partner while the partner is looking at the text. Encourage the students to retell the story as accurately as possible. Retelling stories encourages vocabulary development, story form and performance.
- Cinderella http://www.pitt.edu/~dash/type0510a.html
- On Writing Cinderella Skeleton   http://www.baldric.com/websites/cindy/html/souci.htm
- About Cinderella http://www.shens.com/theme.cgi

Books by Robert San Souci
Brave Margaret: An Irish Adventure
Cut from the Same Cloth: American Women of Myth, Legend and Tall Tale
Fa Mulan: the Story of a Woman Warrior
The Faithful Friend - Caldecott Honor
Feathertop: Based on the Tale by Nathaniel Hawthorne
The Hired Hand: An African-American Folktale
The Legend of Sleepy Hollow
N.C. Wyeth's Pilgrims (see October 22 for more sites about N.C.Wyeth)
Six Foolish Fishermen
Sootface: An Ojibwa Cinderella Story
The Talking Eggs: A Folktale from the American South
Little Gold Star: A Spanish American Cinderella Tale
The Little Seven-Colored Horse: A Spanish American Folktale

October 10, 1942
James Marshall's Birthday
After reading the biographies, have the students prepare a simple PowerPoint presentation about James Marshall. Slide 1 – Title; slide 2 – early life; slide 3 – why he writes, slide 4 – a sample of this books; slide 5 – bibliography.
- Brief Bio http://kalama.doe.hawaii.edu/hern95/pt027/library/marshall.html
- Featured Author: http://www.carolhurst.com/newsletters/42enewsletters.html
- James Marshall http://www.penguinputnam.com/Author/AuthorFrame?0000016794

Web Quest @ James Marshall for 2nd Grade
http://curry.edschool.virginia.edu/go/edis771/webquest2000/student/scheryllynnrussell/home.html

Books by James Marshall
The Cut-Ups
Eugene
George and Martha and the Series
Goldilocks and the Three Bears
Hansel and Gretel
James Marshall's Mother Goose
The Night Before Christmas
Old Mother Hubbard and Her Wonderful Dog
Red Riding Hood
Swine Lake, with Maurice Sendak
All the Way Home
Bumps in the Night
Miss Nelson Is Missing, and the other Miss Nelson Books
The Owl and the Pussycat
The Stupids (Series)
There's a Party at Mona's Tonight

October 11, 1929
Russell Freedman's Birthday

> *"I write history because it ...offers a magic carpet
> to another time and place and
> offers satisfaction that things told are real."*

Russell Freedman

Newbery Award winning author, Russell Freedman is best known for writing biographies. Use the Biography Maker site to help your students write a biography of a historical figure; perhaps Christopher Columbus, Pablo Picasso, Levi Strauss, Charles Schultz, Debbi Fields or Frederic Bartholdi. Scholastic's Writer's Workshop features the work of Patricia and Fredrick McKissack and has a nice format for researching your subject.
- Biography Maker http://www.bham.wednet.edu/bio/biomaker.htm
- Biography: Writer's Workshop http://teacher.scholastic.com/writewit/biograph/index.htm
- Russell Freedman http://www.eduplace.com/kids/hmr/mtai/freedman.html
- ERIC Listing http://www.indiana.edu/~eric_rec/ieo/bibs/freedman.html
- Freedman's Speech @ University of Southern Mississippi
  http://www.pr.usm.edu/prnews/mar99/FREEDMAN.HTM
- Talking with Authors http://www.publishersweekly.com/articles/20000214_84596.asp

Babe Didrikson Zaharias
Eleanor Roosevelt: A Life of Discovery - Newbery Honor 1994
Give Me Liberty: The Story of the Declaration of Independence
Indian Chiefs
Kids at Work: Lewis Hine and the Crusade Against Child Labor
The Life and Death of Crazy Horse
Lincoln: A Photobiography - Newbery Award
Out of Darkness: The Story of Louis Braille
The Wright Brothers: How They Invented the Airplane

Lesson Plans
- Score Teaching Guide for Lincoln; A Picture Biography
  http://www.sdcoe.k12.ca.us/score/linc/linctg.html
- Russell Freedman Biography Web Page http://www.jordan.palo-alto.ca.us/arcylib/authors/a0045.html (this one needs your help)

October 12
Columbus Day, Dia de la Raza, Native American Day

> *"In 1492 Columbus sailed the ocean blue,*
> *And found the land of the free,*
> *Beloved by you,*
> *Beloved by me."*

Winifred Sackwlle Stoner

To honor the quadricentennial of Columbus' arrival, President Benjamin Harrison issued a proclamation appointing a day at the Chicago World's Fair as

> *"...a holiday for the people of the United States...to express honor to the discoverer, and their appreciation of the great achievements of the four completed centuries of American life"*[iv]

But, it wasn't until 1937, that President Franklin Roosevelt proclaimed every October 12th as Columbus Day. President Richard Nixon declared it a federal public holiday in 1971. Today, perhaps no other holiday causes so much passion (and anger), as that of Columbus Day. Some groups feel that these lands had already been discovered and settled by peoples who had their own government, culture, and history. Many Native American people feel this day represents a dark day in their history, when thieves bearing illnesses stole their lands. There is also the controversy between the Spanish and the Italians as to whom should lay claim to this explorer and his discoveries. This poses an interesting debate for your students.
- Columbus Day, Dia de la Raza, Native American Day
  http://www.holidayfestival.com/individual/ColumbusDay.html
No matter how you choose to celebrate this day, there are many Internet sites to get you started. The first list of Internet sites provides an excellent background of information about Columbus and his travels. The second list of Internet sites provide information about how some South American countries and Mexico celebrate the same day, calling it Dia de la Raza or Race Day, a day that commemorates the blending of two peoples, the Europeans and the Native peoples. The third group of Internet sites presents

the Native American point of view with some suggestions for celebrating Native American Day. Use any of these sites or groups of sites individually or together.

Columbus Day – use these sites to write a biography of Christopher Columbus
- Columbus Day http://www.geocities.com/Athens/Acropolis/1465/columbus.html
- Columbus Day http://www3.kumc.edu/diversity/other/columbus.html
- Columbus Navigation homepage http://www1.minn.net/~keithp/
- Columbus Day http://deil.lang.uiuc.edu/web.pages/holidays/Columbus.html
- From About
  http://craftsforkids.miningco.com/parenting/craftsforkids/library/spdays/bloct11th.htm
- COLOMBUS DID NOT LAND IN THE NEW WORLD, A satirical essay by Michael J. Finley
  http://www.thursdaysclassroom.com/15mar01/columbushoax.html

Dia de la Raza

There are at least two interesting things you can do with these Internet sites. First, the Scholastic site has wonderful resources for celebrating Hispanic Heritage, including interviews with famous Hispanic Americans, biographies of famous Hispanic Americans with a very easy to use biography sheet, a multimedia history of Hispanic History in the Americas and a discussion of heritage by Americans of Hispanic descent.
- Hispanic Heritage Month http://teacher.scholastic.com/hispanic/more.htm

The second thing to do is to learn about Dia de la Raza by reading a translation of an Internet site. Look at the site in Spanish and then use the World Translation: Babel Fish site to translate the site. Another neat thing to do at the Babel Fish site is to type in a sentence in English and change it to Spanish. For instance, type in "Hello, my name is _____." Have the students practice greeting each other in Spanish.
- World Translation: Babel Fish http://babelfish.altavista.com/translate.dyn
- Dia de la Raza (race day) http://www.mcye.gov.ar/efeme/colon/
- Columbus Day, Dia de la Raza http://www.holidayfestival.com/individual/ColumbusDay.html
- Dia de la Raza http://world.presidencia.gob.mx/pages/culture/note_12oct.html
- October 12, Dia de la Raza http://www.maristas.com.ar/champa/egb/3grado.htm

Native American Day

What a wonderful opportunity to learn about the culture and history of the indigenous people! It is also an opportunity to discuss point-of-view. After reading the first web site, help students identify the feelings expressed in the article. Discuss why the author feels so strongly about the issue. Are these the same feelings Columbus and the Europeans who followed him would have? Why or why not?
- Christopher Columbus as Seen Through the Eyes of Indigenous People
  http://www.indians.org/welker/columbu1.htm

Work with the students to develop a Native American Day program for parents and / or other classes. One group could tell about famous Native Americans, another could tell about some Native American celebrations and yet another could tell about the different tribes and the fourth group could tell about the history of Native American day.
- Native American Day
  http://www.whitehouse.gov/Initiatives/OneAmerica/Practices/pp_19980804.3413.html
- Native American Indian Resources http://indy4.fdl.cc.mn.us/~isk/mainmenu.html
- Native American Celebrations http://dmla.clan.lib.nv.us/docs/nsla/srp/people/chap4d.htm
- History of Native American Day http://www.doi.gov/bia/namonthist.htm
- 1st American Forefathers http://members.aol.com/circofire/

October 15, 1951
I Love Lucy Premiere

I Love Lucy, which first appeared on TV screens over 50 years ago, is no less than an American institution -- the single most popular and influential TV phenomenon in the history of the medium. Listen to some of Lucy's famous routines. Lucille Ball was a pioneer in TV sitcoms. Since those pioneer days, there have been many changes in television, such as language, theme, and sex. Watch an early I Love Lucy and then a contemporary sitcom. Make a list with your students. Discuss if the changes are better or worse and from what point of view.

- TV's Megahit http://www.lucylibrary.com/Pages/creating-ilovelucy.html
- I Love Lucy http://www.fiftiesweb.com/lucy.htm
- We Love Lucy http://www.lucyfan.com/

October 16
Dictionary Day

Play the daily word puzzle or make one of your own.
- Merriam-Webster Online Language Center http://www.m-w.com/home.htm
- The Puzzlemaker http://puzzlemaker.school.discovery.com/
- Happy Birthday, Noah Webster: Dictionary Activities http://www.education-world.com/a_lesson/lesson206.shtml

Personal Glossary

You and your students can easily make a glossary using any word set with the Glossary Builder at Discovery School. You simply key in the words – spelling list, science vocabulary, etc. and select the options you want. This is an excellent tool for vocabulary development.
- Glossary Builder http://school.discovery.com/teachingtools/glossarybuilder/index.html

Online Dictionaries
- Wordsmyth http://www.wordsmyth.net/
- Merriam Webster http://www.merriam-webster.com/
- Dictionary.com http://www.dictionary.com/
- Oxford English Dictionary http://www.oed.com/
- American Heritage Dictionary http://www.bartleby.com/61/ (this has a very nice collection of illustrations)
- Biographical Dictionary http://www.s9.com/biography/

Wacky Definitions

Give each student a word they may or may not know. Ask them to make up a definition for the word and use it in a sentence or use the correct definition. Have the other students vote 'yes' or 'no' depending on if they believe the definition or not. Have all students look up the 'real' definition.

Pictionary

Use the illustrations from the American Heritage Dictionary. Have each student copy and paste it into a paint program. Using the cutting tool, cut the picture into 4 or 6 pieces. Paste the pieces on a presentation slide. Use the animation tool to expose one piece at a time. As each piece is revealed, have the students guess what the picture is.

October 16
Poetry Day
Listen to people read their favorite poem at the Favorite Poem Project and then read one of your own favorite poems. For a nice list of poetry sites, go to the Campus School Library. You will also enjoy Pass the Poetry, Please.
- Favorite Poem Project http://www.favoritepoem.org/
- Campus School Library http://www.campusschool.dsu.edu/library/poetry.htm
- Pass The Poetry, Please http://www.umkc.edu/imc/poetryin.htm

Also, see April, Poetry Month

October 17
Black Poetry Day

> *Yet do I marvel at this curious thing:*
> *To make a poet black, and bid him sing!*
>
> - "Yet Do I Marvel" by Countee Cullen

From 1920 until about 1930 an unprecedented outburst of creative activity among African-Americans occurred in all fields of art. This African-American cultural movement became known as "The New Negro Movement" and later as the Harlem Renaissance. The Renaissance exalted the unique culture of African-Americans and redefined African-American expression.[v] With your students, read more about the movement and the poetry that is so moving still today.
- Harlem Renaissance http://www.nku.edu/~diesmanj/harlem.html
- Langston Hughes http://search.biography.com/print_record.pl?id=16052
- Langston Hughes Poetry http://www.nku.edu/~diesmanj/hughes.html (the poems change from time to time)

And, for some more recent poetry, look at Maya Angelou, the poet who wrote the famous *On the Pulse of Morning: Inaugural Poem*, for Bill Clinton's inaugural.
- Maya Angelou http://www.mayaangelou.com/
- Maya Angelou http://www.cwrl.utexas.edu/~mmaynard/Maya/maya5.html

For a very nice lesson plan about Robert Hayden, you might enjoy Fooling With Words. Students will learn about his work and have an opportunity to write some of their own poetry.
- Fooling With Words: Robert Hayden http://www.pbs.org/wnet/foolingwithwords/lesson2.html

Poetry Reading
Put on a poetry reading for parents. Have the students find a poem by a black writer. Identify appropriate paintings to project in the background and play Harlem Nocturne. WOW! Be sure to have the students give a little of the history, too.

Painters
- Loïs Mailou Jones http://www.nku.edu/~diesmanj/jones.html
- John Biggers
  - Lesson Plan http://www.artsednet.getty.edu/ArtsEdNet/Resources/Biggers/Looking/index.html
  - Paintings http://www.artsednet.getty.edu/ArtsEdNet/Images/Biggers/index.html

Music
- Harlem Nocturne + lots more http://www.duchessathome.com/index3.html

- Harlem Nocturne http://search.mp3.com/bin/search/
- Other jazz music:
  - Ethel Walters
  - Louis Armstrong

October 22, 1882
N. C. Wyeth's Birthday

Wyeth was not only one of America's most famous painters but also illustrated more than 25 classic books. After reading the short online biography, read a classic to your students.
- Biography http://www.illustration-house.com/bios/wyeth_bio.html

Take an online field trip to an art museum. Visit the sites at Artcyclopedia to view some of N.C. Wyeth's work. You could print out some of the works for a classroom art gallery.
- N.C. Wyeth on the Internet http://www.artcyclopedia.com/artists/wyeth_nc.html

Illustrated by N.C.Wyeth
An American Vision: Three Generations of Wyeth Art: N.C. Wyeth, Andrew Wyeth and James Wyeth, by James H. Duff
The Black Arrow: A Tale of the Two Roses, by Robert Louis Stevenson
The Boy's King Arthur: Sir Thomas Malory's History of King Arthur and His Knights of the Round Table, by Sidney Lanier
The Deerslayer, by James Fenimore Cooper
Kidnapped, by Robert Louis Stevenson
The Last of the Mohicans: A Narrative of 1757, by James Fenimore Cooper
Mutiny on the Bounty, by Charles Nordhoff
The Mysterious Island, by Jules Verne
N.C. Wyeth's Pilgrims by Robert San Souci, (see October 10)
Rip Van Winkle, by Washington Irving
Robin Hood, by Paul Creswick
Robinson Crusoe, by Daniel Defoe
Treasure Island, by Robert Louis Stevenson
The Yearling, by Marjorie Kinnan Rawlings

October 24
United Nations Day

United Nations Day was first recognized as a holiday in 1947 by the United Nations to commemorate the day, October 24, 1945 that the United Nations Charter went into effect. Since then, each president has issued a proclamation asking citizens to reflect on UN Day and the importance the United Nations plays in our lives. The Program site will give you ideas for celebrating United Nations Day.
- Program http://www.unausa.org/programs/unday.htm
- Let's Celebrate http://www.unac.org/unday/celebrate.html

Country Profiles

Learn more about the countries that belong to the United Nations. Divide the students into small groups and have each group research a different UN country. Decide what information you want the students to find, such as flag, continent, date they joined the United Nations and current leader. Have the students share their research using a presentation tool.
- World Fact Book http://www.cia.gov/cia/publications/factbook/index.html
- Embassy Page http://www.embpage.org/

Children's Bill of Rights

Using a word processor or a desktop publishing program and clip art, have the students make a poster for each of the Children's Bill of Rights. Place these in the hallway. Be sure to look at the cartoons of children's rights.

- UNICIF http://www.unicef.org/
  - Cartoons http://www.unicef.org/crcartoons/
- Declaration of the Rights of the Child http://www.unhchr.ch/html/menu3/b/25.htm

Odds and Ends

Make a timeline for the United Nations.

- United Nations Homepage http://www.un.org/
- Milestones http://www.un.org/Overview/milesto4.htm

Additional ideas and lesson plans are provided at the United Nations Cyberschool Bus.

- United Nations Cyberschool Bus http://www.un.org/Pubs/CyberSchoolBus/index.html

October 25
National Denim Day

Everyone wear your jeans today and learn a little of the history of the person who first made them.

- History of Denim http://www.auckland.nl/Levis/levisdenimhist.htm
- Levi Strauss http://www.levistrauss.com/index_sitemap.html
- Jeans: The True Blue Facts http://www.unkc.edu/imc/jeans.htm
- Gold Rush: People to Know http://www.pbs.org/wgbh/amex/kids/goldrush/peopletoknow.html

October 26
Diwali, Hindu

Diwali or Deepavali is the Hindu Festival of Lights. It is held in the Indian month of Kartika and in the United States on October 26. Families decorate their homes and streets with thousands of lights. These lights are to welcome Lakshmi, the goddess of wealth and good fortune to each home. Women and girls take small clay lamps to the river. They light the oil in the lamps and set them a float. If the lamps cross the river safely it is seen as a sign of good fortune.

Five Days of Diwali

After reading the history of Diwali, have the students make a poster for each of the five days of Diwali. Use a word processor or a publishing program to make the poster. Import clip art to illustrate the concept.

- Hindu Festival of Lights http://www3.kumc.edu/diversity/ethnic_relig/diwali.html
- History http://www.indiaexpress.com/faith/festivals/deepavali.html
- Diwali on the Net http://www.diwali.com/
- Build up to Diwali http://www.indolinks.com/websights/diwali/buildup.htm

Holiday Foods

Everyone loves special foods that are featured on special holidays. A delicious rice pudding if featured on the Deepavali Festival of Light site. Your students will need to convert the metric measurement to standard. If you want to do it online, go to the Cooking Measures and Conversion Calculator.

- Deepavali Festival of Light - http://www.diwalimela.com/
- Cooking Measures and Conversion Calculator http://www.globalgourmet.com/cgi-bin/hts?convcalc.hts+usequiv+new

October 26
Steven Kellogg's Birthday
When Steven Kellogg was just a young boy, he used to make up stories for his younger sisters. As he said, he used to call this "telling stories on paper." Have the students use clip art to find pictures of two different people, a place, a thing and an action. Have the students print out cards with their chosen pictures and use the cards to tell a story. Shuffle the cards, and tell another story. A good clip art site is at Discovery School.

- Biography written by children http://coe.west.asu.edu/students/dcorley/authors/Kellogg.htm
- Biography http://www.penguinputnam.com/Author/AuthorFrame?0000013824
- Clip Art @ Discovery School http://school.discovery.com/clipart/index.html

Person	Person	Place	Thing	Action

Clip art from Discovery School.com

Books by Steven Kellogg
The 3 Sillies
A Hunting We Will Go!
Best Friends
Island of the Skog
Jack and the Beanstalk
Johnny Appleseed
The Mystery of the Missing Red Mitten
Pecos Bill: A Tall Tale
Paul Bunyan
Adventures of Huckleberry Finn, by Mark Twain
A Beastly Story
The Day Jimmy's Boa Ate the Wash
Granny and the Desperadoes
How Much Is a Million?
Is Your Mama a Llama?
Yankee Doodle

October 28, 1886
Statue of Liberty's Birthday
Take a field trip to this symbol of liberty. Print a list of the statue statistics and take them out to the playground, football field or to a park. Bring a measuring instrument and some plastic tape like that used by the police. Recreate the statue lying down. You will need a big space!

- National Park Service – Statue of Liberty http://www.nps.gov/stli/

      ○ Your Visit http://www.nps.gov/stli/prod02.htm
- Great Buildings – Statue of Liberty
  http://www.greatbuildings.com/buildings/Statue_of_Liberty.html

October 27, 1728
James Cook's Birthday
Follow the adventures of Captain James Cook, the first European to see the Hawaiian Islands, Antarctica and Australia. While on your journey, learn to tie some basic sailors knots. Use the Glossary of Ship Terms to create a word find puzzle.
- Biography http://www.queensland.co.uk/james.html
- James Cook http://www.geocities.com/Athens/Aegean/7800/cook.html
- Antarctica http://www.bi.k12.ri.us/start/antartic.htm
- Mawson Station Webcam Antarctica http://www.aad.gov.au/stations/mawson/video.asp
- Learn2 Tie Basic Knots http://www.learn2.com/05/0540/0540.asp
- Glossary of Ship Terms http://www.jobxchange.com/shipterms.htm
- Puzzlemaker http://puzzlemaker.school.discovery.com/

October 29, 1929
Black Tuesday
It was on this day in 1929 that the stock market crashed, signaling the beginning of the great depression. Help your students understand the impact Black Tuesday had on not just the United States, but also the world. Then, visit the floor of the New York Stock Exchange and learn the ABCs of the Stock Market. The ThinkQuest activity, Investing for Kids is an excellent way for students to learn about stock market. The Stock Market Game helps students put their newfound knowledge to the test. Have each student select a stock to watch. Set up a spreadsheet and have the student record the price of the stock over a period of time. Use the chart feature and create a line graph for each stock or group of stocks.
- In Black Tuesday's Shadow
  http://www.abcnews.go.com/sections/business/DailyNews/crashanniversary991028.html
- Black Tuesday http://sac.uky.edu/~msunde00/hon202/p4/nyt.html
- New York Stock Exchange http://www.nyse.com/
- ABCs of the Stock Market http://www.abcstockmarket.com/
- Investing for Kids http://library.thinkquest.org/3096/index.htm
- Stock Market Game http://www.prongo.com/stock/
- U.S. Treasury for Kids http://www.treas.gov/kids/

October 31, 1932
Katherine Paterson' Birthday
Unlike many authors, Katherine Paterson did not always want to be a writer. As a child, she wanted to be a movie star or a missionary and as a young woman, she wanted to be a wife and mother of lots of children. After reading Ms Paterson's biography, ask the children to write about what they would like to be when they grow up. Follow a simple outline, such as: what I would like to be, why this job appeals to me, what I need to do to prepare for this job and finally, the special skills or talents I possess that would make me good at this job.
- Katherine Paterson's Homepage http://www.terabithia.com/
- Katherine Paterson http://falcon.jmu.edu/~ramseyil/paterson.htm
- Biography http://www.childrensbookguild.org/kpaterson.html

Books by Katherine Paterson
Bridge to Terabithia - Newbery Medal, 1978
The Great Gilly Hopkins - Newbery Honor, 1979

Jacob Have I Loved - Newbery Medal, 1981
Jip: His Story
The Master Puppeteer

October 31, 1517
95 Theses
Martin Luther mailed the *95 Theses* to local bishops that they might take action against indulgences, inaugurating Protestantism and shattering the structure of the medieval church.

- Martin Luther http://www.wsu.edu:8000/~dee/REFORM/LUTHER.HTM
- Martin Luther and Lutheran Reformation http://www.ultranet.com/~tlclcms/MLuther.htm
- Medieval Times http://historymedren.about.com/library/weekly/aa051799.htm

October 31
Halloween
Our modern celebration of Halloween is a descendent of the 5th century Celtic fire festival called "Samhain". *(Pronounced "sow-in", with "sow" rhyming with cow.)* Samhain, or All Hallowtide, was the feast for the dead in Pagan and Christian times, signalizing the close of harvest and the beginning of the winter season. The word "Halloween," actually has its origins in the Catholic Church. It comes from a contracted corruption of All Hallows Eve. "All Hollows Day" (or "All Saints Day"), is a Catholic day of observance in honor of saints. One story says that, on that day, the disembodied spirits of all those who had died throughout the preceding year would come back in search of living bodies to possess for the next year. It was believed to be their only hope for the afterlife. The Celts believed all laws of space and time were suspended during this time, allowing the spirit world to intermingle with the living.

Not wanting to be possessed, villagers would extinguish the fires in their homes, to make them cold and undesirable. They would then dress up in all manner of ghoulish costumes and noisily paraded around the neighborhood, being as destructive as possible in order to frighten away spirits looking for bodies to possess. Irish immigrants brought the holiday to America in the 1840's[vi].

Five Quick Things To Do
- Learn about werewolves http://www.werewolfpage.com
- Ghosts and Legends http://www.ghostsandlegends.com/index.htm
- Read a story by Edgar Allen Poe http://www.gothic.net/poe/works.html
- Visit a Graveyard of Goodies
  http://craftsforkids.miningco.com/parenting/craftsforkids/library/weekly/aa090400a.htm
- Trick-or-Treat for UNICEF http://www.unicefusa.org/tot2000/what.html http://www.unicef.org

Scary Story
Have the children write a scary Halloween story. Make e-books by using a presentation tool. Use clip art or original drawings to illustrate the story and scary sounds to add to the fun.
Clip Art
- Kids Domain http://www.kidsdomain.com/holiday/halloween/clip.html
- Halloween Clip Art http://rats2u.com/halloween/halloween_clipart.htm
- Calendar for your desktop http://home.wnm.net/~debi/halloween.htm
- Happy Halloween Clip Art http://home.wnm.net/~debi/boo.htm
Sounds
- Sounds of Fear http://www.geocities.com/Heartland/7134/Halloween/halsound.htm
- Pumpkin Caroling http://riceinfo.rice.edu/projects/colleges/wiess/traditions/pumpkin.html
- Halloween Tricks and Treats http://www.night.net/halloween/index.html-ssi
- Halloween Music http://members.aol.com/_ht_a/pumpkinave/music.htm

There are many outstanding Internet sites featuring Halloween customs, games, activities and history. Some of the best are:

History of Halloween
- Halloween History http://members.aol.com/Donnpages/Holidays.html#HALL
- The Origins of Halloween http://homepages.together.net/~joe/origins.html
- Halloween http://wilstar.com/holidays/hallown.htm

Unit Plans
- Ghosts, Ghouls and Goblins http://eduscapes.com/42explore/ghosts.htm (for younger students)
- Halloween Unit Plan: Gothic Literature http://www3.wcu.edu/~mwarner/johnson/warnerpga.html (for older students)

Halloween Stories and Poems
- An extensive list of stories and poems http://rats2u.com/halloween/halloween_books.htm#books
- Little Golden e-Books http://www.goldenbooks.com/fun/emagic/index.html
- Halloween Stories and Nightmares http://www.cavernsofblood.com/halloween_story.html
- Original Halloween Stories and Poems http://christmas-tales.com/hallpg1.html

General Activities
- Everything Halloween http://everythinghalloween.com/index.html
- Happy Halloween http://www.wotch.com/funstuff/halloween.asp
- The Halloween Room http://suzyred.home.texas.net/halloween.html
- Halloween @ Kids Domain http://www.kidsdomain.com/holiday/halloween/index.html
- Halloween @ Alphabet Soup http://www.alphabet-soup.net/hall/halloween.html
- Swan Pumpkin Farm http://www.thepumpkinfarm.com/
- Billy Bear's Halloween http://www.billybear4kids.com/holidays/halowen/halowen.htm
- Absolutely Halloween http://www.geocities.com/Heartland/7134/Halloween/hall.htm
- Cyber Grandma's Halloween http://www.geocities.com/Heartland/2328/hallwen.htm
- Trick or Treat http://www.geocities.com/~5geokids/halloween/index.html
- Halloween on the Net http://www.holidays.net/halloween/
- Happy Halloween from Mrs. Bee http://www.geocities.com/Heartland/Lake/4482/halloween.htm
- Happy Halloween http://www.geocities.com/Athens/Acropolis/1465/halloween.html
- Ghosts of the Castles http://www.nationalgeographic.com/castles/enter.html

Food
- Great Pumpkin Cookies http://www.nestleusa.com/recipes/recipe_template.asp?id=1202
- Black Cat Cookies http://www.cooking.com/recipes/static/recipe2647.htm
- Happy Halloween from Ben and Jerry's Ice-cream http://www.benjerry.com/halloween/index.html
- Fried Pumpkin Blossoms Treats http://www.alphabet-soup.net/hall/pumpkin.html

Arts and Crafts
- Crafts http://www.alphabet-soup.net/hall/hallcraft.html
- Halloween crafts http://www.geocities.com/Heartland/7997/sherri2c.htm
- Art Activities from MailBox
  http://www.sbcss.k12.ca.us/sbcss/specialeducation/ecthematic/halloween/motor.html

Salem Witch Hunt

If you want to take a historical point of view of witches in America, look at these excellent sites about the Salem witch-hunts. Read The Witch of Blackbird Pond by Elizabeth George Speare. Talk about discrimination and judging people by appearance and hearsay and very little evidence.

- Salem Witch Trials 1692 http://www.salemweb.com/memorial/default.htm
- Herstory: Ghosts and Witches http://www7.bcity.com/history/salem.htm
- Salem Witchcraft Hysteria http://www.nationalgeographic.com/features/97/salem/

War of the Worlds

One of the greatest Halloween pranks was on the night before Halloween in 1938. Orson Welles and the Mercury Theater broadcasted a dramatization of H.G. Wells' famous *War of the World*. Although the listeners were informed at the beginning of the program that they were listening to a dramatization, many people who tuned in late believed the tale and panic ensued[vii]. Welles never intended the broadcast to be anything more that a Halloween prank, however the panic and the fallout of the episode certainly changed the broadcasting business. Older students will enjoy reading *War of the World* and listening to excerpts from the radio broadcast. There is also a couple of parodies available. There is even a script available if you want to put on your own radio show. This may also be an opportune time to discuss censorship. Was this the same as yelling "fire" in a movie theater?

- The War of the Worlds by H. G. Wells
  http://www.fourmilab.ch/etexts/www/warworlds/warw.html
- Audio clips http://earthstation1.simplenet.com/wotw.html
- What Happened http://www.phy.syr.edu/courses/modules/SETI/HISTORY/wells.html
- Study guide http://www.wsu.edu:8080/~brians/science_fiction/warofworlds.html
- Radio Listeners in Panic http://members.aol.com/jeff1070/wotw.html
- Parody: War of the Welles http://www.comedyorama.com/radio/parodies.htm

October 31
Dia de los Muetos – Day of the Dead

Many cultures have special days to celebrate or honor the dead. One of those is Dia de los Muetos, or Day of the Dead. Dia de los Muetos is perhaps Mexico's most popular holiday; a day when families come together to honor their ancestors. Death's morbid side is put aside as families celebrate and honor the lives of those who have passed on[viii]. People in Venezuela celebrate Retardo or Day of the Dead on March 20, Retardo. In Japan, the Festival of the Souls or Obon and Bon Matsuri are celebrated during the summer.

Day of the Dead Lesson Plans and Activities
- Day of the Dead Activity for Early Grades http://www.teachingtolerance.org/teachingtolerance/tt-44.html
- Migration and the Spirits of Life: Day of the Dead Activity for Grades 6-12
  http://www.teachingtolerance.org/teachingtolerance/tt-45.html
- Day of the Dead Activities http://www.pentewa.com/lamer.html
- Day of the Dead Lesson Plans http://members.aol.com/Donnpages/2Holidays.html#El
- Day of the Dead Classroom Activities http://www.teachers.net/lessons/posts/758.html

Day of the Dead Celebrations
- Mexico's Day of the Dead – November 1 and 2
  http://www.mexconnect.com/mex_/feature/daydeadindex.html
- Guatemala http://www.kidlink.org/KIDPROJ/MCC/mcc0170.html
- Festival of the Dead (Sicily) – November 2
- Dia de los Muertos (Arizona) – November 1 http://www.azcentral.com/ent/dead/

- Festivals of Souls, Obon and Bon Matsuri
  http://bose.bsd.uchicago.edu/yoshida/Paul_Abramson/jcal0814.htm
- About Obon http://www.geocities.com/Tokyo/Island/6653/obon1.htm
- Lantern Festivals http://asianideas.com/asianideas/lanterns.html

Other cultures honor their ancestors who have passed away with celebrations similar to Halloween. Fastekavnstursday, celebrated on Shrove Tuesday is a Danish holiday. Children dress up in costumes and enjoy candy treats. Sprengidagur, in Iceland, is celebrated in a similar manner. In Slovenia, the holiday is called Pust.

---

[i] Macbeth, Act 4, Scene 1, William Shakespeare
http://www.cs.usyd.edu.au/~matty/Shakespeare/texts/tragedies/macbeth.html#xref023 July 12, 2001
[ii] How We Celebrate Sukkot http://www.vjholidays.com/sukkot/sukkot1.htm Celebrate Sukkot, January 6, 2001
[iii] http://www.fsa.usda.gov/pas/fsanews/html/1999/aug99/factcookiealt.htm Farm Service Agency News, August 1999 newsletter. *by Linda Blum, Program Assistant, Emmet County FSA Office, Iowa*
[iv] Columbus Day
http://americanhistory.about.com/homework/americanhistory/library/weekly/aa101397.htm?terms=Columbus+Day
[v] The Harlem Renaissance http://www.nku.edu/~diesmanj/harlem_intro.html Jill Diesman, January 7, 2001
[vi] History and Customs of Halloween http://wilstar.com/holidays/hallown.htm
[vii] What Happened http://www.phy.syr.edu/courses/modules/SETI/HISTORY/wells.html
[viii] Dia de los Meurtos, Day of the Dead http://www.azcentral.com/ent/dead/about.shtml

5/7/2002

November

Come, ye thankful people, come,
raise the song of harvest-home:
all is safely gathered in,
ere the winter storms begin;
God, our maker, doth provide
for our wants to be supplied:
come to God's own temple, come;
raise the song of harvest-home.

Psalms and Hymns - Henry Alford[i]

Special Month

Stamp Collecting

Stamp collecting is not only a life long hobby, but also an exciting way to bring history alive. Search for stamps about people and events in this month. Have the students nominate a person from their community for honor on a stamp. They will need to describe the person's accomplishments and tell why the person should be commemorated in such a way. Using a paint program, have then design a stamp.

- Stamp 'Cool'lecting: Your Window To The World
  http://www.framed.usps.com/fyi/nscm2000/
- Stamp Collecting for Kids http://www.bnaps.org/stamps4kids/
- Junior Philatelists on the Internet http://www.ioa.com/~ggayland/junior/
- America's 2000 Stamp Program
  http://www.stampsonline.com/gallery/2000/welcome.htm
- Their Stamp On History http://www.stamponhistory.com/
- Stamp Quest http://www.civilization.ca/membrs/npm/stampquest/entree.html

Sign up for daily postcards from all over the United States. Put up a large map of the United States and track the daily progress of your postcards. Be sure to look at the different stamps that come with each postcard.

- Post Cards From http://www.postcardsfrom.com

The Professor's Postcards site also sends your class postcards, but these are from all over the world and the student's have to find out where they are from.

- The Professor's Postcards
  http://www0.un.org/cyberschoolbus/postcards/index.asp

Native American Heritage Month

"Grown men can learn from very little children
for the hearts of little children are pure.
Therefore, the Great Spirit may show to them many things
which older people miss."

Black Elk

By participating in Native American Heritage Month activities and projects, we gain an understanding of the culture and history of the Native American and his or her place in society. Get started by choosing one or more of the Five Quick Things to Do.

Five Quick Things to Do
1. Play a game - Native American Online Games
   http://www.nativetech.org/Nipmuc/kidscorner.html
2. Learn a few words in Lakota – Lakhota Online Language Dictionary
   http://www.lakhota.com/online/order.cgi?go=prev&L=0
3. Make something good to eat - Wojapi (fruit pudding)
   http://www.nativetech.org/food/wojapi.html
4. Discover the true meaning of the word *squaw* - Reclaiming the Word Squaw
   http://www.nativeweb.org//pages/legal/squaw.html
5. Visit a school – Red Cloud Indian School http://www.redcloudschool.com/ or St. Joseph's Indian School http://www.stjo.org/

The Native American Heritage Month homepage has an excellent list of Internet sites with ideas for classroom use. If you are like I am, you're concerned about the way we present materials to students. Appropriate Methods for Teaching About Native Americans and Stereotyping of Native Americas provide valuable information for teachers concerning some do's and don'ts when teaching about Native Americans.
- Native American Month
  http://www.onlineschoolyard.com/schoolmedia/NativeAmerican/NativeAmerican.htm
- National Native American Awareness Month
  http://www.fortunecity.com/victorian/verona/514/14c.html
- Appropriate Methods for Teaching About Native Americans
  http://www.ableza.org/dodont.html
- Stereotyping of Native Americans http://www.unr.edu/nnap/NT/i-10_11.htm

Online Lesson Plans and Activities
The following lesson plans provide many suggestions that will be useful in the classroom.
- Native American Themes
  http://www.connectingstudents.com/themes/nat_amer.htm
- Native American History Archive Inquirer
  http://www.ilt.columbia.edu/k12/naha/inquirer.html
- Exploring Native Americans Across the Curriculum http://www.education-world.com/a_lesson/lesson038.shtml
- Original activities developed by Native American schools http://4directions.org/
- Native American Culture
  http://www.mcps.k12.md.us/schools/argylems/NativeAm.htm
- Native America: Multicultural Arts http://www.pentewa.com/namer.html
- Native Americans http://disney.go.com/educational/cyberlesson_oct.html

Native American Stories and Legends

Storytelling is so important to the Native American. Native American author, Charles Eastman says in <u>Indian Boyhood</u>, 1902, *"Very early, the Indian boy assumed the task of preserving and transmitting the legends of his ancestors and his race. Almost every evening a myth, or a true story of some deed done in the past, was narrated by one of the parents or grandparents, while the boy listened with parted lips and glistening eyes. On the following evening, he was usually required to repeat it."* To carry on this tradition, have the students prepare a story to tell to classmates and parents.

- Native American Storytelling http://disney.go.com/educational/cyberlesson_nov99.html
- The Native American Bedtime Story Collection http://www.bedtime-story.com/bedtime-story/indians.htm
- Dibaajimowinan idash Aadizookaanag http://www.kstrom.net/isk/stories/stories.html
- Zitkala-Sa: Old Indian Legends http://www.inform.umd.edu/EdRes/ReadingRoom/Fiction/Zitkala-Sa/
- True Stories of the Native Americans http://www.kstrom.net/isk/stories/stories.html
- Indian Legends http://www.germantown.k12.il.us/html/legends.html
- Iroquois Oral Tradtion http://www.indians.org/welker/iroqoral.htm
- Online PowerPoint Stories http://www.campusschool.dsu.edu/library/stories.htm
- Creation Stories http://www.lehigh.edu/~amy2/folklore.html
- Native American Cinderella http://www.kstrom.net/isk/stories/cinder.html
- Children's Books with Native American Indian Themes http://www.cynthialeitichsmith.com/nativebooks.htm

A Day In The Life

To help students understand that all Native Americans are not alike, have them prepare a presentation about *A Day In The Life*. A good place to begin is with a great interactive map located at Indian Cultures. Research an individual tribe. Talk about writing from the historical perspective. Look for common elements, such as location, home, food, etc. But, also encourage them to find unique information about 'their' tribe. Depending on the age of the students, this can be a simple project where the students draw a picture on the top of the page and write a sentence about their picture to a multimedia presentation using presentation software. In either case, prepare a rubric for the project. Kathy Schrock has an excellent site about preparing assessments and rubrics for almost any type of project.

- Native American Nations http://www.nativeculture.com/lisamitten/nations.html
- Indian Cultures http://www.germantown.k12.il.us/html/culture.html
- Mitchell Prehistoric Indian Village http://www.mitchellindianvillage.org/
- Sioux Architecture http://web.reed.edu/academic/departments/english/courses/English558/tipi.html
- The First Americans http://www.germantown.k12.il.us/html/intro.html
- Native American Resources at the Smithsonian http://www.si.edu/opa/amind/start.htm
- Native American Midi http://www.greywolfcub.com/

- Native American Web Sites and Links http://www.littleleaf.com/vickyslinks.htm
- American Indian Exposition http://www.indianexpo.org/
- Additional Links
    - Games and Toys (including online activities and instructions for making games) http://www.nativetech.org/games/
- Kathy Schrock's Guide for Educators http://school.discovery.com/schrockguide/assess.html

Native Americans Today

It's important to help our students understand some of the contemporary issues facing Native Americans today. Issues range from poverty to schools to jobs on the reservations to reclaiming land to reconciliation to changing names of sports tribes and many more are worthy or our time and attention. One way to help us see the world from the Native American point of view is to read an online newspaper. Indian Country Today and Canku Ota are two that students would find informative. Canku Ota also has links just for children. Throughout this month, ask students to find relevant articles to post on your current events bulletin board.

- Indian Country Today http://www.indiancountry.com/
- Canku Ota (Many Paths) http://www.turtletrack.org/
- Native Villiage http://www.turtle-tracks-for-kids.org/

A couple of other sites that will help students understand issues facing the Native Americans today, refer to:

- A Line In The Sand http://hanksville.phast.umass.edu:8000/cultprop/
- Bureau of Indian Affairs http://www.doi.gov/bureau-indian-affairs.html

A topic that can be very controversial is the use of Native American words and tribal names in sports and advertising. Have you students write an editorial about this issue.

- American Indian Sports Team Mascots http://members.tripod.com/earnestman/1indexpage.htm

Native American Heroes

"The earth has received the embrace of the sun
and we shall see the results of that love.
He put in your heart certain wishes and plans;
in my heart, he put other different desires."

Sitting Bull

It is right and indeed necessary for all of our students to recognize and honor the contributions and impact Native Americans have made. Brainstorm a list of attributes of a hero to help students define the term. Then, have small groups of students identify a Native American they want to research for their project. Have them prepare a list of questions using the *who, what, when, where and why* format. List these questions using a word processor. At the computer, bring up both the list of questions and the Internet site they are using for their research. Minimize both programs and arrange them on the desktop so that they are side-by-side. This allows the students to see the questions and read the materials at the same time. This is a good way to keep students focused and on-task and helps them spell unfamiliar words. You also want to have students document their sources as they use them. Basically, the important things to include in the documentation are: title of the site, date THEY accessed the site, author (if you know it) and the URL. Pictures also need to be documented. Finally, after the research has been completed, the students need to think of a way to honor their hero. They could write a song, poem, play, or tribute, or make a gallery of significant memorabilia.

- Native American Leaders of the Past
  http://www.americanwest.com/pages/pastldrs.htm
- Indian Heroes and Great Chieftains
  ftp://uiarchive.cso.uiuc.edu/pub/etext/gutenberg/etext95/indhe10.txt
- Native American Heroes http://www.skyfamily.com/cozette/index13.html
- The People Page http://www.tahtonka.com/people.html
- Jim Thorpe http://nascsports.org/JThorpe/index.htm
- Jim Thorpe http://www.cmgww.com/sports/thorpe/thorpe.html
- Eli Parker: A Warrior in Two Worlds
  http://www.pbs.org/warrior/noflash/index.html
- Pomp: The True Story of the Baby on the Sacagawea Dollar (an e-book)
  http://pompstory.home.mindspring.com/index.html
- Geronimo, His Own Story http://odur.let.rug.nl/~usa/B/geronimo/geronixx.htm
- Native America History (many links to famous Native Americans)
  http://www.turtletrack.org/Links/CO_NAHistoryLinks.htm
- Native American Heroes and Heroines
  http://classroomtoday.classroom.com/TeachersLounge/About/Topics/Topic.asp?TopicID=23 (you need to subscribe to this site, but there is a FREE trial period)
- Native American Images http://www.csulb.edu/projects/ais/nae/

For more information about documenting electronic resources, refer to:

- Site Documentation http://faculty.luther.edu/~barrynan/document.htm

Odds and Ends
- Native American Links http://www.geocities.com/RainForest/7694/websites.html
- Native Americans http://www.studyweb.com/culture/natamsioux.htm
- First Nations Histories http://www.tolatsga.org/Compacts.html
- Native American Resources on the Net
  http://www.indolinks.com/websights/diwali/buildup.htm
- Index of Native American Resources on the Internet
  http://www.hanksville.org/NAresources/ (this appears to be a more political site, but it does have good resources for teachers)
- Native Tech http://www.nativetech.org/ (information about art and culture with instructions for making many games, toys and food)
- Native Web http://www.nativeweb.org/
- Carnegie Museum of Natural History: American Indians and the Natural World
  http://www.clpgh.org/cmnh/exhibits/north-south-east-west/
- Create Your Own Native American Board Game
  http://school.discovery.com/lessonplans/programs/nativeamericans/index.html

Special Week

Week 2
National Chemistry Week
Want to do some experiments with your kids but afraid of blowing up the school? Don't worry; try some of these online chemistry activities. But, first, learn about the Scientific Method. I hope you enjoy these experiments and have a safe week.

- Scientific Method
  http://www.brainpop.com/science/matter/scientificmethod/index.weml
- The pH Factor http://www.miamisci.org/ph/default.html
- Bill Nye http://billnye.com/flash_go.html
- Experiencing Chemistry http://www.omsi.edu/explore/online.cfm
- SNL Lab http://www.jsf.or.jp/sln/laboe.html
- Periodic Table http://www.brainpop.com/science/matter/periodictable/index.weml

For the more adventuresome, try some of these off-line experiments. Be sure to follow directions carefully and supervise the students.

- Bizarre Stuff You Can Make in Your Kitchen http://freeweb.pdq.net/headstrong/
  - Stupid Egg Trick http://freeweb.pdq.net/headstrong/egg.htm (my favorite)
- Science Experiments You Can Do http://www.west.net/~science/expindx.htm
- Science Bob http://www.sciencebob.com/
- Edible/Inedible Experiments http://madsci.wustl.edu/experiments/
- Home Experiments
  http://scifun.chem.wisc.edu/HOMEEXPTS/HOMEEXPTS.HTML
- Science Teacher's Resource Center http://chem.lapeer.org/Chem1Docs/
- Delights of Chemistry http://www.chem.leeds.ac.uk/delights/texts/

Odds and Ends
- Science Service Resources on the WWW
  http://www.sciserv.org/isef/teacher/resourc.asp
- National Science Teachers Association http://www.nsta.org/
- Science Learning Network http://www.sln.org/
- National Science Foundation http://www.nsf.gov/home/ehr/start.htm

2nd Week
Children's Book Week
Many Internet sites provide ideas for celebrating Children's Book Week. The following are some that provide a good starting point.

- Celebrate Children's Book Week http://www.education-world.com/a_special/bookweek_99.shtml
- Motivational Ideas for Children's Book Week and National Library Week
  http://falcon.jmu.edu/~ramseyil/bookweek.htm
- Ideas to Celebrate Children's Book Week
  http://npin.org/pnews/pnewn97/pnewn97i.html
- The Children's Book Council http://www.cbcbooks.org/
- 25 Ideas to Motivate Young Readers (by Book-IT) http://www.education-world.com/a_lesson/lesson035.shtml

- Children's Book Week http://www.cbcbooks.org/html/book_week.html

Celebrating Children's Book Week in Other Countries
- Australian Book Week http://www.cbc.org.au/bookweek.htm
- Canadian Book Week http://www3.sympatico.ca/ccbc/
- Japan's Book Week
  http://www.jinjapan.org/kidsweb/calendar/october/bookweek.html

There are literally thousands of children's books online. Books and Authors is a good place to begin. I also like Golden Books for younger children. You can subscribe to this site (free) and they will send you updates for the holidays that are interactive.
- Books and Authors http://www.lapl.org/kidsweb/coolsites/bookauthor-0p.html
- Golden Books http://www.goldenbooks.com
- Children's Storybooks Online http://www.magickeys.com/books/index.html
- Reading Room Book Stacks http://www.dalton.org/libraries/fairrosa/stacks.html
- Creation Stories http://www.ozemail.com.au/~reed/global/mythstor.html
- Folk Legends of Japan http://www.jinjapan.org/kidsweb/folk.html

Things to Do
1) Have your students make a list of their favorite books. Interview students in other classes and record the results on a spreadsheet. Make a graph of your school's favorite books. To see what others recommend, look at:
- 100 Best Children's Books http://www.parenting-qa.com/parentqa/feature_4.html
- Best Books of the Year http://www.acs.ucalgary.ca/~dkbrown/bestbooks.html

2) Why not make a book! Ask the teacher of a younger grade what subject they are learning about, such as dinosaurs or whales. Then, have your students search the Internet for clip art related to that topic. Copy the images into a publishing program, such as MS Publisher. I like to use the card format. That will give you a title page and three other pages in your book. Print out and give to the younger students.
- Make a Coloring Book http://www.ehow.com/eHow/eHow/0,1053,18071,FF.html

Other ideas for books include classroom poetry books, ABC books and counting books. ABC books are particularly good to review any subject at any age level.
- Book Binding http://www.art.eku.edu/bookbinding/page1.html

Did you know that you can find books about any, or almost any topic at Amazon and Barnes and Noble? Simple select books and then the topic, such as dinosaurs or family. This is a great tool if you are looking for books to complement a specific unit.
- Amazon http://www.amazon.com (they found 1447 titles with the keyword dinosaur)**1447 total matches for "dinosaur**
- Barnes and Noble http://www.bn.com (they found 3,401 titles with the keyword dinosaur) I might need to refine my search!!

2nd Week
American Education Week
"For the first time in history, free schooling was offered for all children. Puritans formed the first formal school in 1635, called the Roxbury Latin School. Four years later, the first American College was established; Harvard in Cambridge. Children aged 6-8

attended a 'Dame school' where the teacher, who was usually a widow, taught reading. 'Ciphering' (math) and writing were low on the academic agenda."[ii]

Is this something worth celebrating? You bet! Have your students take a look at the History of American Education. This is an exceptional site with many pictures. Assign small groups to report on the different eras. They could use any presentation tool for their report.

- History of American Education http://www.nd.edu/~rbarger/www7/

Additional sites to help in their research include:

- Racial Desegregation in Public Education
  http://www.cr.nps.gov/history/online_books/nhl/school.htm
- The Horn Book http://www.nd.edu/~rbarger/www7/colonial.html
- History of the horn book http://www.lva.lib.va.us/sb/exhibits/treasures/rare/rar-h5.htm
- McGuffey Reader http://www.ohiokids.org/games/ohv/schoolhs/ch3.html
- McGuffey Readers http://www.nd.edu/~rbarger/www7/common.html
- National Textbook http://www.backgroundbriefing.com/mcguffee.html
- John Dewey http://www.infed.org/thinkers/et-dewey.htm
- Dewey Quotes http://cuip.uchicago.edu/~cac/dewey.html
- Dick and Jane: Illustrations of an American Education
  http://www.tfaoi.com/newsmu/nmus18d.htm
- Reading Deeper: The Legacy of Dick and Jane
  http://www.carlagirl.net/read/dickjane.html

"How happy is he born and taught,
That serveth not another's will;
Whose armor is his honest thought,
And simple truth his utmost skill!"

From "The Character of a Happy Life,"
Sir Henry Wotton
McGuffey's Fifth Eclectic Reader

For additional ideas for celebrating American Education Week, go to the American Education Week Homepage. This will help you get ideas for publicizing your events, also.

- American Education Week http://www.nea.org/aew/

As there are so many concerns about education that lend themselves to debate. This would be an excellent time to introduce debate to your students. Some topics that come to mind include: charter schools, vouchers, testing, homeschooling, and standard-based education. The list goes on. A couple of good places to start looking for information are:

- National Education Association http://www.nea.org/
- American Federation of Teachers http://www.aft.org/
- Achieve+MCREL
  http://www.achieve.org/achieve/achieved.nsf/support/about+Achieve+MCrel

Debate Guidelines

- Parliamentary Debate Guidelines and Conventions
  http://ccdu.mckenna.edu/parl/parli_guidelines.htm
- Literary Debate Guidelines
  http://www.ncteamericancollection.org/literary_debate_guidelines.htm (look at the four different debate formats)
- Debate Criteria
  http://deil.lang.uiuc.edu/class.pages/eil367/webprojects/teamsF98/Team5/debate1.htm

2nd Week

Geography Awareness Week

    George Eagan's Old Grandfather Rode A Pig Home Yesterday
                 GEOGRAPHY

There are so many things to do to celebrate Geography Awareness Week. I have just listed couple of my favorites and some really great sites to whet your imagination and creativity.

    A good place to start is National Geographic for Educators with information and suggestions for Geography Awareness Week. National Geographic also sponsors the Family Geographic Challenge and the Geographic Bee.

- National Geographic for Educators
  http://magma.nationalgeographic.com/education/index.cfm
  - Family Geography Challenge
    http://www.nationalgeographic.com/challenge/cgi-bin/kwquiz.cgi
  - Geographic Bee http://www.nationalgeographic.com/geographybee/
- Helping Your Child Learn About Geography
  http://www.ed.gov/pubs/parents/Geography/
- And, THE BEST GEOGRAHPY site on the Internet,
  A-Z Geography
  http://school.discovery.com/homeworkhelp/worldbook/atozgeography/index.html
- American Geography http://odur.let.rug.nl/~usa/GEO/index.htm

Then, check out Geography Lesson Plans and Ideas
http://www.educationplanet.com/maps/socialstudiesplanet/search/Geography_and_Countries

Travel Agent

Assign each student, or small group, a country to research. Have them look for the following information: Country, Capital, Population, Language, Climate: Summer, Climate: Winter, Money, Activities, etc. When the students have found their information have them enter it into a database program. Then, set up a Travel Agent game. Students can ask questions such as: What country can I go to where the language is Spanish? Or, where can I go where it is warm (>) 50 degrees in the winter? *Note – when setting up a database, be sure to use the same words for the same thing. For instance, use Spanish to mean Spanish, not Hispanic or Mexican. The computer will only sort if you use the same terms, as it doesn't know that Spanish and Mexican might mean the same thing on your database.* There are many sites that would be a ready reference.

- Map Machine http://www.nationalgeographic.com/maps/index.html (look at Flags and Facts)
- Future Culture http://www.wcpworld.com/future/culture.htm (this site also has a neat quiz and a good description of culture traits)
- World Fact Book http://www.cia.gov/cia/publications/factbook/index.html
- Country Profiles http://www.theodora.com/wfb/abc_world_fact_book.html
- World Encyclopedia http://www.emulateme.com/nationalpha.htm
- Countries of the World http://www.factmonster.com/countries.html
- E-Conflict World Encyclopedia http://www.emulateme.com/_vti_bin/shtml.dll/index.htm

Find out how far you are from wherever you want to be at Bali and Indonesia.

- How far is it? http://www.indo.com/distance/

Field Trip

Take a Field Trip! Through the wonders of the Internet, you and your students are no longer limited to the local fire station (although I think this is a great field trip and encourage you to take you students and your digital camera and make you own online field trip on your class web page.) Check out some of the online field trips available to you. A good list is on the Campus School and Are We There Yes?

- Campus School – Field Trip http://www.campusschool.dsu.edu/fieldtrips/
- Are We There Yet? http://www.fieldtrip.com
- The Greatest Places http://www.greatestplaces.org/

"Global Learn uses the Internet to allow children to participate in explorations of places and people that they might never get to know on their own."
—Boston Sunday Globe, September 27, 1998

You and your students can join an exploration and travel to many interesting places, via the Internet. You will need to register, but there is no cost. I particularly like the feature that allows you to participate in investigations. Another neat feature is the noon picture. The team stays with host families and you will get to meet them, learn about their culture, food and money. I think you will enjoy this one.

- Global Learn http://www.globalearn.com/

For the ultimate field trip, you can join a Quest. These are hosted by Classroom Connect and are great! Your students can visit directly with the explorers and get daily updates. There is a fee for these interactive Quests; however, you can participate in any of the past Quests for free!

- The Quest Channel http://quest.classroom.com/

You can also make your own web trip. You choose where you want to go, the sites to visit and the questions to ask. Enter it into a simple to use online database and off you go!

Maps

One of the things I have noticed with students is that they have a hard time visualizing that an abstract map represents a real place. To help them understand this concept, use an aerial or satellite map to identify a well-known place. Then, find a corresponding picture of that place. This would make an interesting bulletin board. Put the maps on one side and the pictures on the other. Connect them with map tacks and string.

Map Sites
- Map Blast http://www.mapblast.com/myblast/index.mb
- Online Map Creations http://www.aquarius.geomar.de/omc/
- Online World Atlas http://www.maps.com/explore/atlas/
- National Atlas of the United States http://www.nationalatlas.gov/
- Color Landform Atlas of the United States
  http://fermi.jhuapl.edu/states/states.html
- National Mapping Information http://mapping.usgs.gov/
- Map Happy http://www.wolinskyweb.com/maphappy.htm (this is a great list of map sites)

Odds and Ends
- **Online Geography Games** http://www.geography-games.com
- **From Asia to Africa to Antarctica** is a complete integrated unit plan about the continents. Besides social studies, there are math, science, language arts and music activities.
  - Continents
    http://www.lightspan.com/teacher/pages/classroomthemes/continents/default.asp?_prod=LS&_Nav=t3_tools_classrmthemes
- **Online Map Games** For some really cool map games, check out Online Map Games http://www.maps.com/learn/games/
- **Degree Confluence Project** The goal of the project is to visit each of the latitude and longitude integer degree intersections in the world, and to take pictures at each location. The pictures and stories will then be posted. http://www.confluence.org/index.php
- **The Globe Program** This interactive online program is a little more involved and would probably take more time than you want to spend for just a quick geography lesson. But, if you are looking for an ongoing project that has your students collecting data and sharing with other class around the world..this is the site for you. http://www.globe.gov/fsl/html/aboutglobe.cgi?intro&lang=en&nav=1

Quick Tip:
To learn more about any state, use the address: http://www.state.sd.us using the two letter abbreviation. This one would take you to South Dakota's Home Page. http://www.state.mn.us would take you to Minnesota's Home Page. Need a reminder about the abbreviations? Check out http://fermi.jhuapl.edu/states/states.html

---

Date Varies

Election Day
1st Tuesday after 1st Monday
(for President, in years equally divisible by 4)

The core concept of our American education system of free, public education is to prepare an informed electorate (see American Education Week, November). In fact, the reason our forefathers provided education for girls (an unheard of thing in the 1700s) was not so they could vote (that wouldn't come for over 200 years) but they might grow up to be mothers of men who could vote and therefore, they needed to have a proper education. With this in mind, it is vital that we as teachers work diligently to help students understand our American system of government and in particular our system of campaigning and voting. Education World provides an excellent starting point for teachers. It includes lesson plans and activities.

- Education World Lesson Plans and Activities http://www.education-world.com/a_special/election_2000.shtml

How does government affect me? The Kids Democracy Project, published by PBS is one of the best and most readable Internet sites about the American system of government I know of. I would suggest you start with this site as a large group presentation. You can quickly learn (or review) the three branches of government and see how government affects our daily lives.

- Kids Democracy Project http://www.pbs.org/democracy/kids/

The President

To begin your discussion of the Presidency, have the students research a president. Take a roll of freezer-wrap paper and make a timeline. Starting with George Washington, have the students print out a picture of their president with certain biographical facts, such as birthday, home state, etc. I would work with the students to identify 5 – 10 facts that they should be able to find. Then, ask the students to think of five additional facts about their particular president that they find interesting. List their facts on a bulleted list to hang with their president's picture. Some really good, basic sites are:

- The Presidents http://www.pbs.org/wgbh/amex/presidents/indexjs.html
- POTUS http://www.ipl.org/ref/POTUS/
- Portraits of Presidents http://lcweb2.loc.gov/ammem/odmdhtml/preshome.html

If you are looking for some interesting, sometime off the beaten path information about our presidents, look at:

- US Presidents Lists http://www.fujisan.demon.co.uk/USPresidents/preslist.htm but be careful at this site, as you and the students might learn more than you care to.

The president's wives have also played an important part in our cultural heritage. An excellent site about the first ladies is:

- First Ladies http://www.firstladies.org/Flbib2.htm

After you have completed your timeline, insert some basic historical references, such as the Civil War, WWII, 1st man to walk on the moon, etc. (For more ideas about the Presidents, see February)

Presidential Campaigns

To learn more about political campaigns, look at the American President. This is a site developed by PBS for their original documentary series. You do not need to have the video series to use this site. It has excellent campaign and election information for the presidents plus brief biographies. There are lesson plans for each of the segments with excellent classroom activities. If you have the PBS series, the lessons tie right in, but many are useful even without the video series.

- American President (PBS series) http://www.americanpresident.org/home6.htm
  Have older students play The War Room: Campaign Simulation Game
  http://www.americanpresident.org/prezgame.htm

All students will enjoy looking at old campaign posters and buttons and listening to campaign songs. Have students prepare a campaign button for themselves using a digital camera. Then, select a song for their theme song. Use a familiar tune and write new words.

- Campaign buttons and memorabilia http://ronwadebuttons.com/ (this is a commercial site)
- Campaign songs
  http://www.leisuresuit.net/Webzine/articles/presidential_songs.shtml
- Campaign songs make or break candidates
  http://www.pub.umich.edu/daily/1996/nov/11-07-96/arts/art05.html

Political Parties
- The Democratic National Committee http://www.democrats.org/index.html
- Republican National Committee http://www.rnc.org/

Voting
To help students understand about the voting process, refer to the Kids Voting Project. This site has classroom ideas and activities for students and teachers. Inside the Voting Booth gives students a historical perspective on some major voting events in our history. And, the Importance of One Vote gives readers an understanding of one of the greatest election problems – lack of voter turnout. Have the students make a list of one-vote actions and send it to a local radio or TV station.

- Kids Voting http://www.kidsvotingusa.org/
- Inside the Voting Booth http://www.pbs.org/democracy/kids/vote/index.html
- Importance of One Vote
  http://www.activedayton.com/community/groups/kidsvoting/How_important_is_o ne.html

Electoral College
What is the Electoral College and how does it work? What is the difference between the Electoral College and popular vote? An excellent site for some basic information is at the Federal Election Commission http://www.fec.gov/

- How the Electoral College Works http://www.fec.gov/pages/ecworks.htm.
- For a list of states and their number of electors, refer to
  http://www.nara.gov/fedreg/elctcoll/votebyst.html.
- There is on online calculator where students can predict which states will vote for which candidate and make predictions http://www.jump.net/~jnhtx/ec/ec.html
- And, to compare different electoral maps, check out the maps at
  http://teachpol.tcnj.edu/amer_pol_hist/_browse_maps.htm

The Evolution of Voter Rights

Over the course of the past 200+ years, our Constitution has changed to include Black and women voters. The age for eligible voters has also changed over the years. An excellent lesson plan for upper elementary grades is *Voting and the U.S. Constitution*. It includes role-play activities, a women's suffrage play and many other activities. *Note: for more information about Women's Suffrage, refer to August 18, the 19th Amendment.* Voting and the U.S. Constitution Have students read Jane Addams, *Why Women Should Vote* as a Reader's Theater. Some of this is quite lengthy, so have students edit their parts. Merge selections from Susan B. Anthony's speech, *Women's Right to Vote*. Students take the part of famous women in history and read their part from their character's point of view.

- Why Women Should Vote http://douglass.speech.nwu.edu/adda_a03.htm
- Susan B. Anthony: Women's Right to Vote http://www.fordham.edu/halsall/mod/1873anthony.html

Read Women Win the Right to Vote! Note that the 19th Amendment passed by just one vote (refer to Voting). Who was president during the critical periods of women's suffrage? Add information from the Chronology of Woman Suffrage Movement Events to the Presidents Timeline.

- Women Win the Right to Vote! http://www.aracnet.com/~histgaz/hgv3n5.htm
- Chronology of Woman Suffrage Movement Events http://teacher.scholastic.com/researchtools/articlearchives/womhst/chrono.htm

Additional Sites about Women's Suffrage

- Suffrage History From PBS http://www.pbs.org/onewoman/suffrage.html
- Living the Legacy: Women's Rights Movement http://www.legacy98.org/
- From Parlor to Politics http://www.umkc.edu/imc/suffrage.htm
- http://ncctest.netreach.net/sections/teacher/lesson_plans/html/10202ag.asp
- U.S. Constitution http://www.law.cornell.edu/constitution/constitution.overview.html

Polls

Often political positions are determined by polling or asking the public how they feel about certain issues. Have the students look at some online polls to get a feel for how they are written and reported. Then, have the students make up polls they could ask other classes such as favorite lunch menu, recess activity, author, etc. Use a spreadsheet such as Excel to record the information and make a chart to display the results. Post these in the hallways. What political platform could candidates for student council run on based on this polling information?

- USAToday Snapshots http://www.usatoday.com/
- The Yuckiest Site on the Internet http://yucky.kids.discovery.com/

Political News

For some general, all purpose information about elections use the following Internet sites:

- Voter.com http://www.voter.com/home/0,1126,2--,00.html
- Election.com http://www.election.com
- Project Vote Smart http://www.vote-smart.org

Thanksgiving - PL 90-363
4th Thursday

Five Quick Things to do for Thanksgiving
1. Color a "Count Your Blessings" picture. Go to the Mary Engelbreit site and with print out copies of the picture or copy and paste it into a paint program and use your electronic colors to color the picture.
   http://www.maryengelbreit.com/WorkShop/Workshop.htm
2. Read the 1st Thanksgiving Proclamation. The First Thanksgiving Proclamation June 29, 1676 http://www.benjerry.com/thanksgiving/thanks-proc.tmpl
   - Continental Congress Thanksgiving Proclamation of 1782
     http://www.night.net/thanksgiving/1782proc.html
   - George Washington's Thanksgiving Proclamation
     http://www.night.net/thanksgiving/kwash-11.html
   - Abraham Lincoln's Thanksgiving Proclamation
     http://tristate.pgh.net/~garyr/linc_doc.html
3. Take a tour of the Mayflower. While you are at this site, also take a look at the timeline.
   - Explore the Mayflower
     http://teacher.scholastic.com/thanksgiving/mayflower/index.htm
   - Timeline http://teacher.scholastic.com/thanksgiving/pictimeline/sep1620.htm
4. Learn the history of the wishbone.
   - Who gets the wishbone?
     http://www.butterball.com/pages/bb_journal.cfm?BID=3&JID=19&PRID=&AID=713&mode=article_display
5. Play a Thanksgiving game. Twelve games to choose from; some noisy and some quiet, some indoors, some outdoors. Enjoy!
   - Thanksgiving Games http://www.night.net/thanksgiving/games11.html-ssi

Online Lesson Plans and Activities
Are you looking for some ready-made lessons for Thanksgiving? These are some of the best. If you don't want or have time to do the complete lesson, pick and choose what will be most beneficial for your class.
- Teaching About Thanksgiving http://www.night.net/thanksgiving/lesson-plan.html This excellent site was developed by the Center for World Indigenous Studies and written by a veteran teacher who is also a Native American. Thanksgiving Lesson Plan for ESL students http://www.everythingesl.net/lessons/gobble.shtml This is primarily a vocabulary lesson
- Thanksgiving Traditions http://www.teacherlink.usu.edu/TLresources/longterm/LessonPlans/Byrnes/thanks.html This is an easy to use, rather simple lesson that would be appropriate for a beginning study of traditions. It does use many interesting teaching techniques.
- A Time to Give Thanks http://www.teelfamily.com/education/thanksunit.html Starting with the discontent with the Church of England through traditional Thanksgiving customs, this unit plan can be adapted for many different purposes.

- Then and Now
  http://www.learningcompanyschool.com/school/prods/kd2plan1.htm Using
  KidPix or another drawing program, have students make a Venn diagram of
  Thanksgiving concepts.
- Education World's Thanksgiving Lesson Plan http://www.education-
  world.com/a_lesson/lesson037.shtml This is a very complete unit plan about
  Thanksgiving. All or parts of it would be useful in most elementary and middle
  school classrooms.
- Awesome Library Lesson Plan: Thanksgiving
  http://www.awesomelibrary.org/Classroom/Social_Studies/Holidays/Thanksgivin
  g.html This site provides web sites, worksheets and suggestions for learning
  about Thanksgiving
- Two Lesson Plans honoring Native American Thanksgiving Celebrations
  - Green Corn Festival
    http://teacherlink.ed.usu.edu/TLresources/longterm/LessonPlans/Byrnes/c
    orn.html
  - Strawberry Thanksgiving
    http://teacherlink.ed.usu.edu/TLresources/longterm/LessonPlans/Byrnes/st
    raw.html
- Test Your Knowledge About Thanksgiving
  - Thanksgiving Cyberchallenge
    http://teacher.scholastic.com/thanksgiving/plygame/hi.asp
  - What Do You Know About Thanksgiving?
    http://wilstar.com/holidays/thanksgv.htm
  - Wampanoag Thanksgiving http://www.teachervision.com/lesson-
    plans/lesson-3359.html
- Choose from many other online lesson plans
  http://www.lessonplanspage.com/Thanksgiving.htm There are some interesting
  math lessons including grocery shopping and graphing to check out.

History of Thanksgiving
There are some wonderful history resources on the Internet. Some I would recommend
to begin with are:
- Thanksgiving in American Memory
  http://memory.loc.gov/ammem/ndlpedu/features/thanks/thanks.html This site
  gives personal memories of Thanksgiving, included are Jewish and African-
  American reminisces. Have students interview family members and record their
  memories of past Thanksgivings.
- History http://www.historychannel.com/thanksgiving/ There is an interesting
  discussion of 17th Century table manners. Have the students write a book of
  manners for the 21st Century. There is also an interview with Miles Standish and
  Ellinor Billington. Have the students use the same format and after researching a
  pilgrim (see What Do We Know About The People On The Mayflower
  http://www.umkc.edu/imc/mayflow.htm and The Mayflower Passenger List
  http://members.aol.com/calebj/passenger.html and the Native Americans
  associated with the Mayflower http://members.aol.com/calebj/indians.html) write

what might have been their answers. This is a good time to talk about the different types of biographies: authentic - all factual information, documented with eye witness accounts and/or written documents; fictionalized – based on research, but the author uses fictionalized conversation; biographical fiction – based on fact, but includes invented dialog and secondary characters.

- 17th Century Games and Activities for Children http://www.plimoth.org/Education/kidspage.htm Make a copy of the Nine Men's Morris game board and the rules for playing. Have groups of children make up a simple board game of their own and write the rules.
- Using the following resources, have the students recreate the early Plimoth settlement. Take a square piece of paper. Fold it in half taco style (corner to corner), unfold it and fold it in half the other way, taco style. Cut on one fold to the center. Bring the two halves together and staple. This forms the base for an easy diorama.

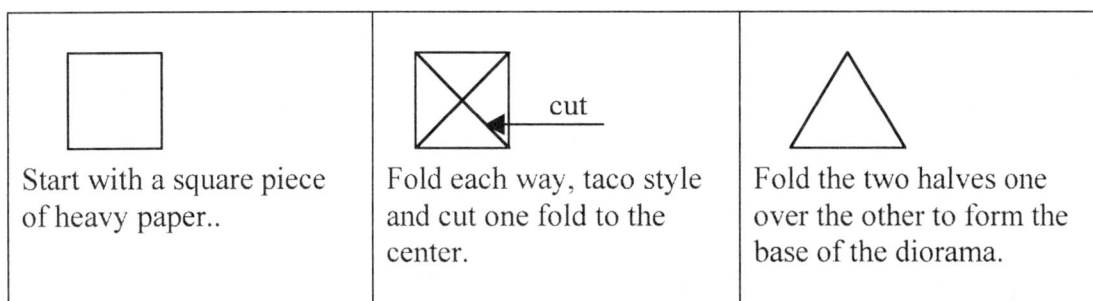

Start with a square piece of heavy paper..	cut Fold each way, taco style and cut one fold to the center.	Fold the two halves one over the other to form the base of the diorama.

Use clip art and drawings to cut out and form the background, objects and the people in the scene. Hint: when cutting out the people, make a little tab on the bottom of each person. Cut a slit in the bottom of the diorama and insert the tab from the person into the slit. This will help the person stand up.
- o The Pilgrims in American Culture http://www.plimoth.org/Library/Thanksgiving/thanksgi.htm
- o The Mayflower Web Page http://members.aol.com/calebj/mayflower.html
- o Pilgrims http://pilgrims.net/plymouth/
- o Daily Life in 1621 http://teacher.scholastic.com/thanksgiving/plimoth/daily.htm

Native Americans
November is Native American Heritage Month. Refer to that heading for lots more information about Native Americans.

For brief biographies about Squanto, Samoset, and Massasoit refer to the following:
- Squanto http://search.biography.com/print_record.pl?id=19676
- Samoset http://search.biography.com/print_record.pl?id=19159
- Massasoit http://search.biography.com/print_record.pl?id=17392
- Massasoit http://www.plimoth.org/Library/massasoi.htm

Food

Thanksgiving celebrations always include food. Spend some time researching foods associated with Thanksgiving.

- Tour a Cranberry Bog http://www.cranberryexpo.com/online_tour.html
- What's the difference between yams and sweet potatoes? http://www.ces.ncsu.edu/depts/hort/hil/hil-23-a.html
- Thanksgiving Turkey http://www.holidays.net/thanksgiving/turkey.htm
- Compare the Thanksgiving 17th Century feast with modern Thanksgiving dinners. What's alike, different or just modernized? Typical Bill of Fare for the Thanksgiving feast http://www.plimoth.org/Library/Thanksgiving/17feast.htm

Table Graces

- Blessings and Graces http://www.night.net/thanksgiving/grace.html-ssi
- Early Table Grace http://www.plimoth.org/Library/manners.htm#grace

Clip Art, Crafts and Games

You and your students will enjoy many Thanksgiving related games and activities on the Internet. Be sensitive to the images portrayed in the clip art and coloring pages. If some of them show Native Americans, ask the students identify and describe the stereotypes. Some of the fun sites to explore include:

- Find Tom Turkey http://www.heathersholidaze.com/thanks/index.html
- Kids Clip Art http://kidexchange.about.com/kids/kidexchange/library/clipart/bltclipart.htm
- Thanksgiving crafts http://www.geocities.com/Heartland/7997/sherri2e.htm#thbook
- Thanksgiving Pictures to Color http://www.night.net/thanksgiving/colorsheets.html-ssi
- Kids Domain Thanksgiving Games and Crafts http://www.kidsdomain.com/holiday/thanks/index.html
- 8 Thanksgiving Day Games http://family2.go.com/features/family_1998_11/famf/famf118games/famf118games.html

Stories and Poems

One-way to enjoy any holiday is to read stories and poem about the special day. Some of the best on the Internet for Thanksgiving are:

- The Spirit of the Corn http://etext.lib.virginia.edu/cgibin/toccer?id=OlcGood&images=images/modeng&data=/lv1/Archive/eng-parsed&tag=public&part=88
- Goodbye Pumpkin Pie: Poem for Readers Theater http://www.dads.com/pumpkin.htm
- Lonesome Turkey (a funny, interactive story) http://www.honeysucklewhite.com/just_for_fun/lonesome_turkey/
- Rosies Thanksgiving Dinner (an online alphabet story) http://www.night.net/thanksgiving/Alpha-Click-Thanks.html-ssi

Write your own Thanksgiving story at Sears Mixed-up Stories
http://www.searsportrait.com/storybook/thanksgiving_99_form.html
And, for the more serious reader, try *Pilgrim's Progress* by John Bunyan.
http://www.ccel.org/b/bunyan/pilgrims_progress/title.html This is the story of a pilgrim or traveler's dream. Have students pretend to be a pilgrim dreaming about a quest. Where might they go, who might they meet and how might they know when they have arrived?

General Thanksgiving Links
- Ben and Jerry http://www.benjerry.com/thanksgiving/
- Chantessy's Happy Thanksgiving http://www.rainbow-magic.com/holidays/thanksgiving/index.html
- Lots of things to do related to Thanksgiving http://www.memphis-schools.k12.tn.us/admin/tlapages/thanksgiving.htm (this has something for everyone!)
- North of Boston Library Exchange Thanksgiving Links http://www.noblenet.org/year/tty11tha.htm
- Kids Domain Thanksgiving http://www.kidsdomain.com/holiday/thanks/index.html
- Billy Bears Thanksgiving http://www.billybear4kids.com/holidays/thanksgiving/thanksgiving.htm
- Thanksgiving on the Net http://www.holidays.net/thanksgiving/

Thanksgiving Celebrations in Other Countries
- Canadian Thanksgiving (2nd Monday in October) http://kidexchange.about.com/kids/kidexchange/library/weekly/aa092898.htm?pid=2775&cob=home
- Labor Thanksgiving Day (Japan) November 23 http://www.jinjapan.org/kidsweb/calendar/november/labor.html

Odds and Ends
- Macy's Thanksgiving Day Parade http://www.nyctourist.com/macys_menu.htm
- Vote for the Greatest Turkey Game on TV http://washingtonpost.com/wp-srv/style/polls/turkeygames.htm
- Where the Boys Are: Bonding Out Back, In The Turkey Bowl http://www.cs.duke.edu/~ola/wsjfootball.html

Special Days

November 1, 1926
Hilary Knight' s Birthday
Hilary Knight, is most famous for his illustrations of the classic *Eloise* books by Kay Thompson. Eloise is a rambunctious, wiser-than-her-years girl who lives with her nanny and an assortment of pets at The Plaza Hotel, New York, New York. The original book, *Eloise*, was followed by *Eloise in Paris, Eloise at Christmastime* and *Eloise in Moscow*.

More than 3 million copies of *Eloise* have been sold worldwide since Simon & Schuster originally published it in 1955.

After reading the Eloise books, visit each of the famous cities on the Internet and have students compare the illustrations with the "real" sites. Example:

Illustration	"Real" Landmark
Cover of Eloise in Paris	artday, Tour Eiffle Tower http://www.artday.com/dayimg.htm

Take an online tour of the famous Eloise cities:
- New York, New York http://travel.yahoo.com/t/North_America/United_States/New_York/New_York_City/
- Paris, France http://travel.yahoo.com/t/Europe/France/Paris/
- Moscow, Russia http://travel.yahoo.com/t/Europe/Russia/Moscow/

Write a class book about Eloise and the sites she would see if she came to your town. Use a digital camera to take pictures of popular sites, and then draw them for the illustrations in your book.

Interviews and Biographical Information about Hilary Knight
- Eloise http://www.gti.net/iksrog/eloise/hilary_knight.htm
- Interview with Hilary Knight http://www.ingrambook.com/Company_info/ibchtml/Resource_Center/Whats_New/bb_hilary_knight.asp
- Meet the Authors and Illustrators http://www.childrenslit.com/f_knight.html
- Eloise Online Activities http://www.itsybitsye.com/kids/eloise/index.html

Selected Books by Hilary Knight
Eloise in Paris
Eloise in Moscow
Eloise at the Plaza
Where's Wallace
Hilary Knight's Twelve Days of Christmas
The Absolutely Essential Eloise
The Best Little Monkeys in the World
A Dog Is Listening: The Way Some of Our Closest Friends View Us
Eloise's Guide to Life: How to Eat, Dress, Travel, Behave and Stay Six Forever!
Happy Birthday
Hello Mrs. Piggle Wiggle
Eloise At Christmastime
Side By Side
The Owl and the Pussy Cat
Sunday Morning

November 1
All Saint's Day
Days remembering and commemorating the dead have been observed by peoples all over the world. All Saint's Day, (known as Allerheiligen in Germany) was at first celebrated to honor all martyrs, later including all saints, known and unknown, and it now honors all those who died in the faith (Catholic.) The feast of All Souls, November 2, (known as Allerseelen in Germany) was to remember those poor souls who were still in purgatory and had not yet reached their full communion with God. Today, relatives gather at the gravesites of the family members to decorate the graves with flowers and lanterns. This is similar to Memorial Day celebrated the last Monday in May.

- Origin of All Saints Day http://www.serve.com/shea/germusa/allsaint.htm
- All Saints Day http://www3.kumc.edu/diversity/ethnic_relig/allsaint.html
- All Saints Day
  http://www.gpc.peachnet.edu/~mhall/mypage/holidays/fall/hallow/saint.htm
- Lithuanians Celebrate All Saint's Day
  http://neris.mii.lt/heritage/lfcc/roots/node48.html
- Decorating Graves in Sweden
  http://www.multifaithnet.org/mfnopenaccess/research/graves/allsaints.htm
- Memorial Day http://home.ptd.net/~nikki/memorial.htm

Note: see Dia de los Muertros Day http://www.allsoulsart.com/ (October 31.)

Take a field trip to a local cemetery. Make rubbings of the gravestones. You might want to have different groups of students look for special graves: those from different wars, the oldest grave/latest grave, those of children, and those before a certain year, such as 1900. Discuss why there were many deaths during certain years (war, epidemic, etc.) Make paper flowers to lie on the graves of children.

- Make Some Paper Flowers http://www.cstone.net/~bry-back/holidayfun/cincodemayocraft.html (these can also be used for Poppies for Veterans Day and for Dia De los Meutros – October 31)

November 2
All Souls Day
Similar to All Saints Day, November 1, All Souls Day is a day for people to remember members of the faith who have died, especially those believed to be suffering in purgatory. Through prayers, masses, and almsgiving, the living pay tribute to the dead and hope to help them enter into heaven. (See All Saints Day, November 1)

- The Day for Celebration in Lithuania
  http://ausis.gf.vu.lt/eka/customs/velines.html
- Hispanic heritage comes alive at All Souls Day celebration
  http://detnews.com/menu/stories/21927.htm
- All Souls Day
  http://www.comptons.com/encyclopedia/ARTICLES/0000/00058880_A.html

November 3, 1718
John Montague, 4th Earl of Sandwich
National Sandwich Day

Legend has it that venerate card player, John Montague, was so engrossed in playing cards that he told his servants to bring his meat between two slices of bread so he wouldn't have to end his game to eat dinner. Alas, some say that due to an old injury, he was unable to eat solid food so would not have asked for such a treat. Whatever the case may be, when you eat your peanut better sandwich for lunch today, thank Sir John for a great idea!

- Happy Birthday, Sandwich
  http://www.smartbread.com/newsroom/happybdaysandpr.html
- The Earl of Sandwich http://www.stratsplace.com/rogov/earl_sandwich.html
- The History of Sandwich
  http://www.waiter.com/wwwsys/togos/historyofsandwich.htm

Sandwiches are sometimes named after famous people. Have each student develop a recipe for an outrageous sandwich named after him of her. Use a word processor for the recipe. This is a good opportunity to practice keying _ , 1/3, _, etc.

November 5
Guy Fawkes Day, England

"Remember, remember the fifth of November.
Gunpowder, Treason and Plot.
I see no reason why Gunpowder Treason
Should ever be forgot."[iii]

On the night of November 5th, bonfires surround cloth manikins or "Guys" and are set on fire in every town and village in Britain. Fireworks are also displayed. Originally, this was to burn in effigy Guy Fawkes, a legendary figure who devised a plot to blow up the House of Parliament and King James I in the early 17th Century. Because gunpowder was to be used, it is called the Gunpowder Treason. Today, children, sometimes dressed in fancy clothes, carry the "Guy" through the neighborhood asking people for "a penny for the Guy." What other holidays do children dress in fancy clothes and ask for candy and treats?

Sites that provide background information:
- Guy Fawkes Night http://www.kidlink.org/KIDPROJ/MCC/mcc0422.html (child's description)
- Guy Fawkes http://www.worldbook.com/fun/holidays/html/fawkes.htm
- Kids Domain http://www.kidsdomain.com/holiday/guyfawkes.html
- Bonfire Night http://web.ukonline.co.uk/conker/archive/gunpowder-plot.htm

Lesson Plans and Classroom Activities:
- North of Boston Library Exchange http://www.noblenet.org/year/tty11guy.htm very complete list of Internet sites, including greeting cards and recipes.
- Gunpowder Plot http://www.britannia.com/history/kaboom.html
- Electronic Classroom http://www.bcpl.net/~cbladey/guy/html/main.html You will need to register for this and get a password, but there is no cost.
- Gunpowder Plot http://www.innotts.co.uk/~asperges/fawkes/indexx.html This site is a very interactive, multimedia site.

Terrorism is not just a thing of the past. Recent acts of terrorism include the bombing of the Federal Building in Okalahoma City and the U. S. Embassy bombings in Africa. Have students use a search engine, such as http://www.google.com and search for *terrorism*. The following site is a good place to start.
- A Summary of Terrorism Events http://www.emergency.com/cntrterr.htm

November 9
Kristallnacht
On Kristallnacht, the Night of Broken Glass or Crystal Night, November 9th, 1938, Nazis vandalized and destroyed 7,500 Jewish businesses and 1000, possibly 2000 synagogues were burned. At least 96 Jews were killed and hundreds more injured. Often people remember a tragedy in the past with the hopes that if people today realize the horror, they will not allow it to happen again. Have the students read the information about Kristallnacht and then use the word processor to write a story about a boy or girl about their same age, who lived through Kristallnacht. Discuss with the students the controversy about the term Kristallnacht. What other horrific events in history do we remember? Think of Pearl Harbor and the Kennedy Assassination.
- Kristallnacht http://www.us-israel.org/jsource/Holocaust/kristallnacht.html
- Kristallnacht http://www.mtsu.edu/~baustin/knacht.html
- What is Kristallnacht? http://motlc.wiesenthal.com/resources/books/kristallnacht/
- A Teacher's Guide to the Holocaust http://fcit.coedu.usf.edu/holocaust/default.htm

November 9, 1934
Lois Ehlert's Birthday
Author and illustrator, Lois Ehlert is best known for her use of collage--the cutting, layering, and pasting of paper, fabric or objects on to a backing. She delights in simple shapes and bold colors. Her books are very popular for use in pre-kindergarten-lower elementary school.

Online Biographies:
- Lois Ehlert http://www.loisehlert.com/
- Author study http://web.t10-laba.mun.ca/~tracy4/lang.htm
- Biography; Lois Ehlert http://powayusd.sdcoe.k12.ca.us/pusdtes/Lois%20Ehlert.htm
- Lois Ehlert http://www.mhhe.com/socscience/education/kidlit/aom/janaom.html

Online Lesson Plans
- Let's Read, Eating the Alphabet http://www.tdh.state.tx.us/kids/CHap10_1.htm
- Cyberguide for Snowballs http://www.sdcoe.k12.ca.us/score/sno/snotg.htm

Shape Book
Have the students use a paint program, such as Paint or KidPix. Use the auto-shape tool to create interesting shapes. Use the fill tool to color the shapes in bright colors. Combine with simple text to create your own class book. When you are finished, fold the book on the lines. Cut the centerline and push the "pages" together. You will have a simple, little book.

Selected Books by Lois Ehlert
Snowballs
Red Leaf, Yellow Leaf
Chicka Chicka Boom Boom, by John Archambault
Circus
Color Farm
Color Zoo
Eating the Alphabet: Fruits and Vegetables
Feathers for Lunch
Fish Eyes: A Book You Can Count On
Growing Vegetable Soup

November 11
Veterans Day, USA
Remembrance Day, Canada, San Martino, Italy and the Netherlands
Armistice Day, England

Veterans Day honors men and women who have served in the U.S. armed forces. In 1919, President Woodrow Wilson proclaimed November 11th as Armistice Day to remind Americans of the tragedies of war. A law adopted in 1938 made the day a federal holiday and, in 1954, Congress changed the name of the holiday to Veterans Day to honor all U.S. veterans.
- Veterans Day http://www.factmonster.com/spot/veteransday1.html
This is a wonderful opportunity to introduce your students to oral histories. There are many online sources of oral histories; one of my favorites is *What did you do during the war, Grandma?* http://www.stg.brown.edu/projects/WWII_Women/tocCS.html For older students, I would invite veterans to the classroom. With a pre-determined list of interview questions, have groups of students interview the guests. Record the interview on audio and/or videotape. Ask the guests to bring in memorabilia including pictures. Scan the artifacts. Have the students prepare a PowerPoint (or other presentation tool, such as ClarisWorks or HyperStudio) presentation about their interviewee using pictures, sounds and responses to the interview questions. On Veterans Day, invite the interviewees back to the classroom and have the students present their presentations.

This can be quite emotional for both the students and the guests. That's okay…it's good to feel strongly about something. But, you might want to warn the students in advance.

Veterans Day Lesson Plan and School Resources
- Veterans Day – Lest We Forget http://www.umkc.edu/imc/vetsday.htm
- Veterans Day Home Page http://www.va.gov/pubaff/vetsday/
- Activities for Veterans Day http://www.va.gov/pubaff/celebAm/acts4vd.htm
- Veterans Day Resource Guide http://members.aol.com/veterans/warlib69.htm

History of Veterans Day
- Veterans Day http://www.usis.usemb.se/Holidays/celebrate/Veterans.html
- VFW Origins of Veterans Day http://www.vfw.org/amesm/origins.shtml
- How It Was Named http://www.crk.umn.edu/newsevents/notices97-98/veteran/veterans.htm
- A Tribute to USA Veterans http://www.geocities.com/EnchantedForest/Tower/8476/

Memorials
- Grief and Loss Memorials http://www.rockies.net/~spirit/grief/grief05.html
- Viet Nam War Memorial http://thewall-usa.com/
- Arlington National Cemetery http://www.arlingtoncemetery.org/
- Korean War Veterans Memorial http://www.nps.gov/kwvm/home.htm

Armed Forces
- Army http://www.army.mil/
- Navy http://www.navy.mil/
- Air force http://www.af.mil/
- Marines http://www.usmc.mil/

Military History
- America's Wars Fact Sheet http://www.va.gov/pressrel/amwars97.htm
- Military History http://www.cfcsc.dnd.ca/links/milhist/index.html
- A World At War http://www.education-world.com/a_lesson/lesson208.shtml
- America's Black Soldiers http://www.historychannel.com/classroom/admin/study_guide/archives/thc_guide.0326.html
- Purple Heart http://www.mdw.army.mil/fs-h17.htm
- Women in the Armed Forces http://www.fas.org/man/crs/92-008.htm
- What did you do in the War, Grandma? http://www.stg.brown.edu/projects/WWII_Women/tocCS.html
- The 21 Gun International Salute http://www.mdw.army.mil/FS-H05.HTM

Music and Poems
- Origins of Taps http://www.mdw.army.mil/FS-H06.HTM
- Story of Taps http://www.va.gov/pubaff/celebAm/taps.htm
- Taps: Butterfield's Lullaby http://www.acronet.net/~robokopp/usa/taps.htm
- American Folk Songs http://www.acronet.net/~robokopp/usat.html

- When Johnny Comes Marching Home
  http://www.contemplator.com/folk/whenjohn.html
- John Phillip Sousa http://dws.org/sousa/works.htm
- Irving Berlin http://www.nodanw.com/biographies/irving_berlin.htm
  - This Is the Army http://www.nara.gov/publications/prologue/berlin1.html
- Glenn Miller Orchestra http://www.glennmillerorchestra.com/history.html
  - Our Musical Heritage
    http://www.dmamusic.org/ourmusicalheritage/glennmiller/
- Military Music and Sound Files
  http://www.usmilitary.about.com/careers/usmilitary/cs/soundsandmusic/
- In Flanders Field http://www.noblenet.org/year/fland.htm
- High Flight http://www.skygod.com/quotes/file18.html
  - Pilot Officer John G. Magee, Jr.
    http://www.wpafb.af.mil/museum/history/prewwii/jgm.htm

Remembrance Day – Canada

Also celebrated on November 11, Canadians remember their war heroes on Remembrance Day. Compare and contrast the celebrations of these two neighboring countries.

- Remembrance Day, Canada
  http://www.cbc4kids.ca/general/time/remembrance/index.html
- Remembrance Day
  http://www.craigmarlatt.com/craig/canada/symbols_facts&lists/remembrance_day.html
- Canada Info http://www.craigmarlatt.com/craig/canada/

Note: See Anzac Day – Australia, April 25

November 13
International Day of Kindness

"Kindness begets kindness."
-- Greek Proverb

Sponsored by Random Acts of Kindness (RAOK), this day is set aside to spread kindness throughout the Internet in hopes that the ripple effect of one simple act of human kindness will affect not only one person but entire communities. Read some of the stories people have sent in about acts of kindness people have bestowed on them. Then have the students brainstorm ideas they could do to show people kindness. Challenge the students to perform an act of kindness, without telling the recipient why they are doing it, and report back. You could also design a class project. Some things would be to adopt a nursing home or the children's ward at your local hospital. Each month, plan some activity, such as tray favors, hall decorations, visits, writing notes or cards or even putting on a simple program.

- Random Acts of Kindness http://theraokgroup.com/

- Random Acts of Kindness Foundation http://www.actsofkindness.org/index.php ideas for all ages of students
- Random Acts of Kindness http://kids.discovery.com/KIDS/adv16.html
- The Generosity Game http://www.generosity.org/ make copies of these cards or design your own, then when you do something for someone hand them a card to encourage them to pass it on. This is especially fun for children. Have then put their name on the back of the card and add new names as the card is passed along. After a week, give the card back to the first person on the list and see how many people have received an act of kindness.
- Australian Random Acts of Kindness http://www.auscharity.org/kind.htm
- Send a Card http://www.randam-art.com/greetings.htm
- Random Acts of Kindness http://www.mpls.k12.mn.us/MCGFDA/mcgfda.page9a.html These are children's accounts of things they did to celebrate Random Act of Kindness Week at their school.[iv]

November 14, 1840
Claude Monet's Birthday
Monet was one of the leaders of the Impressionist movement in art. (The impressionist style of painting is characterized chiefly by concentration on the general impression produced by a scene or object and the use of unmixed primary colors and small strokes to simulate actual reflected light.)[v] Take a virtual tour of an art museum to see some of Monet's famous painting and also enjoy a visit to Monet's garden.
- Welcome to Claude Monet http://giverny.org/monet/welcome.htm
- Visit Monet's Garden http://www.mbam.qc.ca/visite-vr/anglais/
Lesson Plans
- Computer Lesson Plan: Monet's Water Lilies http://www.richland2.org/jke/Monet's%20Water%20Lilies%20Computer%20Lesson%20Plan.htm
- The Claude Monet Project http://members.aol.com/donnajv/monet.html
- Night and Day, a digital art lesson http://www.pixelpixie.net/pixelpixie/nightandday.html

Explore Impressionism
Take a virtual tour of five impressionist paintings.
- Explore Impressionism http://www.biography.com/impressionists/classroom_main.html

November 15
Schichi-Go-Sen – Japan
Shichi-go-san is a day of prayer for the healthy growth of young children in Japan. Shichi-go-san literally means three, five and seven; children of those ages are taken to a shrine to be blessed.

A traditional gift is a paper bag decorated with pine trees, cranes and tortoise for good luck and filled with candy. Have older students prepare small sandwich bags to give to the Kindergarten children.   Bags can be printed using the computer. Create a pleasing design using clip art; add a good luck wish. Tape a sandwich bag to a regular piece of 8 _" by 11" piece of paper and run it through the printer.

- Shichi-go-san http://www.worldbook.com/fun/holidays/html/shichi.htm
- Schichi-Go-Sen
  http://www.jinjapan.org/kidsweb/calendar/november/shichigosan.html

November 16, 1915
Jean Fritz' s Birthday

Author Jean Fritz was born in Hankow, China to missionary parents. She lived in China for 13 years. Her father often told her stories of American heroes, but at the British school she attended, she heard another story. Her American heroes, George Washington, Paul Revere and others were, from the British point of view, the 'bad guys.' She vowed that when she grew up, she would write the 'real' story. Famous for her biographies of famous Americans, her birthday provides a perfect opportunity to discuss point of view.

Online biographies
- Jean Fritz http://www.penguinputnam.com/Author/AuthorFrame?0000008926
- Jean Fritz http://teacher.scholastic.com/authorsandbooks/authors/fritz/bio.htm
- Author study http://www.carolhurst.com/authors/jfritz.html
- Meet the Author http://www.cbcbooks.org/html/jeanfritz.html

Lesson Plans
- Lesson Plans based on books http://www.indiana.edu/~eric_rec/ieo/bibs/fritz.html

Things to do..
1. Locate China on a map http://www.nationalgeographic.com/maps/index.html
2. Research the American Revolution
   http://www.historyplace.com/unitedstates/revolution/
3. Have one student tell a story in the 1st person; maybe about something that happened on the playground. Have another person tell the same story only from a different point of view, such as the playground supervisor or another student. See how things can look differently depending on who is telling the story.
4. Play the game - The Road to Revolution @ http://www.pbs.org/ktca/liberty/game/

Selected Books by Jean Fritz
Shh! We're Writing the Constitution
George Washington's Breakfast
Will You Sign Here, John Hancock
And Then What Happened, Paul Revere?
Around the World in a Hundred Years: From Henry the Navigator to Magellan
Bully for You, Teddy Roosevelt
The Cabin Faced West
Can't You Make Them Behave, King George
The Double Life of Pocahontas
George Washington's Mother

The Great Little Madison
Harriet Beecher Stowe and the Beecher Preachers
Homesick; My Own Story
Just a Few Words, Mr. Lincoln; The Story of the Gettysburg Address
Make Way for Sam Houston
Traitor; The Case of Benedict Arnold
What's the Big Idea, Ben Franklin?
Where Was Patrick Henry on the 29th of May?
Who's That Stepping on Plymouth Rock?
Why Not, Lafayette?
Where Do You Think You're Going, Christopher Columbus?

November 17
Homemade Bread Day

Yes, this is a good day to bring in the bread machine and make a loaf of homemade bread to share with the students. But, while you're waiting for the bread, take this opportunity to learn about the 'staff of life.' Check out the Bread for the World site about world hunger. What can your class do? Baking Bread is an online Field Trip about bread around the world.

- Breadworld – Just for Kids http://www.breadworld.com/justkids/ (with teacher's guide)
- Bread for the World http://www.bread.org/whoweare/bfwi/ (report on world hunger)
- Bread Around the World – Kindergarten Interdisciplinary Unit http://www.prof-dev.okcps.k12.ok.us/coreunits/kinderbread.htm (easily adaptable for upper grades)
- Bread Around the World – 6th Grade Interdisciplinary Unit http://www.prof-dev.okcps.k12.ok.us/coreunits/6bread.htm
- Bread Around the World - http://204.98.1.2/passport/conference/breadpage.html click on different types of bread and learn about the culture that makes it.
- Field Trip: Baking Bread http://www.field-trips.org/sci/bake/index.htm

November 18
Peace Day

> *"Ask not what your country can do for you,*
> *ask what you can do for your country."*
>
> John F. Kennedy, 1961

With these now famous words, President Kennedy called young and old people from all over to share their talents with those in need. Since then, 163,000 Americans have joined the Peace Corps, serving in 135 nations. Visit the Peace Corps Homepage to read about some of the volunteers. Also visit the Kids World for stories, games, food and to learn how kids can make a difference.

- Peace Corps http://www.peacecorps.gov/
  - Kids World http://www.peacecorps.gov/kids/index.html

The United Nations hosts a wonderful site that helps students learn about peace education. It is written from the teacher as learner and the learner as teacher perspective.
- Peace Education http://www.un.org/Pubs/CyberSchoolBus/peace/index.htm
- Peace http://www.peace.org

Listen to *Let There Be Peace on Earth* http://www.personality-creations.com/xmas/SApg105.htm

November 18, 1928
Mickey Mouse's Birthday

"It's kind of fun to do the impossible."

Walt Disney

Everyone loves a party and what would be better than celebrating with the world's most famous mouse! Mickey's career began on November 18, 1928, when he debuted in *Steamboat Willie*, a short black-and-white animated film. Celebrate the day by learning about the mouse and his creator in every subject.

Reading	Science
Read Mickey and the Beanstalk http://asp.disney.go.com/DisneyBooks/RASFirst.asp?id=2322&page=1 Compare this version to the traditional Jack and the Beanstalk http://www-dept.usm.edu/~engdept/jack/inventt.htm Look specifically for characters, setting, plot, text, etc.	Explore how you can 'trick' your eyes. Optical Illusions http://www.illusionworks.com/ Optical Illusions http://www.opticalillusion.cjb.net/ About Your Eyes http://www.aoanet.org/teachers-center.html
Math	**Art**
There are many things you can do related to math depending upon the age and skill level of your students. Compare admission prices at the different theme parks. Ask questions such as: How much would it cost for a family of 4 (mom, dad and two children) to visit the park for one day? If the family bought a year pass, how much would it cost per	Let's Draw Mickey http://disney.go.com/DisneyBooks/activities/1560100877.html?id=2110 Look how Mickey has changed over the years. http://www.intergraffix.com/walt/mkgfx.htm Make your own 'toon! Try your hand at animation.

day? When is the break even day? http://disney.go.com/park/bases/vacationsbase/today/flash/index.html Pretend to shop at the online Disney store. Give each student an amount they can spend (such as $50.00.) See who can purchase the most things and not go over their allotted budget. http://disney.store.go.com/	http://www.mamamedia.com Click on **Surprize** Click on **Frame that 'toon** Have fun!
Language Arts Print out vintage Mickey comics and cut them apart. Have students sequence the comics in an order that makes sense. You might need to copy them into a word program before you print. Mickey Comics http://asp.disney.go.com/DisneyBooks/Comic.asp Use the Mickey clip art to illustrate an original comic strip. Most word processors have a quotation bubble on the draw tool bar. Disney Clip Art http://www.disneyclipart.com/	**Technology** Look at the CyberNetiquette Comix Cyber Safety http://www.disney.go.com/cybersafety/ Write class rules for using the Internet. Check out the web cams http://asp.disney.go.com/disneyworld/db/havefun/hitechfun/index.asp
Social Studies Look at the evolution of Mickey Mouse and make a timeline by printing out the different Mickeys and pasting them on a long sheet of paper. http://www.geocities.com/Hollywood/Set/1344/ Look at the original Steamboat Willie http://disney.go.com/disneyatoz/waltdisney/maincollection/masterworks/steamboatwillie.html Discuss how Mickey's character	**Music** Disney Online music activities http://asp.disney.go.com/DisneyRecords/Activities.asp Listen to Disney music http://asp.disney.go.com/DisneyRecords/ListeningCenter.asp Disney Karaoke http://disney.go.com/disneyrecords/karaoke-player/disney_karaoke.html

has changed with the times. Predict how Mickey will look in 2020, 2050, etc.	
Take a Field Trip Walt Disney Family Museum http://disney.go.com/disneyatoz/waltdisney/home.html	**Additional Internet Sites** Fun With Mickey http://disney.go.com/keywords/special/mickey_special.html Disney for the Classroom http://disney.go.com/educational/classroom.html Mickey Mouse http://www.surfnetkids.com/mickey.htm Hidden Mickeys http://www.hiddenmickeys.org/

November 19, 1863
Lincoln delivers the Gettysburg Address

"The world will little note,
nor long remember what we say here,
but it can never forget what they did here."

Abraham Lincoln

Did President Lincoln really write the speech on the back of an envelop on his way to the dedication? That's the way the story goes. Read the accounts to see for yourself. This speech was not well received at the time, but is considered today to be one of the greatest speeches of all time. The only way to read it is out loud. So, stand tall with your students, and read it together, listening to the beat and the rhythm.

- Gettysburg Address http://lcweb.loc.gov/exhibits/gadd/ (notice the translations into the different languages)
- The Battle of Gettysburg http://www.militaryhistoryonline.com/gettysburg/
- Battle of Gettysburg – Eye Witness Account http://www.ibiscom.com/gtburg.htm
- The Battle of Gettysburg http://americancivilwar.com/getty.html

Refer to July for more ideas about the Battle of Gettysburg and February for more information about Abraham Lincoln.

November 21
World Hello Day

Hola – Aloha - Guten Tag – Bonjour - Shalom

Make a bulletin board using a large map of the world as the background. If one is not available, print a suitable one from National Geographic http://www.nationalgeographic.org/maps/index.html or from ABC Teach http://www.abcteach.com/directory/researchreports/ Have the students make cards saying "hello" in the different languages and clip them to their respective country.

- Say "Hello" to the World http://www.ipl.org/youth/hello/
- Lesson plan for younger children A to Z Kids Stuff (very nice poem)
  http://www.atozkidsstuff.com/novcal3.html
- World Hello Day http://www.worldhelloday.org/ (contains letters from famous people)
- Foreign Languages for Travelers http://www.travlang.com/languages/

Locate a school in another country to send a postcard to. Also, get involved in the e-pals program.

- Hello Postcards http://browse.postcards.org/postcards/cards/1155/
- K-12 Schools on the Internet
  http://connectedteacher.classroom.com/library/states.asp?dir=1216
- Epals http://www.epals.com/

November 22, 1963
John Fitzgerald Kennedy is assassinated in Dallas
This was certainly a heartbreaking day for all Americans and indeed the world. Share your memories of this day with your students and encourage them to talk about their feelings about tragic events that affect us all.

- Short Biography http://search.biography.com/print_record.pl?id=16490
- The President John F. Kennedy - Assassination Records Collection
  http://www.nara.gov/research/jfk/index.html
- The Kennedy Assassination http://mcadams.posc.mu.edu/home.htm

Look up other presidents who have been assassinated or shot during their presidency. Have the students write a newspaper headline for each one.

- List of U.S. Presidents http://www.fujisan.demon.co.uk/USPresidents/preslist.htm

November 25, 1949
***Rudolph, the Red-Nosed Reindeer* appeared on the music charts**
Enjoy listening to and singing along with this great Christmas classic. This will get you in the mood for the holidays ahead.

- Rudolph the Red-Nosed Reindeer Sing-along
  http://www.12days.com/library/carols/rudolph.htm
- Listen to Burl Ives sing Rudolph the Red-Nosed Reindeer
  http://www.tantara.ab.ca/fun_xmas/job_aids/songbook/rudolph.htm
- Read the book http://www.goldenbooks.com/holiday/rudolph_read.html

November 26, 1865
Alice's Adventures Underground
November 26, 1865, Charles L. Dodgson, aka Lewis Carroll, sent a handwritten manuscript to 12-year-old Alice Liddel as an early Christmas present; it was called *Alice's Adventures Underground*--later called *Alice in Wonderland*. Discuss the elements of fantasy, and then use a word processor to write a fantasy story. Give it to a special person for Christmas.

- Alice In Wonderland – An Interactive Adventure http://www.ruthannzaroff.com/wonderland/
- Alice In Wonderland – Original Text http://www.literature.org/authors/carroll-lewis/alices-adventures-in-wonderland/
- Multimedia Version of Alice in Wonderland http://megabrands.com/alice/indexx.html (asks for donation, but you don't have to)
- Background and History of Alice in Wonderland http://www.bedtime-story.com/bedtime-story/alice-background.htm
- Disney Video Clips http://www.disneymania.org/alice.htm
  - Alice's World http://disneywonder.tripod.ca/aliceindex.html
- The Wonderful Wizard of Oz Website http://www.eskimo.com/~tiktok/index.html
- The Oz Encyclopedia http://www.halcyon.com/piglet/
- Elements of Fantasy http://www.d118.s-cook.k12.il.us/east/media/fantasies.htm
- Literary Elements in Fantasy http://library.ucok.edu:10020/Cyber/Waits,%20Dr.%20Patsy/LME%204163%205233/Ch%207%20fantasy/tsld010.htm

November 28, 1931
Ed Young's Birthday
Ed Young was born in Tienstin, China, but came to America as a young man to attend art school. He won the Caldecott Award in 1990 for *Lon Po Po*, the Chinese version of Little Red Riding Hood.

- Ed Young, Biography http://www.edupaperback.org/authorbios/Young_Ed.html
- Biography http://teacher.scholastic.com/authorsandbooks/authors/young/bio.htm
- Author Visit http://hastings.ci.lexington.ma.us/projects/edyoung/index.html

In one of his interviews, Ed Young said, "A Chinese painting is often accompanied by words. They are complementary. There are things that words do that pictures never can, and likewise, there are images that words can never describe."[vi]

Have the students look at traditional Chinese paintings. There are many interesting sites on the Internet. Notice the use of nature and animals. Compare these to Young's illustrations.

- Chinese Painting http://kaladarshan.arts.ohio-state.edu/exhib/gug/intr/innovintr.html
- Art of Traditional Chinese Painting http://www.gio.gov.tw/info/culture/culture4.html

- Chinese Traditional Painting
  http://china.pages.com.cn/chinese_culture/painting/paint.html
- Chinese Painting Gallery http://www.chinapage.org/painting.html

Then, have the students select a short story from Classical Chinese Story Simulate a Chinese painting by combining the text of the story with a nature/animal painting. You can use any photo program, such as PhotoShop to create your 'painting.' Or, use the Kodak play station. You will need to register, but there is no cost. Select a photo of a scene that illustrates the story. A good place to find photos on the Internet is Alta Vista. You will need the URL of the picture you select. Right click on the picture and go to Properties. Copy the URL. At the Kodak site, Up Load a Picture. There are many different techniques you can choose from, but the one I like best is Oil Paint. After your painting is ready, copy it to a word or publishing program. Enlarge it to almost fill the paper. Create a text box and copy and paste the story. Be sure to make the text box transparent. (right click on the text box, choose format, and the no fill option.) Choose an interesting font and ta da, your Chinese painting, combining text and art is complete.

- Classical Chinese Story http://www.chinapage.org/story/story.html
- Kodak http://playground.kodak.com/cgi-bin/filterFactory/asCgi.pl?app=home
- AltaVista Images http://www.altavista.com

November 29, 1832
Louisa May Alcott's Birthday

*"Far away in the sunshine are my highest aspirations.
I may not reach them, but I can look up and see their beauty,
believe in them, and try to follow where they lead."*

Louisa May Alcott

One of the best loved and most widely read books of all time is Louisa May Alcott's *Little Women*. Not only a best selling author (even 100 years after her death), but also a Civil War hero (no, it was not Father who went off to the war, but Jo, Louisa, herself!) Read her fascinating biography, meet the real-life 'little women' and tour her home. Read passages from *Hospital Sketches*. Then, study other women involved in the Civil War.

- Lousis May Alcott Homepage http://www.alcottweb.com/
- Civil War Women http://scriptorium.lib.duke.edu/women/cwdocs.html
- Women in the Civil War http://userpages.aug.com/captbarb/femvets2.html
- Women Soldiers in the Civil War
  http://www.nara.gov/publications/prologue/women1.html
- Sarah Sampson http://www.geocities.com/acw_women/brave_ss.html
- Not Just A Man's War http://score.rims.k12.ca.us/activity/manswar/

Prepare a glass of Switchel and enjoy reading passages from her books. Her words are often so lyrical, they read like poetry. Have the students copy a passage from one of the books. Rearrange the text to *look* like poetry and read it as a reader's theater.

Little Women Chapter One – Playing Pilgrims	The Happiest Hour
While making these maternal inquiries Mrs. March got her wet things off, her warm slippers on, and sitting down in the easy chair, drew Amy to her lap, preparing to enjoy the happiest hour of her busy day. The girls flew about, trying to make things comfortable, each in her own way. Meg arranged the tea table, Jo brought wood and set chairs, dropping, over-turning, and clattering everything she touched. Beth trotted to and fro between parlor kitchen, quiet and busy, while Amy gave directions to everyone, as she sat with her hands folded.	Narrator: Mrs. March got her wet things off, her warm slippers on, and sat down in the easy chair. Reader 1: Meg arranged the tea table Reader 2: Jo brought wood and set chairs, dropping, over-turning, and clattering everything she touched. Reader 3: Beth trotted to and fro between parlor kitchen, quiet and busy, Reader 4: while Amy gave directions to everyone, as she sat with her hands folded. Narrator: And Marmee enjoyed the happiest hour of her busy day

Switchel

- 1 gallon of fresh spring water
- 2 cups refined sugar
- 1 cup dark molasses
- 1 cup apple cider vinegar
- 1 teaspoon ground ginger

Mix well, jar, and chill in a running stream, down a well, in a springhouse, or icehouse.[vii]
And, for a last minute book report on Little Women, watch Disney's Little Women Last Minute Book Report.

- Last Minute Book Reports: Little Women
http://disney.go.com/family/lastminute/women/index.html

November 30, 1835
Mark Twain' s Birthday

> *"The man who does not read good books*
> *has no advantage over the man who can't read them."*
>
> Mark Twain

Another author of classic American literature is Mark Twain. Born Samuel Langhorne Clemens, this humorist and author have had a place in American literature for well over 150 years. An excellent site to begin a study of Mark Twain is Mark Twain, In His Times. After reading his biography and sampling some of his writings, play Mark Twain's Memory Builder Game, fashioned after the game he designed and patented to help people remember historical facts.

- Mark Twain, In His Times http://etext.virginia.edu/railton/
- Mark Twain in Cyberspace http://salwen.com/mtcyber.html

Although his books are read and studied today, they are not without controversy. This would be an excellent time to discuss racism and prejudice with your students. Begin by reading *Only a Nigger*, an essay written by Twain for the *Buffalo Express*. Discuss satire and how Twain was using the word, *nigger*. Then, read Mark Twain and Racism. *Huckelberry Finn* has been highly criticized, again for the numerous use of the word, nigger. Have the students go to *Huckelberry Finn*, Chapter XXXIV, and count how many times he uses the word. By holding down the Ctrl+F key, you can find all of the instances.

- Only A Nigger http://www.boondocksnet.com/twaintexts/onlynigger.html
- Mark Twain and Racism http://www.gms.ocps.k12.fl.us/biopage/t-z/twainm.html
- Huckelberry Finn http://users.telerama.com/~joseph/finn/finntitl.html
  Chapter XXXIV

For more information about racism in Children's Literature, refer to the following Internet sites:

- Professional Guidelines, Kay Vandergrift
  http://www.scils.rutgers.edu/special/kay/guidelines.html
- 10 Quick Ways to Analyze Children's Books
  http://birchlane.davis.ca.us/library/10quick.htm
- Tolerance, Racism and Prejudice, Carol Hurst
  http://www.carolhurst.com/products/booksetstol.html

---

[i] This favorite Harvest Festival hymn was written by Henry Alford (1810-1871) and first published in his *Psalms and Hymns* (1844). http://www.stpetersnottingham.org/hymns/thankful.htm Listen to the midi http://www.cyberhymnal.org/htm/c/o/comeytpc.htm July 12, 2001

[ii] Puritans http://www.nd.edu/~rbarger/www7/puritans.html History of American Education Web Project, January 5, 2001

[iii] Bonfire Night and Guy Fawkes http://web.ukonline.co.uk/conker/archive/gunpowder-plot.htm February 11, 2002

[iv] Different communities celebrate random Acts of Kindness Week on different days. Many communities choose to celebrate in February.

[v] WebMuseum http://www.ibiblio.org/wm/paint/glo/impressionism/ July 12, 2001

[vi] Ed Young's Biography http://teacher.scholastic.com/authorsandbooks/authors/young/bio.htm January 3, 2001 Scholastic

[vii] Women and the American Civil War http://www.geocities.com/acw_women/ November 10, 2000 Mary Kindred

5/7/2002

December

"God gave us memory so that we might have roses in December."

James Barrie

Special Month

Read A New Book Month

Not only do books provide research materials and stimulation, they are also a wonderful form of entertainment. During the month of December, read reviews of new books, look at how books can be purchased via the Internet and check out the latest in e-books.

All America Reads is a wonderful new web site for middle school and high school teachers and students. It is an online reading discussion group with lesson plans and reading strategies. Contemporary authors are chosen. The first selection was Wish You Well by David Baldacci. The suggestions for reading really encourage in-depth reflection.

- All America Reads http://allamericareads.org/

Book Reviews Online

With over 7000 children's books published annually, it is very hard to keep up with what's the best. Two of the most respected journals that review children's literature are the Horn Book and the School Library Journal.

- Horn Book http://www.hbook.com/mag.shtml
- School Library Journal http://slj.reviewsnews.com/

Another excellent web site is the Carol Hurst site. Not only does she provide reviews, but also suggested themes and classroom activities.

- Carol Hurst Children's Literature Site http://www.carolhurst.com/

The New York Times provides reviews of adult and children's books plus sample chapters and best selling lists.

- New York Times Book Reviews http://www.nytimes.com/pages/books/

Other Book Review Sites

- Parent's Council http://www.parentcouncil.com/
- The Boston Book Review http://www.bookwire.com/bbr/children/children.html
- Book Hive http://www.bookhive.org/bookhive.htm
- Writers Write http://www.writerswrite.com/books/rchild.htm

Buying Books Online

Booksellers online offer much more than just books. They provide thematic lists, author sites, and sample chapters to name a few. Have the students use the search feature to locate specific books, authors and books about a specific topic or theme such as dinosaurs or mystery. Use these sites to discuss online buying safety. Have the students make consumer brochures with the information provided using a publishing program to take home to their parents. These sites also provide information for authentic math problems in anything from simple addition to percentages.

- Amazon http://www.amazon.com
- Barnes and Noble http://www.bn.com
- Half http://www.half.com
- Online Buying Safety http://www.stretcher.com/stories/00/000731L.cfm
- CyberBuying http://www.capitalone.com/credit101/cyberbuying/

E-books Online

Electronic books are here! They are in the libraries, bookstores and in people's pockets and purses. They can be downloaded to palms or desktops. But, are they the way of the future or a passing fancy? You be the judge! Download some of these e-books. Do a little classroom research project about reading online compared to reading a hard copy. You could use either a simple questionnaire – which do you like better? Or, have half of the students read text online and the other half read hard copy. Evaluate amount of time taken to read the same content to reading comprehension, to eyestrain or any question you may have. For a discussion of e-books, read the article about e-books and libraries.

- Awe-Struck http://www.awe-struck.net/
- Tumble Books http://www.tumblebooks.com/asp/home_tumblebooks.asp
- E-books.org http://e-books.org/
- TeleRead http://www.teleread.org/
- The Online Books Page http://onlinebooks.library.upenn.edu/
- Ebooks on the Net http://www.ebooksonthe.net/
- Can e-books improve libraries? http://skyways.lib.ks.us/central/ebooks/

Book Publishers

Many publishing companies maintain excellent Internet sites. Besides information about the newest books, they also provide curriculum resources, kids pages, author interviews and parent pages. These are just a few. Use a search engine to find a company not listed here.

- Random House http://www.randomhouse.com/teachers/
- DK Publishers http://www.dk.com/store_select.asp
- Harper Collins http://www.harperchildrens.com/hch/
- Houghton Mifflin Trade Books http://www.houghtonmifflinbooks.com/hmcochild/
  - Kids Place http://www.eduplace.com/kids/
- Little Brown and Company http://www.twbookmark.com/children/
- North South Books http://www.northsouth.com/
- Penguin Books http://www.penguin.co.uk/static/packages/uk/children/intro.html
- Puffin Books http://www.puffin.co.uk/
- Scholastic http://scholastic.com/
- Simon Says Kids http://www.simonsays.com/subs/index.cfm?areaid=183

Human Rights Month

On December 10, 1948 the General Assembly of the United Nations adopted and proclaimed the Universal Declaration of Human Rights. From then on, December 10th has been celebrated as Human Rights Day. We now proclaim the whole month of December – Human Rights Month. The Assembly asks that the Universal Declaration of Human Rights be "disseminated, displayed, read and expounded principally in schools and other educational institutions, without distinction based on the political status of countries or territories."[i] As you and your students read this Declaration, compare it to the United States Bill of Rights.

- Human Rights http://www.un.org/rights/

For an excellent Q&A about the Universal Declaration of Human Rights refer to the 50th Anniversary Press Kit information.

- Human Rights at Your Fingertips http://www.un.org/rights/50/game.htm

The United Nations also has an excellent web site for young people that pertains to the issue of human rights. This site has the Universal Declaration of Human Rights and a translation in 'plain' language and a really neat illustrated version of each of the rights. Each right also has classroom activities that more fully explain it. You could take a different Article each day to explore.

- Human Rights in Action http://www.un.org/Pubs/CyberSchoolBus/humanrights/index.html

Bill of Rights Day

December also is the anniversary month of another famous document – the Bill of Rights. The Bill of Rights is first 10 Amendments to the Constitution of the United States. So fresh in citizen's minds were the British violations of human rights, they demanded that a list of these rights be included in the Constitution before some would vote to ratify the Constitution. On September 25, 1789, the First Congress met to define and propose a list of human rights, now known as the "Bill of Rights." December 15th is Bill of Rights Day. Have the students make posters illustrating each Amendment. Using a publishing program, students can select either clip art or photographs to illustrate their poster.

- The Bill of Rights http://www.nara.gov/exhall/charters/billrights/billmain.html
- Historical Documents: Bill of Rights http://memory.loc.gov/const/bor.html
- Web Quest: Bill of Rights http://www.plainfield.k12.in.us/hschool/webq/webq68/
- Quiz http://insight.dcss.mcmaster.ca/org/efc/pages/law/canada/BillofRights.html

I've also included the Canadian Bill of Rights for comparison purposes.

- Canadian Bill of Rights
  http://insight.dcss.mcmaster.ca/org/efc/pages/law/canada/BillofRights.html
- Comparison Chart Graphic Organizer
  http://www.abcteach.com/kidsclub/graphicorganizers/CompareChart.htm

Human Rights begin with Student's Rights

Help students counteract some of the negative words they hear every day on the school bus or playground by having them use encouraging words. Encouraging words protect one of our most basic rights – the right to be happy.

- Encouraging Words http://www.noogenesis.com/malama/encouraging_words.html

Date Varies

Winter Solstice

December 21 or 22 is the 1st day of winter, the winter solstice, the shortest day of the year. Winter in South Dakota means long nights, cold, blustery winds and snow. What about winter in your state? The Seasons Investigation offers an excellent lesson plan for researching weather patterns.

- Seasons Investigation http://www.globe.gov/sda-bin/wt/ghp/tg+L(en)+P(seasons/Temperatureregion

What is Winter Solstice?

The word 'winter' comes from the German word meaning 'time of water' referring to the amount of precipitation during the season. For an excellent explanation of the winter solstice, refer to the following Internet site.

- The Winter Solstice http://windows.ivv.nasa.gov/cgi-bin/tour_def/the_universe/uts/winter.html

Legends and Myths

Many different legends and myths are about the winter solstice – the darkest time of the year. Explore some of these stories.

Native American -

- A Reason for the Season http://www.nationalgeographic.com/xpeditions/activities/07/season.html
- Lakota Winter Solstice Stars http://indy4.fdl.cc.mn.us/~isk/stars/starwint.html

Europeans and Early Christians -

- Winter Solstice and Christmas http://home.ccil.org/~kmiles/dln/12-95/decsol.html
- The Winter Solstice http://familyeducation.com/topic/front/0,1156,1-4205,00.html
- Solstice http://www.candlegrove.com/home.html

Diamante Poetry

A diamante poem compares two different things, therefore making it a perfect format for comparing winter and summer. Have your students write a poem using the diamante format. Illustrate their poem with clip art.

- Diamante Poems
  http://www.geocities.com/EnchantedForest/5165/pages/poetry_samples.html#diamonte

Odds and Ends

- Winter Begins http://rs6.loc.gov/ammem/today/dec21.html
- Winter Fun http://www.kidsdomain.com/holiday/winter/
- Frosty the Snowman http://www.frostythesnowman.ws/

Advent

Advent, meaning the coming or arrival, is the time in the Christian church season that precedes Christmas. It begins on the fourth Sunday before Christmas Day, nearest November 30, and ends on Christmas Eve. Advent is a time of expectation, of anticipation, of preparation, of longing. Use these sites to learn more about the Advent season.

- Advent Celebrations http://www.cresourcei.org/adventnaznet.html
- The Season of Advent http://www.cresourcei.org/cyadvent.html
- Advent, A Season of Preparation http://www.cptryon.org/prayer/adx/adprep.html
- The Season of Advent http://www.sundayschoollessons.com/advent.html

Time of Anticipation and Preparation

To help students prepare for Christmas, open a gift each day at the *Advent Calendar* site and learn about a different Christmas custom. Read the story about Tate, the cat as each day a different part of the story is revealed.. The *Advent Calendar Activity Calendar* has a new craft or activity for each day. And, yes, you guessed it, the *Cookie Calendar* has a new cookie recipe for each day. Don't forget, recipes make practical and authentic math problems. Organize a cookie sale with your students and give the proceeds to the American Red Cross or the Salvation Army. The *Musical Advent Calendar* is just that, plus a prayer for each day. This site is changed every year, so you may have to search a little. The *Smile A Day Calendar* also has a new song for each day. And, for the younger students, enjoy *Billy Bear's Advent Calendar*. It has a new picture for each day and new wallpaper for you computer also. The *Artcyclopedia Advent Calendar* features a different painting each day with the story behind the painting. The history site has an online museum of Advent calendars.

- Advent Calendar http://www.algonet.se/~bernadot/christmas/calendar.html
- Tate is a Lucky Cat http://www.advent-calendars.com/index.html
- Advent Calendar Activity Calendar
  http://www.geocities.com/Heartland/7134/Christmas/chradvent.htm
- Cookie Calendar http://www.cookierecipe.com/cat/christmas.asp
- Musical Advent Calendar
  http://acweb.colum.edu/users/agunkel/homepage/xmasweb/adventcal.html
- Smile A Day Calendar http://www.smile-a-day.com/advent-calendar.shtml
- Billy Bear's Advent Calendar
  http://www.billybear4kids.com/holidays/christmas/advent/advent4.htm
- Artcyclopedia Advent Calendar http://www.artcyclopedia.com/feature-2000-12.html
- History of the Advent Calendar http://www.sellmer-verlag.de/history.htm

Advent Around the World

In many parts of Europe, Advent is also a time for markets and festivities. Take a field trip!

- Salzburg http://goswitzerland.about.com/library/weekly/aa991115.htm
- Germany http://www.weihnachtsmarkt.german-christmas.com/ (needs to be translated)

- German Christmas Markets http://www.german-christmas.com/

Odds and Ends
- Advent Devotions http://www.frtommylane.com/adventchristmas.htm
- How to Make an Advent Wreath http://www.kencollins.com/question-10.htm

Hanukkah
24th night of the Jewish month of Kislev
Hanukkah or Chanukah, the Festival of Lights, is a Jewish festival that celebrates the victory of the Maccabees. It commemorates the miracle of the oil that burned for 8 days. It is a holiday that means, "Never Give Up."[ii] Read the story of Chanukah with your students.
- The Story of Chanukah http://www.holidays.net/chanukah/story.html
- Hanukkah Stories http://www.night.net/kids/hanukkah.html-ssi

Learn More About It
To learn more about Hanukkah, refer to these sites. Ask students to complete a Venn diagram comparing Hanukkah, Christmas and Kwanzaa customs.
- Virtual Hanukkah http://www.virtualchanukah.com/
- Learn More About Hanukkah http://www.torah.org/learning/yomtov/chanukah/
  - The On-line Menorah http://www.torah.org/chanukah.html
- Festivals: Chanukah http://www.jajz-ed.org.il/festivls/hanuka/index.html
- Triple Venn Diagram http://www.abcteach.com/GraphicOrganizers/trivenn.htm

Learn more about the history and traditions of Christmas, Hanukkah and Kwanzaa at the History Channel. History Channel http://www.historychannel.com/cgi-bin/frameit.cgi?p=http%3A//www.historychannel.com/exhibits/holidays/hanukkah/history.html

Hanukkah Games and Music
As with most holidays, Hanukkah is also celebrated with games and music. Your students will enjoy spinning a dreidel and singing the dreidel song.
- Torah Tots http://www.torahtots.com/holidays/chanuka/chanuk.htm
- Hanukkah http://www.holidays.net/chanukah/index.htm
- How to Play the Dreidel Game http://www.night.net/kids/hanukkah-dreidel.html
- I Have a Little Dreidel http://www.night.net/kids/hanukkah-s-dreidel.html

Hanukkah Foods
In my family, celebrations and food go together. Enjoy these special Hanukkah treats. I think your students will really enjoy the Holiday Mix.
- Chanukah Recipes http://www.holidays.net/chanukah/recipes.htm
  - Honey Roasted Holiday Mix http://www.holidays.net/chanukah/recipes/holmix.htm
- Potato Latkes http://www.harperchildrens.com/holiday/hanu4.htm
- Hanukkah Recipes http://128.138.129.27/library/bpl/child/season/hanukk3.html

Special Days

December 1, 1949
Jan Brett's Birthday
Children's author and illustrator Jan Brett is popular with children and adults alike. As a child, Jan spent many hours reading. She says, "I remember the special quiet of rainy days when I felt that I could enter

the pages of my beautiful picture books. Now I try to recreate that feeling of believing that the imaginary place I'm drawing really exists."[iii] Read more about her life, listen to her read from her books and watch videos about how she illustrates among other topics at her web site. This is an excellent month to study Jan Brett as she has written and illustrated many Christmas stories.

- Jan Brett http://www.janbrett.com/

Jam Brett maintains one of the most extensive web sites. It has games, coloring pages, calendars, alphabets – you name it! She has many activities and projects based on her Christmas books. Enjoy!

Additional Sites about Jan Brett
- Jan Brett Teacher Resource File http://falcon.jmu.edu/~ramseyil/brett.htm
- Authors Online: Jan Brett http://teacher.scholastic.com/authorsandbooks/authors/brett/bio.htm

Books by Jan Brett
Gingerbread Baby
The Night Before Christmas
The Hat
The Mitten
Comet's Nine Lives
Armadillo Rodeo
Town Mouse Country Mouse
Christmas Trolls
Trouble With Trolls
The Owl and the Pussycat
Berlioz the Bear
The Wild Christmas Reindeer
Goldilocks and the Three Bears
The Twelve Days of Christmas
The First Dog
Annie and the Wild Animals
Christmas Treasury

December 4
Know Your State Capital Day

"What is the capital of Wyoming? 'W'"

Spend today as a "capital blitz!" Challenge your students to learn as many state capitals as possible. Approach the project by learning the states and their capitals in alphabetical order – Alabama, Alaska, Arizona, etc or by region – northeast, southwest. Do a pre and posttest, give awards for the most improved, most learned, highest percentage learned, etc. These are some sites that provide quick information about our states.

- The State Capitals http://www.homeworkspot.com/ask/statecapitals.htm (just the facts - no flash!)
- States and Capitals http://www.50states.com/ (be sure to look at the map)
- Any state: http://www.state.sd.us (substitute the 2 letter abbreviation for the sd – South Dakota)
- Stately Knowledge http://www.ipl.org/youth/stateknow/skhome.html (this one has a good quiz)
- State Information http://libraryspot.com/state/

Cool Stuff
- US Capitals http://observe.ivv.nasa.gov/nasa/gallery/capitals/capital.html (NASA pictures from space)
- State and Capital Game http://www.scottforesman.com/resources/statescapitals/

- Quia State and Capital Games http://www.quia.com/jg/4.html (word search, flashcards, etc.)
- State Capital Quiz http://www.maps.com/learn/games/capquiz2.html
- State Capital Game http://www.funschool.com/current/games/ges_uscapquiz.36
- States and Capitals Games
  http://www.schoolexpress.com/funtime/states_capitals/states_capitals.asp (you can select to see the state and name the capital or see the capital and name the state)
- State Capital Game http://www.triv.net/html/Geography/uscap1.htm (keep track of your score!)

Looking for something a little more in-depth? Check out the My State Report site at abcteach. This has everything from graphic organizers to coloring pages of state birds to maps and mobiles.

- My State Report http://www.abcteach.com/States/StateTOC.htm

December 5
International Volunteer Day

In 1985, the United Nations General Assembly designated December 5th as an annual celebration of communities, peoples and governments for all that is achieved by voluntary effort -- by volunteers -- around the world.[iv] Kids of all ages are great helpers. Enlist their sense of community by brainstorming a list of volunteer projects your class could do this month. Have the students vote for one (or you choose depending upon what is on the list.) One idea might be to have your class put on a puppet play based on one of Jan Brett's Christmas books for the local day care center or nursing home or both. Learn more about volunteering at the following sites.

- United Nations Volunteers http://www.unv.org/
- Volunteer Connections http://www.volunteerconnections.org/
- Points of Light Foundation http://www.pointsoflight.org/
- Get Warm and Fuzzy http://kids.discovery.com/KIDS/adv30.html

December 6
St Nicholas Day

It doesn't matter what you call him – St. Nicholas, Sinterklass, Mikulas, Santa Claus or something else, this jolly old elf symbolizes joy, happiness and giving. St. Nicholas was a 4th century saint. Legend tells us that Nicholas was from a wealthy family. One day he heard that a man who had lost all of his money was going to sell one of his daughters so he could provide for the rest of his family. That night, Nicholas took a bag of gold and tossed it through the man's window. Later, Nicholas became a priest who continued to give anonymous gifts and small treats to young children. It is not hard to see how his name came to be associated with Christmas and giving. Read the Story of St. Nicholas.

- The Story of St. Nicholas http://www.cptryon.org/prayer/adx/adnick.html
- St. Nicholas for Young Children http://www.cptryon.org/prayer/child/nick.html
- St. Nicholas http://www.geocities.com/EnchantedForest/Meadow/8272/stnick.html

December 6th is the feast day for St. Nicholas. Children often receive small gifts on that day.

- Frequently Asked Questions About St. Nicholas
  http://www.santaclaus.com/faq.html#Historical%20Questions
- St. Nicholas Day http://www.umkc.edu/imc/stnick.htm
- St. Nicholas Day http://www.algonet.se/~bernadot/christmas/6.html
- Christmas in Germany http://www.pastrywiz.com/cookies/christmas.htm

Santa Claus

Our modern version of St. Nicholas, known as Santa Claus, is attributed to Clement C. Moore's 1823 poem, *A Visit From St. Nicholas*.

- Santa Links http://www.night.net/christmas/santa.html-ssi
- Santa Claus http://www.umkc.edu/imc/santa.htm
- Pine Cone Santa Claus http://www.victoriana.com/christmas/craft1-99.htm

- Christmas Coloring Book http://www.christmas.com/pe/46
- Christmas Paper Dolls http://www.makingfriends.com/f_holiday.htm#Christmas%20Friends

If your class exchanges gifts at Christmas time, why not have a Secret Santa. Have the students draw names but do not tell whose name they have. Ask the students to think of small gifts, such as a pencil, a candy cane, or sticker to give to their classmate. Students leave one gift each day on the desk or locker without letting the recipient know who did it. You decide if you want to start on St. Nicholas Day and end the day you leave for holiday break or some other time frame. I suggest a shorter period of time, such as a week. Then, have the students 'guess' their Secret Santa.

Songs About Santa

Sing some of these songs about Santa. Do the lyrics sustain the image we have of St. Nicholas? Have the students make a music video using PowerPoint, or another presentation tool, based on a song about Santa Claus or St. Nicholas.

❖ Christmas Songs *I Saw Mommy Kissing Santa Claus* Midi
http://www.catholic.net/RCC/music/midi/christmas/
September 30, 2001

❖ Christmas Songs *I Saw Mommy Kissing Santa Claus*
http://www.nevada.edu/~blake/Christmas.songs.html#1
%20Saw%20Mommy%20Santa%20Claus
Septmeber 30, 2001

- Songs of the Season http://www.night.net/christmas/songs12.html-ssi
- Christmas Songs http://www.nevada.edu/~blake/Christmas.songs.html
- Online Christmas Songbook http://rememberjosie.org/carols/
- Christmas Songs http://www.homestead.com/stnick/christmassongs.html
- Christmas Clip Art http://christmas-clipart.net/
- Clip Art: Christmas http://www.kidsdomain.com/holiday/xmas/clip.html

December 7, 1941
Pearl Harbor Day

On December 7, 1941, the Japanese unexpectedly attacked the United States bases at Pearl Harbor, Hawaii. This act brought the United States into World War II. *Remembering Pearl Harbor* is an excellent, interactive site that takes the viewer step by step through the attack on Pearl Harbor. On the day after the attack on Pearl Harbor, the Library of Congress sent archivists around the country to record the thoughts and fears of the American people. These accounts are online at the Sound Portraits site. Compare these with the thoughts of people after the attacks on the World Trade Center and the Pentagon on September 11, 2001.
- Remembering Pearl Harbor http://www.nationalgeographic.com/pearlharbor/
- Pearl Harbor http://plasma.nationalgeographic.com/pearlharbor/index.html
- The Day after Pearl Harbor http://www.soundportraits.org/on-air/the_day_after_pearl_harbor/

The Four Freedoms

Almost a year earlier, January 6, 1941, President Roosevelt gave his State of the Union address to congress and the nation. In this address, he outlined four freedoms that American's hold dear. These four freedoms were to become a battle cry during World War II.

- Four Freedoms: Roosevelt's State of the Union Address
  http://gi.grolier.com/presidents/ea/side/4freedms.html
- Hear Roosevelt http://www.nara.gov/exhall/powers/freedoms.html

Popular illustrator Norman Rockwell translated President Roosevelt's words into images. After viewing these illustrations and working through the *Four Freedoms Web Quest*, have the students use a digital camera to capture pictures of four freedoms in your community.

- Norman Rockwell's 4 Freedoms http://www.nara.gov/exhall/powers/freedoms.html
- Four Freedoms Web Quest http://www.broward.k12.fl.us/summWebquest00/MNewman/
- The Four Freedoms http://www.history-matters.org/TACT/selling%20the%20american%20dream/Four%20Freedoms.htm

December 12
Guadalupe Day - Mexico

About 450 years ago, Juan Diego, a Mexican laborer, saw was walking by a hill when he saw a vision of the Virgin Mary. She told him that she wanted a shrine built there. Juan Diego told the priest who at first didn't believe him. But when roses suddenly appeared, everyone believed. The shrine is known at the Lady of Guadalupe. This is one of the most holy days celebrated in Mexico. The day is marked with pilgrimages, feasts and gifts. Puppet shows reenact Juan Diego's vision. Have your students make puppets and tell the story of Juan Diego.

- Guadalupe Day http://www2.worldbook.com/features/holidays/html/guadel.htm
- About this Holiday http://hicards.com/bizarre/guadalupe.shtml
- Guadalupe http://www.ptreyeslight.com/stories/dec21/virgen.html
- Puppet Building http://www.sagecraft.com/puppetry/building/

December 12
St. Lucia Day – Italy, Norway, Sweden

The origins of St. Lucia Day are varied. Broadly speaking, the day is considered the first day of the Christmas celebration. In many communities, a young girl is dressed in white with an evergreen wreath on her head. The wreath has lighted seven candles. The girl awakens each member of the family by bringing them coffee and buns. The candles represent the return of light to countries that are in the darkest period of the year. Read more about the history and customs associated with St. Lucia Day at the following sites. *Note: add this custom to your Around the World Custom Tree. See December 25.*

- St. Lucia Day http://www.umkc.edu/imc/stlucia.htm
- St. Lucia Day http://www2.worldbook.com/features/holidays/html/lucia.htm
- St. Lucia http://www.whitington.com/write/alucia.htm

December 12
Poinsettia Day

Poinsettias were first used as a Christmas decoration by Franciscan priests in Mexico. They were introduced into the United States in 1825 by Joel Robert Poinsett, the first United States ambassador to Mexico Today, Poinsettia Day, December 12, marks the anniversary of the death of Joel Robert Poinsett. Have the students color poinsettia pictures. Cut them out and cut some of the individual petals almost to the center. Curl these petals around a pencil to give the flower depth. String your flowers together and make a garland for your door.

- National Poinsettia Day http://www.ecke.com/html/h_corp/corp_pntday.html
- Poinsettia Day http://aggie-horticulture.tamu.edu/greenhouse/guides/poinsettia/history.html
- The Facts About Poinsettias http://www.rabbit.org/care/poinsettia.html
- Poinsettia Day http://www.holidayinsights.com/other/poinsettia.htm
- Color a Poinsettia http://www.myhome.org/hoho/cpoinset.gif
- Poinsettia Day Cards http://www.123greetings.com/events/poinsettiaday/

December 15, 1891
Basketball Invented

Dr. James Naismith, a Canadian minister, invented the game of basketball while he was working in a school for young men in Springfield, Massachusetts. As a strong believer in "healthy body, healthy mind", he was determined to get the young men in his class actively involved in sports. He asked the school janitor to hang two peach baskets, one on each end of the school gym. As they say, "the rest is history." Visit the *Life and Times of Dr. James Naismith* site to learn more about this amazing Canadian. This site also has an excellent 'kids page' with many interesting and educational activities for students.

- The Life and Times of Dr. James Naismith http://collections.ic.gc.ca/naismith/index.htm
- James Naismith http://www.allsands.com/Entertainment/People/jamesnaismith_byx_gn.htm

Invent a Game

Dr. Naismith wanted a game that could be played indoors in all kinds of weather. He tried to modify existing games such as soccer and football, but thought they were too rough to play on a hard wood floor. Soon after he posted his 13 rules for playing basketball, the game became a favorite. Ask the students to invent a new game or modify an existing game. You might want to start with something simple such as a new game of tag. Writing rules for games is an excellent task for sequencing and word choice.

Odds and Ends

- Basketball Hall of Fame http://www.hoophall.com/index.htm
- USA Basketball http://usabasketball.com/usab/index.html
- NBA http://www.nba.com interactive games
- WNBA http://www.wnba.com/
- Harlem Globetrotters http://www.harlemglobetrotters.com/

December 16, 1770
Ludwig Von Beethoven's Birthday

Ludwig Von Beethoven was born in Bonn, Germany to working class parents. He was very young when his musical genius was discovered. His father exploited his talent and demanded perfection by often 'boxing' his ears when he made a mistake. Nonetheless, Beethoven loved music and performing. Beethoven composed whole pieces of music in his head before writing it on paper. His music was passionate and dramatic, full of feeling and emotion. His new style music lead to a new period of music known as the Classical Era. There are many excellent Internet sites about Beethoven. These are some of my favorites.

- Ludwig von Beethoven http://www.classical.net/music/comp.lst/beethoven.html
- Beethoven http://www.edepot.com/beethoven.shtml
- Beethoven http://www.beethoven.de/ (needs to be translated)

Ode to Joy

During this holiday season, have the students draw and scan or take digital pictures of things that make them joyful. Use them to illustrate Beethoven's 4th movement of the 9th symphony – Ode to Joy.

- Ode to Joy http://www.edepot.com/beetsym.html (with Schiller's Poem in English)
- Winter Morning http://musictoons.tripod.com/wintertoons/wintermorn.html
- Ode to Joy http://members.tripod.com/~discodor/index-26.html
- Beethoven's 9th Symphony http://www.geocities.com/Vienna/1636/9.html

Odds and Ends

- 9th Symphony Lesson Plan http://www.csrnet.org/csrnet/substitute/beethoven9.html
- Composer Road Rally http://www.lessonplanspage.com/MusicBeethovenBachInfo.htm

- Multimedia Beethoven http://www.geocities.com/Vienna/1636/
- Trans Siberian Orchestra: Beethoven's Last Night http://www.trans-siberian.com/noflash/xmas-eve.htm

December 16
Los Posadas - Mexico
Los Posadas is celebrated in remembrance of Joseph and Mary's search for shelter in Bethlehem. In the evening, there is a candlelight procession through the town. Children stop at homes and ask if there is room at the Inn. Of course, there is not, but the walkers are often asked in for refreshments and to see the family's display of nativity scenes. The procession ends at the church where there is a service and piñata party for the children. Learn more about the Los Posadas traditions at the following sites. Use the *Nativity Paper Dolls* to make a nativity scene for your classroom. Invite another class to tour your classroom to see your Nativity Scene and play the piñata game.
- Mexico http://www.azcentral.com/culturesaz/hispanic/posadas.shtml
- Los Posadas http://www.mexonline.com/xmas.htm
- Feliz Navidad http://clnet.ucr.edu/holiday.html
- The Nativity Paper Dolls http://www.makingfriends.com/f_holiday.htm#Nativity%20Friends
- Learn2 Make a Piñata http://www.learn2.com/04/0402/0402.asp

December 17, 1843
Charles Dickens's Published *A Christmas Carol*
One of the best-loved Christmas stories is Charles Dickens's *A Christmas Carol*. Read this classic to and with your students. It makes a wonderful reader's theater. Copy and paste into a word processor. Assign readers. I suggest you have a couple of 'narrators' besides the main characters. Invite other classes to your performance.
[exhibit 102]

- A Christmas Carol http://www.literature.org/authors/dickens-charles/christmas-carol/
- A Christmas Carol http://etext.lib.virginia.edu/cgibin/toccer?id=DicChri&tag=public&images=images/modeng&data=/lv1/Archive/eng-parsed&part=0

For a more in-depth study of *A Christmas Carol*, you will enjoy using the following CyberGuide. It is quite extensive, but you can pick and choose the parts that will work with your class.
- CyberGuide http://www.nashville-schools.davidson.k12.tn.us/CyberGuides/CC/ChristmasCarol.html

December 19, 1928
Eve Bunting's Birthday
Award winning author Eve Bunting was born in Maghera, Ireland. She came to the United States in 1959 with her husband and became a naturalized citizen in 1969. Although as a child she loved writing assignments in school she never considered becoming an author. It wasn't until she was in her 40s that she took a class in Writing for Publication, which began her writing career. Today, besides writing, she now teaches a class for adults who are interested in writing. Learn more about Eve Bunting at the following sites:
- Eve Bunting, Biography http://www.edupaperback.org/authorbios/Bunting_Eve.html
- A Talk With Eve Bunting http://www.bookpage.com/9705bp/childrens/evebunting.html
- Eve Bunting http://dept.kent.edu/virginiahamiltonconf/bunting.htm
- Kidsread: Eve Bunting http://www.kidsreads.com/authors/au-bunting-eve.asp
- Teacher's Resource File: Eve Bunting http://falcon.jmu.edu/~ramseyil/bunting.htm

Short Story

Eve Bunting says writing is a gift and that no one can be "taught to write" but students can be taught how to structure a story.[vi] In her class, she also teaches students how to develop a plot and how to create characters that are real. Have your students write a short story. Print copies of the *Story Grammar* for each student to use to outline their story. Then, have the students put 'meat' on the bones of the story. Eve Bunting has always been fascinated with the magic of words. Encourage the students to use the word processor's Thesaurus to change some of the tired words, such as *very*, with 'magic words.' *Note: Bunting often writes about social injustices or family problems. Think about having students write about families in homeless shelters or children whose father/mother are serving in the armed forces during the holidays.*

- Story Grammar http://www.abcteach.com/Reading/storygrammar.htm
- Student Writing Checklist http://www.abcteach.com/Writing/checklist.htm
- Creating Memorable Characters http://www.poewar.com/articles/characters.htm
- Teaching Creative Writing http://teacher2b.com/creative/createwr.htm

It is often hard for children to understand that the author and the illustrator often do not know each other and do not collaborate on the book. Look at the books that another December birthday girl, Jan Brett, illustrated for Eve Bunting. To explore how this process works, have students exchange their stories and have another student illustrate their story. Remind them that the illustrator cannot change anything the author has described, such as "Jim had bright red hair." But if the author did not mention the color of Jim's hair, illustrator is free to make it any color he or she chooses. Post your stories on your Internet site.

Lesson Plans About Teaching Writing From ERIC

- Creative Writing – Before, During and After http://askeric.org/cgi-bin/printlessons.cgi/Virtual/Lessons/Language_Arts/Writing/WCP0011.html
- Creative Writing – Beginning, Middle and End http://askeric.org/cgi-bin/printlessons.cgi/Virtual/Lessons/Language_Arts/Writing/WCP0009.html
- Creative Writing – Using Writing Prompts http://askeric.org/cgi-bin/printlessons.cgi/Virtual/Lessons/Language_Arts/Writing/WCP0010.html
- Creative Writing – Using Comics http://askeric.org/cgi-bin/printlessons.cgi/Virtual/Lessons/Language_Arts/Writing/WCP0013.html

Field Trip to Ireland

Eve Bunting was born and raised in Ireland, in fact, attended school in Belfast. Have the students take a virtual field trip to Ireland. See if they can find Christmas customs unique to Ireland. Use Google or another search engine to search for [Ireland+Christmas]

- Ireland http://www.ireland.travel.ie/home/
- Go Ireland http://www.goireland.com/
- Cam Vista http://www.camvista.com/
- Google http://www.google.com

Some Books by Eve Bunting

Smoky Night – Caldecott, 1995
The Blue and the Gray
Butterfly House
Cheyenne Again
Dandelions
The Day Before Christmas
A Day's Work
December

Ducky
Fly Away Home
The Girl in the Painting
Going Home
Happy Birthday, Dear Duck (illustrated by Jan Brett)
Moonstick: The Seasons of the Sioux
The Mother's Day Mice (illustrated by Jan Brett)
Night of the Gargoyles
Noche De Humu
Scary, Scary Halloween (illustrated by Jan Brett)

December 21, 1913
1st Crossword Puzzle Published
Celebrate this anniversary by making a crossword puzzle of words associated with December. Have the students help by brainstorming a list of words. Use the *Puzzlemaker* to make your puzzle. *Note: You have many different options for word puzzles besides crossword puzzles.*
- Puzzlemaker http://puzzlemaker.school.discovery.com/

One of the most famous crossword puzzles is the *New York Times* crossword puzzle. Check these out. There are puzzles for younger students, too.
- New York Times http://www.nytimes.com/diversions/

Online Crossword Puzzles
- The Night Before Christmas http://www.newsword.com/christmas/thenightbefore/
- Crossword Puzzles for ESL Students http://www.aitech.ac.jp/~iteslj/cw/
- Crossword Puzzle Links http://www.crossword-puzzles.co.uk/
- Online Crosswords http://www.clearlight.com/~vivi/xw/
- Lists of Crossword Puzzles http://www.primate.wisc.edu/people/hamel/cp.html
- Crossword Puzzles http://www.nytimes.com/learning/teachers/xwords/index.html
- Kid Crosswords http://www.kidcrosswords.com/
- Clue Master: 1000 Crossword Puzzles http://www.cluemaster.com/
- Early American Crossword Puzzle http://www.earlyamerica.com/crossword/

Test Your Knowledge About Crossword Puzzles
- Crossword Puzzle Quiz http://www.nanana.com/xwordhist/crosswordquiz.html
- The World's First Crossword Puzzle http://www.crosswordtournament.com/more/wynne.html

December 23, 1937
Avi's Birthday
Avi was born in New York City and lived in Brooklyn. His twin sister called him Avi and that is the name he has always used. He was not a very good student, in fact, when he was in high school he failed all of his courses. His parents finally enrolled him in a small school that emphasized reading and writing. As writing was important to his family, it became important to him. He became a playwright and didn't begin writing for children until he had children of his own. Avi say's that if you want to be a writer, you need to be a reader. "I believe reading is the key to writing. The more you read, the better your writing can be."[vii] Help your students record, respond and reflect on the books they read by keeping a **Book Log**.
- Avi http://www.avi-writer.com/
- Avi http://www.ipl.org/youth/AskAuthor/Avi.html
- Avi http://www.booksnbytes.com/authors/avi_.html
- Featured Author: Avi http://www.carolhurst.com/newsletters/23dnewsletters.html
- Teacher Resource File: Avi http://falcon.jmu.edu/~ramseyil/avi.htm

- Book Logs http://www.occdsb.on.ca/~jam/read.htm

Photography

Avi believes that no matter how much you enjoy something, you need to take a break from it. When, he takes a break from writing, he enjoys his hobby -- photography. Digital cameras are wonderful classroom tools. There are many low cost models available that make them affordable for classroom use. Search for digital cameras to see which ones would be best for your classroom. Have the students experiment with different techniques by taking pictures of each other. Then, save their pictures to the desktop. If you don't have a photo finishing program, you can download a sample of PhotoStudio. Have the students bring in their picture and try using the different effects. Hang a display of your portraits in the hallway. Take your students on a virtual field trip to a couple of museums of photography to learn a little about the history of photography.

- PhotoStudio http://www.arcsoft.com/support/downloads/index.html
- 411 Photography http://www.411photography.com/
- Learn2 Take Better Pictures http://www.learn2.com/04/0475/0475.asp
- California Museum of Photography http://www.cmp.ucr.edu/
- American Museum of Photography http://www.photographymuseum.com/
- History of Photography http://www.rleggat.com/photohistory/

Reading Chapter Books

Students are always excited about reading chapter books as it is an indication that they are growing up. Here are a couple of suggestions for helping students read chapter books.

- Chapter Books http://www.knownet.net/users/Ackley/chapter.html
- Personal Responses to Novels http://www.knownet.net/users/Ackley/readnovel.html
- Reading a Literary Text Scoring Guide http://www.nwrel.org/assessment/pdfRubrics/littextscoringguidest.PDF

Nicknames

Avi's sister was about a year old when she gave him the nickname Avi. Have the students use the nicknames sites to find common nicknames based on their given name. The last site provides the given name for some famous people.

- Nicknames http://www.tngenweb.org/franklin/frannick.htm
- Nicknames http://www.rootsweb.com/~pacumber/nick.htm
- Nicknames of Famous People http://www.execpc.com/~jamesf/zone/nickname.html

Some Books by Avi (go to his homepage for a complete list with descriptions)
Midnight Magic
History of Helpless Harry
Who Was that Masked Man Anyway?
Who Stole the Wizard of Oz?
Poppy
The True Confessions of Charlotte Doyle – Newbery Honor
The Barn
Captain Grey
The Christmas Rat
Nothing But the Truth
Abigail Takes the Wheel

December 23, 1823

A Night Before Christmas **Published**

Legend tells us that Clement Moore wrote the *Night Before Christmas* for his daughters Margaret and Charity in 1822 and published it anonymously in the New York *Sentinel* the following year. However, some feel Moore couldn't have written this famous poem and the actual author was probably Major Henry Livingston, Jr. What do you think?

- Moore or Less http://www.snopes2.com/holidays/xmas/moore.htm
- Literary Sleuth Casts Doubt on the Authorship of an Iconic Christmas Poem http://www.nytimes.com/learning/general/featured_articles/001027friday.html (with lesson plan)
- Selected Poetry of Clement C. Moore http://www.library.utoronto.ca/utel/rp/authors/moorec.html
- Selected Poetry of Major Henry Livingston, Jr. http://www.library.utoronto.ca/utel/rp/authors/livingston.html

Regardless of the true authorship, reading *A Night Before Christmas* or *A Visit From St. Nicholas* is one of our best-loved Christmas traditions. It also makes an effective coral reading with a few solo parts, or try singing it to a familiar melody such as *The Yellow Rose of Texas*.

- The Night Before Christmas http://www.christmas-tree.com/stories/nightbeforechristmas.html
- The Night Before Christmas http://www.childrenstory.com/christmas/b41.html (listen to this very nice version with classic illustrations)
- Another excellent version: The Night Before Christmas http://www.max-designs.com/holiday/stories/night-b-4.html (read by Basil Rathbone, 1939)
- 1914 Version http://www.winternet.com/~swezeyt/NBXmas/nbx0.htm
- Night Before Christmas Web Maze Game http://www.onenorthpole.com/gamcintro.html
- The Yellow Rose of Texas midi http://www.melodylane.net/songlist.html

Note: If you still haven't found just the right version, use any search engine and search for "The Night Before Christmas"

Different Versions of The Night Before Christmas

Many people have written parodies based on the *Night Before Christmas*. Have your students write a parody using one of these themes: the Night Before Hanukah, The Day After Christmas, The Day Before Vacation, or have the students think of their own.

- Night Before Christmas http://www.thursdaysclassroom.com/09dec99/teachnight.html (space version and cloze procedure)
- The Night Before Christmas: An African Christmas Story http://www.night.net/christmas/night-before-africa.html-ssi
- The Night Before Christmas: Mexican Version http://www.teachers.net/lessons/posts/761.html

Make Your Own Book

Use Flip Album to publish your own version of *The Night Before Christmas*. Don't forget to add background music.

- An Example Your Students Could Do http://members.tripod.com/christmas_dec25/stories/nightb4/
- Flip Album http://www.flipalbum.com
- Christmas Songbook http://rememberjosie.org/carols/
- Classic Clip Art http://www.tssphoto.com/vt/xmas5/

Not For Children

- 'Twas the Night Before Christmas – Childhood Disease http://www.geocities.com/griefpoetry/christmas.html
- Politically Correct Version http://paul.merton.ox.ac.uk/xmas/pc-night-before.html
- Many Different Versions http://www.geocities.com/NapaValley/2049/nb4.htm

- More Parodies http://urbanlegends.miningco.com/library/bltwas.htm

December 24
Christmas Eve

The night before Christmas is a very special, magical time. It is celebrated with religious services, parties and family celebrations. In the tradition of Jewish holidays, celebrations begin at sundown and end at sundown. So, the Christmas celebration begins the evening before Christmas. Modern celebrations of Christmas Eve usually refer to the day before Christmas, not just the evening. Many people from different countries have longstanding Christmas Eve customs. Have small groups of students research a different country's Christmas Eve customs. Write a short explanation of the celebration and attach to the world map with ribbon and map tacks.

- Christmas in Poland http://www.polishworld.com/christmas/
- Italian Christmas Eve http://www.globalgourmet.com/food/egg/egg1297/buonatale.html
- Lithuanian Christmas Eve http://neris.mii.lt/CHRISTMAS/christmas_eve.html
- Lithuanian Christmas Eve http://www.lithuanian-american.org/educat/tradicijos/kucios.html
- Germany http://www.californiamall.com/holidaytraditions/traditions-germany.htm
- A Polish Christmas Eve http://wings.buffalo.edu/info-poland/CMK.html
- Poland Christmas Eve Customs http://www.kresy.co.uk/pol_christmas.html
- Christmas Eve Pre-Christmas Traditions http://www.abcog.org/xmas2.htm
- Christmas Traditions from Around the World http://www.soon.org.uk/country/christmas.htm
- Christmas Eve in Finland http://virtual.finland.fi/finfo/english/joulueng.html
- French Christmas Eve Yule Log http://www.culture.fr/culture/noel/angl/buche.htm

Christmas Eve From Outer Space

The Apollo 8 Christmas Eve broadcast remains one of the most meaningful and inspirational events in our history. Have your students illustrate it using a presentation tool such as PowerPoint.

- The Apollo 8 Christmas Eve Broadcast
  http://nssdc.gsfc.nasa.gov/planetary/lunar/apollo8_xmas.html

December 25
Christmas, Navidad, Juleafton

Many words are used to signify this joyous holiday celebrating the birthday of the Christ child. Today, Christmas is a legal holiday in all fifty states, but that was not always the case. Louisiana and Arkansas were the first states to observe Christmas as a legal holiday in 1831. In fact, the Massachusetts General Court ordered a fine of 5 shillings for "observing any such day as Christmas" in 1651.

- Christmas in the United States (1700-1900) http://www.umkc.edu/imc/christmas.htm

To get in the Christmas spirit, here are five quick things you can do.

- Put on a class play: Santa Knows About Rudolph's Nose
  http://www.macscouter.com/Skits/ThemeSkits.html#SANTA%20KNOWS%20ABOUT%20RUD
  OLPH'S%20NOSE
- Follow the December Holiday Scavenger Hunt
  http://www.angelfire.com/ks/tonyaskinner/dechunt.html
- Learn about the Reindeer http://www.umkc.edu/imc/reindeer.htm
- Learn to say Merry Christmas in different languages http://christmas.com/pe/1427
  http://www.flw.com/merry.htm or other holiday messages
  http://users.aol.com/WSCaswell/message.htm and listen to Christmas Greetings
  http://www.holidays.net/christmas/voices.htm
- Open a Gift Box http://bbs.scholastic.com/holiday.asp

Religious Celebrations

Christian celebrations center around the biblical story of the nativity. Enjoy this beautiful story illustrated with old masters and highlighted with classical music. You can read the Christmas Story according to St. Luke in English or many different languages. The *12 Voices of Christmas* is an audio Christmas play based on 12 biblical characters and the *Biblical Accounts of Christmas* has different versions of the Christmas story plus a quiz. I've also included a unit plan that focuses on the religious aspect of this holiday and a word find puzzle.

- The Birth of Christ: St. Luke http://www.night.net/christmas/luke-intro.html-ssi
- The 12 Voices of Christmas http://www.backtothebible.org/christmas/12home.html
- Biblical Accounts of Christmas http://www.execpc.com/~tmuth/st_john/xmas/scrip.htm
- Christmas Unit Plan http://hometown.aol.com/MomCaroe/Christmas.html
- The Christmas Story Word Find Puzzle http://www.annieshomepage.com/decemberpuzzle.html

Christmas Stories

Of course, there are many other wonderful Christmas stories. You can read these to the students, have the students read them in a reader's theater format, make them into plays for puppets or make illustrated books for the library or younger students in your school. I hope you find some old friends and make some new ones here. I suggest you start by making a Christmas ABC Book or frieze for your room or to share with the library. I used PowerPoint but you could use any word processor or publishing program also.

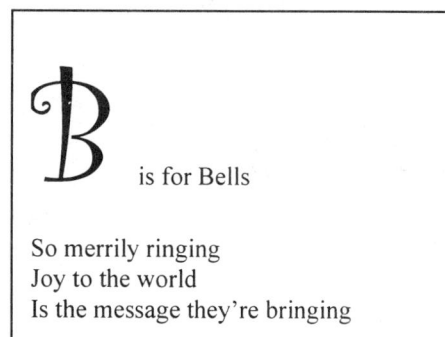

A is for Angels

With halos so bright
Whose carols were heard
On that first Christmas Night

B is for Bells

So merrily ringing
Joy to the world
Is the message they're bringing

- ABC's of Christmas http://www.myholidayplace.com/christmas/poems/43.html
- Christmas Poems http://www.myholidayplace.com/christmas/poems.html
- Grandpa Tuckers Christmas stories http://www.grandpatucker.com/christmas/index-txt.html-ssi
- Stories and Poems http://www.night.net/christmas/poems12.html-ssi
- Rosie's Christmas Tongue Twisters http://www.night.net/christmas/f-twisters1.html
- Stories http://www.ucalgary.ca/~dkbrown/christmas.html
- Good Stories for Great Holidays http://etext.lib.virginia.edu/cgibin/toccer?id=OlcGood&images=images/modeng&data=/lv1/Archive/eng-parsed&tag=public&part=100

Music

Singing carols and listening to holiday music is a big part of our celebrations. Here are some sites that will help with those lyrics you can't remember. Use these to add a multimedia dimension to other projects or just enjoy the background music as you and the students do your other work.

- Online Song Book http://rememberjosie.org/carols/
- Christmas Songs http://www.night.net/christmas/songs12.html-ssi
- Name That Tune http://www.night.net/christmas/f-name-tune.html#Q4
- Silent Night http://www.lessonplanspage.com/MusicMDStretchSilentNight36.htm
- Elycia's Real Audio Hollydazzle http://www.elycia-webdesign.com/seasonal/christmas.html#3e

Christmas Custom's Tree

Christmas is a wonderful time to learn about other countries and how they celebrate this special day. Ask small groups of students research one country and report to the rest of the class during a social studies class or take a different country each day and during a large group time such as home room or opening exercises share your research.

- Christmas Around the World http://www.night.net/christmas/traditions.html-ssi
- Christmas Around the World http://library.thinkquest.org/10007/text/christ.html
- World View of Christmas http://christmas.com/worldview/
- Christmas Symbols Teach the Children http://www.geocities.com/~lightoflove/teachchild.htm
- Christmas Around the World http://www.santaclaus.com/world.html

One of our favorite Christmas customs is the Christmas tree – a symbol of everlasting life. Decorate your classroom tree with ornaments the students have made. Each ornament describes a different Christmas custom. I suggest the students use an outline of the country for the shape of their ornament. On one side of the ornament place an appropriate clip art or photo and on the other side a paragraph describing the custom. Cut out the ornament, punch a hole in the top, place a ribbon through the hole and hang on your tree.

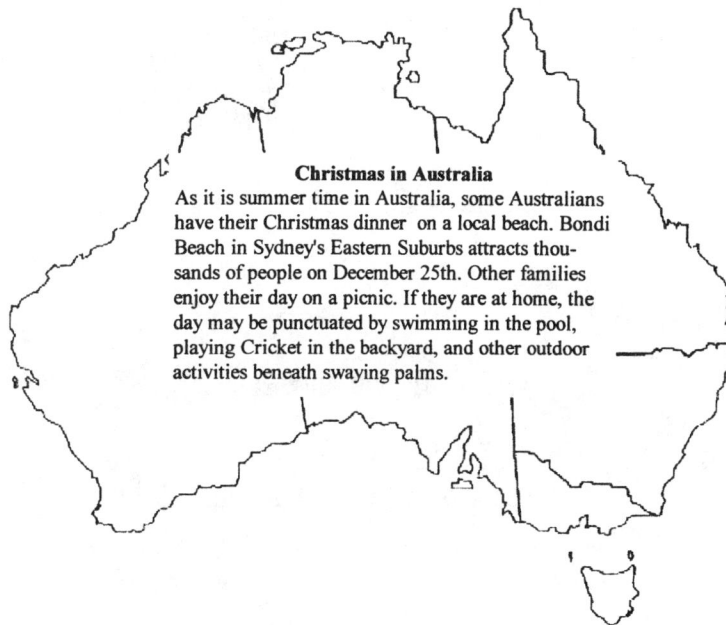

Christmas in Australia
As it is summer time in Australia, some Australians have their Christmas dinner on a local beach. Bondi Beach in Sydney's Eastern Suburbs attracts thousands of people on December 25th. Other families enjoy their day on a picnic. If they are at home, the day may be punctuated by swimming in the pool, playing Cricket in the backyard, and other outdoor activities beneath swaying palms.

- Outline Maps http://www.abcteach.com/Maps/mapsTOC.htm

More about Christmas Trees…
- Christmas trees http://www.christmastrees.on.ca/ednet/lesson1.html
- The Christmas Tree
  http://www.teacherlink.usu.edu/TLresources/longterm/LessonPlans/Byrnes/christmas.html

- Trees of Christmas http://photo2.si.edu/ctree/ctree.html
- National Christmas Tree http://www.realchristmastrees.org/
- Christmas Facts http://www.maui.net/~mcculc/xmas.htm
- Christmas Quiz http://familygames.com/features/quizzes/qzx/questions.html?11

Lesson Plans

There are many wonderful lesson plans about Christmas on the Internet for your use. This is a list of some of them.

- Christmas Lesson Plans http://www.lessonplanspage.com/Christmas.htm
- Holiday Lesson Plans http://www.cloudnet.com/~edrbsass/edholiday.htm
- All Purpose Lesson Ideas for Christmas http://members.aol.com/Donnpages/Holidays.html#XMAS
- Christmas in Williamsburg http://www.history.org/other/teaching/colxmas.htm
- Shopping Lesson Plan Using Spreadsheets http://www.tamu-commerce.edu/coe/shed/espinoza/s/tschoerner-h-lp1.html
- Christmas Activities and Lessons http://www.trumbull.k12.oh.us/teachers/Christmas.html
- Holiday Geography http://www.education-world.com/a_lesson/TM/WS_holiday_geography.shtml
- Spreading Christmas Cheer Using Spreadsheets http://www.tamu-commerce.edu/coe/shed/espinoza/s/tschoerner-h-lp1.html

Odds and Ends

The Internet also has lots of games, crafts, and recipes and other projects to make your celebration festive. These sites are just a few of my favorites.

- Merry Little Christmas Page http://www.kate.net/holidays/christmas/
- Black Dog's Christmas Fun and Games http://blackdog.net/holiday/christmas/
- How Stuff Works: Christmas http://www.howstuffworks.com/christmas.htm
- A Christmastime Celebration http://www.myholidayplace.com/christmas/
- Christmas Clip Art http://www.myholidayplace.com/christmas/images/11/
- The Legends of Christmas http://www.hoover.nara.gov/gallery/legends/legends-intro.htm
- Christmas.com http://christmas.com/
- Christmas on the Net http://www.holidays.net/christmas/index.htm
- It's Christmas http://www.itschristmas.com/
- Merry Christmas http://merry-christmas.com/
- Kids Domain: Activities http://www.kidsdomain.com/holiday/xmas/print.html
- Holiday Fun from Sears Portrait Studio http://www.searsportrait.com/contest/xmas_00_activity.html
- Christmas Trivia Quizzes http://www.familygames.com/features/quizzes.html

December 25 – January 5
The 12 Days of Christmas

The twelve days of Christmas refers to days between Christmas and Epiphany, January 6th.

- The Origins of the 12 Days of Christmas http://www.cin.org/twelvday.html
- Drennon's 12 Days of Christmas (read before or if you share this one with the students) http://www.cvc.org/christmas/12days.htm
- Lyrics and Midi http://www.12days.com/library/carols/12daysofxmas.htm
- 12 Days of Christmas (artwork by children) http://www.12days.net/
- 12 Days of Christmas Screen Saver http://www.40splusimages.com/12days.html

It can sometimes be hard to keep children busy after Christmas. These games and such will keep the little one entertained. Have the older students work with the little ones so you can have a little rest. You can also have the students work together to write another version of the 12 Days of Christmas.

- 12 Days of Christmas http://www.12days.com/scene.htm games and stories
- Cybergrandma's 12 Days of Christmas http://www.geocities.com/Heartland/2328/xmas.htm

December 26
Boxing Day
Boxing Day is a British holiday that has to do with giving presents or gratuities to the less fortunate or those who work in a service capacity. It is celebrated in England, Canada, Australia and other countries with English roots. There are many different legends about what the day is and how it was started, but most agree that it began as the day the upper classes gave Christmas gratuities or gifts to their servants. After reading the different versions of the story and about the ways it is celebrated, have your students collect canned foods, place them in boxes and take them to your local food pantry.
- Origins of Boxing Day http://www.snopes2.com/holidays/xmas/boxing.htm
- Boxing Day at Web Holidays http://www.web-holidays.com/boxing/
- Happy Boxing Day http://www.rosebriar.uk.com/holidays/boxingday.html
- Annie's Boxing Day http://www.annieshomepage.com/boxingday.html

December 26
St. Stephen's Day
December 26th is also St. Stephen's Day. St. Stephen was the first Christian martyr. He was stoned to death shortly after the death of Christ. This holiday is primarily celebrated in Ireland. Children, known as Wren boys, go from home to home asking for coins. The money that has been collected is used for community or school projects. Most of us, however, know of this holiday because of an old Christmas carol, Good King Wenceslas, that tells the story of a nobleman who is on his way to the feast of St. Stephen.
- St. Stephen's Day http://www.noblenet.org/year/tty12sts.htm
- Good King Wenceslas http://www.noblenet.org/year/wenc.htm
- Good King Wenceslas http://www3.bc.sympatico.ca/st_simons/cr9212.htm

December 26 – January 1
Kwanzaa
The Kwanzaa celebration is based on African harvest traditions. Kwanzaa means first fruits in Swahili.[viii] Dr. Maulana Karenga established Kwanzaa in 1966 as a way to demonstrate black pride. It stresses history, values, family, community and culture. The seven day celebration is based on seven basic values of African culture: unity, self-determination, collective work, cooperative economics, purpose, creativity and faith. Learn more about meaning and conception of this holiday at these Internet sites.
- Official Kwanzaa Web Site http://www.officialkwanzaawebsite.org/
- Kwanzaa http://www.whyy.org/smc/allen/ZwanWeb/kwanzaa.html
- Kwanzaa Information Center http://melanet.com/kwanzaa/

Kwanzaa Activities and Projects
There are many ways to help students learn the principles of Kwanzaa. These sites provide some excellent activities and projects pertaining to Kwanzaa.
- Make a Kwanzaa Gift http://www.pentewa.com/kwaanzaa.html
- Billy Bear http://www.billybear4kids.com/holidays/kwanzaa/kwanzaa.htm
- Kwanzaa – An African American Holiday
  http://www.afroam.org/children/fun/kwanzaa/kwanzaa.html
- Kwanzaa Cards http://www.bluemountain.com/eng/kwanzaa/
- A Kwanzaa Story http://www.searsportrait.com/storybook/kwanzaa_97_form.html

Odds and Ends

Read how one girl celebrates Kwanzaa and then have students submit their own Kwanzaa traditions.

- Tessa's Kwanzaa Celebration http://www.agirlsworld.com/amy/pajama/winter/Kwanzaa.html

Use this site to complete the Triple Venn Diagram from the Hanukkah section.

- Kwanzaa on the Net http://www.holidays.net/kwanzaa/

Play games while learning about Kwanzaa.

- Kulture Kidz Kwanzaa Fun and Games
  http://www.kulturezone.com/kidz/center/kwanzaa/kwactivities.html

December 29, 1890
Battle of Wounded Knee

On a cold winter day in a ravine near Wounded Knee Creek, South Dakota, the United States Army, attacked and killed approximately 300 Lakota men, women and children. Chief Spotted Elk (Big Foot) was dying of pneumonia. A flag of truce was flying in his encampment when 470 soldiers attacked the Indians. When the "battle" was over, 31 soldiers had been killed, many by "friendly fire" of fellow soldiers.[ix] Later, twenty-seven soldiers would receive the Congressional Medal of Honor for their "bravery" during that massacre. As you can imagine, there are multiple perspectives on this issue. As the students read these accounts, have them compare the information given in each one by using a matrix. Have them identify the information that is fact and can be collaborated and the information that is opinion or that may be fiction. This is a good time to discuss the validity of information on the Internet. Some things for students to look for include: authorship, hosting server, supporting documentation and date published. When there is conflicting information, such as number of soldiers or date many teachers suggest either providing the range (300 to 350 Sioux) or using the one that is stated in most of the documents. What conclusions do your students draw from their critical reading?

- Massacre At Wounded Knee http://www.ibiscom.com/knee.htm
- Wounded Knee Massacre http://memory.loc.gov/ammem/today/dec29.html
- A Massacre Survivor Speaks http://www.dickshovel.com/DwyBrd.html
- Newspaper Account http://www.geocities.com/braintanning/battlewounded.html
- Wounded Knee http://msnbc.com/onair/msnbc/TimeandAgain/archive/wknee/telegrams.asp
- Comparison Matrix Graphic Organizer http://www.graphic.org/commat.html

The Battle Continues

During the last quarter of the last century through today, the Sioux people have worked toward reconciliation. Simply stated, their demand is an apology from and the resending of the Congressional Medals of Honor by the United States government. What do your students think?

- The Siege of 1973 http://msnbc.com/onair/msnbc/TimeandAgain/archive/wknee/1973.asp
- Wounded Knee – A Wound That Won't Heal http://www.dickshovel.com/hill.html

Odds and Ends

- Wounded Knee: Past and Present – a Lesson Plan
  http://nuevaschool.org/~debbie/library/cur/wk97.html
- A Twisted Footnote to Wounded Knee http://www.dickshovel.com/TwistedFootnote.html (L. Frank Baum editorials from the Aberdeen Pioneer)

December 31
New Year's Eve

Great Britain and her colonies, including America, adopted the Gregorian calendar in 1752, in which January 1st was restored as New Year's Day.[x] The festivities begin the evening before with parties and parades. It is a time to wish each other good luck and make resolutions to do better in the following year.

- New Year's Eve in the United States http://www.usis.usemb.se/Holidays/celebrate/newyears.html
- Happy New Year http://wilstar.com/holidays/newyear.htm

After learning a little about the customs and history of New Year's Eve, make a party hat and play some games while you wait to watch the revelers in Times Square. You can also see how New Year's Eve is celebrated around the world via web cams and by reading about worldwide traditions. Learn how to wish each other a Happy New Year in one of 37 different languages.

- Party Hat http://www.kinderart.com/seasons/newyearshat.htm
- Black Dog's New Year's Eve Celebration http://www.blackdog4kids.com/holiday/newyear/
- New Year's Eve In Times Square http://www.timessquarebid.org/new_year/
- New Year's Eve Web Cams http://www.earthcam.com/newyears/2000-2001/
- New Year Around the World http://www.fathertimes.net/traditions.htm
- Learn to Say "Happy New Year" http://www.theholidayspot.com/newyear/wishes.htm

---

[i] Universal Declaration of Human Rights http://www.un.org/Overview/rights.html September 30, 2001

[ii] Torah Tots: Chanukah http://www.torahtots.com/holidays/chanuka/chanstr.htm September 22, 2001

[iii] Jan Brett http://www.janbrett.com/biography.htm September 30, 2001

[iv] International Volunteer Day http://www.unv.org/events/ivd/ivd.html, May 25, 2001

[v] The Life and Times of Dr. James Naismith http://collections.ic.gc.ca/naismith/index.htm October 6, 2001

[vi] Educational Paperback Association *Eve Bunting* http://www.edupaperback.org/authorbios/Bunting_Eve.html October 7, 2001

[vii] Avi *Questions and Answers About Avi* http://www.avi-writer.com/QandA.html October 7, 2001

[viii] Kwanzaa http://www.familyculture.com/holidays/kwanzaa.htm September 29, 2001

[ix] Professor Robert Venables, Northeast Indian Quarterly *Looking Back At Wounded Knee* http://www.dickshovel.com/TwistedFootnote.html September 29, 2001

[x] Celebrate Holidays in the USA *New Year's Day* http://www.usis.usemb.se/Holidays/celebrate/newyears.html September 29, 2001

5/7/2002

January

Should auld acquaintance be forgot,
And never brought to mind?
Should auld acquaintance be forgot,
And auld lang syne!ⁱ

Robert Burns

Special Month

Thank You Month

There are three little magic words
That will open any door with ease.
Two little words are "Thank you!"
And the other little word is "Please!"

- Learn to say thank you in 15 different languages http://kids.discovery.com/KIDS/adv15.html
- Say Thank You http://www.factmonster.com/ipka/A0769407.html

Thank You Notes

The obvious thing to do here is to write thank you notes for the holiday gifts students were given. It is a good thing. Use your computer to make thank you cards. There are many software packages that provide templates. MS Publisher and Printshop are just a couple. You can also use your word processor. Have the students fold a piece of scratch paper first and label the cover, inside, and back. Then, lay it out flat so they can see where to place those things on the page. Or, you can send online thank you cards. These are a couple of sites you might find helpful.

- Learn2 Write a Thank You Note http://www.learn2.com/05/0547/0547.asp
- Thank You Cards http://www.afreegreetingcard.com/postcards/jthanks.shtml
- Blue Mountain Cards http://www.bluemountain.com/eng3/thnx/
- Hallmark http://www.hallmark.com/hmk/Website/hallmark_home.jsp (you need to register, but there is no cost)

Manners

Mid-winter is also a good time to just refresh and reinforce good manners in general. The first site is just a good article for teachers and parents about the importance of teaching manners. The next two are lesson plans about manners and the last one is an online scavenger hunt for children.

- Helping Children With Manners http://childdevelopmentinfo.com/parenting/manners.shtml
- Good Manners Are Fun http://henson.austin.apple.com/edres/ellesson/elem-goodmanners.shtml
- Students Learn Respect http://www.education-world.com/a_curr/curr232.shtml
- Manners http://www.childfun.com/themes/manners.shtml

For older students you might want to compare the etiquette of the past with the more relaxed expectations of today. A Venn diagram would be a useful organizer for this activity.

- Manners and Customs in the Times of Jane Austin
  http://www.stpt.usf.edu/~runge/MasonJA1.html
- M.I.P. Minors in Possession of Bad Manners http://library.thinkquest.org/2993/ (this is a site developed by teens)
- Etiquette for Today http://www.nljc.com/previous.asp
- Venn Diagram http://www.sdcoe.k12.ca.us/score/actbank/svenn.htm

128

Our Book of Manners

Have students write their own book on manners. Brainstorm a list of good manners. Have each child select a good manner from the list and have them key it on the computer and illustrate with either clip art or their own drawing. Collect all of them and make into a book. If you aren't quite sure of what is the right thing to do, Ask Miss Manners.

- Ask Miss Manners http://underwire.msn.com/underwire/itspersonal/miss/104manners.asp

Netiquette

When thou enter a city, abide by its customs.

-- The Talmud

As we work with students on the Internet and with e-mail, we need to help them learn the proper 'rules of the road.' Make a bulletin board, titled 'Rules of the Road'; use a roadmap for the background. Have each student print out a rule and hang on the bulletin board. For older students, have them prepare a brochure using a publisher program titled 'Rules of the Road'. List the rules they think are important. Make copies for your computer lab.

- Core Rules of Netiquette http://www.in.on.ca/tutorial/netiquette.html

"No act of kindness, no matter how small, is ever wasted."
--Aesop

Thank You Tea

Have your students think of the support staff and bus drivers at your school. Encourage them to write 'thank you' notes. Invite them to a tea (where students can practice their good manners) and have the students sing *Thank You Very Much*. Students can make simple tea sandwiches. After cutting the bread into fancy shapes, spread with simple spreads available at most grocery stores.
Thank You Very Much – song nominated for Academy Award, 1970 (Scrooge)

- Midi http://www.tooninn.com/tv/
- Tea Sandwiches http://www.seedsofknowledge.com/teatime.htm

National Soup Month

"Beautiful soup, so rich and green,
Waiting in a hot tureen!
Who for such dainties would not stoop?
Soup of the evening, beautiful Soup!
Soup of the evening, beautiful Soup!
Beau--ootiful Soo--oop! Beau--ootiful Soo--oop!
Soo--oop of the e--e--evening, Beautiful, beautiful Soup"

The Mock Turtle's Song...Lewis Carroll[ii]

Nothing warms you up so much as a hot bowl of soup. Whether you use 'soup' as your monthly theme or just for a day, there are many ways you and your students can enjoy soup.
Learn the Soup Song, and get started!

- Soup Song http://www.niehs.nih.gov/kids/lyrics/soupsong.htm

International Soups and Recipe Book

Soup is an international dish; each country having their own specialty. Take that world map and investigate different country's soups and customs. Make a recipe book of favorite soups. You could call it Alphabet Soup finding a different soup for each letter of the alphabet. Use your word processor to type in the recipes. For younger students, I would make a template, for older students, use a style sheet that gives the font, print size, margins, etc.

- International Soups http://www.soupsong.com/iinterna.html
- Soup Customs Around the World http://www.soupsong.com/isoupta.html
- Campbell Soup Around the World
  http://www.campbellsoup.com/center/around_the_world/default.cfm

"Waiter, there's a fly in my soup!"
"Be quiet, or everyone will want one."
Old Joke

Medicinal Qualities of Chicken Soup

"I told you once
I told you twice
all seasons of the year are nice
for eating chicken soup with rice!"
Rhyming Book of Months …Maurice Sendak[iii]

Does chicken soup really help cure the common cold? Well, let's do some research. Students need to become careful Internet users. This means, they can't believe everything they read on the net. As the students look at these web pages, have them identify the author, the site sponsor, and the last date it was updated. These are some things that will give them a clue that this may be a reliable site.

- Chicken Soup, Vital Medicine http://www.jewishsf.com/bk000121/ichickensoup.shtml
- Is Chicken Soup an Essential Drug? http://www.cma.ca/cmaj/vol-161/issue-12/1532.htm

The researchers found that chicken soup and many of its ingredients were
an aid to neutrophils, the white blood cells that help remove and destroy
bacteria and cellular debris.

Well, it may or may not help us stay well, but we will feel better after reading *Chicken Soup for the Soul.*

- Chicken Soup for the Soul http://www.chickensoup.com/

For younger students, read, Sendak's Chicken Soup with Rice. There are a couple of good lesson plans you might want to use.

- Lesson Plan http://www.eduplace.com/tview/tviews/smith53.html
- Book Ideas: Chicken Soup with Rice http://www.preschooleducation.com/rice.shtml
- Unit Plan: Chicken Soup with Rice http://libweb.uncc.edu/cimc/integration/Units/ChckSoup.htm

By the way, the Greek version of chicken soup is Avgolemono.

- Avgolemono http://www.globalgourmet.com/destinations/greece/avgolemo.html Put it in your Alphabet Soup Recipe Book.

Stone Soup

A wonderful folktale, told all over the world is *Stone Soup*; the story of a village that overcomes their fear and together to make a tasty pot of soup. There is a project for the needy called stone soup, where restaurants make a nourishing soup using leftover vegetables and donating it to homeless shelters. After reading *Stone Soup* and other stories, and learning about the Stone Soup Project, help your students make some soup. Each child brings a vegetable and puts them together with some broth to make the soup. Find a couple of large rocks, wash them in Clorox and run them through the dishwasher to put in the bottom of your Crock-pot. You could do a couple of things here. One, you could donate the soup to a shelter for the homeless, or you could have a soup supper for the parents, sell your Alphabet Soup Recipe Books, put on a play of Stone Soup, sing your Soup Song and donate the money to the shelter. Either way, students will feel good about helping those in need.

- Stone Soup http://spanky.triumf.ca/www/fractint/stone_soup.html
- Other stories and poems about soup http://www.soupsong.com/isoupta.html
- How to Make Stone Soup http://sites.tier.net/stonesoup/instructions.htm

Have your students write a story or poem about helping someone in need and submit it to Stone Soup.

- Stone Soup, the Magazine http://www.stonesoup.com/home.html

M'm M'm Good!

We have been eating Campbell's soups since 1867! There is an excellent timeline of the history of Campbell's Soup that could serve as a starting place for talking about advertising, as many of the original ads are shown. Extend this study to include other advertising slogans. Make a list of those the students know. Now, have the students plan an advertisement for a new product they dream up – it could be a new drink, candy, article of clothing, toy or mode of transportation. Use a graphics program to create their ad.

- Campbell's Soup M'm M'm Good! http://www.campbellsoup.com/
- History http://www.campbellsoup.com/center/history/default.cfm
- Advertising Slogans http://advertising.utexas.edu/research/slogans/
- Coca Cola Advertising Slogans http://www.gds.co.za/klerksdorp/coca-cola/slogans.html
- Burma Shave Rhymes http://www.paturnpike.com/traveler/summer97/page5.htm
- Columbian Coffee http://www.juanvaldez.com/menu/advertising/index.html
- Famous Milk Famous http://www.whymilk.com
  - Got Milk? http://www.gotmilk.com/game.html (play the game)
- Chefboy http://www.chefboy.com/ (visit the Arcade and make a commercial)
- Television Commercials http://www.televisioncommercials.com/home/home_main.asp (look at the classics)

On a more serious note, the same techniques Campbell's or the Dairy Council uses to sell your students soup or milk are the same techniques drug dealers use to sell them drugs. Make your students aware of common selling techniques: everyone is doing it, famous people (maybe a popular school ball player or student) use it, you deserve it, it makes you feel better, and you will be part of the crowd.

Other ideas

- Use your spreadsheet to compare the nutrients and calories on the soup labels. Graph your results.
- Survey students, parents, school personnel about their favorite soup and graph the results using a spreadsheet.
- Collect soup labels for you school.
  Campbell's Labels For Education http://www.labelsforeducation.com/
- Make a bulletin board similar to Andy Warhol's painting. Put up big letters that say "M'm M'm Good!" and have students write on soup can shaped paper, what makes them feel good.
  Andy Warhol's Campbell's Tomato Soup http://www.warhol.org

Ramadan

Ramadan is the ninth month of the Moslem calendar. It is called the Fast of Ramadan and lasts the entire month. It is a time of worship and contemplation. A time to strengthen family and community ties. Depending on the Muslim calendar - can be celebrated in November, December, January, or February. Beginning celebration depends on the sighting of the moon. Help your students understand the Muslim faith by learning about the Five Pillars of Faith. Create a poster for each pillar to display in your room.

- The Five Pillars of Faith http://www.holidays.net/ramadan/pillars.htm

One of the pillars of faith is to fast in order to concentrate on faith and spend less time on the concerns of everyday lives. During Ramadan, it is forbidden to tell a lie, slander, talk behind someone's back, give a false oath or be greedy or envious. Not bad rules to live by all the time. Discuss these rules with your students and post them in your room. Challenge your students to obey these rules during the month of Ramadan.

- The Fast of Ramadan http://www.holidays.net/ramadan/story.htm

Data Varies

Super Bowl Sunday
Last Sunday in January
More people, world wide, watch the Superbowl than any other event on television. So take advantage of Superbowl Fever to encourage research, writing and oral communication.

- SuperBowl http://www.superbowl.com/
- Play Football for Kids http://www.playfootball.com/indexflash.html
- Sports Illustrated for Kids http://www.sikids.com/index.html

Rules of the Game
Writing rules for any game is not an easy task, but provides an excellent opportunity for practicing sequencing, clear and concise writing. It also lends itself to the 6+1 Traits for Writing format, especially organization and voice. Select a simple game that the students know well. Something like checkers or 4 Square would work. Have the students write an introduction to the game and then list the rules. To check their work, have the students exchange their rules with another group and see if they can play the game.

- Playing the Game http://www.football.com/rulesabc/play_game.shtml
- Learn2 Understand American Football http://www.learn2.com/05/0544/0544.asp
- 6 + 1 Traits of Writing http://www.nwrel.org/eval/writing/definitions.html

Play-by-Play Commentator
Get a videotape of a game played by one of your middle school or high school teams. If this is not available, video tape your class playing a game. Show segments of the game have students provide the play-by-play commentary. This activity really makes students think on their feet. I would keep the segments short to begin with, as this is very difficult. To get a feel for what play-by-play commentary is, go to any of the major news sites and listen to their 'real time' sports. These are not just sites for children, so you might want to talk about Internet safety and appropriate viewing materials.

- ABC sports http://espn.go.com/abcsports/ (has audio and video achieve)
- CBS sports http://cbs.sportsline.com/u/cbs/sports/
- NBC sports http://www.msnbc.com/news/spt_front.asp?ta=y
- EPSN http://espn.go.com/

Online Research
Teach students to be effective Internet surfers. Go to a popular search engine. I like Google because it has a simple, clean presentation. Prepare a handout for the students to use similar to this:

Search for	Number of hits	Technique
football		Word in lower case
footballs		Plural
football+history		Use the + sign
"football history"		Use quotation marks

"origins of football"		Use quotation marks, and specific term

Some search engines are case sensitive, so you might want to try using a capital letter. Try it with another sport. *Note for teachers: try typing in football+ lesson plan. Surprised?*
- Origins, A Brief Look At Football History http://www.football.com/rulesabc/origins.shtml

Play Power Football Math
- Power Football http://www.funbrain.com/football/index.html

Special Days

January 1
New Year's Day

Five Quick Things To Do
1. Change your desktop - Calendar Wallpaper http://www.mamselle.ca/calendars.html or http://www.billybear4kids.com/desktop/calendar/program.html
2. Play a game - BrainPOP: New Year http://www.brainpop.com/specials/newyears/
3. Learn a little about the history of New Years - Annie's New Year History Page http://www.annieshomepage.com/newyearshistory.html
4. Find out how the Tournament of Roses Parade first started - http://www.tournamentofroses.com/
5. Eat something lucky - Lucky Food Around the World http://allrecipes.com/cb/w2m/seaspec/holiday/newyear/lucky/default.asp

After you have sung "Auld Lang Syne" and found out what it means, learn to say "Happy New Year in different languages. Cards with pictures of the country and the saying would make an excellent bulletin board. I like to give the students the lyrics for "auld Lang Syne" and have them translate, before we share what it really means. One verse is probably enough. Note that Robert Burns' birthday is later this month. The Happy New Year site is just a good overview of the history and customs associated with the holiday.
- Traditional Auld Lang Syne http://www.chivalry.com/cantaria/lyrics/auldlang.html
- What About Auld Lang Syne? (Translation) http://www.worldburnsclub.com/newsletter/auld_lang_syne_what_about.htm
- The Story Behind the Song http://www.robertburns.org/encyclopedia/AuldLangSyne.5.html
- Happy New Year http://wilstar.net/holidays/newyear.htm
- Learn to say "Happy New Year" in different languages http://www.merpy.com/newyear/
- World Encyclopedia http://www.emulateme.com/alphanationtext.htm

Eduplace has a very nice list of classroom activities related to the New Year. Note the multicultural activities. I think students would really enjoy playing Fuku Warai. You could use clip art to find face pictures and enlarge them. Then, look at ways people in other countries celebrate the New Year now and in ancient times.
- Eduplace Classroom Activities for January http://www.eduplace.com/monthlytheme/january/newyear.html
- New Year Celebrations Around the World http://www.geocities.com/Heartland/Plains/7214/newyear.htm
- Ancient New Year's Customs http://www.worldbook.com/fun/holidays/html/ancient.htm
- New Year's Celebrations Around the World http://www.rice.edu/projects/topics/internatl/holidays/new-years-page1.htm

- Celebrate! Holidays in the USA New Year
  http://www.usis.usemb.se/Holidays/celebrate/newyears.html

Ever wonder how the months and days of the week got their names? These make for good storytelling.

- Janus and January http://www.cs.utk.edu/~mclennan/BA/JO-DSJT.html#janus
- Mythology in the ESL Classroom
  http://www.yale.edu/ynhti/curriculum/units/1983/2/83.02.09.x.html#top

Calendars
History of the Calendar

Have you ever wondered how we came to have the calendar we have? Who was the first one to even think of a calendar? Check out these sites to see how the calendar has changed through the ages. Happy New Year, Or Is It? Offers an excellent, easy to read and understand article about how the modern calendar developed.

- Happy New Year, Or Is It? http://www.education-world.com/a_lesson/lesson045.shtml
- Calendars – Counting the Days
  http://www2.worldbook.com/features/calendars/html/calendars.htm
- Calendars Through the Ages http://webexhibits.org/calendars/calendar.html
- Gregorian Calendar http://es.rice.edu/ES/humsoc/Galileo/Things/gregorian_calendar.html
- Egyptian Origin of the Gregorian Calendar http://www.egypt-tehuti.org/articles/gregorian-calendar.html
- The British Switch to the Gregorian Calendar http://www.crowl.org/Lawrence/time/britgreg.html
- Calendars; Counting the Days http://www.worldbook.com/fun/calendars/html/calendars.htm
- Calendar Trivia http://www.furrfu.com/magpies/calendars.html

Classroom Calendars

Thirty days hath September,
April, June and November.
All the rest have thirty-one
Save February alone
Which hath twenty-eight, in fine,
Till leap-year gives it twenty-nine.
Richard Grafton, 1570[iv]

I look forward to the New Year and changing my calendar. There is something about a fresh start, clean page, and anticipation of things to come that energizes me. I hope some of these calendar ideas will get your creative juices flowing, also. The Clickable Calendar is the best calendar I know for classroom use. If your class does a daily opening that includes the day of the week…put this one on your favorites list and use it daily. What fun! Then, post a quote of the day.

- Clickable Calendar http://www.clickablecalendars.com/click.htm
- Quotes of the Day http://www.quotationspage.com/qotd.php3
- Calendar Quotes, Thoughts, Songs and Stuff http://www.calendarzone.com/quotes/

Calendars on the Net

The Internet has many, many calendars some that relate to the curriculum, such as This Day in History and others that are multicultural, such as the Aztec Calendar and still, others that are just interesting.

- Curriculum Tie-ins – I find these are very helpful in meeting standards that require the history of the discipline. Start out your lesson with a personal glimpse of one of the pioneers in the field.
  - This Day in History http://www.historychannel.com/thisday/
  - Mathematicians Throughout the Year http://www-groups.dcs.st-and.ac.uk/~history/Day_files/Year.html

o This Day in Music History http://datadragon.com/day/select.shtml
o Women in History and Art http://www.wic.org/cal/idex_cal.htm
o Famous Birthdays http://www.famousbirthdays.com/
- Multicultural Calendars – The first site on the list of holidays that have been submitted by children in different countries. There is a place where you can have your students write about one of their favorite holidays and send it in. The One World Global Calendar is probably the most extensive multicultural calendar on the net. The other sites on the list describe different calendar systems. Some are no linger in use, but other, such as the Chinese Calendar are used today. (See February for suggestions about celebrating Chinese New Year)
  o Multicultural Calendar http://www.kidlink.org/KIDPROJ/MCC/ (entries sent in by children)
  o The One World Global Calendar http://www.zapcom.net/phoenix.arabeth/1world.html
  o Aztec Calendar http://www.azteccalendar.com/
  o Mayan Calendar http://tim.to/maya.html
  o Islamic Calendar http://webexhibits.org/calendars/calendar-islamic.html
  o Chinese Calendar http://webexhibits.org/calendars/calendar-chinese.html
  o Jewish Calendar http://webexhibits.org/calendars/calendar-jewish.html
- Calendars on the Net – some of these are just for fun, like the Game A Day calendar, but the others have a wealth of information for classroom use.
  o A to Z Calendars to Print Out http://www.enchantedlearning.com/calendar/
  o Game A Day http://www.agameaday.com/kidshome.htm
  o The Calendar Zone http://www.calendarzone.com/
  o Daily Almanac http://erebus.phys.cwru.edu/~copi/events.html
  o Great Dates http://www.fi.edu/qa98/dates/dates.html
  o Inquiry Almanac http://www.fi.edu/qa96/archive.html
  o Earth Calendar http://www.earthcalendar.net/

Make Your Own Calendar

Use the calendars listed above to make your own classroom calendar. Divide your class into 12 groups. Give each group a month to research. Have them make a calendar for their month. You can use a spreadsheet program, such as Excel or a desktop publishing program for the template. Some graphics and word processors also come with a calendar template. Or, you can use an online calendar maker. I have found that these are somewhat limited in what you can do with them, but worth looking into. For younger children, you might want to make a Calendar Timeline. Hang the names of the months on your trusty clothesline. Add holidays and birthdays to the timeline. This could go all around the room. Take digital pictures of the classroom and/or birthday boy or girl when the time comes as a personal reminder of the day. Hang up the pictures.
- Make an online calendar for your classroom/school http://www.localendar.com/elsie
- Make a calendar online Billy Bear's New Year http://www.billybear4kids.com/holidays/newyears/fun.htm
- Jan Brett http://www.janbrett.com/calendars.htm
- Make a calendar http://www.primarygames.com/holidays/new_years/crafts.htm

Timelines

Need another idea for teaching time? Try a timeline. Education World has an excellent lesson plan about timelines. Check out some of the great timelines at AlternaTime – you will find a timeline on just about any subject!
- Timelines – A Timeless Teaching Tool http://www.educationworld.com/a_lesson/lesson044.shtml#tips
- AlternaTime http://www2.canisius.edu/~emeryg/time.html

January 2, 1920
Isaac Asimov

"What's so amazing that keeps us stargazing
And what do we think we might see?
Someday we'll find it, the rainbow connection,
The lovers, the dreamers, and me."

The Muppet Movie - Kermit[v]

Isaac Asimov, writer, scientist, teacher, was born on January 2, 1920 in Russia, but moved to America with his family in 1923. An avid reader, he wrote his first story at age 11. Read his essay on science fiction to gain a better understanding of this genre. Always a dreamer and a scientist, he merged these two loves in his numerous short stories and novels. In his biography, his three laws of robots are defined. Other writers since have used these laws.

- The meaning of science fiction http://www.asimovs.com/_issue_9908/asimov_name.shtml
- Biography http://search.biography.com/print_record.pl?id=12396
- Imperial Trantor http://home.interstat.net/~slawcio/foundation/cover.html

Asimov's fictional character, Lucky Starr, agent of the interplanetary law enforcement agency the Council of Science and his faithful sidekick, John Bigman Jones, a short, tough man born and raised on the great agricultural farms of Mars, have had many adventures. Have your students use a word processor to write another episode. For inspiration, refer to the artwork of Michael Whelan and the Encyclopedia Galactica. You can also use images to illustrate their stories.

- Michael Whelan: Gallery of Art Work based on Asimov's work
  http://www.glassonion.com/gallery/archive/authors/asimov/
- Encyclopedia Galactica http://www.geocities.com/Area51/Dimension/1136/

Asimov's Three Laws of Robots

1. A robot may not injure a human being or, through inaction, allow a human being to come to harm.
2. A robot must obey the orders given it by human beings except where such orders would conflict with the First Law.
3. A robot must protect its own existence as long as such protection does not conflict with the First or Second Laws.

Robots
Often it is the dreamer or artist or writer that inspires the scientist. Asimov's robots have inspired a number of real-world robots. Look at how robots are being used today. This would be a great time to use LogoWriter or LegoLogo software and the to learn how to program a robot. You can download a public domain version at Logo Software. Ask students to write a description of a robot that they would like to own, maybe one that does homework or mows the yard or carries out the garbage. Use a paint program to draw their robot.

- NASA: Cool Robot of the Week http://ranier.oact.hq.nasa.gov/telerobotics_page/coolrobots.html
- Honda: Humanoid Robot http://world.honda.com/robot/
- Robot Zoo http://www.thetech.org/exhibits_events/traveling/robotzoo/
- Robot Information Central http://www.robotics.com/robots.html
- Logo Software http://el.www.media.mit.edu/groups/logo-foundation/products/software.html

January 3, 1953
Happy Birthday, Alaska
Take a trip to the last frontier; visit Alaska. The following Internet sites provide lots of information and activities to help you learn about our 49th state.

- Alaska for Kids http://www.state.ak.us/kids/
- Alaska Curriculum Ideas http://www.education-world.com/a_curr/curr112.shtml
- The Teel Family Web Site http://www.teelfamily.com/

Use a publisher program to create a travel brochure highlighting Alaska's wonders. Look for additional information about the Alaska Gold Rush and dog sleds on Jack London's birthday, January 12.

January 4
Phyllis Reynolds Naylor, Newbery Award Winner, 1992

Phyllis Reynolds Naylor has been writing stories and book since she was in Kindergarten and sold her first manuscript when she was 16. Even though she has published 100 books and many articles and short stories, she has had 10,335 rejections. As she says, "That's ten-thousand three hundred and thirty five! I sure bought a lot of stamps and envelopes. But if I hadn't stuck with it, if I hadn't tried to make my next story better than the one before, I probably wouldn't ever have got up the courage to write books."[vi] The following are a couple of brief biographies of Ms. Naylor.

- Phyllis Reynolds Naylor http://www.childrensbookguild.org/PhyllisNaylor.html
- Author Interviews http://www.teachingk-8.com/html/fs_author.html
- de Grummond Collection http://www.lib.usm.edu/~degrum/findaids/naylor.htm
- Alice Fan Club http://www.simonsays.com/subs/txtobj.cfm?areaid=183&pagename=newalice
- Phyllis Naylor, Internet Public Library http://www.ipl.org/youth/AskAuthor/Naylor.html

Writer's Notebook

Phyllis Reynolds Naylor is often asked where she gets the ideas for her stories. Her answer is from things that have happened in her life and things she sees or reads about. This is one of the hardest things for students to do..come up with something to write about. Ms Naylor keeps a notebook of ideas and as she gets more information or finds pictures or maps, she puts them in the notebook until she is ready to write. Have you students begin a writer's notebook. Use a desktop publishing program to design a cover for the notebook. Staple the cover to blank pieces of paper. Take legal size paper and fold up the bottom so that it is the same size as a regular 8 _ by 11. Staple it to make a pocket. Now you're ready to start collecting ideas.

Lesson Plans
- Shiloh Lesson Plan #1 http://www.umcs.maine.edu/~orono/collaborative/shiloh.html
- Shiloh Lesson Plan #2 http://www.planetbookclub.com/kids/archive/shiloh/shilohmain.html
- Shiloh Teaching Guide http://www.randomhouse.com/teachers/guides/shil.html
- Reluctantly Alice Lesson Plan http://www.umcs.maine.edu/~orono/collaborative/reluctantly.html

Some books by Phyllis Reynolds Naylor
    Shiloh – Newbery Award
    Saving Shiloh
    Shiloh Season
    The Alice Series, including:
    The Grooming of Alice
    Alice the Brave
    All But Alice
    The Agony of Alice
    Alice in Between
    Reluctantly Alice
    Achingly Alice
    Alice in Lace
    A Spy Among the Girls

A Traitor Among the Boys
The Boys Start the War: The Girls Get Even
Boys Against Girls
Walker's Crossing
The King of the Playground
Sang Spell
The Fear Place
The Healing of Texas Jake
Peril in the Bessledorf Parachute Factory

January 4, 1809
Louis Braille

An accident in his father's shop caused this young French boy to loose the sight in both of his eyes. But, being both creative and intelligent, he continued with his schooling and learned to play the cello and organ. He heard about an alphabet code being used by the army. This code was a series of raised dots and dashes so the soldiers could 'read' with their fingers in the dark, therefore not giving away their position to the enemy. Braille improved on this code to create a smaller, easier to use code he called Braille. Here are a couple of nice biographies.

- The Story of Louis Braille http://www.his.com/~pshapiro/braille.html
- Louis Braille - A Light in the Dark http://www.brailleinstitute.org/Education-Louis.html
- Facts about Louis Braille's Birthplace http://www.blind.net/bg410002.htm

The Eye

Learn a little more about the eye and sense of sight by looking at the following Internet sites. The National Eye Institute offers some great graphics to explain the anatomy of the eye and various eye diseases. These can either be viewed online or saved for off line viewing. You can view the dissection of a cow's eye, but as this site says, it doesn't replace the real thing. For some great experiments, try the innovative ideas at Sight. And finally, the last site is a quick overview of how the eye works.

- Photograph, Image and Video Catalog http://www.nei.nih.gov/photo/index.htm
- Cow Eye Dissection http://www.exploratorium.edu/learning_studio/cow_eye/
- Sight: Vision Experiments and Models http://faculty.washington.edu/chudler/chvision.html
- Sense of Sight http://yucky.kids.discovery.com/flash/body/pg000142.html

Braille

Learn about the Braille alphabet. You can also download a demo copy (fully functional) of BrailleMaster. This will translate any word document into Braille. You can also download a Braille font to install on your computer.

- The Braille Alphabet http://thinkquest.phillynews.com/tq1997/11799/data/blind2.html
- BrailleMaster http://www.braillemaster.com/download.htm
- Braille Font http://www.tsbvi.edu/Education/fonts.html

Odds and Ends

- Bob Miller's Light Walk http://www.exploratorium.edu/light_walk/index.html
- VI Guide for Parents and Teachers http://www.viguide.com/
- Courtesy Rules of Blindness http://www.blind.net/bg000001.htm
- The Magic Eye http://www.magiceye.com/ (this is really cool!)

- The Seeing Eye http://www.seeingeye.org/
- Information about Eye Disease http://www.blind.net/bg200001.htm

January 5 – 7
Epiphany

The season of Epiphany begins with the arrival of the three kings in Bethlehem to visit the baby Jesus and ends the day before Lent. Many cultures celebrate the arrival of the kings or Magi with gifts and parties. In old English, it was known as 12th Night and is remembered in the song "The Twelve Days of Christmas." This is the Christmas celebration for the Eastern Orthodox Church. It is known as Dia de los Santos Reyes in Spain and other Spanish speaking countries. Three Kings Day is also celebrated in France and Italy.

- For images portraying the Magi, refer to http://www.textweek.com/art/magi.htm
- Epiphany Traditions Around the World http://anglicansonline.org/resources/epiphany.html
- 12 Days of Christmas (lyrics and midi file) http://www.12days.com/library/carols/
- Origin of the Twelve Days of Christmas http://www.cin.org/twelvday.html
- A rebuttal of the Origin of the Twelve Days of Christmas http://128.242.205.65/holidays/xmas/12days.htm#origins

January 8
Elvis Presley's Birthday

What can I say? I've been an Elvis fan since 54,000,000 other viewers and I first saw those swiveling hips on the Ed Sullivan Show in 1956! He sang *Hound Dog* and *Love Me Tender*. I even have a Basset hound. But I only sing *Hound Dog* to her in the privacy of my own home! You, however, can listen to Elvis sing it on a number of Internet sites. My favorites are:

- Broadcast Elvis http://www.broadcastelvis.com/
- Elvis Discography http://www.elvispresleyonline.com/html/elvis_discography.html (this one provides the lyrics, in case you have forgotten!)

Song lyrics provide material for analyzing syntax. Have the students copy and paste a song lyric into a word program. Then, rewrite the lyrics correcting the grammar.

Original Lyrics	Correct Copy
Hound Dog *words & music by Jerry Leiber and Mike Stoller* http://www.musiclinks.nl/songteksten/Elvis_Presley/5164.html	Hound Dog You are not a hound dog that cries all the time. Well, you have never caught a rabbit and you are not my friend. When they said you were high classed, they told a lie. You have never caught a rabbit and you are not my friend.

Want to learn a little bit more about the King?
- Official Elvis Web Site http://www.elvis.com/
- Unofficial Elvis Homepage http://www.ibiblio.org/elvis/elvishom.html

In 1955, RCA Records paid the unheard of sum of $25,000 to Elvis for the rights to the music and gave a pink Cadillac to his mother. What do recording stars of today earn? You do the math!
- The Billboard http://www.billboard.com/

Interview parents and grandparents about favorite singers; make a spreadsheet of your class top billboard. What trends to you see? What is the all time favorite recording star?
- Music Hall of Fame http://www.epluri.com/TSA/AMHall/AmericanMusicHall.html
- Rock and Roll Hall of Fame http://www.rockhall.com/

January 8, 1815
Battle of New Orleans
During December 1814 through January 1815, a diverse force of soldiers, sailors, and militia, including Indians and African Americans, defeated Britain's finest white and black troops drawn from Europe and the West Indies. This victory forced the British to recognize United States claims to Louisiana and West Florida and to ratify the Treaty of Ghent.[vii] A truly amazing account of this battle, illustrated with artwork and artifacts is online at the first site. There is also a complete lesson plan available at the same site.
- The Battle of New Orleans http://lsm.crt.state.la.us/cabildo/cab6.htm
- Lesson Plan: The Battle of New Orleans http://lsm.crt.state.la.us/museum/education/lesson5.htm

Another good resource is an article by A. Wilson Greene for the History Traveler. To get a better idea of the location, superimpose the map of the battle onto a modern map of New Orleans by bringing both into a paint program. Label the maps important places and strategic events.
- The Battle of New Orleans
  http://www.thehistorynet.com/HistoricTraveler/articles/1998/03989_cover.htm
- Map of the Battle http://www.thehistorynet.com/HistoricTraveler/images/02972_map.htm
- Map Quest http://www.mapquest.com/
- Jackson's account of the battle
  http://www.hillsdale.edu/dept/History/Documents/War/America/1812/South/1815.01.19-Jackson.htm
- The Scottish Regiment http://www.argylls.co.uk/93norleans.html
- Winning the Battle of New Orleans
  http://www.americaslibrary.gov/pages/jb_0108_jackson_1_e.html

Bonus - trace the route Jackson would have taken from Nashville to New Orleans. With Map Quest, check the driving distance and the travel time it would take today.
- MapQuest http://www.mapquest.com

Old Hickory and the Pirate
One of the great stories stemming from that battle is that of Andrew Jackson, Old Hickory, and the Pirate, Jean Lafitte. Lafitte was a well-known pirate, a buccaneer. But, he was also a hero of the Battle of New Orleans. This is an exciting adventure story about two men, who came together to save the new nation. Enjoy this story with your students. Have them make a picture book using presentation tools, such as PowerPoint or HyperStudio. Add music and background pictures and of course, pirate ships.

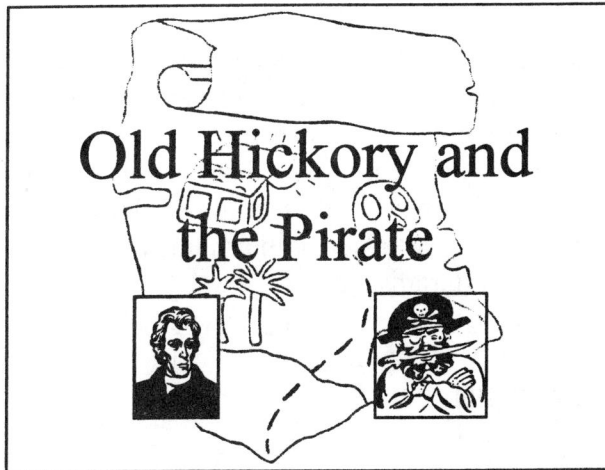

Old Hickory and the Pirate

- Andrew Jackson http://www.whitehouse.gov/history/presidents/aj7.html
- Jackson http://odur.let.rug.nl/~usa/P/aj7/about/bio/jackxx.htm
- Jean Lafitte http://www.crimelibrary.com/americana/lafitte/main.htm
- Beej's Pirate Images http://www.ecst.csuchico.edu/~beej/pirates/

Music and Memory

Jimmy Driftwood was a principal and history teacher who wrote the song, Battle of New Orleans to help his students remember facts about the battle. Listen to the music and sing the verses. Music often helps us remember basic facts. Have the students write a song about something they are currently studying. You could use a familiar melody, such as Twinkle, Twinkle Little Star.

- Jimmy Driftwood's Battle of New Orleans
  http://www.geocities.com/Heartland/Ranch/9198/war1812/w1812f.htm

Odds and Ends

- ThinkQuest: War of 1812
  http://www.thinkquest.org/library/lib/site_sum_outside.html?tname=22916&url=22916/orleans.html
- America's Wars http://www.multied.com/wars.html

January 11, 1815
John MacDonald – 1st Prime Minister of Canada

"One people, Great in Territory, Great in Resources,
Great in Enterprise, Great in Credit, Great in Capital."[viii]

Sir John MacDonald

Use this day to learn more about Canada's 1st Prime Minister, John MacDonald and the country he loved. Begin by reading his biography. Put MacDonald's history in perspective by aligning it with what was happening in the United States during the same time he was prime minister.

- Canada's 1st Prime Minister http://macdonald.egate.net/sirjohn/sir.html
- A Teacher's Tribute http://macdonald.egate.net/sirjohn/birthday.html
- Sir John Alexander MacDonald http://www.nlc-bnc.ca/2/18/h18-229-e.html

Scottish Plaids or Tartans

There are three days this month that we celebrate and honor Scotsmen; January 8 at the Battle of New Orleans, January 11, John MacDonald's birthday (he was born in Glasgow, Scotland) and January 25 Robert Burns Night. All of these men would have worn a distinct plaid. (see A Teacher's Tribute.) This is a type of material unique to each family or clan. Learn more about the history of the Scottish Tartans. Look at the Land's End catalog for plaid shirts to see how these traditional tartans are used today. Have the students use a paint program to design a tartan or plaid for their family.

- Tartan http://www.scotland-calling.com/tartans.htm
- Scottish Tartans Museum http://www.scottishtartans.org/museum.html
- Highland Dress http://www.namehistory.co.nz/index_l.htm?inner_page_l.htm$high_dressem.htm
- Land's End Catalog http://www.landsend.com

Canadian Resources

What do we know about our neighbor to the north? For instance, did you know that it is the second largest country in the world? Can you name her 10 provinces and 3 territories? Check out these two sites to learn more. Have your students develop a trivia game of Canadian facts and see if they can stump each other.

- About Canada http://www.emulateme.com/canada.htm
- Canadiana http://www3.sympatico.ca/goweezer/cnadiana.htm
- Lesson Plan for Sir John MacDonald's Birthday http://canadateachers.about.com/library/weekly/aa011101.htm

January 12, 1876
Jack London

Popular novelist, Jack London, lived as exciting a life as he wrote about in his many stories of adventure. In his words,

> *"I would rather be ashes than dust!*
> *I would rather that my spark should burn out in a brilliant blaze*
> *than it should be stifled by dryrot.*
> *I would rather be a superb meteor,*
> *every atom of me in magnificent glow,*
> *than a sleepy and permanent planet.*
> *The proper function of man is to live, not to exist.*
> *I shall not waste my days in trying to prolong them.*
> *I shall use my time"*[ix]

Between 1900 and 1916, London completed over fifty books. Many of his books were about dogs. In *Call of the Wild*, Jack London tells the story of Buck the dog, dognapped from his comfortable home in California to the gold fields of Alaska. But Buck was not a pampered house pet. *"And this was the manner of dog Buck was in the fall of 1897, when the Klondike strike dragged men from all the world into the frozen North."*

Dog Breeds Spreadsheet

After reading a biography of Jack London to learn more about his short, adventurous life, and about his intense writing style, study the magnificent dogs that were so important to him.

- Jack London http://www.parks.sonoma.net/JLStory.html
- American Kennel Club http://www.akc.org/index.html
- All About Dogs http://www.a2zofpets.com/dogs/index.shtml
  - Breeds of Dogs http://www.a2zofpets.com/dogs/breeds.shtml

Use a spreadsheet to make a graph of the kinds of dogs people in your class, grade level or school have. Identify the pets by breed and group (collie, working dog).

Dogs Enrich Our Lives

Dogs are an important part of our lives. Whether they are working dogs, show dogs or just our pet. Learn more about 'mans best friend.' Begin with Working Dogs.

- Working Dogs http://www.fbi.gov/kids/k5th/kidsk5th.htm

1. Westminster Dog Show

The first Westminster Dog Show was held from Tuesday, May 8 to Friday, May 11, 1877 in Gilmore's Gardens, located at Madison Avenue and 26th Street in New York City. There were 1,201 dogs shown in that first show.[x]

- Westminster Dog Show
  http://www.petsmart.com/dog/answers/behavior/articles/article_6888.shtml
- Car Dogz http://cardogz.com/columns/vet/archive/2000_02_23.shtml

2. Guide Dogs

Since 1946, the Guide Dog Foundation for the Blind, Inc. has provided guide dogs free of charge to people who are blind or visually impaired.

- Guide Dog Foundation http://www.guidedog.org/
- Guide Dogs of America http://www.guidedogsofamerica.org/
- The Seeing Eye http://www.seeingeye.org/

3. Iditarod Race

Buck was a working dog. Today, there are many sled dogs still at work. One of the most famous dog sled races is the Iditarod. You can learn all about the Iditarod write to the mushers and follow the races. Have you students write a fictional, historical story in first person about the first dog sled run from Anchorage to Nome in 1925 that transported the life-saving serum that saved a town. There is an excellent map that describes each leg of the race students can use for description of setting.

- The Iditarod Race http://www.workingdogweb.com/Iditarod.htm
- Iditarod Home page http://www.iditarod.com/
- The Iditarod Trail http://www.cabelasiditarod.com/trail.html
- The Iditarod Lesson Plan http://www.education-world.com/a_lesson/lesson103.shtml
- Nature: Sled Dogs http://www.pbs.org/wnet/nature/sleddogs/

Alaskan Gold Rush

Gold Rush Days are celebrated in August. Many more Internet sites and activities are provided there, but for a quick reference, refer to The Official Student Information Guide to Alaska. Note that Alaska became the 49th state on January 3, 1959. Ask you students to find out when their state was awarded statehood.

- Gold Rush http://www.dced.state.ak.us/tourism/student.htm

Some books by Jack London
Call of the Wild
White Fang

The Sea Wolf
Klondike and Other Stories
Martin Eden
To Build a Fire and Other Stories
The Iron Heel
The Best Short Stories of Jack London

January 13, 1910
1st radio broadcast
What a difference radio brought to the lives of people worldwide. Enjoy this day by making a radio broadcast of your own or recreating a vintage broadcast. There are many different scripts available at the Old Time Radio Script Collections site; my favorite is the Lone Ranger. Use the recorder on your computer to record your own sound effects or save those downloaded from the Internet, combine that with background music.

- Old Time Radio Script Collections http://www.genericradio.com/
  - Clayton Moore – The Lone Ranger http://members.tripod.com/~ClaytonMoore/ (download the original theme and opening)
- Old Time Sound Effects http://www.old-time.com/sfx.html
- Background Music http://www.midcoast.com/~lizmcl/dramusic.html

Learn more about old time radio at these sites.

- Old Time Radio http://www.old-time.com/
  - Timeline with audio clips http://www.old-time.com/golden_age/index.html
- Museum of Television and Radio http://www.mtr.org/

Radio Makes a Difference
Radio not only brought news to people across the country, but sports and entertainment. Look at these sites to see how radio brought the nation together.

- Grand Ol' Opry http://www.old-time.com/sfx.html
- President Franklin Roosevelt: Fireside Chats http://www.mhric.org/fdr/fdr.html
- Radio Commercials http://www.old-time.com/commercials/index.html
- Library of Congress: Recorded Sound Reference Center http://lcweb.loc.gov/rr/record/
- Old Time Radio Sites http://www.old-time.com/
- Big Bands http://old-time.com/music/index.html
- List of Radio and Television History Sites http://www.rtvf.unt.edu/links/histsites.htm
- Radio Days http://www.otr.com/index.shtml

National and International Radio Broadcasts
Listen to radio from around the world. Compare the lead story from different countries.

- National Public Radio http://www.npr.org/
- Public Radio International http://www.pri.org/PublicSite/home.html
- British Broadcasting Company http://www.bbc.co.uk/radio1/

Odds and Ends

- National Geographic and National Public Radio have teamed up to bring exciting adventures to your radio. Listen in…. http://www.nationalgeographic.com/features/radiox/frame.html
- Make a Radio Documentary http://www.soundportraits.org/education/how_to_record/

January 15, 1929
Martin Luther King

In 1983, the 98th Congress passed Public Law 98-144 to honor the birthday of Martin Luther King, Jr. This was first celebrated as a Federal legal holiday on January 20, 1986 and has been observed on the third Monday of January since that time. For a guide to the holiday and suggestions for celebrating refer to the following Internet sites:

- Martin Luther King Day http://www.mlkday.com/
- The King Center http://www.thekingcenter.com/
- Celebrate! Holidays in USA: Martin Luther King
  http://www.usis.usemb.se/Holidays/celebrate/mlk.html

Timeline Game

After researching the life and times of Martin Luther King, Jr., have the students make a board game based on the timeline of his life. Use a layout similar to Monopoly, and yes, have "Go To Jail." Rules I have used are, 1) if you land on a positive event, such as *1953, Martin and Coretta are married*, jump for joy – move two spaces 2) if you land on negative events, such as *1959, King's home is bombed*, miss 1 turn, 3) when a space marks an event when a person was arrested, Go To Jail and miss two turns, then return to that space on the board, and 4) if you land on a question space, draw a card from the pile. If the student answers the question correctly, get another turn. I start with his birth and end when congress declares the Martin Luther King holiday. This way, you can include his death, but not end with such an unhappy event. Divide the students into small groups assigning each group a specific job. Group One, prepare the game board, Group Two, write the rules of the game, Group Three, write the trivia questions for the question spaces. All students will need to study Martin Luther King's biography to play the game successfully. Note: I use a publishing software program to make the game board. You can rotate the text and use pictures. Limit the number of spaces and keep the game board to an 8 _ X 11 piece of paper so you can print many copies of the game.

Martin Luther King on the Net http://www.holidays.net/mlk/index.htm
- AFRO-Americ@ Salute to Martin Luther King
http://www.afroam.org/history/mlkpage/mlkmainpage.html

Martin Luther King's Speeches
King is remembered for his moving and inspiring speeches. There are many Internet sites where you can read the text of his most famous speeches, but at the Standford site, you can hear his powerful voice. Use the format provided at the Thinkquest site to have students write their own "I Have A Dream" speech.
- Martin Luther King, Jr. Homepage http://www.stanford.edu/group/King/
- Martin Luther King, Jr. http://www.seattletimes.com/mlk/holiday/index.html
- I Have A Dream http://web66.coled.umn.edu/new/MLK/MLK.html
- Write a Speech http://library.thinkquest.org/10320/Starter.htm

Additional Activities
- Classroom Activities http://www.eduplace.com/monthlytheme/january/activities_mlk.html
- Web Quest http://www.fayette.k12.il.us/techcurr/shayla/mlk.htm

One of the legacies Martin Luther King, Jr. left us is the call to make a difference, to stand up for what is right. At Do Something, your students can join with students around the world to look at issues that still concern society.
- Do Something http://www.dosomething.org

January 15
Coming of Age – Japan
In Japan, twenty is the age of majority. This means that twenty-year-olds have both responsibility and privileges; they are now considered an adult. Coming of Age ceremonies are held in communities and in family homes. Research the history and traditions surrounding this cultural holiday.
- Coming of Age Ceremony http://www.tokujo.ac.jp/Tanaka/WWW97/Hello4/megumi.html
- Japanese Coming of Age Ceremony and History
http://www.personal.psu.edu/users/j/e/jeh227/COAday.html

Read personal stories about the Coming of Age ceremony.
- Coming of Age Day Celebration http://www.rice.edu/projects/topics/internatl/holidays/coming-of-age1.htm
- Coming of Age Day - Seijin-no-hi http://www.kidlink.org/KIDPROJ/MCC/mcc0268.html

Many cultures recognize the significance of a particular time when young people enter the adult world. Read Coming of Age Ritual in Other Cultures for a cross-cultural perspective of this time in a young person's life. Use a Spider Map graphic organizer to record the different culture's ceremonies.
- Coming of Age Ritual in Other Cultures http://www.mjoe.org/cultures/index.html
- Coming of Age Ritual http://www.mjoe.org/cultures/japan1.html
- Spider Map http://www.ncrel.org/sdrs/areas/issues/students/learning/lr1grorg.htm

For most young people in the United States, there is no clear-cut day when they become an adult. We have many different birthdays that are associated with achieving adult rights and responsibilities. Have the students use the Internet to research the driving age in different states. Drinking laws also vary from state to state. Have them look up the date for registering for the draft and voting. How old do people have to be in your state before they can marry without their parent's consent? Discuss the idea of having one date, nationwide for these events. What are the pros and cons? Write a journal entry where they can record their ideas, feelings and personal experiences.

Karaoke

One way young people in Japan celebrate their Coming of Age is karaoke. You can enjoy karaoke in your classroom. Download a Midi Karaoke Player. Add some tunes and you're set. If you just want quick and easy kids songs, try eatsleepmusic and for television themes, go to Midi Karaoke.

- Computer Karaoke Homepage http://www.teleport.com/~labrat/karaoke.shtml
- Eatsleepmusic http://www.eatsleepmusic.com/
- Midi Karaoke http://www.geocities.com/Broadway/3386/

Challenge the students to use a presentation tool, like PowerPoint, and develop their own karaoke.

January 16, 1919
18th Amendment – *repealed by 21 Amendment (December 5, 1933)*

The 18th Amendment prohibited the manufacture, sale, or transportation of intoxicating liquors. The "noble experiment" was undertaken to reduce crime and corruption, solve social problems, reduce the tax burden created by prisons and poorhouses, and improve health and hygiene in America. However, alcohol became more dangerous to consume; crime increased and became "organized"; the court and prison systems were stretched to the breaking point; and corruption of public officials was rampant. The amendment was repealed in 1933 by the 21st Amendment. Read about the history of temperance and prohibition in the United States to see what lead up to the passing of this amendment. Then, read the exact amendment. I've included an essay about the 18th Amendment and a reference to the Encyclopedia Britannica: amendments. Another day during this month was set by an amendment, the 20th Amendment. What is it?

- Temperance and Prohibition http://www.cohums.ohio-state.edu/history/projects/prohibition/Contents.htm
- Amendment 18 http://www.nara.gov/exhall/charters/constitution/18th/18th.html
- Amendments to the Constitution http://www.law.emory.edu/FEDERAL/usconst/amend.html
- Policy Analysis http://www.cato.org/pubs/pas/pa-157.html
- Encyclopedia Britannica: Amendments http://www.britannica.com/eb/article?eu=2753&tocid=0

In ratifying the 18th Amendment, people tried to legislate morals. We know that there are many things that are legal, but could be harmful. Discuss with your students the passing of an amendment that forbad the use of cigarettes, for instance. We are faced with a similar situation today in that the use of drugs is forbidden. Many feel that if they were legalized there would be control of the production and distribution, therefore making the consumption safer. Gun control is similar, but different because of the 2nd Amendment. This is an interesting discussion for your students.

How Laws Are Made

If your students did feel there should be a law against the *manufacture, sale, or transportation* of cigarettes, how would they do it? The first site is a simple step-by-step description of how laws are made; the second one is more detailed.

- How Laws Are Made http://bensguide.gpo.gov/3-5/lawmaking/index.html
- How Our Laws Are Made http://thomas.loc.gov/home/lawsmade.toc.html

January 17, 1706
Benjamin Franklin

"If you would not be forgotten
As soon as you were dead and rotten
Either write things worth reading
Or do things worth the writing."

Benjamin Franklin

Benjamin Franklin not only wrote these words, he lived them. To learn more about his amazing life, enjoy looking at The World of Benjamin Franklin. The article describes seven different things Benjamin Franklin is known for. Divide your class into seven groups and assign each group a different topic. Have them develop a presentation about their topic using PowerPoint or another presentation tool. For many different and interesting classroom activities, visit the Franklin Institute Online.

- The World of Benjamin Franklin http://sln.fi.edu/franklin/rotten.html
- Franklin Institute Online http://sln.fi.edu/learning.html

Franklin is known for his many wise sayings. Have the students each take a different saying and make a poster using clip art to illustrate the saying. The sayings are in alphabetical order so that when you print them out; display them in your room for alphabet cards.

- Words of Wisdom http://sln.fi.edu/franklin/printer/abc.html

Odds and Ends

- Autobiography of Benjamin Franklin http://odur.let.rug.nl/~usa/B/bfranklin/frankxx.htm
- Benjamin Franklin http://www.english.udel.edu/lemay/franklin/
- Think Quest: Benjamin Franklin
  http://www.thinkquest.org/library/lib/site_sum_outside.html?tname=22254&url=22254/home.htm
- Benjamin Franklin Resource Guide http://tlc.ai.org/franklin.htm
- The Electric Franklin http://www.ushistory.org/franklin/ (with the famous kite experiment)

January 18, 1882
A. A. Milne

"I am a Bear of Very Little Brain, and long words bother me."
A. A. Milne, Winnie-the-Pooh

Alan Alexander Milne was born in London on January 18, 1882. As a father, Milne wrote stories for his son, Christopher Robin, about a little black bear in the London zoo. A soldier returning to London from Canada gave the bear, Winnipeg, Winnie for short, to the zoo. Christopher was so fond of the bear; he renamed his stuffed bear, Edward Bear, Winnie the Pooh. For more information about Milne and his classic stories, refer to these biographies:

- A. Milne http://www.kirjasto.sci.fi/aamilne.htm
- A. Milne http://www.penguinputnam.com/yreaders/pooh/pooh3.htm
- A Selection of Poetry http://ingeb.org/songs/thekingb.html
- A Word For Autumn, by A. Milne http://www.bartleby.com/237/16.html (an essay for older students.)

Fan Sites

Winnie the Pooh and his friends are so popular among children and adults alike that there are many Internet sites developed and maintained by fans – people who love the "chubby little cubby old bear."

You will find coloring pages, online activities, maps, character sketches and much more. I have listed some sites, but there are new ones being developed as we speak. One of my favorites is listed first because you can listen to Charles Kuralt read "Winnie the Pooh."

- Winnie the Pooh http://www.penguinputnam.com/Pooh/start.htm
- Winnie the Pooh and Friends http://worldkids.net/pooh/
- Winnie the Pooh – Mr. Sanders Home http://www.just-pooh.com/home.html
- Winnie the Pooh Character Guide http://www.poohguide.com/
- Winnie the Pooh http://www.winniethepoohbear.net/
- The Literary World of Winnie the Pooh http://www.bright.net/~kbaumle/
- Winnie the Pooh http://www.angelfire.com/bc/WINNIE/

Classroom Projects

1. Have your students bring one of their favorite stuffed animals to school and use a word processor to write a story about an adventure they have with their stuffed animal. This is a good time to emphasize character development. As a prewriting activity, divide students into pairs and have them tell their partner about their animal, then have the animals introduce themselves.
   - Creative Writing Tutorial – Character Development http://www.teenwriting.about.com/teens/teenwriting/library/blextras/blextra134.htm
2. Tour Winnipeg, Canada
   - Winnipeg, Canada http://www.tourism.winnipeg.mb.ca/
3. Join the Teddy Bear Project
   - The Teddy Bear Project http://www.ne.com.au/~mwells/teddybear.htm
4. Learn about the black bear- the original Winnipeg was a black bear from Canada.
   - American Black Bear http://species.fws.gov/bio_bear.html
   - Black Bear Facts http://www.geocities.com/Yosemite/Trails/1470/bears.html

Some Books by A.A. Milne
Winnie the Pooh
The House at Pooh Corner
When We Were Very Young
Now We Are Six
The Red House Mystery

January 19, 1807
Robert E. Lee

> *"Duty then is the sublimest word in the English language.*
> *You should do your duty in all things.*
> *You can never do more,*
> *you should never wish to do less."*
>
> General Robert E. Lee

Robert E. Lee was the commander of the Southern armies. As a graduate of West Point, Lee distinguished himself in service to his country. But, when President Lincoln offered him the command of the Union army, he replied, "...though opposed to secession and a deprecating war, I could take no part in the invasion of the Southern States."[xi] Read a biography of this American hero. Note his views on slavery. Students will be interested in his horse, Traveller. Have the students use a search engine to look for other famous horses.

- Biography http://www.stratfordhall.org/rel.htm
- Biography http://odur.let.rug.nl/~usa/B/relee/relee.htm
- Biography http://www.civilwarhome.com/leebio.htm
- Traveller http://www.cavalry.org/traveller.htm
- Google http://www.google.com (search: "famous horse")

Of course, to do justice to studying the Civil War would take more in-depth study than what I am suggesting, but these sites will give you a quick overview.

- American Civil War http://americancivilwar.com/civil.html
- The American Civil War Overview http://www.civilwarhome.com/overview.htm
- The American Civil War Homepage http://sunsite.utk.edu/civil-war/

Take a Field Trip
Visit Lee's Boyhood Home Stratford Hall and then tour West Point.

- Tour Lee's Boyhood Home http://members.aol.com/rphs44/leetour.htm
- West Point http://www.usma.edu/

January 19, 1809
Edgar Allan Poe

"Those who dream by day
are cognizant of many things
which escape those who dream by night."

Edgar Allan Poe, *'Eleanora'* 1842

Orphaned at the age of 3, this soulful writer has been entertaining and chilling readers for over a century and a half with his dark, macabre storytelling. He has been given credit for inventing the detective story. The Mystery Writers of America's annual award for the best mystery is called the Edgar. Read more about his unhappy, sad life to better understand how it may have influenced his writing.

- The Edgar Allan Poe Society of Baltimore http://www.eapoe.org/
- Index to Edgar Allan Poe's Biography http://www.poedecoder.com/Qrisse/bioindex.html

Use a presentation tool, such as PowerPoint, to make a multimedia book of one of his famous poems. I think Annabel Lee or the Raven would be good ones to do. Use backgrounds, sounds, pictures and clip art to make the book come alive.

- Works of Edgar Allan Poe http://bau2.uibk.ac.at/sg/poe/Work.html
- Tales of Mystery and Imagination http://bau2.uibk.ac.at/sg/poe/Tales.html
- Edgar Allan Poe: Works http://www.gothic.net/poe/works.html

Classic Mysteries for Young People
The mystery genre may be attributed to Edgar Allan Poe, but most mystery writers of today say that they became interested in mysteries the first time they read a Hardy Boys or Nancy Drew book. Enjoy reading one of these classics with your class. Help them understand the mystery genre by looking for the classic traits of a mystery book. Also, refer to January author Phyllis Reynolds Naylor, January 4, for some of her mystery books.

- The Making of a Mystery
  http://www.sonic.net/~mk/work/broderbund/programs/galaxy/sample/lesson.html
- The Mystery http://lee.boston.k12.ma.us/d4/curr/stand/genres/mysterykey.asp
- Helping Children Understand Literary Genres
  http://www.ed.gov/databases/ERIC_Digests/ed366985.html
- What Is A Mystery http://www.mysterynet.com/learn/lessonplans/
- Challenging Children with Mystery Stories
  http://www.yale.edu/ynhti/curriculum/units/1989/4/89.04.06.x.html
- Kids Love a Mystery http://www.mysterywriters.org/kidsloveamystery/index.html
- Sisters in Crime http://www.sistersincrime.org/

The Hardy Boys
- The Hardy Boys http://www.larilana.com/stratemeyer/hardy/hardy.htm
- The Unofficial Hardy Boys Homepage http://www.geocities.com/fwdixon/
- The Hardy Boys Casefiles http://home.columbus.rr.com/skywarppro/HardyBoys/index.html

Nancy Drew
- The Unofficial Nancy Drew Homepage http://www.geocities.com/nancydrewpage/
- Around the World with Nancy Drew http://www.geocities.com/Athens/crete/4048/
- Nancy Drew – A Brief History http://www.larilana.com/stratemeyer/drew/nancydrew.htm
- Nancy Drew http://www.bookloversden.com/series/girls/Drew/Drew.html

Odds and Ends
- The Edgars and Other MWA Awards http://www.mysterywriters.org/awards.html
- Free Mini Book: The Raven http://www.wotch.com
- Youth Sleuths Backgrounds
  http://www.fortunecity.com/meltingpot/missouri/1008/sleuthbgsindex.html

January 20
Inauguration Day (every 4th year)
20th Amendment

> *"I do solemnly swear*
> *that I will faithfully execute*
> *the Office of President of the United States,*
> *and will try to the best of my ability,*
> *to preserve, protect and defend*
> *the Constitution of the United States."[xii]*

Note: George Washington added the phrase, "So help me God."
Although it only happens every 4th year, the Inauguration of the President is an event unique to the United States – the orderly transference of power. It is always fun to look back to the history of the inauguration and the ceremonies and celebrations that mark the day. Certainly, this provides an opportunity to develop a timeline that could be continued in February when you celebrate President's Day. The facts are made personal with the many human-interest stories that accompany them.
- Inauguration Day http://www.pbs.org/inaugural97/index.html
- The PBS Newshour http://www.pbs.org/newshour/inauguration/
- History of the President's Inauguration
  http://www.whitehouse.gov/history/presidents/index.html

- Inaugural History and Trivia http://inaugural.senate.gov/history/index.cfm
- Inaugurations http://americanhistory.si.edu/presidency/6b_frame.html
- 20th Amendment http://gi.grolier.com/presidents/aae/side/20amend.html

Reading the Inaugural speeches that former presidents have delivered provide a framework for a discussion of speech writing. First, have the students read a favorite speech aloud. (I wouldn't have them choose William H. Harrison as it lasted 1 hour and 45 minutes!) Then, have them write a speech that they would like to see the President deliver. Most people report public speaking is their biggest fear. By giving students some skills and opportunity to develop them, we are giving them a gift that lasts a lifetime.

- Great American Speeches http://www.pbs.org/greatspeeches/timeline/index.html
- Presidential Inaugurations http://lcweb2.loc.gov/ammem/pihtml/pihome.html
- Learn to Write a Speech http://www.learn2.com/06/0694/0694.asp
- Toastmasters International: 10 Tips for Successful Public Speaking http://www.toastmasters.org/tips.htm

Not to be ignored, the president's wives have played an important and memorable role in the history of the presidents and their inaugurations.

- First Ladies of the United States http://www.geocities.com/Athens/Parthenon/1402/preswife.html

January 24, 1848
California Gold Rush

> Miner #1: I'm not feeling too well today. You better take my temperature.
> Miner #2: What's the matter?
> Miner #1: I think I have 'gold fever!'
>
> Eric's Jokes – WayBack, PBS[xiii]

Neither John Marshall, an employee at the Sutter Sawmill on American River, nor his employer, John Sutter, had any idea how his discovery of a few flakes of gold would effect the nation. Before it was over, nearly half a million people would come to California seeking their fortune. Begin your discovery at the Gold Rush Museum in Oakland. You will find wonderful stories and artifacts and curriculum ideas. One of the coolest things at this site if the 360-degree pictures that put you on the spot! Another, are the Gold Rush stories. Then, visit the other two museums in San Francisco and Sacramento, and, don't forget the ladies…

- Gold Rush: Oakland Museum http://www.museumca.org/goldrush/
- San Francisco Museum http://www.sfmuseum.org/hist1/index0.1.html#gold
- Gold Rush: Sacramento Bee http://www.calgoldrush.com/
- Women in the Gold Rush http://www.goldrush.com/~joann/

Submit your student's Gold Rush jokes.

- The American Experience: California Gold Rush http://www.pbs.org/wgbh/amex/kids/goldrush/index.html

January 25
Robert Burns Night – Scotland, England, Newfoundland
We started this month by singing one of Robert Burns most famous songs, *Auld Lang Syne*. Now is the time to celebrate this much-loved poet's life with a traditional Robert Burns Night Celebration! This holiday, celebrated world wide, wherever Scots or those of Scottish heritage gather, commemorates the

life, times and writing of Scotland's favorite bard. Plan your event to include a tour of Scotland, a brief biography, some Scottish bag pipes, some traditional foods and, of course, some poetry reading. You could divide your class into groups, giving each group a job to do. If you need more jobs, add more things to make the event special, such as invitations, decorations and hosts. End your event by holding hands and singing *Auld Lang Syne*.

A Traditional Burns Night
- The Burns Supper http://www.worldburnsclub.com/supper/burns_supper_1.htm

Biography
- The Beginners Robert Burns http://www.worldburnsclub.com/begin/robert_burns.htm#Fuss
- Burns Country http://www.robertburns.org/
- The Bard http://www.rabbie-burns.com/index.cfm

Scotland
- Scotland http://www.scotland.org/
- Welcome to Scotland http://www.geo.ed.ac.uk/home/scotland/scotland.html
- Tour Scotland Tour Ireland http://www.earthwisdom.com/irelandmain.html

Music
- Comin Thro the Rye http://www.worldburnsclub.com/poems/poems.htm (lyrics)
- Scottish Tunes http://www.contemplator.com/tunebook/scotmidi.htm
- Folk Music of England, Ireland, Scotland and America http://www.contemplator.com/folk.html

Foods
You may not have the ingredients readily available for Haggis, a traditional Scottish delicacy, but you can read about it. You easily can make scones. Tea is a traditional drink.
- Haggis http://www.robertburns.org/suppers/haggis.shtml
- Scones http://www.joyofbaking.com/scones.html
- Grandma's Shortbread http://www.geocities.com/Heartland/Farm/7446/granshort.html
- Scottish Shortbread http://www.cookierecipe.com/az/ScotishShortbread.asp

Poetry

> *Rabbie Burns was born in Ayr*
> *And noo he stands in Geordie Square*
> *And if you want to see him there*
> *Take the bus and pay your fare.*
> An Old Schoolyard Rhyme

Some of the poems that I think are the easiest for children to read are "My Love Is Like a Red, Red Rose", "The Book Worms", and "Rantin Rovin Robin." "The Marriage of Robin Red Breast and The Wren" is harder to read because of the dialect, but it would make a great reader's theater. The quote that we all remember, *The best laid schemes o' mice an' men, Gang aft a-gley,* is from "To a Mouse." This has a difficult dialect, but is a must!
- List of Poems http://www.worldburnsclub.com/poems/poems.htm
- Robert Burns' Poems and Songs http://www.bath.ac.uk/~exxdgdc/poetry/poets/rab1.html

- Robert Burns, Scotland and Auld Lang Syne http://www.worldburnsclub.com/index.htm

Curling

O curlers, come, we're brithers a',
Come join the curling game;
Our eyes are keen, our arms are true,
Our courage is aflame;
I n winter air, and sport so rare,
T he stones our weapons be,
We'll make the fight with honest might,
To gain the victory:
A man who is a curling man,
No better man than he.[xiv]

Although there is a lively debate about the origin of curling, millions of people around the world are involved in the sport today. And it has been an Olympic event since 1924.
Both the Scots and the Flemish who immigrated to Scotland during the reign of James VI, claim to be the inventors of the game. After reading a little about the origins and history of the game, play an online version. Then, visit a curling rink in your neighborhood or invite a curler to visit you classroom. Print the flags of the countries that curl and place them on that world map that you've used before. On the playground, make a curling court. Adapt the court to your climate and use whatever stones you have at hand.

- What is Curling? http://cbs.sportsline.com/u/olympics/nagano98/features/kidzone/kid_curling.html
- Description of the Game http://icing.org/game/descript/index.htm
    - Play the game online http://cbs.sportsline.com/u/olympics/nagano98/curling/i_game.html
- History of the Game http://icing.org/game/history/historya.htm
- Curling History Page http://home.istar.ca/~rockroll/curling.html (information about countries that curl)

January 26, 1788
Australia Day

Australia Day commemorates the day in 1788 that Captain Arthur Phillip took formal possession of the colony of New South Wales and became its first governor. That day was honored as Australia Day in 1808. Go to the National Australia Day site to learn more about modern and historical Australia Day celebrations. What a good excuse to visit the "land down under" where it is summer now and get to know the people, their stories and history, and of course, see their wonderfully unique animals. Learn a few words of Aussie slang, too. Put up a large map of Australia on the bulletin board with "G'Day, mate." for the title. Use this as a backdrop for student reports and projects. Divide the class into small groups. Give each group a different topic. Be sure to visit the National Geographic site for koalas, boomerangs and kangaroos.

- National Australia Day http://www.nadc.com.au/home/
- Australia Day History http://www.adc.nsw.gov.au/history.htm
- Map http://www.auslig.gov.au/facts/map.htm
- Australian Slang http://www.koalanet.com.au/australian-slang.html
- Geography and History http://www.koalanet.com./australian-geography-history.html

- Australia @ National Geographic http://www.nationalgeographic.com/downunder/
- The Australian People http://www.ozemail.com.au/~enigman/australia/people.html
- Guide to Australia http://www.csu.edu.au/australia/
- Picture Australia http://www.pictureaustralia.org/
- Unique Australian Animals http://home.mira.net/~areadman/aussie.htm
- Creation Stories and Traditional Wisdom http://www.ozemail.com.au/~reed/global/mythstor.html
- One Week Australia Unit Plan http://panther.bsc.edu/~lrcrook/australia.htm

January 27, 1756
Wolfgang Amadeus Mozart

Born into a happy family, Mozart was the son of a court musician. From an early age, he showed extreme musical talent. He was to blossom into one of most gifted composers and performers the world has ever known. To help your students understand the life and times of Mozart, have them prepare a musical timeline. Refer to the Mozart Project for a chronology of both Mozart's life and world events. Using a presentation tool, assign each student a time frame to research and prepare. Develop a template for students to use that will provide uniformity. Put all of the slides together for a musical timeline.

Wolfgang Amadeus Mozart	
A Musical Timeline	• Serenade in D, "Haffner" is performed in Salzburg for the marriage of Elisabeth Haffner and Franz Xaver Spaeth.
• Mozart is born at Salzburg. • Treaty of Westminster between Britain and Prussia guarantees neutrality of Hanover.	Click here to listen to a midi clip
	• Declaration of Independence is approved by Congress.
January 27, 1756	**July 1776**

Develop a Standard Template
1. Use the same background
2. Use the same timeline bar across the bottom
3. Use the same color scheme
4. Put the Mozart information on the left and the 'world' information on the right
5. Use the same box and clip art for musical clips

Because you will be using information from the Internet, teach the students the correct format for documenting the sources they use.
- How to compile a bibliography http://www.intac.com/~aroldi/biblio.html

Mozart Links
- Wolfgang Amadeus Mozart http://w3.rz-berlin.mpg.de/cmp/mozart.html
- The Mozart Project http://www.mozartproject.org/
- Wolfgang Amadeus Mozart Index
  http://radio.cbc.ca/programs/takefive/composers/MOZART/WA_MOZART.html

Mozart and Brain Development

Does listening to Mozart make you smarter? If so, how? In what way? Is this claim real or just hype? Put on some Mozart while you browse through these links to research on the subject. It can't hurt.

- The Mozart Effect http://parenting-baby.com/Parenting-Baby-Music-Research/Music-Research.html

January 29
National Puzzle Day

You know what to do.

- One Player http://www.oneplayer.com/PuzzleRing.asp
- Jigsaw Puzzles http://www.squirrel-rehab.org/puzzle/index.html
- Puzzle Depot http://www.puzzledepot.com/
- The Ultimate Puzzle Site http://www.dse.nl/puzzle/index_us.html
- Bonus.com http://www.bonus.com (search for puzzles)
- Interactive Mathematics and Miscellany Puzzles http://www.cut-the-knot.com/games.html (these are great!)

January 31
Gerald McDermott

Gerald McDermott won the Caldecott medal for <u>Arrow to the Sun</u> and the Caldecott Honor for <u>Anansi the Spider</u> and <u>Raven, A trickster Tale from the Pacific Northwest</u>. McDermott's beautiful and striking retelling of traditional folktales gives us an opportunity to use the auto-draw feature on simple paint programs. Find a folktale that you really like. Read or tell it to your class. Discuss the characters and setting. Also discuss the country of origin. Look at Gerald McDermott's illustrations noting his use of color and geometric shapes. Give each student a strip of paper with the text they are to illustrate. Then, have them use a paint program to make their illustration. Collect all of the pages and make your own book. Most computers have a simple paint program built in.

- Myths and Legends http://pubpages.unh.edu/~cbsiren/myth.html
- Folktales and Fables http://faculty.billerica.mec.edu/~classpage/folktale.html

Additional Links

- CyberGuide for Arrow to the Sun http://www.nashville.k12.tn.us/CyberGuides/arrow/arrow.html
- The Reading Room http://showcase.netins.net/web/reading/juvmcd.html
- Gerald McDermott http://www.geraldmcdermott.com/

Some books by Gerald McDermott
Arrow to the Sun – Caldecott Award
Anansi the Spider – Caldecott Honor
Zomo the Rabbit: A Trickster Tale from West Africa
Musicians of the Sun
Tim O'Toole and the Wee Folk
Raven: A Trickster Tale from the Pacific Northwest – Caldecott Honor
Coyote: A Trickster Tale from the American Southwest
The Fox and the Stork
The Stonecutter: A Japanese Folk Tale
Daniel O'Rourke

January 31, 1919
Jackie Robinson

> *"A life is not important except in the impact it has on other lives."*
>
> Jackie Robinson

Jackie Robinson was the first black man to "officially" play in the big leagues in the 20th century. He led the Brooklyn Dodgers to six National League titles and one victorious World Series. When he retired from the game, Jackie Robinson went on to champion the cause of civil rights.

- National Baseball Hall of Fame http://baseballhalloffame.org/
- Jackie Robinson Scrapbook http://www.sportingnews.com/archives/jackie.html

Timeline

Next month, February, is African American Month. You could not choose a better person to begin your celebration than Jackie Robinson. I would begin by looking at Baseball, the Color Line and Jackie Robinson. Assign each student, or small group, an athlete to research. Make a timeline and fasten the report to the timeline. The Dodgers have an excellent timeline of Jackie Robinson's life with quicktime movies.

- African American Barrier Breakers in Sports
  http://www.utexas.edu/students/jackie/robinson/barriers.html
- Jackie Robinson and Other Baseball Highlights http://lcweb2.loc.gov/ammem/jrhtml/
  - Baseball, the Color Line and Jackie Robinson
    http://memory.loc.gov/ammem/jrhtml/jrabout.html
- Jackie Robinson's 50th Anniversary
  http://www.dodgers.com/archive/1997/dodgers97/jackietl.html

Lesson Plan: Civil Rights

Beyond the Playing Field is a wonderful collection of primary documents with easy to use lesson plans about Civil Rights, Character Development and Civic Responsibility.

- Beyond the Playing Field http://www.nara.gov/education/teaching/robinson/robmain.html

Newspaper Writing Activity

After the students have had an opportunity to learn about Jackie Robinson, have them write a newspaper article as if they had interviewed him. Use your word processor to create a newspaper by using the column option or if you have a publishing software program, use the newspaper feature.

- Stealing Home: A Tribute To Jackie Robinson http://www.sound.net/~vivian/jackie2.html
- The Jackie Robinson Interview http://www.inthegardenstate.com/unionmedia/robinson/Intro.htm
- The Jackie Robinson Society http://www.utexas.edu/students/jackie/

The Science and Math of Baseball

To tie into your science curriculum, the Exploratorium has an excellent project called the Science of Baseball. The Dodgers have math problems for all grade levels related to baseball.

- Exploratorium's Science of Baseball http://www.exploratorium.edu/baseball/
- Baseball Math http://www.dodgers.com/kids/classroom/

Need to learn more about the game? Check out Learn2 Understand Baseball.

- Learn2 Understand Baseball http://www.learn2.com/05/0542/0542.asp

[i] Auld Lang Syne http://www.wilstar.com/xmas/auldlangsyne.htm January, 15, 2001 (a nice audio version)

[ii] Lewis Carroll http://www.fortunecity.com/meltingpot/nicaragua/1105/carrolpage1.html February 5, 2001

[iii] Maurice Sendak http://homearts.com/depts/relat/sendakf1.htm February 7, 2001
http://www.eyeontomorrow.com/embracingthechild/Bookspecialsendak.htm February 9, 2002

[iv] A Rhyme and A Reason, http://www.geocities.com/Athens/Forum/3041/september.html January 15, 2001

[v] The Rainbow Connection http://www.geocities.com/aequum/rainbowconnection.html July 14, 2001

[vi] Phyllis Reynolds Naylor http://www.childrensbookguild.org/PhyllisNaylor.html January 15, 2001

[vii] Cabildo, The Battle of New Orleans http://lsm.crt.state.la.us/cabildo/cab6.htm July 14, 2001

[viii] John A. MacDonald http://collections.ic.gc.ca/charlottetown/fathers/jmacdonald.html July 14, 2001

[ix] Jack London, His Life and Books http://www.parks.sonoma.net/JLStory.html January, 20, 2001

[x] 125th Westminster Kennel Club http://www.usanetwork.com/sports/wm2001/fastfacts.html August 10, 2001

[xi] Robert E. Lee http://www.stratfordhall.org/rel.htm July 13, 2001

[xii] Article II, Section 1, of the U.S. Constitution

[xiii] WayBack, PBS, Eric's Jokes http://www.pbs.org/wgbh/amex/kids/goldrush/jokesreaderics02.html July 15, 2001

[xiv] The Game History http://icing.org/game/history/historya.htm February 3, 2001

5/7/2002

February

"How do I love thee? Let me count the ways."

Elizabeth Barrett Browning

Special Month

Black History Month
In February 1926, Dr. Carter G. Woodson and others sought a way to recognize the achievements and contributions of African Americans. Originally, the observance was one week. Since 1976 the entire month of February has been set aside to celebrate Black History Month. For Black History Month posters, refer to the Diversity Store http://www.hmsdc.com/

History

"I believe that any man's life will be filled with constant and unexpected encouragement, if he makes up his mind to do his level best each day, and as nearly as possible reaching the high water mark of pure and useful living."

Booker T. Washington

One way to begin the month's celebration is to see how much your students know about African American history. At the AA History Challenge site, students can take a quiz to assess their knowledge. Teachers can request a class code so they can save their student's scores. Take the challenge again at the end of the month. To help students gain knowledge about important historical figures and events in African American history, refer to the additional Internet sites. To help students put people and events in perspective is to use a chain of events graphic organizer. In this case, I would literally have the students record the event on a strip of paper about 1-_ inches wide and 8 inches long. Students key in the information using a word processor. Link all of the pieces of the chain together. See how long you can make the chain by the end of the month.
- African American History Challenge http://www.brightmoments.com/blackhistory/
- Chain of Events Graphic Organizer http://www.sdcoe.k12.ca.us/score/actbank/tchain.htm

Additional Internet Sites
- The African American Mosaic http://www.loc.gov/exhibits/african/intro.html
- Black History Month Who Am I Calendar
  http://teachervision.com/tv/features/calendar/february_01.html
- Black History: Exploring African American Issues on the Web
  http://www.kn.pacbell.com/wired/BHM/AfroAm.html
- Black History Timeline http://home.nbci.com/LMOID/resource/0,566,-576,00.html?tag=p-lv.mi.s-1035.p-lv.s-576
- African American firsts http://www.umkc.edu/imc/blackfir.htm
- Black History http://www.blackhistory.com/
- Black History on the Internet http://www.education-world.com/a_curr/curr056.shtml
- Black History http://www.kn.pacbell.com/wired/BHM/AfroAm.html

Lesson Plans and Activities
For additional lesson plans to use throughout the month refer to these excellent sites.
- 10 Activities Celebrate the Achievements of African Americans http://www.education-world.com/a_lesson/lesson159.shtml

- Preschool Activities http://www.preschoolrainbow.org/black-history.htm
- Black History in Boston http://teachervision.com/lesson-plans/lesson-4557.html
- Black History Treasure Hunt http://www.education-world.com/a_lesson/lesson052.shtml
- Stamp on Black History http://library.thinkquest.org/10320/Stamps.htm#anchor305420
- Black History Tour http://library.thinkquest.org/10320/Tourmenu.htm
- Afro-American History http://www.umkc.edu/imc/blackhis.htm
- Black History Month http://www.infoplease.com/spot/bhm1.html

Road to Freedom

One of the most difficult events in our history to help students understand is the issue of slavery. There are many interesting web pages to use with the theme of freedom. Many of these have activities and lesson plans. The drinking gourd sites work very well combined with a science unit on stars and the universe.

- The Road to Freedom http://www.education-world.com/a_lesson/lesson101.shtml
- Slave Narratives http://ancestry.nbci.com/search/rectype/biohist/slavnarr/promo.htm
- Harriet Tubman http://www.gale.com/freresrc/womenhst/tubmanh.htm
- Taking the Train to Freedom http://www.nps.gov/undergroundrr/contents.htm
- The Underground Railroad http://www.nationalgeographic.com/features/99/railroad/
- The Underground Railroad http://www.cr.nps.gov/nr/travel/underground/thhome.htm
- Underground Railroad http://www.cr.nps.gov/aad/ugrnhl.htm
- Follow the Drinking Gourd http://www.contemplator.com/folk2/gourd.html
- Guide to Follow the Drinking Gourd http://www.madison.k12.wi.us/planetarium/ftdg1.htm
- Astronomy Background http://www.madison.k12.wi.us/planetarium/ftdg2.htm

Arts and Letters

For an outstanding resource of classic African American literature, refer to the first Internet site. My favorite and one I feel all students should read or have read to them during this month is Heroes in Black Skins by Booker T. Washington. This fits in so well not only with Black History Month, but also with Hero Week.

- African American Literature Links
  http://curry.edschool.virginia.edu/go/multicultural/sites/aframdocs.html

Refer to the Quotes page to read and hear the inspiring quotes of contemporary as well as historical African Americans. Have the students make posters for each of the quotes, add a picture of the speaker and a brief commentary about who the person is or was. Display them in your school cafeteria.

> "I am America. I am the part you won't recognize.
>   But get used to me. Black, confident, cocky;
>   my name, not yours; my religion, not yours;
>   my goals, my own; get used to me."
>
> - Muhammad Ali
> - Born: Cassius Clay
>   January 17, 1942
> - Boxer

- African American Quotes http://www.factmonster.com/spot/bhmquotes1.html

View the works of African American Artists. Make a collage in the style of Romare Bearden and learn about a wonderful African American photographer, Teenie Harris and view the life and times she documented with her camera.

- Art History 101 http://www.artnoir.com/history101.html
- Romare Bearden-Style Collages http://www.education-world.com/a_lesson/01-1/lp221_10.shtml

- Teenie Harris
    - Interview http://www.pbs.org/blackpress/film/transcripts/harris.html
    - African Americans in Pittsburgh Photos by Teenie Harris
      http://www.pitt.edu/~elwst2/teenie.htm
    - Obituary http://www.post-gazette.com/magazine/20000223kids9.asp

Music

You can't do justice to studying about African Americans without taking pleasure in the contributions they have made to American music. Sit back and enjoy!

- Red Hot Jazz http://www.redhotjazz.com/
- Blues Midi Jukebox http://members.aol.com/WASC/blues/midi.htm
- The Blues http://www.geocities.com/BourbonStreet/Delta/6625/
- Old Time Gospel http://members.tripod.com/~RoseMcK/Jukebox-Gospel.html

Odds and Ends

- Down Home Healthy, Family Recopies of Black American Chefs
  http://familyhaven.com/health/dnhealth.html
- Black History Museum http://www.afroam.org/history/history.html
- Afro Americ@ http://www.afroam.org/index.html
- Black World Today http://www.tbwt.com/content/commentaries.asp
- Encyclopedia Smithsonian: African Americans http://www.si.edu/resource/faq/nmah/afroam.htm
- Black American Coloring Book http://teachervision.com/lesson-plans/lesson-4951.html
- African Heritage Cards http://www.bluemountain.com/eng3/african/
- African American Calendar for February
  http://www.enchantedlearning.com/calendar/blackhistory/feb.shtml

Heart Month

In 1963, Congress recognized the need to focus national attention on heart health when it mandated that the president of the United States issue a proclamation annually designating February as American Heart Month.[i] Heart Month is a time to acknowledge the ongoing efforts of the American Heart Association and other noteworthy health organizations to reduce the deadly risks and consequences of heart disease and stroke. How can you further their efforts in your classroom?

Learn How the Heart Works

Begin with a large group presentation using the Virtual Tour of the Heart. The BrainPOP Heart also has movies. Click on Experiments and Activities for heart-related off-line activities. Click on additional Internet sites for more information and activities.

- Virtual Body: Virtual Tour of the Heart http://www.medtropolis.com/VBody.asp
- BrainPOP: The Heart http://www.brainpop.com/health/circulatory/heart/index.weml
- The Heart, Online Exploration http://sln.fi.edu/biosci/heart.html
    - Enrichment Activities http://sln.fi.edu/biosci/activity/activity.html
- How the Body Works http://kidshealth.org/misc_pages/bodyworks/bodyworks.html
- The Life Pump http://www.imcpl.org/kids_circ.htm
- Virtual Body http://www.medtropolis.com/VBody.asp
- Your Gross and Cool Body: Cardiovascular System
  http://yucky.kids.discovery.com/flash/body/pg000131.html
- How Your Heart Works http://www.howstuffworks.com/heart.htm

Healthy Hearts

Challenge yourself and your students to a healthier life-style during the month of February. Set goals for eating healthier and getting more exercise. Keep track of your progress daily by recording your data on a spreadsheet. Check in daily by asking the students to show you a happy face or a sad face if they met or didn't meet their daily goal. Be sure to get the parent's permission before beginning this activity.

- Nutrition for Kids http://www.kelloggs.com/nutrition/nutritioncamp/learning/main.html
- Healthy Refrigerator http://www.healthyfridge.org/mainmenu.html
- Jump Into a Healthy Life http://tqjunior.thinkquest.org/5407/
- Physical Activity in Your Daily Life http://www.americanheart.org/catalog/Health_catpage9.html
- Healthy Heart Lesson Plan http://www.phdimensions.com/samplelesson.htm

Healthy Heart

My goal is to eat 5 fruits and vegetables, drink 3 glasses of milk and 6 glasses of water.
My goal is to sleep eight hours and exercise 30 minutes.

Week 1	# fruits and vegetables	# glasses of milk	# glasses of water	# hours of sleep	# minutes of exercise	
Monday	5	3	6	8	30	😊
Tuesday	4	2	6	8	0	😞
Wednesday						
Thursday						
Friday						
Week 2						
Monday						
Tuesday						
Wednesday						
Thursday						
Friday						
Week 3						

Wear Your Heart On Your Sleeve

Maybe because the heart is central to our physical well-being, we use 'heart' related terms to describe emotions also. Ask the students to define and illustrate each of these terms. Use either a word processor or presentation tool.

- ♥ heart-throb
- ♥ have a heart
- ♥ change of heart
- ♥ to know something by heart
- ♥ broken hearted
- ♥ heartfelt
- ♥ have your heart in the right place
- ♥ cry your heart out
- ♥ heavy heart
- ♥ faint of heart
- ♥ have your heart set on

American History Month

History In Your Hometown

Do you know the National Historic Landmarks in your state? Or, the buildings in your town that are on the National Register of Historic Places? Take a tour. Put up a state or city map and visit these important historical sites. With your digital camera, take a walking tour of your town looking for buildings or sidewalks or fence posts that have dates on them. Take pictures and when you return to the classroom, make a timeline of your hometown using the pictures and the landmarks you found on the Internet. *Note: the National Register of Historic Places site is a little difficult to navigate. To locate the historic building in your town, go to* **Research**, *and then click on* **database**. *If you don't know what you're looking for, go to* **location**. *When the database open, click on the* **queries** *icon. Then, simply key in your state and city.*

- National Register of Historic Places http://www.cr.nps.gov/NR/
- National Historic Landmarks http://www.cr.nps.gov/nhl/
- MapMachne http://plasma.nationalgeographic.com/mapmachine/

The 4th graders in my hometown put on a bus tour of our little city. Groups of students research the buildings and other important areas. The students act a tour leaders telling about the important events and people. Parents and guests are asked to purchase the tickets that go toward the expense of school buses. At the end of the tour, the busses return to our local museum for refreshments.

History Through Headlines

PBS offers an excellent activity that uses the local newspapers of three cities to look at the changes over time. You could have the students search your local newspapers archives to see the headlines of the times listed on your timeline (see above.)

- History Through Headlines
  http://www.nationalgeographic.com/xpeditions/activities/18/headlines.html

Then and Now

The Turn of the Century Child site offers stories, pictures and guiding questions about children from the early 1900. Explore this site with your class as a large group. Then, ask the students to make a Then and Now Book. Copy a picture from then of the school or children playing a game or whatever you like. Take a digital picture of students in your class doing the same thing – your school, playing on your playground, etc. Write captions for each picture. Be sure to document your source. I would not put these pictures on your web page without getting permission from the Turn of the Century Child site and the parents of your students. If you have access to old yearbooks, you could scan pictures of your school. Under no circumstances, use children's names or addresses. Does your school have a policy about putting student pictures and information on web sites? If not, you need one.

- Turn of the Century Child http://nuevaschool.org/~debbie/library/cur/20c/turn.html
- Federal Communications Commission CIPA Rules
  http://www.fcc.gov/Bureaus/Common_Carrier/Orders/2001/fcc01120.doc
- Federal Trace Commission Kidz Privacy Initiatives
  http://www.ftc.gov/bcp/conline/edcams/kidzprivacy/

Then	Now
Typing class, circa 1942	Computer class, circa 2002

International Friendship Month

"The only reward of virtue is virtue; the only way to have a friend is to be one."
- Ralph Waldo Emerson

"Make new Friends but keep the old;
One is Silver but the other Gold."

Author Unknown

What better month to celebrate friendship than February! There is a very nice Internet site from Australia that has lots of poems, quotes and activities. Other friendship sites follow.
- The Friendship Page http://www.friendship.com.au/
- Suite 101: Friendship http://www.suite101.com/welcome.cfm/friendship
- Friends and Friendship Web http://www.cyberparent.com/friendship/
  - Conversation Tips http://www.cyberparent.com/friendship/converse.htm
- National Association of Friendship CentresYouth Websites http://www.auysop.com/

Music

"Celebrate the happiness
that friends are always giving,
make every day a holiday
and celebrate just living!"

-- Amanda Bradley

Lots of songs reflect the need for and pleasure we take in our friends. Have your students brainstorm a list of 'friend' songs. I hope you enjoy some of my favorites:
- You Got a Friend in Me… http://www.mickey-mouse.com/soundfiles.htm
- That's What Friends Are For…
  http://orion.spaceports.com/~mmp/letras/ThatsWhatFriendsAreFor.html
- I get by with a little help from my friends…
  http://homepage.tinet.ie/~colinhawkes/songs/withalittlehelp.html

Language Arts Ideas
Reader's Theater
Copy and paste Judith Viorst's poem *Since Hannah Moved Away* into a word processor. Add reader at appropriate places. For older students, use *Friendship* from the Prophet.
- Since Hannah Moved Away http://www.poets.org/poems/poems.cfm?prmID=1660
- The Prophet: Friendship by Kahlil Gibran http://www.geocities.com/Athens/5484/Gib19.htm
Writing Ideas
Write an essay about man's best friend.
- Companion Dogs
  http://www.enchantedlearning.com/subjects/mammals/dog/companiondogs.shtml
- True Life Lassie Dogs http://ncnc.essortment.com/lassiedogs_ppw.htm
- American Kennel Club http://www.akc.org/
Write a list of instructions on how to be a friend.
- How to grow a friend…12 step program
  http://www.cyberparent.com/friendship/growdirectory.htm
Copy the first part of the proverb to a word document. Have the students complete the proverb and then check to see how close they were to the one at the Internet site.
- Friendship Proverbs http://www.friendship.com.au/quotes/quopro.html
Write an ABC Book about friendship.
- ABC's of Friendship http://www.paradiseawaits.com/Ties6.html
Make a list of synonyms for friend, such as chum, buddy, and pal. Copy the lyrics of Disney's *A Friend Like Me* to your word processor. Have the students use the find/replace feature of the word processor to

164

change the word friend to one of the synonyms. For fun, go to the Magic Songs and Music site and listen to *A Whole New World* in different languages.

- Disney Music Achieve: Aladdin - Friend Like Me http://www.geocities.com/mash_malene/musikarkiv/midiindex.html
- Aladdin's Magic Songs and Music http://www.agrabah.org/music.html

Read online books about peace.

- Kidz Care Story Center http://members.aol.com/kidz4peace/stories/

Crafty Things

Learn to make friendship bracelets, friendship lanterns and origami peace doves.

- Peace Pals Projects http://members.aol.com/_ht_a/pforpeace/peacepals/projects.htm
- Friendship Bracelet http://www.amazingmoms.com/htm/artfriendshipbracelet.htm

Lots of friendship ideas including GREAT paper dolls.

- Making Friends http://www.makingfriends.com/f_Friends.htm

Create a friendship poster with the word friend in English and in other languages. Decorate with hands, flags or pictures. I used PowerPoint but you could a publishing program or even a word processor.

- AltaVista.com http://www.altavista.com (click on **translate**)
- Poster to color http://members.aol.com/pforpeace/WorkItOut/color.htm

And for the teacher, join the friendship quilt web and make some new quilts and some new friends.

- Friendship Quilts http://thebunnie.tripod.com/FriendshipQuilt.html

Penpals

Find a penpal through Penpal and send him or her a friendship greeting card.

- Penpal.net http://www.penpalnet.com/
- Friendship Cards http://www.bluemountain.com/eng/frnd/
- Cuddlecards http://www.cuddlecards.com/
- Friendship Connection http://www.friendshipconnection.net/

Research

Planet Friendship encourages people to take a stand that will create a positive ripple effect in the world, like a stone dropping into a pond, that will help reduce the negativity and suffering on our planet and create new possibilities for people and the planet. One of the programs they sponsor is a cyberfair competition. Refer to the one titled Values. This was done by a group of high school students in Solvenia. They asked other students and adults around the world and in their home school and town to send in to then what they value, such as family, friends, etc. Replicate this research project in your school and compare your results with theirs.

- Planet Friendship http://www2.arnes.si/~sskkssb6s/
  - o Values that mean a lot to me http://www2.arnes.si/~sskkssb6s/values/values.htm

Teaching About Anger and Hate

The Teaching Tolerance site has many wonderful lessons for different multicultural holidays, but the one I want you to look at is the one about hate. Unfortunately, in today's world there is so much anger that is acted out homes, schools and playgrounds. Help students understand hate and how to deal with their own anger. These sites will be very helpful.

- Teaching Tolerance http://www.splcenter.org/teachingtolerance/tt-index.html
- Get Your Angries Out http://members.aol.com/AngriesOut/
- We Can Work It Out http://members.aol.com/pforpeace/WorkItOut/

Special Week

Hero Week, 2nd

"A hero is simply someone who rises above his own human weaknesses, for an hour, a day, a year, to do something stirring."

Betty Deramus, Detroit News

February is full of heroes; from presidents to African Americans to authors and scientists to everyday people, honor those and learn from them traits that can make all of us everyday heroes.

Lesson Plans and Ideas

- Heroes for our Planet http://216.12.138.32/index.html
- Heroes Online: Looking to the Web for Those We Can Look Up To http://www.education-world.com/a_lesson/lesson157.shtml
- Heroes http://www.education-world.com/a_sites/sites002.shtml
- Kids Can Make a Difference
  http://www.lightspan.com/kids/pages/makediff/cyberfair.asp?_prod=LS&_nav=T3_proj_makediff
  true stories about kids world wide, making a difference in their community

What Makes A Hero?

What makes a Hero? The Giraffe Project say that heroes are "people with vision and courage, people who are willing to stick their necks out and take responsibility for solving tough problems, on the planet and on the block."[ii] Begin this discussion by following the lesson plan outlined at Giraffe Project.

- Giraffe Project http://www.giraffe.org
  - Giraffe Lesson Plan http://www.giraffe.org/k12_3.html

Then, brainstorm a list of characteristics that make a hero. One list, from the Basic School in Obristvi[iii], Czech Republic includes:

Honesty	To know what is right and what is wrong, to follow these principles
Initiative	To do something because it is necessary to do it
Perseverance	To make progress in spite of difficulties
Flexibility	Ability to change a plan, to seek for different solutions
Organizing	To plan, arrange and carry out things in an organized way, always to seek for coherences, to keep order
Sense of Humor	To be merry and playful, to be able to enjoy life
Common Sense	To use good judgment, to weigh up the reality of the solution
Solution to a problem	To seek for a solution to a problem or situation
Responsibility	To feel and accept responsibility for oneself, one's decisions, for one's surroundings, nature and environment
Patience	To wait peacefully for somebody or something, to listen to people
Friendship	To make friends and keep on good terms with them by mutual trust and care, to be able to show friendship
Inquisitiveness	Desire to get to know the surrounding world, to discover new things
Cooperation	To work together on the same task, to accept the role in the group to be useful according to one's abilities, to help
Care	To show interest in other people, to imagine oneself in other person's place to help

Integrity	Balance of all personal roles, equilibrium

Have your students identify a person (famous or not, living or not) that they think is a hero. Read a biography or interview people who know that person. Identify the hero characteristics the person possesses based on the list generated. Have the students write why their person qualifies as a hero citing specific examples. Use the graphic organizer at the Hero of the Year site. Submit their story to My Hero.

- Character Counts http://www.charactercounts.org
- Role Model of the Month http://www.rolemodel.net/
- Hero of the Year http://w3.nai.net/~chewie/mainhero.htm
- My Hero http://www.myhero.com/home.asp
- Amazing Kids http://www.amazing-kids.org/
- Heroes of History http://www.heroesofhistory.com/index.html
  - Values of Heroes http://www.heroesofhistory.com/page3.html nice explanation with a Christian influence
- Heroes and Such, A Poem http://www.du.edu/english/calamus/fall95/heros.html
- Wind Beneath My Wings, by Bette Midler http://home.earthlink.net/~pwmurray/wind.htm
- Cape and Fancy Tights Not Required http://kids.discovery.com/KIDS/adv25.html
- Medal Of Honor Coloring Book http://www.homeofheroes.com/coloringbook/index.html

Superhero Cartoons

Superman, Batman and Robin, and other super heroes all have powers that help them fight crime and protect those in need. Have your students develop a superhero for today. Identify a problem, think of a way to solve that problem and develop a superhero that has the powers to solve the problem. Have the students design a storyboard using index cards. On each card, sketch out the scene, the text, the animation and sound. Reinforce the basic story map by arranging the storyboard cards in these categories: Introduction, problem, solution, climax. Use a presentation program, like PowerPoint to develop the cartoon.

- Superhero Database http://www.pazsaz.com/scotlink.html
- History of the Superhero Comic Book http://www.geocities.com/Athens/8580/frames.html
- Superhero Dictionary http://shdictionary.tripod.com/pages/all.html
- Superhero Art http://www.spitfiresvcs.com/sh.htm

Cereal Box Heroes

Wheaties, the Breakfast of Champions, has been honoring sports heroes for over 75 years. Have your students honor their hero on a box top they design. First, look at some of the old Wheaties boxes. Talk about design, color, font, and other design features. Then have the students find a picture of the person they want to honor. I would encourage them to think of historical people, scientists, inventors, entertainers, authors, artists, people in their family, etc. Find a picture of that person or take one with a digital camera. Use a publishing program to design the box top. Add a cereal character. On the back of the box, publish an 'interview" with their hero. On one side of the box, include basic facts about the person, and on the other side, list resources that were used.

- Wheaties http://www.wheaties.com/
- Cereal Box Characters http://www.geocities.com/EnchantedForest/3278/cereal-guide.html
- What Makes a Hero Interview form http://www.education-world.com/a_lesson/TM/WS_heroes.shtml
- Color Wheel http://hort.ifas.ufl.edu/teach/floral/color.htm
- Color Matters http://www.colormatters.com/colortheory.html

National Engineers Week, 3rd

The goal of National Engineers Week is to stress the importance of engineering, technology and science and to get more people into the profession's "pipeline" sooner, so that they have enough secondary math and science education to enter college engineering programs. Engineers have teamed up with educators and the producers of PBS's Zoom to explore the fun and fascination of engineering. Encourage your students by viewing some of the following Internet sites. Many have interactive or hands-on activities.

- National Engineers Week http://www.eweek.org Look at the resources for students and teachers as well as 50 engineers you should know.
- Discover Engineering http://www.discoverengineering.org/eweek/default.asp
- A Sightseer's Guide to Engineering http://www.engineeringsights.org/
- ZOOM http://www.pbs.org/wgbh/zoom/

Date Varies

Chinese New Year
Kung Hey Fat Choi (Prosperous Wishes)
The Chinese New Year falls on a different date each year based on the 2nd new moon after winter solstice. It usually occurs in January or February. No matter when you are celebrating this year, you are bound to have a great time and learn some fascinating things about the Chinese culture. Chinese New Year is celebrated for fifteen days so, get started.

FYI
- 15 Day Celebration http://www.educ.uvic.ca/faculty/mroth/438/CHINA/15-day_celebration.html
- How do we celebrate Chinese New Year? http://www.phila.k12.pa.us/schools/lowell/newyr.html
- New Year's Eve and Chinese New Year http://www.gio.gov.tw/info/festival_c/html_e/spring.htm
- Origins of Chinese New Year http://www.indiana.edu/~chasso/newyear.html#origin
- Chinese New Year http://homex.coolconnect.com/member/crescent/index.htm
- Chinese New Year http://www.lunabase.org/~bpod/ppcce/1999-02-08.htm
- Chinese New Year http://www.familyculture.com/Chinese_new_year.htm

Crafts and Foods
Any holiday is an excuse for good food and Chinese New Years is no exception. Oranges are a traditional food thought to bring good luck. So, eat some orange slices while you make some of these traditional Chinese crafts. For the more skilled, try some of the recipes.

- Chinese New Year Paper Cuttings
  http://www.rice.edu/projects/topics/internatl/holidays/newyrchinapaper.html
- Chinese New Year Crafts http://www.kidsdomain.com/craft/_chin-ny.html
- Chinese New Year Recipes http://www.familyculture.com/newyear_food.htm
- Red Envelopes and Oranges
  http://allrecipes.com/cb/w2m/seaspec/holiday/Chinesenewyear/default.asp
- Chinese Food
  http://zone.cps.k12.il.us/Showcase/Student_Projects/China/Chinese_20Food/chinese_20food.html

12 Lucky Animals
In the Chinese lunar calendar each of the 12 years is named after an animal. According to one legend, Lord Buddha asked all the animals to come to him before he left the earth. Only 12 animals came to wish him farewell, and as a reward Buddha named a year after each one.[iv] Many Chinese believe that the year of a person's birth is the primary factor in determining that person's personality traits, physical and mental attributes and degree of success and happiness throughout his lifetime. What is your sign? Check it out

at the Chinese Horoscope site. Have the students find their sign and make a poster about themselves listing their character traits. Use the animal sign to illustrate their year.

- Chinese Horoscope http://www.index.force9.co.uk/mayflower/zodiac.htm

Other Astrological Sites

- Chinese Astrology http://cat.nyu.edu/liaos/horoscope_old.html
- Horoscope http://www.hkta.org/horoscopes/index.html
- The Chinese Calendar http://www.infoplease.com/ipa/A0002076.html
- Chinese Calendar http://webexhibits.org/calendars/calendar-chinese.html
- The Chinese Zodiac http://www.lausd.k12.ca.us/Haskell_EL/calendar%20past%20events/chinesenew%20year%20gifs/chinesenewyear.htm

Write Numbers in Chinese

Have the students make a counting book in Chinese similar to that found on this site. Use Chinese clip art to represent the number. Print out the pages for the book. Make a simple calligraphy pen with small dowels. Cut the dowel into lengths about the size of a pencil. With a sharp knife (don't have the children do this) taper the end on both sides to form a flat surface. Dip the end in ink and draw the appropriate character on each page, hold the pen perpendicular to the page or, use the number's clip art.

- Write Numbers in Chinese http://www.fi.edu/fellows/fellow1/apr99/number/num1.html

Chinese Clip Art

- At About http://chineseculture.about.com/library/clipart/blscliparts.htm
- Chinese Clip Art http://www.in4mation.org/clipart.html
- Numbers http://www.ocrat.com/ocrat/chargif/numbers.html
- Chinese New Year's Clip Art http://all4freegraphics.com/chinese.html (this also has sounds and music so if you make your book with a presentation tool, you could have animations and sound!)

三　3 fish kites

五　5 men in a parade

Lantern Festival
Celebrated on the 15th day of the Chinese New Year

Make a colorful lantern and then gather for a big" lantern fair". Have a traditional riddle-guessing contest to add to the festivity of the occasion and sing the Dragon Song. Refer to the first Lantern Festival site for stories about the origins of the Lantern Festival and the second Lantern Festival site to learn how to make a lantern. Don't forget to add a riddle.

- Lantern Festival http://english.peopledaily.com.cn/features/festivals/yuanxiao.htm
- The Lantern Festival http://artsedge.kennedy-center.org/nso/asian/activities/lanternact.html
- The Dragon Song http://artsedge.kennedy-center.org/nso/asian/culture/culture.html (If you don't play the piano, Chinese music is based on a *pentatonic* 5-note scale, so if you play only the black keys on the piano, it will sound pretty good.)
- Riddles http://www.cartooncorner.com/funnyfolder/riddles/riddles.html
- Squigly's Jokes and Riddles http://www.squiglysplayhouse.com/JokesAndRiddles/

Take an online field trip to a Lantern Festival.

- The Lantern Festival http://www.gio.gov.tw/info/festival_c/html_e/glue.htm
- Let there be light http://www.asianweek.com/061898/latern.html

Shrove Tuesday also known as Fat Tuesday
Tuesday before Ash Wednesday
The French term *Mardi Gras* means "Fat Tuesday" in English. It began at a time when Christians had to use up all the animal fat in their homes before Lent started.[v] This, of course means that we need to do some cooking today. I suggest either doughnuts or pancakes because they are traditional Shrove Tuesday foods.

Doughnuts
- Doughnut History (don't believe everything you read on the web!) http://www.elliskaiser.com/doughnuts/history.html
- Krispy Kreme http://www.krispykreme.com/

For 10-minute doughnuts take a tube of refrigerator biscuits, cut a hole in the middle with a thimble (save the holes) and fry in hot oil. Turn once when the bottoms look golden brown. Fry the holes. Dust with granulated or powdered sugar. *Note: be careful with the hot oil. I make these in an electric frying pan and really have had no trouble with spattering.*

Pancakes
- Shrove Tuesday Pancakes http://www.emmanuelfellowship.org/easter/shrovetuesday.html
- Pancake Day http://www.kidsdomain.co.uk/kids/activities/about_pancake_day_shrove_tuesday.html
- International Pancake Day http://www.pancakeparlour.com/Special_Events/Shrove/shrove.html

Mardi Gras
Tuesday before Ash Wednesday
Also know as Carnival in Portugal, Laskiaistiistai in Finland, Fastelavnstirsday in Denmark
It's time for a party! To prepare for the six long weeks of Lent, people put all of their efforts into creating a huge celebration. There are parties and parades and of course, food. Learn about the history of Mardi Gras in New Orleans, the American capital of Mardi Gras and compare it to the Mexico Online site. *Note: Mardi Gras is basically an adult celebration, so view the sites first to see if they are appropriate for your students.*
- History of New Orleans Mardi Gras http://www.mardigrasneworleans.com/history.html
- Mardi Gras Live http://www.mardigrasneworleans.com/mardlive.html
- Carnival http://www.mexonline.com/carnaval.htm

Masks
One of the most beautiful and sometimes frightening features of Mardi Gras celebrations is the masks worn by the party goers. People have used masks for centuries for ceremonial purposes. Have the students create a world tour that focuses on masks. Assign small groups of students different cultures' masks to research. Put all of the projects together for your world tour. You could use either a presentation tool like PowerPoint or make a web page for your final project. These sites will get you started and most will lead to additional Internet resources.
- Mardi Gras Masks http://www.mardigrasmasks.com/
- Simple Mardi Gras Masks http://www.earlychildhood.com/crafts/index.cfm?FuseAction=Craft&C=52
- Japanese Noh Masks http://www.pasar5.com/NOH_MASK/
- Wixarica/Huichol Art: The Masks of God http://www.themasksofgod.com/
- Artistry of African Masks http://harlemm.com/nokbeta/exhibit/artistry/main.html
- El Otro Lado Mexican Masks http://elotrolado.org/
- Ceremonial Masks (Pacific Rim) http://www.art-pacific.com/artifacts/indonesi/masksjbc.htm

- Jacob Simonoff Native American Mask Maker
  http://www.conexus.si.edu/yupik/simeonoff/?pos=99999 watch slide show of him making a mask
- Native American Masks and Collectibles http://www.americanindiancollectibles.com/Masks.htm

Lesson Plans About Masks
- Encarta: Mask http://encarta.msn.com/find/concise.asp?ti=05F3E000
- Mask Unit Plan http://www.cln.org/themes/masks.html
- Power of Masks Lesson Plan http://www.curriculum.edu.au/download/lesspln/masks.htm
- Masks: The Face Tells the Story
  http://www.artsednet.getty.edu/ArtsEdNet/Resources/Aeia/cultur-lp.html
- Jan Brett's Masks http://www.janbrett.com/activities_pages_masks.htm
- Arthur Masks http://www.pbs.org/wgbh/arthur/francine/playmaker/masks/
- Noh Masks http://www.pasar5.com/NOH_MASK/index.html
- Milwaukee Public Museum: Masks http://www.mpm.edu/collect/mask.html

Ash Wednesday
1st day of Lent
7th Wednesday preceding Easter

"for dust thou art, and unto dust shalt thou return".

Genesis 3:19

Many Christians worldwide go to church on this day in preparation for the Lenten season. During the service, the priest or pastor will make the sign of the cross with ashes on the forehead of the churchgoer. Ashes are a biblical symbol of mourning and penance and a reminder of our own mortality. Use these sites to help students understand this important day in the Christian year.
- Dates of Ash Wednesday and Easter http://aa.usno.navy.mil/AA/data/docs/easter.html
- Ash Wednesday http://www.theholidayspot.com/ash_wednesday/
- Origin and History of Ash Wednesday http://www.theholidayspot.com/ash_wednesday/origin.htm

100th Day of School
Usually, sometime in February
Recently, schools have started celebrating the 100th Day of School. The Internet offers lots (maybe even 100) ideas for you to use in your school or classroom. Make a list of 100 ideas to celebrate the 100th Day of School on your school web site. Ask teachers and students to contribute ideas. To get you started, check out these sites.
- A – Z Teacher Stuff http://atozteacherstuff.com/themes/100days.shtml
- Mrs. Alphabet's 100 Day Activities http://mrsalphabet.com/100thday.html
- 100th Day E-mail Project http://www.siec.k12.in.us/~west/proj/100th/
- 100th Day of School Activities http://www.iup.edu/~njyost/KHI/Days.html
- This Day in History http://www.historychannel.com/today/
- Internet Field Trip: 100 Day Activities http://teacher.scholastic.com/fieldtrp/math/100th.htm
- 300 Teacher Suggested Activities for 100th Day of School
  http://users.aol.com/a100thday/ideas.html
- 100th Day of School http://exit3.i-55.com/~vickib/100th.html

Snow Festival
Japan
For many people around the world, February means snow. You can either curse it or celebrate it. The people in Sapporo, Japan, choose to celebrate it by hosting Japan's biggest snow festival. Take a field trip

to Japan to see some of the extraordinary ice sculpture and snow lanterns. Then, try making some of your own. Take digital pictures of your snow artwork to post on your class web page. Send an e-mail to a class in Japan inviting them to view your snow festival.

- Snow Festival http://www.jinjapan.org/kidsweb/calendar/february/snow.html
- Snow Lantern Festival, Japan http://www.compusmart.ab.ca/fenske/float143.htm
- Celebrating the World of Festivals: Sapporo http://festivals.com/~gallery/sapporo/
- Make a backyard snow sculpture http://kids.discovery.com/KIDS/adv18.html
- E-pals http://www.epals.com/index_en.html

Odds and Ends

- Snow Activities http://www.teelfamily.com/activities/snow/
- SNOW http://www.niksula.cs.hut.fi/~mnikkane/
- Questions and Answers About Snow http://nsidc.org/NSIDC/EDUCATION/SNOW/snow_FAQ.html
- Snow Castles http://www.snowcastle.net/
- There's Snow Time Like Now http://www.explorescience.com/news/march2001.cfm#snowtime
- Eskimo Snow Words http://www.inquiry.net/outdoor/okpik/snow&ice/eskimo_snow.htm (what's outside your windows today?)

President's Day
3rd Monday

Until the mid-1970s, the birthday of George Washington (February 22), first president of the United States was observed as a federal holiday. In addition, the birthday of Abraham Lincoln (February 12), president during the Civil War, was observed as a holiday in many states. In the 1970s, Congress declared that in order to honor all past presidents, a single holiday, to be called Presidents' Day, would be observed on the third Monday in February. In many states, however, the holiday continues to be known as George Washington's Birthday. President's born in February are Ronald Regan, William Harrison, Abraham Lincoln and George Washington.

Presidential Trading Cards

Teacher Vision suggests a lesson plan that has each student making a trading card about a president. What a good idea!

Born: 9 February 1773 **Birthplace:** Charles City County, Virginia **Death:** 4 April 1841 (pneumonia)	*Old Tippecanoe* -Hero of the early Indian Wars -Remembered for giving longest inaugural speech and serving the shortest term of office. -Grandson, Benjamin Harrison, was 23rd president.

William Henry Harrison
9th President

- Teacher Vision http://teachervision.com/lesson-plans/lesson-24.html

Internet Resources about Presidents
- The American Presidency http://gi.grolier.com/presidents/preshome.html
- Presidential Trivia http://www.umkc.edu/imc/prestriv.htm
- The American Presidency http://www.virtualblackboard.com/modules/history/prez/prz-o.htm
- Nicknames of the Presidents http://www.quia.com/jg/65621.html
- The Presidents http://odur.let.rug.nl/~usa/P/index.htm
- Presidential Portraits http://www.historyplace.com/specials/portraits/presidents/index.html
- U.S. Presidents http://www.infoplease.com/ipa/A0873867.html
- U.S. President Facts http://teachervision.com/lesson-plans/lesson-4409.html

Presidential Database
To have the students learn a little bit more about databases, make a Presidential Database. I like to use a spreadsheet and filters for younger students as they can 'see' how a database works. Open President Data Base @ Infoplease. Highlight the complete table and paste it in Excel or another spreadsheet. You may need to adjust the format. Add additional columns for more information if you want. Set the filters so you can look for specific information. For instance, how many presidents were born in Virginia? Or who were the presidents who died on the 4th of July? Have the students think of additional queries. An excellent source for additional information to add to the database is Presidents of the United States.
- President Data Base http://www.infoplease.com/ipa/A0194030.html
- Presidents of the United States http://www.netcolony.com/news/presidents/

President's Day Lesson Plans
For additional lesson plans related to President's Day, refer to these Internet sites.
- Presidential Speeches Lesson Plan
  http://school.discovery.com/lessonplans/activities/presidentialspeeches/index.html
- President's Day Resource Guide
  http://www.atozteacherstuff.com/themes/febholidays.shtml#President's
- Education World, Presidents Day http://www.education-world.com/holidays/archives/february_2000.shtml#president
- President's Day Activities
  http://www.alfy.com/teachers/teach/thematic_units/Presidents_Day/PD_1.asp
- President's Day Virtual Field Trip http://score.rims.k12.ca.us/activity/presidentsday/
- Some cool 'presidential' activities http://www.field-trips.org/ss/prez/tr.htm

Test Your President's IQ (Information Quizzes)
Online games and quizzes provide a fun way to learn presidential facts and trivia. After practicing by taking some of these quizzes, test your knowledge by making headbands for each student with the name of a president written on the front of each one. Students guess who they are by asking other students questions that can be answered with yes or no. All of these presidents make a big data pool with lots of facts, so you may need to limit the field by selecting a few of the presidents and posting their names before the big event.

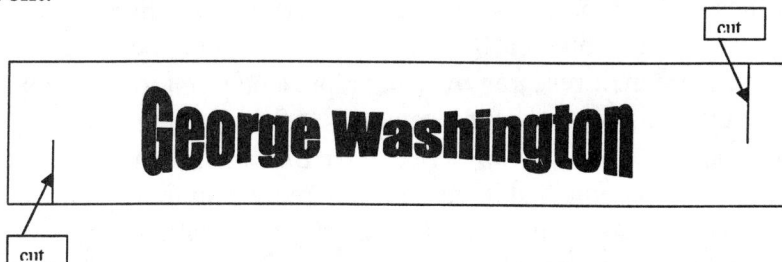

- Online Quizzes http://www.quia.com/dir/hist/
- First Ladies Quiz http://www.infoplease.com/spot/quiz/firstladies/1.html
- President's Day Quiz http://www.factmonster.com/spot/quiz/IPKApresidents1/1.html
- Presidents and Their Dogs Quiz http://www.factmonster.com/spot/quiz/prespets/1.html
- U. S. President Games http://www.quia.com/jg/66016.html
- President Hangman http://www.quia.com/hm/22746.html

Odds and Ends
- Coloring Posters http://www.dltk-kids.com/usa/mpresidentposter.html
- The White House http://www.whitehouse.gov/
- The White House for Kids http://www.whitehouse.gov/kids/index.html
- POTUS http://www.ipl.org/ref/POTUS/
- Sounds of the Presidents http://www.historyplace.com/specials/sounds-prez/index.html
- Political Clip Art http://members.nbci.com/_XMCM/jograham/politics.htm

Tu B'Shevat
15th day of Jewish Month of Shevat
Tu B'Shevat is the new year for the purpose of calculating the age of trees for tithing. The fruit from trees may not be eaten during the first three years; the fourth year's fruit is for God, and after that, you can eat the fruit.[vi] (Do your students know what *tithing* means? http://www.dictionary.com/) Today, Tu B'Shevat has become a tree planting festival for Jews throughout the world and in Israel. No, you don't have to cut down a tree to count its rings. There are a number of Internet sites with great pictures of tree rings and explanations of tree growth patterns.
- Tu B'Shevat http://uahc.org/va/bnai_shalom/tubshvat.html
- Tu B'Shevat Holiday Guide http://www.tricityjcc.org/family_life/holidays/tubshevat.html
- National Arbor Day http://www.arborday.org/
- Carly's Kids Corner http://www.arborday.org/carly/carlyskidscorner.html
- American Forests http://www.americanforests.org/
- Oldest Tree Images http://www.nyu.edu/projects/julian/websources.html
- Tree Ring Research http://web.utk.edu/~grissino/gallery.htm#Rings
- Comparing Tree Rings http://www.bsu.edu/burris/iwonder/realities/activities/ctr.html
- Tree Rings – A Study of Climate Change http://www.athena.ivv.nasa.gov/curric/land/global/treestel.html (with Teacher Talk)

Special Days

A Month of Birthdays
For being such a little month, February has a plethora of famous birthdays, and not just the presidents! They include: Langston Hughes, Rosa Park, Galileo Galilea, Toni Morrison, Ansel Adams, Thomas Edison, Frederick Douglas and Susan B. Anthony. At the beginning of the month, assign small groups of students to research a famous person. Then, on their birthday, have the group present information to the rest of the class. The students can share their research by using a presentation tool, a web page, or Internet field trip. Use Who2 for the initial source of information. After each presentation, have the students add to a large classroom bulletin board – *Happy February Birthdays!* At the end of the month, ask the students what traits, if any, these people had in common. Are they similar to the other birthdays we celebrate in February? *Note: Frederick Douglas was presumably born in February, but the actual date is unknown. However, he died on February 20th.*
- Who2 http://www.who2.com/

February 1
National Freedom Day
PL 80-842
This is a great way to start your month-long discussion of Black History. National Freedom Day commemorates the date President Lincoln signed the resolution proposing the 13th Amendment. Introduce your students to your Black History study by looking at the American Experience: Slavery and Freedom site for a quick overview.

- National Freedom Day http://www4.law.cornell.edu/uscode/36/156.html
- 13th Amendment http://www.mscode.com/usconst/a-13.html
- The American Experience: Slavery and Freedom
  http://www.pbs.org/wgbh/amex/lincolns/slavery/index.html

February 1, 1902
Langston Hughes' Birthday
- Who2: Langston Hughs http://www.who2.com/langstonhughes.html

February 2
Groundhog Day

WEATHER
Whether the weather be fine
Or whether the weather be not,
Whether the weather be cold
Or whether the weather be hot,
We'll weather the weather
Whatever the weather,
Whether we like it or not.

-- Anonymous

What is our fascination with Groundhog Day? I think that it's just that we've finished a long, cold month and we need to hope that spring is coming or we just need an excuse to celebrate something fun. Whatever the real reason, we are certainly not the first people to do it. The legend of Groundhog Day is based on an old Scottish couplet: "If Candlemas Day is bright and clear, there'll be two winters in the year."[vii] So, let's see what we can do. First, learn the history of Groundhog Day by reading these Internet sites. Americans are not the only ones concerned with the length of winter. The Canadians are also worried that there will be six more weeks of winter. Learn about Wiarton Willie, Canada's version of Punxsutawney Phil.

- History of Groundhog Day http://www.stormfax.com/ghogday.htm
- Happy Groundhog Day http://homepages.rootsweb.com/%7Emaggieoh/Holidays/G/g_index.html
- Wiarton Willie http://www.wiarton-willie.org/index.cfm (Canada's Groundhog Prognosticator)

Groundhogs
When the early settlers came to America, they were used to looking at a hedgehog's shadow to predict the end of winter. As there were no hedgehogs in the New World, they choose the 'next best thing' – the groundhog. What is a groundhog anyway? Is he related to a hedgehog? Do they even know each other? Check out these Internet sites.

- The Groundhog or Woodchuck http://www.geocities.com/Heartland/7134/Shadow/ghfacts.htm
- Groundhogs http://www.groundhogs.com/
- Groundhogs http://www.groundhog.org/

- British Hedgehog Preservation Society http://www.software-technics.co.uk/bhps/
- Jan Brett http://www.janbrett.com/ (draw and color hedgehogs, pick up your heggie screensaver)

Shadows

Of course the main thing about the whole day is to see if the groundhog sees his shadow. Spend the day exploring shadows.

Shadow Math
- Me and My Shadow Math Lesson http://www.tandl.vt.edu/mcass/ShadowMathLessonPlan.htm
- Proportional Reasoning Math Lesson http://www.nde.state.ne.us/NMSI/mathvantage/proportional/lesson.html

Shadow Science
- Moon Phases http://www.googol.com/moon/
- What Are Shadows? http://www.geocities.com/Heartland/7134/Shadow/ghshadows.htm
- Shadow Clock http://www.acsamman.edu.jo/~el/5A/science/opaque.html

Shadow Art
- Still Life http://www.geocities.com/Athens/8020/dbaeup2.html

Shadow Language Arts
- Have students define these 'shadow' phrases:

"to be in someone's shadow"

"to shadow someone"

"to cast a big shadow"

"without a shadow of a doubt"
- Write a play script for the Shadow, Chapter 2 or Peter Pan. (copy and paste to a word processor) Make shadow puppets for your actors.
  - Shadow Puppets http://family2.go.com/features/family_1999_01/famf/famf19puppet/famf19puppet5.html

Shadow Social Studies
- Shadow Puppets http://www.itdc.sbcss.k12.ca.us/curriculum/puppetry.html

Shadow PE
- Shadow Tag http://www.malvernschool.com/shadow.htm
- Shadow Buff http://family2.go.com/games/famf/famfcmas_shadow/famfcmas_shadow.html
- Shadow Puppets http://kidsfun.co.uk/Finished%20pages/handshad.html

Shadow Music
- The lyrics are best on the 1st site, but use the 2nd site for the midi
  1. Me and My Shadow http://www.smickandsmodoo.com/aaa/lyrics/shadow.htm
  2. Me and My Shadow http://www.midnitesun.freeserve.co.uk/songsm.htm

Superstition

"If birds fly low
Expect rain and a blow."

"Red sky in the morning
Sailors take warning.
Red sky at night
Sailor's delight."

"If the rooster crows on going to bed,
You may rise with a watery head." [viii]

Of course, we would say that a groundhog being able to predict the weather is just a superstition. What are some other superstitions? Is there any truth to the matter?

- Superstitions: Weather http://www.sandiego-books.com/weather.htm
- Common American Superstitions http://www.globalpsychics.com/lp/Superstition/menu.htm
- Japanese Superstition http://www.japan-guide.com/e/e2209.html
- Weather Proverbs Quiz http://www.infoplease.com/spot/quiz/weatherprov/1.html

Weather

Faced with another six weeks of winter, we need to have some weather-related Internet sites in out back pocket. These should see you through till spring.

General Weather Sites

Use one of these sites when you do your opening exercises when the students tell about the daily weather.

- AccuWeather http://www1.accuweather.com/adcbin/index?partner=accuweather
- The Weather Channel http://www.weather.com/
- Weather Bug http://www.weatherbug.com
- Weather Resources on the Internet http://www.factmonster.com/ipka/A0772916.html
- EarthWatch Weather http://www.earthwatch.com/

Snow and Storms Sites

- Snowflakes – A Thematic Unit http://www.wsanford.com/~wsanford/exo/snowflakes.html
- Wonderland Snow http://www.wxdude.com/page11.html
- Snow Crystals http://www.cco.caltech.edu/~atomic/snowcrystals/
- Snowflake Bentley http://www.jericho-underhill.com/bentley.htm
- Stormy Stories http://www.nationalgeographic.com/xpeditions/activities/07/stormy.html
- NOAA Storms http://www.nws.noaa.gov/om/tpsterm.htm
- Winter Storms http://teacher.scholastic.com/activities/wwatch/winter/index.htm

Predicting the Weather

Compare your predictions with your local TV weatherperson.

- Weather Or Not http://davem2.cotf.edu/ete/modules/weathernot/wonsituation.html
- Predicting Weather Lesson Plan http://www.sasked.gov.sk.ca/docs/elemsci/gr4udesc.html
- Long Range Forecast: Farmers Almanac http://www.almanac.com/weather/weather.html
- Sky Watch: Signs of Weather http://wilstar.com/skywatch.htm

Odds and Ends

Dan's Wild Wild Weather site has fantastic information, games and activities. Enjoy!

- Dan's Wild Wild Weather http://www.wildwildweather.com

Never could figure out how to convert Fahrenheit to Celsius? This will help!

- Fahrenheit and Celsius (Centigrade) Scales http://www.infoplease.com/ipa/A0001731.html

Use the Average Daily Temperature site to play a wishful thinking game. Copy the table and paste in into a spreadsheet. Activate the filter and ask queries such as hottest place in January, coldest place in July, etc.

- Average Daily Temperatures http://www.infoplease.com/ipa/A0004587.html

Lesson Plans and Activities

Pick and choose lessons for your classroom from these wonderful resources.

- Groundhog Day Movie http://teflchina.com/teach/general/groundhogDay.htm (lesson plan for teaching English)
- Groundhog Day Activities
  http://www.atozteacherstuff.com/themes/febholidays.shtml#Ground%20Hog

- Lesson Ideas http://www.umkc.edu/imc/groundho.htm
- Groundhog Day http://www.education-world.com/holidays/archives/february_2000.shtml#groundhog
- The Day of the Shadow http://www.geocities.com/Heartland/7134/Shadow/groundhog.htm
- Wiarton Willie Curriculum http://www.wiarton-willie.org/aboutwillie/getpage.cfm?title=Groundhog%20Day%20Curriculum

Candlemas

If Candlemas be fair and bright,
Winter has another flight.
If Candlemas brings clouds and rain,
Winter will not come again.

Candlemas commemorates the ritual purification of Mary, 40 days after the birth of Jesus.
- Catholic Encyclopedia: Candlemas http://www.newadvent.org/cathen/03245b.htm
- Candlemas http://www.theholidayspot.com/groundhogday/candlemas.htm
- Imbolic http://www.louisville.edu/~aoclar01/ancient/holidays/imbolic.htm

February 2, 1931
Judith Viorst's Birthday

"Brevity may be the soul of wit,
but not when someone's saying, "I love you."

Judith Viorst

It's been over 30 years since Judith Viorst taught us that when we were having a really bad day, we could consider moving to Australia; advice I often wish I could take. Children and adults alike can commiserate with Alexander, who is having a terrible, horrible, no good, very bad day. Learn more about Ms Viorst at the following sites. Have the student's make a list of things that would make them feel they were having a very bad day. Read Life Isn't Fair. Viorst says 'often it's….changing the angle of our perception which makes things seem more bearable.' In the column next to the list of bad things, have the students key what might be good about that by just twisting it a little. Example: got a bad grade on the spelling test, there will be a 2nd chance test tomorrow.
- Judith Viorst http://www.edupaperback.org/authorbios/Viorst_Judith.html
- Biography http://www.annonline.com/interviews/980112/biography.html
- Life Isn't Fair http://www.dreamscapes.co.za/Daydream/dd073

Poetry
Have the students copy and paste one of the poems into a word processor. Add readers for a Reader's Theater presentation.
- Judith Viorst http://www.poets.org/poets/poets.cfm?prmID=62
- Mother Doesn't Want a Dog
  http://pub2.ezboard.com/fhunt4lifepoetry.showMessage?topicID=396.topic

Dealing With Death
In The 10th Good Thing About Barney, a child deals with the loss of
his pet by listing what he liked about his cat. This book is often read to and with children who are suffering loss. I list the following sites for your reference if you know children who are in need of help dealing with the death of a loved one or who have a fatal illness.
- Talking To Children About Death http://www.hospicenet.org/html/talking.html

- Helping Children Cope With Death http://www.madd.org/VICTIMS/children-cope.shtml
- How to Talk to Children About Death http://txtx.essortment.com/howtotalktoc_rhxr.htm
- Helping Children Understand Death http://www.nncc.org/Guidance/understand.death.html

Odds and Ends

Listen to Judith Viorst read
- Kennedy Center: Alexander and the Terrible, Horrible, No Good, Very Bad Day http://kennedy-center.org/programs/family/alexander/

Have students write a review of one of her books and send to -
- KidViews http://www.eduplace.com/kids/rdg/chall.html

These are for you....
- Creative Quotations http://bemorecreative.com/one/1263.htm

For an extensive writing lesson based on Alexerdar, etc, etc, etc, refer to
- Lesson Plan http://www.wavcc.org/wvc/cadre/LiteratureDrama/wellpinit/jscottwriting.htm

Some Books by Judith Viorst (for Children)

Alexander and the Terrible, Horrible, No, Good, Very Bad Day

Absolutely Positively Alexander: The Complete Stories

Super-Completely and Totally the Messiest

Alexander, Who Used to Be Rich Last Sunday

The Good-bye Book

Rosie and Michael

The Tenth Good Thing About Barney

My Mama Says There Aren't Any Zombies, Ghosts, Vampires, Creatures, Demons, Monsters, Fiends, Goblins, or Things

If I Were in Charge of the World and Other Worries

Sunday Morning: A Story

Alexander, Who's Not (Do You Hear Me? I Mean It!) Going to Move

Earrings

The Alphabet from Z to A

I'll Fix Anthony

Sad Underwear and other Complications

(Books for Adults)

Necessary Losses

Suddenly 60: and other Shocks of Later Life

How Did I Get To Be Forty and Other Atrocities

Forever Fifty and other Negotiations

February 3, 1868
15th Amendment

Another great way to celebrate Black History Month…The 15th Amendment is the last of the three so-called Reconstruction amendments ratified in the aftermath of the Civil War to abolish slavery and firmly establish minority civil. The 15th Amendment prohibits federal or state governments from infringing on a citizen's right to vote "on account of race, color, or previous condition of servitude." Henry Adams remarked that the 15th Amendment was "more remarkable for what it does not than for what it does contain."[ix] Before they read the second article, ask the students to speculate what Adams was referring to – women's suffrage perhaps… If women's suffrage had been included, how would history have been changed? Ask students to refer to Amendments 13 and 14 to see the progression. Could everything have been included in Amendment 13?

- 15th Amendment http://gi.grolier.com/presidents/aae/side/15amend.html
- 15th Amendment http://civilwar.bluegrass.net/SlaveryAndEmancipation/15thamendment.html

February 4, 1913
Rosa Parks' Birthday
- Who2: Rosa Parks http://www.who2.com/anseladams.html

February 6, 1903
Crayolas 1st Appeared on Market

Who developed these remarkable tools that have entertained us all since early childhood? How were they made? How have they changed over the years? Inquiring minds want to know. Go to Crayola History to find out! Crayola also offers outstanding activities for your students. I hope you enjoy them all!
- Crayola History
  http://www.crayola.com/factory/preview/factory_floor/bs_history/bs_timeline.htm
- Activities http://www.crayola.com/index.cfm

Just in time for Valentine's Day….go to Jan Brett's wonderful site. Click on Activities and find Hedgie's Valentine Mailbox. Have the students print out the pattern. Because we are talking about crayons, you probably should have the students color Hedgie in the traditional manner, but you could have them copy and paste it into a paint program and 'color.'
- Jan Brett http://www.janbrett.com

Coloring Books
There are many coloring books online or, make your own using clip art.
- Coloring.com http://www.coloring.com
- Kendra's Coloring Book http://www.geocities.com/EnchantedForest/7155/
- Childfun Coloring Pages http://www.childfun.com/color/ (look for cute Valentine pictures)
- Coloring 4 Kids http://www.coloringpage.org/
- Let's Get Ready to Color http://www.preschoolcoloringbook.com/
- Coloring Pages http://coloring-page.com/ (Disney and other familiar characters)

February 7, 1867
Laura Ingalls Wilder's Birthday

"I had no idea I was writing history."

Laura Ingalls Wilder

What fond memories, Laura Ingalls Wilder brings to mind. Every teacher I ever had in grade school would read a Little House book after recess as we rested with our heads on our desks. My grandmother and grandfather were friends of Laura and Almanzo. I had the opportunity to meet her one day when she 'called' on my grandmother. The following sites will give you a little information, a little more information, still more information and more information than you'll know what to do with. Any of them offer great browsing for LIW fans.
- FactMonster: Laura Ingalls Wilder http://www.factmonster.com/ipka/A0801303.html
- Laura Ingalls Wilder http://www.umkc.edu/imc/wilder.htm
- World Wide Guide to the Little House
  http://www.worldwideguide.net/guides/index.cfm?guideID=1

- K-12 TLC Guide http://tlc.ai.org/wilder.htm
- Laura Ingalls Wilder Teacher Resource File http://falcon.jmu.edu/~ramseyil/wilder.htm
- Laura Ingalls Wilder Timeline http://hoover.nara.gov/education/liw/timeline.html

Tour Laura's Homes
Refer to Frontier Girl for a map of Laura's homes. Recreate the map for your bulletin board. Have small groups of students research the different home sites. Scan a picture from the book written about that site and have the students search the Internet for a contemporary picture of their site to compare then and now. How far would you travel from your school to her home? How far would you travel if you visited all of her homes? Check it out with MapQuest's Driving Directions.
- Laura's Travels http://www.lauraingallswilderhome.com/ (very nice printable map)
- Frontier Girl http://webpages.marshall.edu/~irby1/laura/frames.html
- Laura Ingalls Wilder Home Sites http://lauraingallswilder.com/homesites.asp
- Map Quest http://www.mapquest.com

Keep a Diary

"History is a form of story telling about the past. The way we write history, the stories we tell, will reflect our own preoccupations, our own interests, our own understandings of what is important now, and in the past as well. Much history writing in this country has involved an active, but selective process of remembering and forgetting."[x]

Even though Laura says she didn't know she was writing history, her books certainly contain vivid word pictures of the life and times of early pioneers on the western frontier. Have your students begin a diary. For some advice and suggestions about student diaries, look at these sites. One of the things I ask my students to do is to take the last five minutes of our lab time to write about what we did in class. It isn't long, but gives them an opportunity to synthesize their thoughts.
- Diary Writing http://www.keyadvice.com/lil/Files/diary.htm
- Diary Writing www.srkvs.org/dist_feat/diary.html
- Approaches to Diary Writing http://education.leeds.ac.uk/~edu/wblp/landt/chk1.htm
- Journal Writing with Virginia Hamilton http://teacher.scholastic.com/writewit/diary/index.htm

Lesson Plans
Pick and choose what will work best in your classroom.
- Author Study: Laura Ingalls Wilder http://www.teachersfirst.com/winners/wilder.htm
- Laura Ingalls Wilder Teaching Unit http://hoover.nara.gov/education/liw/liw_teaching_unit.html
- Laura Ingalls Wilder Webquest http://webtech.kennesaw.edu/mlipold/webquest.htm
- Laura Ingalls Wilder Lesson Plan
  http://teacherlink.ed.usu.edu/TLresources/longterm/LessonPlans/famous/wilder.html
- Laura Ingalls Wilder Teaching and Learning Center http://tlc.ai.org/wilder.htm

Odds and Ends
This is a hyperlinked site for those who are interested in further research about pioneers.
- Laura Ingalls Wilder http://memory.loc.gov/ammem/today/feb07.html
This is one of the first (and best) fan sites. It has lots of pictures and information about the family and their homes. It also has some neat activites based on the books that could be used in the classroom.

- The Definitive Laura Ingalls Wilder Site http://carver.pinc.com/~jenslegg/
- Little House Activities http://carver.pinc.com/~jenslegg/activity.htm

Just what it says…

- Songs and Musical Memories of Laura Ingalls Wilder http://www.geocities.com/~prairiehome/

This site will fit right in with Hero Week. It contains short writings by students about Laura Ingalls Wilder.

- Writer Heroes http://www.myhero.com/hero.asp?hero=lauraIngallsWilder

Some Books by Laura Ingalls Wilder
Little House In the Big Woods
Little House On the Prairie
Little Town On the Prairie
On the Banks of Plum Creek
Farmer Boy
The Long Winter
These Happy Golden Years
The First Four Years
By the Shores of Silver Lake
On the Way Home
West From Home

February 11, 1847
Thomas Edison's Birthday

- Who2: Thomas Edison http://www.who2.com/thomasedison.html

And a couple more….

- A Spark of Brilliance http://www.fi.edu/qa98/attic12/attic12.html
- Power Lab http://www.edisonkids.com/index.htm
- Inventing Entertainment http://memory.loc.gov/ammem/edhtml/edhome.html

February 12, 1809
Abraham Lincoln's Birthday

Who2: Abraham Lincoln http://www.who2.com/abrahamlincoln.html
And a couple more….
I've often heard that we as teachers are so busy helping students see that 'everyone's a winner' that we don't spend enough time teaching children how to face the inevitable failures and disappointments we all have to face in life. Look at the timeline of Lincoln's life. Here was a man that certainly knew failure and loss. Print a timeline of his life and have the students decide if each event needs a happy face or sad face.

- Lincoln Timeline with Web Sites http://www.abrahamlincoln.cc/timeline.htm
- Assassination and Mock Trial http://members.aol.com/RVSNorton/Lincoln.html
- Abraham Lincoln http://www.siec.k12.in.us/~west/proj/lincoln/index.html

February 12
Lost Penny Day

How many pennies are produced every day? How long does the penny last? What was the first U.S. coin to feature a historic figure? Learn the answers to these and other fascinating facts at Americans for Common Cents.

- Americans For Common Cents http://www.pennies.org

Next take a field trip to the United States Mint and be sure to stop at Pocket Change: History in Your Pocket for games, history, cartoons, time machine and lots more. This is a great site for kids. Visit Inspector Collector to learn about coin collecting. Spelling word for the week: numismatics. Start a coin collection and learn what it is worth at CoinWorld. Learn about presidents on coins, currency and stamps.

- The United States Mint http://www.usmint.gov/
  - o Pocket Change: History in Your Pocket http://www.usmint.gov/kids/
- CoinWorld http://www.coinworld.com/
- Coins, Currency and Stamps Featuring Presidents
  http://www.netcolony.com/news/presidents/coinsstamps.html

Penny Drive

Ask the students to collect pennies. Challenge the other classes in your school to see which one can collect the most pennies. Donate all of the pennies to a shelter or food pantry in your area. To learn the value of a penny, read the Lesson From a Penny.

- The Lesson From a Penny
  http://skywebsite.com/moneynow/sitebuildercontent/sitebuilderfiles/penny.html

A Penny for Your Thoughts

Put together a class book called: A Penny for Your Thoughts. Ask each student to complete the sentence starter: I think….. Illustrate your book with original drawings using a paint program. And, just for fun, for some of the tricks with coins, click on Coins @ Mickey's Fun With Stuff
http://disney.go.com/activities/funstuffcollection/index.html

February 12, 1938
Judy Bloom's Birthday

More than 75 million copies of popular children's author, Judy Bloom books have been sold, and her work has been translated into twenty-something languages. Now second generation children are enjoying the life and times of Margaret, Super Fudge and others. Share her web site with your students

- Judy Blume http://www.judyblume.com/

Censorship

Judy Blume's books are often found on the most censored books for children lists. Judy speaks about censorship on her web site. After your students have read a Judy Bloom book, ask why they think the book might be censored. Compare other books from the list.

- Judy Bloom: Censors http://www.judyblume.com/
- Censored Children's Books http://www.csulb.edu/library/subj/banned.html
- Banned Books and Censorship http://www.luc.edu/libraries/banned/
- Office of Intellectual Freedom http://www.ala.org/alaorg/oif/
- Most Frequently Censored or Controversial Books in America
  http://www.indiana.edu/~eric_rec/ieo/bibs/censor.html

Note: See Banned Book Week in September for more ideas.

Writing Process

Judy Bloom is often asked where she gets her ideas, how she writes her books, what is her favorite part about writing. Read her discussion about writing. Have the students compare her writing process to the ABC's of the Writing Process. Judy Bloom says that rewriting or revising is her favorite part of the process. Have the students open a word document with an early draft of a paragraph. Ask the students to rewrite the paragraph. Compare the final paragraphs. I suggest using a Nursery Rhyme such as Little Miss Muffet or Little Boy Blue.

- Judy Bloom: On Writing http://www.judyblume.com/
- ABC's of the Writing Process http://www.angelfire.com/wi/writingprocess

Little Miss Muffet By Mother Goose	Little Miss Muffet By Linda
Little Miss Muffet Sat on a tuffet Eating her curds and whey. Along came a spider Who sat down beside her And frightened Miss Muffet away.	Once upon a time there was a little girl named Mary Muffet. One bright spring day, she decided to eat her breakfast outside. She sat down on her little pillow and began eating her delicious bowl of curds and whey. When, what do you think happened? Etcetera, etcetera, etcetera....

February 14
Valentines Day

Roses are red,
Violets are blue,
Sugar is sweet
And, so are you!

Traditional

5 Quick Things to Do

1. Play a Game - Heart Pounding Fun
   http://www.bonus.com/bonus/list/holiday_valentines.right.html
2. Send a Valentine Post Card - RosieGrams
   http://rosieo.warnerbros.com/pages/rosieo/rosiegrams/index.jsp
3. Make some cool crafts – Printsville: Valentine's Day
   http://www.hp.com/printing_ideas/seasonal_gallery/s_01.html
4. Put on a puppet play - Boris and the Valentine Fairy
   http://www.kidsdomain.com/holiday/val/stories/boris.html
5. Write a love letter - Ben and Jerry's Valentine Note Generator
   http://www.benjerry.com/holidays/gladlib/

General, all purpose sites with crafts, clip art and more
- Annie's Valentine Day for Kids http://annieshomepage.com/valentineskids.html

- Valentine's Day Resource Guide
  http://www.atozteacherstuff.com/themes/febholidays.shtml#Valentine's
- Billy Bear's Playground: Valentine Day http://www.billybear4kids.com/holidays/valentin/fun.htm
- Valentine Fun and Kid's Domain http://www.kidsdomain.com/holiday/val/
- Valentine's Day at Alphabet Soup http://alphabet-soup.net/val/valentine.html
- Happy Valentines Day http://www.cstone.net/~bry-back/holidayfun/valentine.html
- Valentine's Day @ Child Fun http://www.childfun.com/valentine/

Valentine's Day Around the World
Click on these sites to learn the history and customs of Valentine's Day in different parts of the world.
- History of Valentine's Day http://www.infoplease.com/ce6/society/A0843155.html
- Valentines day http://www.pictureframes.co.uk/pages/saint_valentine.htm
- Valentines day around the world
  http://www.rice.edu/projects/topics/internatl/holidays/valentines/day.htm
- San Valentin in Mexico http://www.inside-mexico.com/SAN.htm#serenata (listen to *Despierta*, a love song)

Valentine Candy
One of my favorite reasons for this season is chocolate! Learn about the history of chocolate, where is comes from, how it's made and then do some math and science lessons. Take a candy quiz and make some chocolate love letters. Yum!
- History of Chocolate http://www.candyusa.org/chocstry.html
- The Cacao Tree http://www.chocolate.org/choctree.html
- Chocolate http://eduscapes.com/42explore/choclat.htm
- Hershey Factions http://forum.swarthmore.edu/paths/fractions/hershey.frac.html (math lesson plan)
- Coming to Our Senses http://sln.fi.edu/qa97/me9/ (science lesson)
- Candy Quiz http://www.infoplease.com/spot/quiz-candy1.html

Candy Hearts
Okay, there may be some folks out there who prefer those little candy hearts. These sites have games and crafts to meet your needs.
- Candy Hearts http://www.infoplease.com/spot/candyhearts1.html
- Write your own sayings http://www.himonkey.net/holiday/v/sh/index.html
- It's Candy Time http://207.197.202.83/indexcur.html
- Kids Candy http://www.kidscandy.org/

Make Love Letters
You will need a box of Alphabets cereal, chocolate chips, a small bar of paraffin and some aluminum foil. Melt the chocolate chips and a bar of paraffin. Be very careful, as paraffin gets very hot! Allow it to cool slightly and dip the Alphabets into the chocolate. Place them on the foil until they are hard. Arrange your letters into words and sayings to give to your 'loved' one.

Write Your Own, *Roses Are Red* Poem
Author Bruce Lansky has a cool lesson on how to have students write their own words for the traditional Roses Are Red poem. You will like this one and so will your students.

- Roses Are Red http://www.poetryteachers.com/poetclass/lessons/rosesrred.html

St. Valentine's Day Massacre

There comes a time in every student's life when they are either too old for traditional Valentine's Day activities and not yet old enough to appreciate Valentines from that certain someone – somewhere around middle school. This is probably a great time for cops and robbers! Have your students research the St. Valentine's Day Massacre. This age student has lots of ideas, so leave it open-ended how they share the information with the rest of the class. To provide a little structure, you might want to give small groups of students a topic to report on, such as – the people involved, what lead up to the event, the actual 'massacre', lessons learned, etc. and then, put the whole thing together in jigsaw manner.

- Crimes of the Century http://www.apbonline.com/crimesofthecentury/stories/stvalentines.html
- Freedom of Information Act: Gangsters http://foia.fbi.gov/gangster.htm
- InfoPlease http://www.infoplease.com/spot/valmassacre1.html
- The Jigsaw Classroom http://www.jigsaw.org/

Odds and Ends

Read about famous couples at The History of Valentine's Day http://www.historychannel.com/exhibits/valentine/ and learn about more couples at Famous Lovers http://encarta.msn.com/list/famouslovers.asp

Read classic love poems and print them on a Valentine card for your favorite person. Or just send an electronic greeting card.

- Classic Love Poems http://www.infoplease.com/spot/lovepoems1.html
- Victorian Valentines http://www.scrapalbum.com/stvalent.htm
- Valentine Art Project Lesson Plan http://www.pacificnet.net/~mandel/TheArts.html
- Valentine Clip Art http://www.geocities.com/Heartland/Hills/7060/valentine.htm
- Valentine Cards @ Blue Mountain http://www2.bluemountain.com/eng/valentine/index.html

What makes us fall in love? Do other animals do it? What is the mating game? You'll know the answers to these and other thought-provoking questions after reading - The Science of Love http://whyfiles.org/033love/index.html

Need some new games for your Valentine Party. Check these out. My favorite - musical hearts. And, for some terrific online games, go to Bonus.com, Heart Pounding Games.

- Game Kids: Valentine Day http://www.gamekids.com/gkval1.html
- Heart Pounding Games http://www.bonus.com/bonus/list/holiday_valentines.html?referrer=KG15

February 15, 1564
Galileo Galilei

Who2: Galileo Galilei http://www.who2.com/galileo.html

February 15, 1820
Susan B. Anthony

- Who2: Susan B. Anthony http://www.who2.com/susanbanthony.html

And a couple more…..

- Susan B. Anthony Paper Doll http://www.myschoolonline.com/printables/piece/0,2357,3-12463-792-1,00.html
- Suffrage History From PBS http://www.pbs.org/onewoman/suffrage.html

February 18, 1931
Toni Morrison
Who2: Toni Morrison http://www.who2.com/tonimorrison.html

February 19, 1942
Executive Order 9066 Japanese Internment

...May it serve as a constant reminder of our past so that Americans in the future will never again be denied their constitutional rights and may the remembrance of that experience serve to advance the evolution of the human spirit...
- Plaque at the Pooston Relocation Center

Following the Japanese attack on Pearl Harbor in December 1941, the United States was gripped by war hysteria.[xi] What were these camps and who had to go? Share with your students this dark side of American history, *so that Americans in the future will never again be denied their constitutional rights...*
- History http://www.geocities.com/Athens/8420/main.html
- Japanese American Interment Camps http://www.lib.utah.edu/spc/photo/9066/9066.htm
- Japanese American Internment Online Exhibit
  http://www.scu.edu/SCU/Programs/Diversity/exhibit2.html

February 20, 1902
Ansel Adams
- Who2: Ansel Adams http://www.who2.com/anseladams.html
- Photography Field Trip http://www.field-trips.org/cross/photo/index.htm

February 20, 1895
Anniversary of Frederick Douglas' Death
- Who2: Frederick Douglas http://www.who2.com/frederickdouglass.html

February 21, 1885
Washington Monument Dedicated
The Washington Monument was begun in 1848 to honor the 1st President of the United States, George Washington. It was not completed until 1885. At the time of completion, it was the tallest structure in the world. It retains its world record for being the tallest world's tallest freestanding masonry structure, constructed entirely of stacked granite and marble blocks with no metal structural supports. Take a tour of the Washington Monument and other monuments on the National Mall. Have students choose another person they feel should be honored by a national memorial. Use a drawing program to design an appropriate monument. *Note: Did you know that Federal law prohibits any structure in Washington, D.C. to be taller than the Washington Monument? How tall is it? Compare it to the Empire State Building in New York or a tall structure in your neighborhood.*
- National Park Service http://www.nps.gov/wamo/
- Sightseers Guide to Engineering http://www.engineeringsights.org/ (search for Washington Monument)
- Teaching Historic Places: Washington Monument
  http://www.cr.nps.gov/nr/twhp/wwwlps/lessons/62wash/62wash.htm
- Washington Monument Live Cam http://travel.discovery.com/cams/monument.html?ct=3b5b2d25

- Plan a Trip: Washington, D.C. http://travel.discovery.com/dest/weisdb/usa/dc/intro.html

February 22, 1732
George Washington's Birthday
Who2: George Washington http://www.who2.com/georgewashington.html
And a couple more…..
- The Real Face of George Washington http://earlyamerica.com/georgexdsl.html movie
- Washington Picture Gallery http://www.historyplace.com/unitedstates/revolution/wash-pix/gallery.htm
- The Life of George Washington http://earlyamerica.com/gwlifemovie.htm movie
- Where's George? http://www.wheresgeorge.com/

February 24, 1786
Wilhelm Grimm
- Who2: Brother's Grimm http://www.who2.com/thebrothersgrimm.html
And one more…..
- Grimm Brothers http://www.nationalgeographic.com/grimm/

February 27, 1807
Henry Wadsworth Longfellow's Birthday

> *Between the dark and the daylight,*
> *When the night is beginning to lower,*
> *Comes a pause in the day's occupations,*
> *That is known as the Children's Hour.*[xii]
>
> The Children's Hour by Henry Wadsworth Longfellow

Henry Wadsworth Longfellow is probably the best loved of American poets the world over. Many of his verses are as familiar as nursery rhymes.[xiii] For a biography and poetry links, refer to Longfellow's Biography and Poetry Pages. Many of Longfellow's poems were narratives – poems that tell a story. Some of the classics include the Paul Revere's Ride, the Song of Hiawatha, the Courtship of Miles Standish and the Village Blacksmith. Read selected verses from these poems and related Internet sites.
- Henry Wadsworth Longfellow Biography http://eclecticesoterica.com/longfellow.html
- Poetry Pages: http://www.theatlantic.com/unbound/poetry/longfel/hwlindex.htm
- Song of Hiawatha: Hiawatha's Childhood http://classicreader.com/toc.php/sid.4/bookid.147/
  - Song of Hiawatha Pageant http://www.pipestone.mn.us/pageant/
- Paul Revere's Ride http://www.paulreverehouse.org/events/poem.html
  - Boston's Old North Church http://www.cityofboston.gov/freedomtrail/oldnorth.asp
  - Paul Revere's House http://www.paulreverehouse.org/
  - Paul Revere's Ride – The Real Story http://www.city-net.com/~davekle/revere.htm
- The Village Blacksmith http://www.blupete.com/Literature/Poetry/Blacksmith.htm
  - Horseshoeing http://www.equiresource.com/villagesmith/
  - The American Blacksmith http://www.americanblacksmith.com/
  - Lesson Plan: Blacksmith Shop http://www.angelfire.com/journal/millrestoration/blacksmith.html
- Courtship of Miles Standish http://members.aol.com/calebj/courtship.html

- Miles Standish http://www.encyclopedia.com/articles/12264.html
- The Pilgrims and Plymouth Colony http://www.rootsweb.com/~mosmd/
- The Plymouth Colony Archive http://etext.lib.virginia.edu/users/deetz/
- Plymouth Thanksgiving Story http://www.2020tech.com/thanks/temp.html#story

The Blacksmith Rap

Today's version of the narrative poem is a rap. They have many things in common – story line, expressive language, a definite rhythm or beat. Have your students rewrite *The Village Blacksmith* as a rap. Copy the poem and paste it in a word processor. Write the rap in the second column.

- The Village Blacksmith http://www.blupete.com/Literature/Poetry/Blacksmith.htm

Under a spreading chestnut tree The village smithy stands; The smith, a mighty man is he, With large and sinewy hands; And the muscles of his brawny arms Are strong as iron bands.	Out under that tree The blacksmith stands He's a strong old man With great big hands And the muscles in his arms Are strong as iron bands. Yes, strong as iron bands. Strong as iron bands.

Poetry to Prose

Copy *Paul Revere's Ride* to a word processor. Have the students rewrite the poem as if it were a newspaper account.

Listen, my children, and you shall hear Of the midnight ride of Paul Revere, On the eighteenth of April, in Seventy-Five; Hardly a man is now alive Who remembers that famous day and year.	**Revere Warns of Impending Invasion** At midnight on April 18, 1775, Paul Revere, rode out to warn the neighboring villages of the British invasion.

Books by Henry Wadsworth Longfellow
The Complete Poetical Works of Henry Wadsworth Longfellow
Favorite Poems
Poems and Other Writings
Henry Wadsworth Longfellow (poetry for Young People Series)

February 29
Leap Day

In Scotland, leap year was an important event. A law was passed in 1288 allowing women to propose marriage to the man of their choice in that year.[xiv]

For an explanation and history of leap year, refer to the following sites, then, take the quiz at the Leap Year Lesson Plan site.

- Leap Year http://aa.usno.navy.mil/faq/docs/leap_years.html

- Royal Observatory Greenwich: Leap Year
  http://www.rog.nmm.ac.uk/leaflets/leapyear/leapyear.html
- Lesson Plan http://www.lessonplanspage.com/MathScienceCIOLeapYearDayWebsite48.htm

Leap Year Birthdays

Do you have leap year birthday students in your class? As you know, they sometimes feel left out. They won't after participating in these great web sites.
- Lesson Plan: Great Leap Forward:
  http://www.nytimes.com/learning/general/featured_articles/000224thursday.html
- Famous Leap Year Babies http://www.mystro.com/leap.htm#Famous%20Leap%20Year

Sadie Hawkins Day

Based on Scottish and Irish tradition, women are allowed to propose marriage to the man of their dreams, only on Leap Day. This myth was popularized by cartoonist Al Capp and his characters Li' Abner and Sadie Hawkins. Plan an all school Sadie Hawkins Dance with parents, brothers and sisters of all ages, teachers and other school personnel and, students. Go with a Dogpatch theme and, of course, have lots of dances where the girls ask the boys. Have students from the highest grade be the disk jockeys.
- Sadie Hawkins Day http://www.care2.com/gates/holidays/leapyear/leapyear.html
- Al Capp http://www.lil-abner.com/cappbio.html
  - Sadie Hawkins http://www.lil-abner.com/cappbio.html

---

[i] American Heart Association http://www.americanheart.org/Whats_News/ahm/info.html July 22, 2001
[ii] Giraffe Country http://www.giraffe.org July 22, 2001
[iii] Obristvi http://www.zs-obristvi.cz February 10, 2001 (you will need to translate)
[iv] Scholastic http://teacher.scholastic.com/holiday/factsfun.htm February 9, 2001
[v] Scholastic http://teacher.scholastic.com/holiday/factsfun.htm February 9, 2001
[vi] Judaism 101: tu B'Shevat http://www.jewfaq.org/holiday8.htm July 19, 2001
[vii] Groundhog Day http://www.gojp.com/groundhog/ February 24, 2001
[viii] Sky Watch: Signs of the Weather http://wilstar.com/skywatch.htm#indicators February 24, 2001
[ix] Slavery and Emancipation http://civilwar.bluegrass.net/SlaveryAndEmancipation/15thamendment.html July 20, 2001
[x] Women Writing: Views and Prospects http://www.nla.gov.au/events/holmes.html July 20, 2001
[xi] Japanese Americans Internment Camps http://www.lib.utah.edu/spc/photo/9066/9066.htm July 19, 2001
[xii] The Children's Hour http://members.nbci.com/_XMCM/darsie/library/kid_poems.html May 27, 2001
[xiii] Henry Wadsworth Longfellow, by Roberto Rabe http://eclecticesoterica.com/longfellow_bio.html July 22, 2001
[xiv] Leap Year, The Untold Story http://kalama.doe.hawaii.edu/hern95/pt011/virtualview/leap.html February 10, 2001

5/7/2002

March

May the road rise up to meet you,
May the wind be always at you back,
May the sun shine warm upon your face,
And the rain fall soft upon your fields,
And until we meet again,
May God hold you in the palm of His hand.

Irish Blessing

March offers many opportunities for wonderful adventures using technology. For all of us who have been housebound most of the winter, this is a time that we can travel to exciting places, even if we are 'virtual' travelers. This month, we will travel to Mexico for Benito Juárez's birthday, Ireland for St. Patrick's Day, and Greece for Greek Independence Day. A professional photographer has created a wonderful Internet site, Magical Places, for us armchair travelers. Use your large world map for the background for your bulletin board. Have the students take the virtual tours of these countries and print out pictures that interest them. Use map tacks and string to connect the pictures to the 'real' location. Do this as an introduction to the month's adventures or as you come to the special days.

- Magical Places http://www.earthwisdom.com/
- World Atlas http://www.sitesatlas.com/Atlas/PolAtlas/index.htm

As you look through this month's activities, you will notice other days that we celebrate other countries, such as St. David's Day, March 1st, Girls Day in Japan on March 3 or Mem Foxes birthday on March 5th. Assign different groups of students to search the Internet for a virtual tour of those countries to add to the bulletin board.

A month of interesting patents..

March is home to a number of interesting patents for objects that have enriched our lives. Besides the telephone, there is Monopoly, the Barbie doll, false teeth, earmuffs and the pencil. Assign small groups of students to research a different patent. Then, on the day it was patented, ask them to share what they have learned about their object. I've included some Internet sites to get them started but encourage them to use a search engine designed for young people such as Ask Jeeves for Kids or Searchopolis to find out more. These search engines are not only user friendly, but lead the user to 'safe' sites.

- Ask Jeeves for Kids http://www.ajkids.com
- Searchopolis http://www.searchopolis.com

Special Month

Women's History Month

"Reserve your right to think,
for even to think wrongly
is better than not to think at all."

Hypatia, Natural Philosopher
(355? - 415 CE)[i]

Just about 30 years ago, an Education Task Force in California, decided to take a week to recognize the contribution women have made to history, science, arts and literature and our nation in general. They choose the week of March 8 to coincide with International Women's Day *(see March 8.)* The event was very well received and soon spread to other communities and states. In 1987, the National Women's History Project petitioned Congress to proclaim March, Women's History Month. For more information about Women's History Month refer to:

- National Women's History Project http://www.nwhp.org/
- Congressional Resolution http://www.tulane.edu/~wc/months/whm.html
- Women Who Changed History http://teacher.scholastic.com/activities/women/index.htm

Make a long timeline for your hallway, listing the 1st in Women's Achievements.

- A List of 1st in Women's Achievements http://www.umkc.edu/imc/womenfi.htm

Partner Research

Women have contributed to every walk of life – it's just that their contributions have not until recently made the history books. Challenge your students to learn about our amazing fore-mothers. Pair a female student with a male student. Ask each pair to identify a person they would like to research. The same basic research can be presented in any or all of the following ways: Autobiographical Incident, TV Talk Show, and Web Page. Teach the students another Internet search technique. Use the *Link* feature. When you find an Internet site that you like, it is likely that other good sites will be linked to it. You can search for other sites by using a search engine such as Altavista and keying in Link:and the URL.

Altavista.com
Link: http://www.greatwomen.org

http://www.geocities.com/Hollywood/1858/ella.html

http://lkwdpl.org/wihohio/low-jul.htm

http://www.glenbrook.k12.il.us/gbs/imc/choices/womnhist.html

Autobiographical Incident

This activity was originally prepared for an author study, but could work just as well for a woman in any walk of life study.

- Explanation and rubric http://www.sdcoe.k12.ca.us/score/actbank/tautoinc.htm

TV Talk Show

Have the pair develop an interview for a TV Talk Show, with the female student taking the part of the woman, and the male student the interviewer. Certainly, they may want to ask some knowledge questions, but focus the interview on higher level thinking questions.

- Bloom's Taxonomy http://www.coun.uvic.ca/learn/program/hndouts/bloom.html
- TV interview famous women interview tips
  http://www.soundportraits.org/education/how_to_record/#interviewing_tips

Web Page

Ask each pair to develop a web page about their person for you class web site: Our Famous Fore-Mothers.

- Web Page Evaluation Rubric http://207.73.196.251/documents/WebRubric.htm

Basic Women's History Sites on the Internet

- Children's Encyclopedia of Women http://www2.lhric.org/pocantico/womenenc/womenenc.htm
- Distinguished Women, Past and Present http://www.distinguishedwomen.com

192

- 4000 Years of Women in Science http://www.astr.ua.edu/4000WS/4000WS.html
- Women's Early Art – Music – Poetry http://music.acu.edu/www/iawm/pages/
- Places Where Women Made History http://www.cr.nps.gov/nr/travel/pwwmh/
- National Women's Hall of Fame http://www.greatwomen.org/
- Distinguished Women Past and Present http://www.distinguishedwomen.com/
- The First Ladies http://www.whitehouse.gov/history/firstladies/index.html
- Women in Sports Timeline http://www.northnet.org/stlawrenceaauw/timeline.htm
- National Women's Hall of Fame http://www.greatwomen.org
- Notable Women of Early America http://earlyamerica.com/earlyamerica/notable/index.html
- National Women's Hall of Fame http://www.greatwomen.org

Quilts

"From necessity to art form,
quilts are woven into the fabric of American life."[ii]

Quilts have been referred to as the only true women's art. Making quilts was such a necessary part of the woman's life of clothing and making a home for her family; seeing that the family was kept warn during the winter months, that it seemed more practical than artistic. But, she could take bits and scraps of old pants and shirts or left over materials and make something not only practical, but also beautiful. My grandmother said that pioneer women could not marry without 12 quilts in their hope chest – at least the quilt tops. And, quilting bees were held to help the young woman prepare for the big day.

The Complete Quilt	Abigail Adams block	Eleanor Roosevelt block

Famous Women's Quilt

To honor this tradition and the women you've studied throughout the month, have your students make a Famous Women's Quilt. Ask each student to find a picture about a woman they have studied this month. Copy the picture to a word processor or publishing program. I would give the students specific measurements. For instance, to print two pictures on a standard 8 _ " x11" piece of paper, have the students make their pictures no bigger than 4"x 5". This allows for the space needed to cut the pictures apart and also give _ " seam allowance. To prepare the 'paper', iron 100% white cotton material to the shinny side of regular freezer-wrap paper. Cut the now material bonded paper to the exact measurements of 8 _ "x11". Feed the material bonded paper through the printer when you print the pictures. Remove the freezer-wrap backing and wa-la, you have the picture transferred to a piece of material that can be put together with strips of material and other pictures to create a beautiful quilt. When we made this one, we added quotes from the women (transferred the same way) and buttons and bits and pieces of laces and trims. Learn more about quilting at the following sites.
- American Quilter's Society http://www.aqsquilt.com/
- America Quilts http://www.pbs.org/americaquilts/
  - Quilts in the Classroom http://www.pbs.org/americaquilts/classroom/index.html
- Aids Quilt http://www.aidsquilt.org/
- Harriet Powers' African American Bible Quilts http://womensearlyart.net/powers/

And, for some math lessons about quilts, you will enjoy using these lesson plans.
- Quilted Math http://www.riverdeep.net/riverdeep_today/news_2001/march/030701_quilts.html
- Shape and Space in Geometry
  http://www.learner.org/teacherslab/math/geometry/shape/quilts/index.html
- Mosaic Magic http://www.kindermagic.com/mosaic.html

Odds and Ends
- Rosie the Riveter Puzzle
  http://lcweb2.loc.gov/ammem/ndlpedu/activity/puzzle/rosie/rospuz1.html
- Women in History Stationery http://www.eduplace.com/monthlytheme/march/stationery.pdf
- Women's History Crossword Puzzle
  http://www.nytimes.com/learning/teachers/xwords/print/19990301.html
- Ada B. Lovelace
  http://www.pbs.org/teachersource/mathline/concepts/womeninmath/activity2.shtm
- National Museum of Women's History http://www.nwhm.org/
- Storied Women http://thealamo.net/~jeffket/storiedalt.html
- Women World Leaders http://www.libraryspot.com/features/womenworldleaders.htm
- Quotes by Women http://www.umkc.edu/imc/quoteswo.htm
- Notable Women Ancestors http://www.rootsweb.com/~nwa/alpha.html

Note: For information about Women's Suffrage, refer to August 18, 19th Amendment.

Music In Our School's Month

"I hear America singing,
The varied carols I hear...
Singing with open mouths
Their strong melodious songs."

-Walt Whitman

This is such a perfect month to celebrate music in our school! Besides all of those wonderful Irish melodies, it's Bach's birthday! To get started, look at the following lesson plans. You don't have to be a music teacher to have music in your classroom, but if your school has a music teacher, ask her to collaborate with you as you plan your month's celebration.
- Music In Our School's Month
  http://www.teachervision.com/tv/theme/Music%20in%20Our%20Schools%20Month?s14
- Tune Up For Music In Our Schools http://www.education-world.com/a_lesson/lesson226.shtml
- Make a Music Video http://www.education-world.com/a_lesson/01-1/lp226_05.shtml
- Children's Music Web http://www.nj.com/yuckykids/

Vocal Music
The Internet offers opportunities for your students to listen to wonderful vocalists or to sing along. I hope you enjoy using these sites with your students.
- Sing A-Long Songs http://www.niehs.nih.gov/kids/music.htm
- I Hear America Singing http://www.pbs.org/wnet/ihas/
- KiDiddles http://www.kididdles.com/ (2000 children's songs)
- Avenue Two: Music From Different Cultures http://www.leeron.com/avetwo.htm
- Songs and Musical Memories of Laura Ingalls Wilder
  http://www.geocities.com/~prairiehome/index.html

Okay, this one might be a little more challenging for us non-music teachers. I just wanted you to see a sample of the amazing things on the Internet.
- Sing Harmony: Music Lesson http://www.emplive.com/create/hrmny_lsn/harmony.asp

Instrumental Music

A friend of mine recently asked me if I knew of any piano lessons on the Internet. Well, I had no idea. To me, remembering long hours of sitting next to Miss Brown as she told me to sit up straight and hold my palms up, I just couldn't imagine such a thing. But, I told my friend I would look. And, lo and behold, there are! Minus Miss Brown, of course. But, if you just want to listen to a master play, you will enjoy Internet Piano Midis.

- Music Magic http://library.thinkquest.org/15060/data/lessons/
- Piano Nanny http://www.pianonanny.com/index.html
- Online Piano Lessons http://www.swv.ie/tono/
- Play a virtual piano http://www.frontiernet.net/~imaging/play_a_piano.html
- Internet Piano Midis http://www.geocities.com/Paris/3486/

You can learn about other instruments online as well.

- The Symphony Orchestra http://library.thinkquest.org/22673/orchestra.html
- Instrument Encyclopedia http://www.si.umich.edu/CHICO/MHN/enclpdia.html
- Play Music http://www.playmusic.org/
- Dallas Symphony Orchestra: Kids Activities http://www.dsokids.com/1/kids.html

Stop by and visit the Shrine to Music at the University of South Dakota.

- American's Shrine to Music http://www.usd.edu/smm/links.html

Things to Do

I am not a music teacher, so forgive me all of you who are. These are a couple of ideas I thought of that anyone could do with their students.

1. History You Can Sing To

With all of the midi and wav files available on the Internet, your class could create a musical timeline of American History. How the West Was Sung @ The Music Room site will get your creative juices flowing.

- The Music Room
  http://www.empire.k12.ca.us/capistrano/Mike/capmusic/music_room/themusic.htm

2. Name That Tune

When I was growing up one of my favorite television shows was Name That Tune. Use a program like PowerPoint and make a game board. Have different categories such as kids songs, cowboy songs, classical music, etc. Import the appropriate midi clips and set them to play on the mouse click. After the game board is set up with the appropriate buttons, have the students add the clips. For something a little grander (and harder), use the Music Memory Game.

Game Board – click on the speaker icon to listen to the clip	A click on the ? stops the music and takes you to this slide. The house icon takes you back to the game board.	The page icon takes you to the answer.

- Music Memory Game
  http://www.austin.isd.tenet.edu/campuses/schools/elem/doss/classic/mmgame.htm

Music Appreciation

In honor of the new millennium, National Public Radio held a contest asking listeners to vote on the most important American music of the 20th Century. See if you agree. These can also be used for your History You Can Sing To project.

- 100 Most Important American Musical Works of the 20th Century
  http://www.npr.org/programs/specials/vote/list100.html#S

For the Teacher
- National Association for Music Education http://www.menc.org/
- National Standards and What They Mean to Music Educators
  http://www.menc.org/publication/books/prek12st.html
- K-12 Resources for Music Educators
  http://www.isd77.k12.mn.us/resources/staffpages/shirk/k12.music.html

Odds and Ends
The EMPlive site is an online museum, archive, chronology, and studio rolled into one of modern music from Blues to HipHop.
- Experience Music Project http://www.emplive.com/index.asp

Learn about the great eras, themes and composers in music history. This is a wonderful site with many excellent sound clips.
- Essentials of Music http://www.essentialsofmusic.com/

Are you looking for a site that teaches music theory and note value? This activity is just what the doctor ordered.
- Adding Note Values http://www.education-world.com/a_lesson/01-1/lp226_04.shtml

Art Education Month
To me, art and music are such wonderful partners, both illuminating the human spirit that it seems very appropriate they are both celebrated in the same month. To set off on the right foot, refer to the Art Education Month sites.
- Art Education month http://familyeducation.com/topic/front/0,1156,24-13135,00.html?efc_h03142
- National Art Education Association http://www.naea-reston.org
- National Endowment for the Arts http://arts.endow.gov/

Art Activities
If you are looking for some simple art ideas for your students, you'll find some cool ones at these sites:
- Art Studio Chalkboard http://www2.evansville.edu/studiochalkboard/
- Recipes for Art http://www.geocities.com/Heartland/3893/Goo.html
- Elmers Arts and Crafts http://www.elmers.com/
- Crayola http://www.crayola.com/

But, if you want some really cool, online activities, lessons and games, these sites will help you out.

Online Art Adventures
- Educational Web Adventures http://www.eduweb.com/
- Eyes on Art http://www.kn.pacbell.com/wired/art2/
- Artful Minds
  http://www.thinkquest.org/library/lib/site_sum_outside.html?tname=50072&url=50072/
- Sanford Art Education Resources http://www.sanford-artedventures.com/

Visit an Art Gallery
Whether you are just looking for are looking for some ideas, enjoy visiting these online art galleries.
- Art Museum.net http://www.artmuseum.net/default.asp
- The Getty http://www.getty.edu/
  - ArtsEdNet http://www.getty.edu/artsednet/

- Smithsonian American Art Museum http://www.nmaa.si.edu/
- The Metropolitan Museum of Art http://www.metmuseum.org/home.asp
- Web Museum http://www.ibiblio.org/webmuseum/
- Musee du Louvre http://www.paris.org./Musees/Louvre/
- Pushkin http://www.museum.ru/pushkin/
- Galleria degli Uffizi http://www.televisual.it/uffizi/

If you haven't found what you're looking for, the WW Art Resources probably has it.
- World Wide Art Resources http://www.wwar.com/categories/Museums/Countries/

Clothesline Art Gallery

Put us a clothesline in your classroom. Allow each student to print out one of his or her favorite paintings to hang on your gallery. Have them write a word document listing the artist, museum where the 'real' painting can be found. You can also have the students make an online personal art museum. *Eyes on Art* offers a free tool that allows anyone to create an online art gallery. You do need to choose from a pre-selected set of paintings, but you can write annotations.
- Eyes on Art: You Choose http://www.kn.pacbell.com/wired/art2/choose/index.html

Combined Art and Music Project

To culminate your celebration of Art and Music Education Month, have the students develop a visual musical tour through the ages. Divide the class into groups assigning each group a historical time period such ad renaissance, baroque, classical, romantic, 20th Century. Have one person on the team be the music director, another the artistic director, a third, the technical advisor and the 4th, the producer. The team is to develop a visual musical tour of their time period. Using a presentation tool, such as PowerPoint, the students will combine the music of the period with artistic representations. The students may choose one composer and one artist to represent the period, or, a selection of composers and artists. The qualifier is to match the composition with the painting. For instance, Liszt's *Piano Sonata in B minor* would be an appropriate partner for a Monet painting, but Wagner's *Ride of the Valkyries,* even though they are all from the same time period (1825-1900) would not. Students should write a description of their presentation listing composer and composition and artist and painting and what they are trying to represent. Put the descriptions together in a program for the combined performance. Project the presentations on a big screen with your best speaker and invite the whole community. WOW!
- Essentials of Music http://www.essentialsofmusic.com/
- Eyes on Art: No Fear of Eras http://www.kn.pacbell.com/wired/art2/eras/index.html
- Artcyclopedia http://www.artcyclopedia.com/index.html

Irish-American Month
PL 103-379

"Irish Americans have distinguished themselves in every sector of American life. We are all enriched, strengthened, and blessed by their service to our country."

- President George W. Bush[iii]

- Irish-American Heritage Month http://www.state.sc.us/dmh/culturalaction_fact6.htm

For a great list of online resources, lesson plans, and web-based activities, refer to:
- Themes http://www.teleport.com/~dleahy/themes/ireland.htm

The Irish in America

Although the Irish have been in America since early exploration, the greatest immigration occurred during the potato famine in Ireland. To learn more about Irish Immigration refer to the following Internet sites. A timeline will help students put events in order.

- The Irish in America http://www.pbs.org/wgbh/pages/irish/index.html
- The Irish Immigration to America http://www.aihs.org/History/history1.htm
- Irish History http://wwwvms.utexas.edu/~jdana/irehist.html

Famous Irish-Americans

According to President Bush's 2001 Irish-American Proclamation...

"Nine of the signers of the Declaration of Independence were of Irish origin, and 19 Presidents of the United States have proudly claimed Irish heritage -- including George Washington, Andrew Jackson, John F. Kennedy, and Ronald Reagan." Irish-Americans have contributed to the arts, music, theater, business and all other areas of American culture. The Famous Irish-Americans database is under construction, but will lead you to many distinguished Irish-Americans for research, posters, and other activities. The PBS site is an excellent lesson plan about the contributions immigrants have made. And, although not famous, many of us claim a little Irish blood. If you want to trace your roots, the last two sites might help.

- Famous Irish-Americans http://www.aihs.org/famedatabases/Fame_1.html
- The New Americans http://www.pbs.org/kcet/newamericans/6.0/html/immcontributions.html
- There's a Bit of Irish in All of Us http://www.umkc.edu/imc/stpats.htm
- Lucky Leprechaun Lane http://www.usacitylink.com/lucky/default.html

Tour the Emerald Isle

Wouldn't we all like to visit this beautiful place..this Emerald Isle. Well, what we can't have it in reality, we can in virtual reality. Put on *Danny Boy* and enjoy your tour.

- Tour Ireland http://www.earthwisdom.com/irelandmain.html
- Access Ireland: Visitor Guide http://www.visunet.ie/
- Irish Midi Collection http://www.blackshade.net/midi/midi.html
  - Danny Boy http://www.blackshade.net/midi/bmidi/dannyboy.htm
- Irish Midis http://www.laurasmidiheaven.com/Irishmidi.htm

Odds and Ends

- Ireland.com http://www.ireland.com
- Irish Recipe Collection http://www.ibmpcug.co.uk/~owls/irishlst.htm

Note: See St. Patrick's Day, March 17

Special Week

Newspapers In Our Schools, 1ˢᵗ

"Where the press is free and every man able to read, all is safe."

Thomas Jefferson

Jefferson, the author of the United States Constitution was talking about the 1ˢᵗ Amendment. *"Congress shall make no law respecting an establishment of religion, or prohibiting the free exercise thereof; or abridging the freedom of speech, or **of the press**, or the right of the people peaceably to assemble, and to petition the Government for a redress or grievances."*

This, of course has been challenged many times. One of the earliest was The United States v Thomas Cooper. Thomas Cooper had published a broadside (newspaper) criticizing President John Adams. He was brought to trial under violation of the Sedition of Act of 1798. For an excellent lesson plan based on this case and the 1st Amendment, refer to this site:

- The 1st Amendment: The United States v Thomas Cooper
  http://www.nara.gov/education/cc/cooper.html

Note: The Sedition Act was repealed after Thomas Jefferson became president. Does that surprise you?

Newspapers in the Classroom
There are so many ways newspapers can be used in the classroom. From current events to point of view, to various writing activities, newspapers enrich the classroom everyday. How many ways can you use a newspaper this week?

Today's Headlines
We now have the tools to immediately read the headlines of all of the major newspapers in the country. Have the students check to see how the news is 'playing' in different parts of the United States. You can also check to see what the headlines are in different capital cities around the world. On you world map, copy the headline and tack it to the appropriate city or state.

- Newspaper Links http://www.newspaperlinks.com/home.cfm
- US Newspaper Links http://www.usnewspaperlinks.com/ (with links to national online news sources)
- Online Newspapers http://www.onlinenewspapers.com/ (links to newspapers around the world)
- Reading a Newspaper http://ericir.syr.edu/Virtual/Lessons/Interdisciplinary/INT0060.html

Parts of the Newspaper
The newspaper offers many opportunities for writing using different styles. Of course, there is the standard 'news' story: who, what, when, where, why. But there are also editorials, letters to the editor, advertisements, advice columns, TV guides, movies, book, restaurant reviews, comics, etc. Using the theme of whatever book your class is reading, have the students write a newspaper about that book. My class wrote a newspaper about Harry Potter. It was great!

- News Writing http://teacher.scholastic.com/writewit/news/index.htm

Creating a Classroom Newspaper Online
There are a number of sties on the Internet that will allow you to make online classroom newspapers. You will need to register, but there is no fee.

- CRAYON (Create Your Own Newspaper) http://crayon.net/
- Scholastic http://www.scholastic.com
- My School Online http://www.myschoolonline.com/
- Learning Network http://familyeducation.com/k12/
- Create a Newspaper http://ericir.syr.edu/Virtual/Lessons/Language_Arts/Writing/WCP0041.html

Odds and Ends
Newspapers In Education (NIE) is a non-profit program funded by the Argus Leader and community sponsors. Newspapers are distributed to area schools to be used as a "living textbook". Search your local newspapers to see what their NIE program is.

- Newspapers in Education http://www.nieworld.com/
- The New York Times Teacher Connection http://www.nytimes.com/learning/index.html
- Current Events Poster http://www.abcteach.com/Elections/events.htm
- Newspapers Online Field Trip http://teacher.scholastic.com/fieldtrp/childlit/newbery.htm

*What's black and white
and read all over?
The Newspaper!*

Bubble Gum, 2nd

Sometimes we just need something silly. Well, this is it! National Bubble Gum Week! Have fun!

How To Blow Bubbles

Writing instructions is not as easy as it might appear. Give the students a stick of bubble gum and have them write step-by-step instructions. Then, check out some of these sites:
- The Giant Bubble Gum Page http://www.dimensional.com/~bkelly/bgpage/
- Great Bubble Blowing http://members.tripod.com/~bubblegum22/gum.html
- How to Blow Bubbles http://www.bubblegum.com/qanda/blowingbubbles/

…and see some celebrity bubble blowers….
- Bubble Gum http://www.geocities.com/SouthBeach/Lagoon/4623/

Who Invented Bubble Gum?

Who ever thought of such an idea? Don't know? Well, have someone check it out for you.
- Chewing Gum and Bubble Gum http://inventors.about.com/library/inventors/blgum.htm
- Invention of Bubble Gum http://www.ideafinder.com/history/inventions/story084.htm

These bubble gum companies have some good information plus, even more fun, some cool games and stuff.
- Bubble Yum http://www.candystand.com/BubbleYum/default.htm?
- Bazooka http://www.topps.com/Confectionery/Bazooka/index.html
- Bubble Gum.com http://www.bubblegum.com/

How about those baseball cards and gum wrappers?

- Beatles Singing Bubble Gum Wrapper http://www.timtv.com/beatles.html
- Topps Company http://www.topps.com/
- MyGum.Com http://come.to/my.gum.world/

…of course, we probably should think of a way to justify all of this as I can't think of a National Standard any of this would meet…
- Bubble Gum Science Project
  http://spidey.sfusd.k12.ca.us/schwww/sch773/review/gumproject.html
- Bubble Gum http://www.worldkids.net/bubblgum.htm

National Library Week, 2nd

The American Library Association (ALA) and libraries nationwide, annually sponsor National Library Week to promote library services. To learn about the yearly theme and resources go to the American Library Association site.
- American Library Association http://www.ala.org/
  - National Library Week http://www.ala.org/pio/presskits/nlwkit/nlw2000release.html
  - Celebrating America's Libraries http://www.ala.org/celebrating/

No more having to run out in the middle of a downpour to run to the neighborhood library. Now, many libraries are at your fingertips! Tour these online libraries.
- WWW Virtual Library http://www.vlib.org/
- Internet Public Library http://www.ipl.org/
- Library of Congress http://www.loc.gov/
- Library Spot http://www.libraryspot.com/

- Libweb http://sunsite.berkeley.edu/Libweb/
- ibiblio (the public's library) http://www.ibiblio.org/

Give the students a topic to look up at the library such as Andrew Carnegie. Have the students visit the different libraries to see what materials are available at each location.

Site	# of hits	Title	Description	Rating	Ease in Navigation
WWW Virtual Lib	70	yes	yes	Yes	good

KidsClick

Although not strictly speaking a 'library', KidsClick is a web search site developed by librarians. I really like this site because it is arranged like a library, using the same categories. In fact, look at it 'through a librarians eyes' to see the Dewey Decimal numbers. The other thing I like is each site is given a readability score. I find this very helpful when looking for sites for young elementary students.

- KidsClick! http://sunsite.berkeley.edu/KidsClick!/

Andrew Carnegie

Andrew Carnegie's story is a real 'rags to riches' story. Born to a poor Scottish family, he began working at a very young age. He and his family soon immigrated to America. Although he had no formal education, he had access to his employer's personal library. It was at this time he developed the philosophy that in America, anyone who could read and was willing to work hard could get ahead. He certainly practiced what he preached and became the richest man in the world. Why are we talking about him during National Library Week? He gave public libraries to more than 2000 communities in the United States alone, plus more to other English speaking countries. Does you town have a Carnegie Library? Ask you students to write an essay about what they would do if they were the 'riches person in the world.' The current 'richest man in the world' is Bill Gates. Find out what charities and projects he supports.

- The Richest Man in the World: Andrew Carnegie http://www.pbs.org/wgbh/amex/carnegie/
- The Carnegie Museum: Dunfermline http://www.carnegiemuseum.co.uk/
- Biography http://www.carnegie.org/sub/about/biography.html
- America's Story: Andrew Carnegie http://www.americaslibrary.gov/cgi-bin/page.cgi/aa/carnegie
- Andrew Carnegie and the Carnegie Libraries http://www.lib.msu.edu/lorenze1/carnegie.htm
- Bill Gates http://www.microsoft.com/billgates/bio.asp

Date Varies

Purim – Israel

Purim is the most festive of Jewish holidays, a time of prizes, noisemakers, costumes and treats. It recounts how Queen Esther saves the Jewish people from their enemy Haman, the king's chief advisor. For an excellent online, interactive version of the story, visit Purim on the Net. Children will enjoy coloring the character's masks and making a gragger or noisemaker, and eating some traditional foods. There are also games and coloring pages available.
- Purim on the Net http://www.holidays.net/purim/index.htm
- Virtual Purim http://www.chabadonline.com/default.asp
- Purim Festival http://www.his.com/~chabad/purim/
- Purim games and stories http://www.torahtots.com/holidays/purim/purim.htm

- o   Lil' Fingers: Purim Sweets http://www.lil-fingers.com/purim/
- o   Mask and Crown http://www.zigzagworld.com/mask/home.htm
- Purim Goodies http://www.geocities.com/Heartland/Hills/1259/goodies.htm

For more in-depth study of Purim:
- Judaism 101: Purim http://www.jewfaq.org/holiday9.htm
- Purim, Origins http://www.everythingjewish.com/Purim/Purim_origins.htm
- Purim http://www.torah.org/learning/yomtov/purim/
- General Index for Purim Educational Materials http://www.jajz-ed.org.il/festivls/purim/

Purim is celebrated on the 14th day of Adar. To learn more about the Jewish calendar, go to Months of the Jewish Year http://www.jewfaq.org/calendar.htm#Months

Vernal Equinox - 1st Day of Spring
March 20, 21?

When is that first day of spring? The Vernal Equinox site is great all purpose introduction giving both the scientific and mythology explanation. For the scientific answer, refer to the math chat explanation @ That Shifting 1st Day of Spring and The Length of Day and Night at Equinoxes by the U. S. Navy Observatory, but for a more romantic, if not exactly factual account, you'll want to read about the Sphinx and Persephone.
- The Vernal Equinox http://www.celestia.com/SRP/MA96/Html/VernalEquinox.html
- That Shifting 1st Day of Spring http://csmonitor.com/cgi-bin/getasciiarchive?script/98/03/19/031998.feat.feat.1
- Length of Day and Night at Equinoxes http://aa.usno.navy.mil/AA/faq/docs/equinoxes.html
  - o   Earth's Seasons http://aa.usno.navy.mil/data/docs/EarthSeasons.html
- The Rite of Spring http://www.infoplease.com/spot/riteofspring1.html
- The Great Sphinx of Giza http://guardians.net/egypt/sphinx/
- The Great Sphinx of Giza http://www.pbs.org/wgbh/nova/egypt/explore/sphinx.html
- Persephone and Demeter http://pages.ancientsites.com/~Torrey_Philemon/thalassa/winter.htm
- http://www.csd4.k12.ny.us/J99/resource/Myths/Persephone%20and%20Demeter/persephone.html
- Persephone and the Seasons http://library.thinkquest.org/23057/persephone.html

Divide your class into two groups, the scientists and the mythologists. Have each group research their point of view and think of a way to present it to the other half of the class.

Special Days

March 1

Of course, we all watch the weather on March 1st to see if March will come in as a lion or a lamb. If you are looking for some fun projects related to lions and lambs or just needing a couple of new pictures to color, these sites should get you started.
- Lion and Lamb Projects http://members.nbci.com/MarchProverb/art.html
- Lion / Lamb Proverb contest http://kinder.cmsd.bc.ca/kinder-1/1998/9802/0204.html
- Color lion and lamb http://www.abcteach.com/Activities/MarchColoring.htm   (Don't forget to copy and paste these into the Paint program that is standard on your computer and have the students color with the computer.)

To check out the accuracy of the familiar saying, you can go to the Hourly U.S. Weather Statistics for today and keep that printout until March 31. Another good site for current weather information for your town is at the National Weather Service Homepage. Click on the Interactive Weather Information Network, your state and then, your town. For your monthly project, have the students select cities in other states that they predict will have very different weather than the weather in their city. Weatherbase will show you the weather anywhere in the world, so you can see if the saying it true worldwide. The National Weather Service Homepage has current and historical weather information. For older students, have them copy and paste the table of temperature and precipitation into a spreadsheet program. Then, they can quickly find highs and lows and graph trends.

- Hourly U.S. Weather Statistics http://www.ems.psu.edu/wx/usstats/uswxstats.html
- National Weather Service Homepage http://www.nws.noaa.gov/
    - http://iwin.nws.noaa.gov/iwin/iwdspg1.html
- Weatherbase http://www.weatherbase.com/

If you want to do this 'scientifically' follow the steps of the Scientific Method. The second site, Steps to Prepare a Science Fair Project, is an excellent resource for preparing any science project.

- Scientific Methods Steps http://www.usd.edu/~msemmler/scientific_method.html
- Steps to Prepare a Science Fair Project http://www.isd77.k12.mn.us/resources/cf/steps.html

Because of the climate changes that occur in March, it can be a severe weather month. This might be a good time to check out the severe weather statistics.

- Severe Weather Statistics http://www.nws.noaa.gov/er/btv/html/sevstats.html

March 1
St. David's Day – Wales, UK

"To be born Welsh is to be born privileged, not with a silver spoon in your mouth, but with music in your blood and poetry in your soul."

-Old Welsh Proverb

Saint David is the patron saint of Wales. He was a Celtic monk who lived in the sixth century. During his life, he was one of many early saints who helped to spread Christianity among the pagan Celtic tribes of western Britain. Today, St. David's Day is a celebrated throughout Wales with songs, dances and traditional Welsh poetry reading. For more information about St. David and St. David's Day, refer to:

- St. David's Day http://www.davidmorgan.com/CATALOGS/DM/dm78
- Land of My Fathers – Wales http://www.cyberbeach.net/~slucas/wales-dewi.html
- Saint David and Saint David's Day http://www.sucs.swan.ac.uk/~rhys/stdavid.html

March 1
Get Caught Reading Day

This is really a time to "practice what we preach." Invite the principal, the gym teacher, the mayor, a parent or grandparent, a fireman or police officer to the classroom to talk about their favorite book as a child and to read a selection from it to the class. Another group of people who may be more impressive to your younger students is the high school football team, the gymnastics team, band members and the theater group. Ask them to read their favorite book to your students. Make a list of favorites. And, catch people reading! Have the students take the digital camera to 'catch' people reading. Bring the picture into a publishing program or photo program that will allow them to add text to their picture. Key "'name' was caught reading!" Hang your pictures in the hallway. Title your wall of readers DEAR for Drop Everything And Read or BEAR for Be Excited About Reading.

- World Book Day http://www.worldbookday.com/
- Child Lit http://www.mhhe.com/socscience/education/kidlit/
- Best Books of the Century http://www.amazon.com/exec/obidos/ts/feature/11295/102-9945013-2973728

March 2, 1904
Theodore Geisel's (Dr. Seuss) Birthday

"I like nonsense; it wakes up the brain cells."

- Dr. Seuss

Join millions of children across America by reading Dr. Seuss books. Make some green eggs and ham and make a tall red and white striped hat. For more ideas, refer to the following Internet sites:
- Read Across America Day http://www.nea.org/readacross/resources/index.html
- CyberSeuss http://www.afn.org/~afn15301/drseuss.html
- Dr. Seuss's Seussville! http://www.randomhouse.com/seussville/

Some books by Dr. Seuss
     Oh, the Places You'll Go
     One Fish Two Fish Red Fish Blue Fish
     The Cat in the Hat
     Green Eggs and Ham
     The Lorax
     Dr. Seuss's ABC
     Horton Hears a Who
     Horton Hatches the Egg
     Gerald McBoing Boing
     And To Think That I Saw It On Mulberry Street
     Hop On Pop
     Fox in Socks
     Yertle the Turtle
     Marvin K. Mooney, Will You Please Go Now
     The Sneetches and Other Stories
     The Butter Battle Book
     How the Grinch Stole Christmas

March 3
National Anthem Day
President Hoover signed the bill in 1931 making *The Star Spangled Banner* our national anthem. But, do you know who wrote it and why? Read the history of our national anthem.
- Star Spangled Banner Web Site http://www.americanhistory.si.edu/ssb/
- Original Copy http://www.azstarnet.com/~rgrogan/flag3.htm
- Francis Scott Key http://www.icss.com/usflag/francis.scott.key.html
- Star Spangled Banner http://www.150.si.edu/chap3/flag.htm
- Star Spangled Banner and the War of 1812 http://www.si.edu/resource/faq/nmah/starflag.htm

Words to Lyrics
Key wrote the words to *The Star Spangled Banner* during that dark night as he looked back to shore, but at that time, it was just a poem. Dolly Madison, wife of President James Madison, encouraged him to set it to music. He used the tune from a popular song of the day. Practice setting a poem to music. Carol Hurst says that you can sing almost any Emily Dickinson poems to the tune of *The Yellow Rose of Texas.* Give it a try.

I'm nobody! Who are you?
Are you nobody, too?
Then there's a pair of us -- don't tell!
They'd banish us, you know.
How dreary to be somebody!
How public, like a frog
To tell your name the livelong day
To an admiring bog![iv]

- Yellow Rose of Texas Midi http://www.lsjunction.com/midi/songs.htm
- Emily Dickinson Complete Poems http://www.bartleby.com/113/

Publisher and poet Bruce Lansky has a wonderful web site that helps students get involved in poetry, but the part I want to use for this exercise is Yankee Doodle and make up new lyrics.

- Yankee Doodle http://www.poetryteachers.com/yankeefib.html

Star Spangled Banner Glossary

In Beverly Cleary's *Ramona the Pest*, Ramona misunderstands the lyrics of *The Star Spangled Banner* and asks her sister to turn on the dawnzer to get some light. I can imagine Ramona singing loudly and proudly, "Oh say, can you see by the dawnzer, the light." The details are in *Ramona the Pest* by Beverly Cleary. Have the students write a glossary for the Star Spangled Banner. Include the parts of speech as well as the definition.

National Anthem Survey

Our national anthem, *The Star Spangled Banner*, is a difficult song to sing. Some people think *America the Beautiful* would be a better National Anthem. Make a list of as many patriotic songs as you and your students can think of. Take a poll of other classes, school personnel and parents to see which song they think would be a better national anthem or if we should keep *The Star Spangled Banner*. Enter your data in a spreadsheet and graph your results.

- USA Patriotic Heritage http://home.t-online.de/home/Gert.Fechner/patriot.htm
- Patriotic Music http://www.azstarnet.com/~rgrogan/flagmusic.htm

Internet Sources for the Star Spangled Banner

Are you just looking for the lyrics or the music to the Star Spangled Banner? For a wonderful rendition, listen to the United State Army Band and for a very nice, simple, easy to sing to version, refer to the second version.

- United State Army Bands Online: National Anthem http://www.bands.army.mil/anthem.asp
- The Star Spangled Banner http://www.azstarnet.com/~rgrogan/usa1.htm

National Anthems of the World

Listen to some of the beautiful and stirring national anthems of other countries. Then, have your students listen to and add a verse to the International Anthem written by middle school students from Vaksalaskolan, Sweden.

- National Anthems of the World http://www.emulateme.com/anthems/
- World Anthem Database http://www.geocities.com/CollegePark/Library/9897/ (lyrics)
- Listen to the National Anthems of the World http://homepage.renren.com/midistation/anthem.htm
- International Anthem http://www.jp.kids-commons.net/vc96/vc-05/internat.htm

March 3, 1847
Alexander Graham Bell's Birthday
Little known facts -

- In 1878, Rutherford B. Hayes was the first US president to have a telephone installed in the White House. And to whom did the commander-in-chief place his first call? Alexander Graham Bell, of course, who was waiting for the call some 13 miles away from the White House. The president's first words were said to have been, "Please speak more slowly."

- When Alexander Graham Bell died on August 4, 1922, millions of phones went dead. In Bell's honor, all phones served by the Bell System in the USA and Canada went silent for one minute. [v]

For most of us, we couldn't imagine a world without the telephone. Whether it's an emergency call to the doctor or 911, to place an order or ask for information or just a friendly chat with friends or relatives, the phone has become an integral part of our daily lives. Who was this man who changed our lives so completely? For an excellent introduction, go to Brain Spin and read the brief biography. Refer to the other sites for more in-depth biographies to see why communication was so important to him.

- Brain Spin http://www.att.com/technology/forstudents/brainspin/
- Biography http://web.mit.edu/invent/www/inventorsA-H/graham_bell.html
- Alexander Graham Bell http://www.ideafinder.com/history/inventors/bell.htm
- Family Papers http://memory.loc.gov/ammem/bellhtml/bellhome.html
- World Book: Alexander Graham Bell http://www.worldbook.com/fun/tty/html/bell.htm
- Bell Images http://bell.uccb.ns.ca/images/

We all know that the telephone was invented by Alexander Graham Bell, but did you know that he was the president of the National Geographic Society? Check it out! And then, take a virtual tour of Bell's home at Cape Breton.

- President of the National Geographic Society
  http://www.nationalgeographic.com/infocentral/fact/biobel.html
- Birth of a Society http://www.nationalgeographic.com/birth/nfor5at.html
- Driving Tour of Cape Breton
  http://www.nationalgeographic.com/destinations/Cape_Breton/Cape_Breton.html

Telephone Etiquette
Have the students write a mini book about phone manners. Be sure to add chapters on web cam phones, cell phones and phone safety. You can download a sample FlipAlbum for you book.

- Telephone Etiquette http://library.thinkquest.org/2993/phone.htm
- Business Phone Etiquette http://www.lcc.whecn.edu/cpes/SEPManuals/Telephone.htm
- Miss Stacey's Mind Your Manners
  http://199.17.178.123/en3930/steinkopf/manners/Telephone.html
- FlipAlbum http://www.flipalbum.com

How Does It Work?
Take the mystery out of the phone. These sites not only have the real scoop, but some interactive things for your students to do.

- How Stuff Works: Telephone http://www.howstuffworks.com/telephone.htm
- The Invention of the Telephone http://jefferson.village.virginia.edu/albell/homepage.html
- Telephones Through the Years http://www.pbs.org/wgbh/amex/telephone/gallery/index.html

- Video and Audio of 1st telephone
  http://www.att.com/technology/history/chronolog/1876telephone.html
- Cyber Telephone Museum http://www.museumphones.com/
- AGB Games http://bell.uccb.ns.ca/kids/kidsindex.htm

Learn More About the Deaf and Hard of Hearing
Bell's family members influenced and encouraged his interest in helping people with hearing problems. This tradition continues today through the Alexander Graham Bell Association for the Deaf and Hard of Hearing. Have the students learn to finger spell their names. Students will also enjoy learning to count and to 'say' a few phrases such a 'hi, what is your name? my name is…'
- AGBell Association for the Deaf and Hard of Hearing http://www.agbell.org/
- Deaf World: Sign Language http://dww.deafworldweb.org/asl/
- Sign Language Cards http://www.abcteach.com/ABC/signTOC.htm

Odds and Ends
- Find a Phone Number http://www.switchboard.com/
- Robert Frost poem "Telephone" http://www.lit.kobe-u.ac.jp/~hishika/frost.htm

March 3
Girl's Day Hinamatsuri – Japan

Akari o tsukemasho bonbori ni
Ohana o agemasho momo no hana
Go-nin bayashi no fue taiko
Kyo wa tanoshii Hinamatsuri

Let's light the lanterns
Let's set peach flowers
Five court musicians are playing flutes and drums
Today is a joyful Dolls' Festival^{vi}

Hina Matsuri is a special day in Japan, when families pray for the happiness and health of the girls. A significant part of the celebration is to set up a display of special dolls. To learn the history of Hinamatsuri, refer to the following Internet sites. The last two offer personal accounts of how the day is celebrated.
- Hina Matsuri http://www.jinjapan.org/kidsweb/calendar/march/hinamatsuri.html
- Hinamatsuri http://www-japan.mit.edu/mit/culture-notes/Mar/hinamaturi.html
- Hinamatsuri http://ua1vm.ua.edu/~mlc/japanese/celebrations/hinamatsuri/hinamatsuri.htm
- Girls Festival in Japan http://www.rice.edu/projects/topics/internatl/holidays/girls.festival.html
- Girls Day http://www.kidlink.org/KIDPROJ/MCC/mcc0277.html

Listen to Hinamatsuri
Of course, most holidays are associated with special songs. Listen to Hinamatsuri and learn to sing along.
- Music and lyrics http://www.caves.net/~cmmeyer/Hinamatsuri.html
- Joyous Girl's Festival http://home2.highway.ne.jp/hinachan/ureshihina_e.html

The Dolls

One of the important features of this festival is a doll display. Many families give the first set of dolls as a baby gift to the newborn little girl. The collection grows over the years. The dolls are displayed only a few days a year, so are very special. According to legend, paper dolls were made representing each member of the family. At the end of the day, the dolls were floated down the river, taking the bad luck that may have happened to the family member with them, so the rest of the year would be free of misfortune. View some of the exquisite dolls and then, have the students make paper dolls for your classroom display. I don't know that you will be able to talk the students into floating their dolls down a river, though.

- Hina Visual Japan http://www.harapan.co.jp/english/JPImage_e/hina_e.htm
- Dolls http://www.kyohaku.go.jp/mus_dict/hd04e.htm
- All About Japanese Hina Dolls http://www.kyohaku.go.jp/mus_dict/hd04e.htm
- Origami Paper Doll http://www.askasia.org/image/drawing/i000303.htm
- Doll Book Mark http://crayola.com/activitybook/display.cfm?id=545
- Paper Dolls http://www.ushsdolls.com/paperdoll/pdarc.html

Note: if you remember playing with paper dolls when you were little, like I do, and think they are a thing of the past, check out some of these paper dolls and links @

- Marilee's Paperdolls http://www.ameritech.net/users/macler/paperdolls.html

Navaratri

Navaratri is a Hindu holiday celebrated in India. The festival honors the different gods. Households set up a display of doll-like ornaments called Golu. As this is mainly a womens and girls festival, small gifts are given to the female visitors.

Navaratri http://library.thinkquest.org/11719/vasishtfiles/navaratri.html

March 5, 1946
Mem Fox's Birthday

Mem Fox has one of the most extensive web sites of any children's author I know. You will not only find her biography and list of likes and dislikes, the background for many of her books, but also you will be able to listen to her read some of her most loved books. You will really find this a treasure.

- Mem Fox http://www.memfox.net/
- Mem Fox http://coe.west.asu.edu/students/dcorley/authors/Fox.htm (student site)

I just called to say, "I love you…."

Mem Fox is very concerned that children hear the words, *"I love you."* Recognizing that many people have trouble expressing how they feel, she often writes those words in her books, so that when children are being read to, they hear the words – 'I love you.' Have your students brainstorm a list of how people say 'I love you' without using words…hugs, smiles, serving a favorite food…etc. The idea for brainstorming is to be fast and non-judgmental. I like to have students work with a computer for this and give them a time limit of say 5 minutes. Each student makes his or her own list with only the computer to see what he or she is writing. Then, have the students edit a little for spelling, etc. Go around the room with each student reading one thing from the list. If the other students don't have it on their list, they can add it. Do this until everyone has a very long list of ways to say, 'I love you.' Replace the word 'called' in the song with one of the words or phrases form the list. Help students see that by smiling at someone or picking up their toys, they are saying 'I love you.'

- Stevie Wonder: I Just Called To Say I Love You
  http://orion.spaceports.com/~mmp/letras/IJustCalledToSayILoveYou.html

Field Trip to Australia

Mem Fox often tells her stories through the animals native to Australia. Through the Travel Buddies Project, your students can share stories, local history and customs with children around the world. The other sites listed invite you to learn about Australia through photographs and webcams. In Possum Magic, a grandmother and small child travel across Australia. Recreate their journey by finding pictures of the places they visit. Mount these on a map of Australia. Have your students rewrite this story using the United States as the setting. Locate regional foods and locations. Send your story to the children at Wangaratta Primary School and invite them to get to know America. Include the recipes.

- Travel Buddies Project: Koala Chris http://www.rite.ed.qut.edu.au/oz-teachernet/projects/travel-buddies/index.html
- Explore Australia – Photo Gallery http://www.nationalgeographic.com/explorer/australia/abell/
- National Geographic on Australia http://www.nationalgeographic.com/downunder/
- Creature Features on Koalas
  http://www.nationalgeographic.com/kids/creature_feature/0008/index.html
- WebCam View of Sydney Harbor http://www.viewsydney.com/index3a.htm
- Wangaratta Primary School http://members.ozemail.com.au/~wprimary/wps.htm

Some books by Mem Fox
Wilfrid Gordon McDonald Partridge
Koala Lou
Time for Bed
Book to a Goose
Possum Magic
Whoever You Are
Zoo Looking
Shoes from Grandpa
Hattie and the Fox
Tough Boris
Night Noises
Sleepy Bears
Harriet, You'll Drive Me Wild!
Sophie
Wombat Divine
Feathers and Fools
Guess What?

March 6, 1475
Michelangelo de Lodovico Buonarroti-Simoni
"His contemporaries spoke about his terribilità, *which means, of course, not so much being terrible as being awesome. There has never been a more literally awesome artist than Michelangelo: awesome in the scope of his imagination, awesome in his awareness of the significance--the spiritual significance--of beauty."* [vii] To learn more about the life and times of Michelangelo, refer to the following Internet sites.

- Web Museum http://www.ibiblio.org/wm/paint/auth/michelangelo/

- Michelangelo http://www.michelangelo.com.br/ (use AltaVista: Babel Fish to translate)
- Michelangelo http://www.worldbook.com/fun/tty/html/michelangelo.htm

Drawing People

Michelangelo is famous for his drawing and painting of the human form. To learn some techniques for drawing the human form these sites will be very helpful. If you have the students use a Paint program, they will be able to 'erase' the lines they don't need to complete their drawings.

- Learn to Draw http://www.learnhowtodraw.com/
- Hiro's Drawing Class http://susanooh.anime.net/Art/Class/

Okay, if people are your thing, maybe the kids will enjoy drawing cartoon characters. My apology to Michelangelo!

- Gary Harbo http://www.garyharbo.com/

Visit the Sistine Chapel

Michelangelo's most famous work is the Sistine Chapel in the Vatican . The Sistine Chapel is where major papal ceremonies take place. Explore this beautiful work of art and faith.

- Cappella Sistina http://www.christusrex.org/www1/sistine/0-Tour.html
- Exploring the Sistine Chapel Ceiling http://www.science.wayne.edu/~mcogan/Humanities/Sistine/
- Sistine Chapel
  http://www.twingroves.district96.k12.il.us/Renaissance/SistineChapel/Michelangelo/Ceiling.html
- Visit the Sistine Chapel http://www.kfki.hu/~arthp/tours/sistina/
- Medici Villa
  http://www.twingroves.district96.k12.il.us/Renaissance/SistineChapel/Michelangelo/Michelangelo.html

March 7, 1876
Telephone Patented
See March 3 – Alexander Graham Bell's Birthday

For the students' research project, you might want to ask them to do the biography or how the telephone works. Decide this before you participate in other Alexander Graham Bell Birthday projects.

March 7, 1933
Monopoly Patented

You might want to offer the following questions to guide the student research.

1. What is the history of monopoly?
2. Are there really the streets and avenues named in Monopoly? Where are they? Can you find a map on the Internet?
3. What is a monopoly?
4. Is there an online version of the game?
5. What other board games have become popular over the years?
   - Monopoly http://www.monopoly.com/

March 8
International Women's Day

The first women's day was held on March 8, 1857, when women working in clothing and textile factories (called 'garment workers') in New York City, in the United States, staged a protest. They were fighting against inhumane working conditions and low wages. Police quickly broke up the demonstration. But, again on March 8, 1908, 15,000 women marched through New York City demanding shorter work hours; better pay, voting rights and an end to child labor. Through their efforts and those of others, women's rights in the workplace have improved. International Women's Day, sponsored by the United Nations, main focus is *"to recognize that peace and social progress require the active participation and equality of women, and to acknowledge the contribution of women to international peace and security."*[viii] The United Nations Cyber School Bus site maintains a very helpful resource for teachers with history, lesson plans, current events and suggestions for successful International Women's Day celebrations.

- International Women's Day http://www.un.org/Pubs/CyberSchoolBus/womensday/index.html

Note: See March 25 – the Triangle Shirtwaist Fire and other Women's History Month activities.

March 9
Holi

Holi is a holiday in India that signifies the end of winter and the beginning of spring. The celebration begins the night before when bonfires burn the dead sticks and limbs that have fallen during the winter. Often an effigy of Pootna, a mythological demon is burnt. Does this remind you of Guy Fawkes? Holi is a joyous festival celebrated with the bright colors of clothing, decorations and colored powders. To learn more about this holiday, refer to these Internet sites.

- About Holi http://www.colorsofindia.com/aboholi.htm
- Holi http://www.indolink.com/Kidz/holi.html
- Holi http://www.ahmedabad.com/travel/fairfest/holi.htm
- Holi Festival http://www.swaminarayan.org/festivals/holi/index.htm

Word Choice – Holy Vehicles

Hindu gods have their own vehicles which they ride as they go about their tasks. Look at these beautiful paintings. Have the students key in descriptive words and phrases for each of the paintings. Make lists of uncommon color words – such as red = vermilion, scarlet, rose, etc. This will help them develop word choice, one of the 6+1 Writing Traits.

- Holy Vehicles http://www.kamat.com/kalranga/vehicles/index.htm
- 6+1 Writing Traits http://www.nwrel.org/eval/writing/definitions.html

March 9, 1454
Amerigo Vespucci's Birthday

Amerigo Vespucci was the navigator on at least two explorations to the New World, a term he was the first to use. Often belied as a fraud, Vespucci actually wrote the most interesting account of explorations in the Americas that had appeared up to that time renewing the people's interests. It was however, German mapmaker, Waldseemueller, who used Vespucci's name, Amerigo (changing it to the Latin – America) on maps and in books to identify this New World. Travel with Vespucci to the land he recognized as a New World.

- Amerigo Vespucci: Account of His First Voyage, 1497
  http://www.fordham.edu/halsall/mod/1497vespucci-america.html
- Amerigo Vespucci http://tqjunior.thinkquest.org/4034/vespucci.html
- Why Was America Named After Amerigo Vespucci?
  http://www.straightdope.com/classics/a4_021.html
- Vespucci's Career Compared to Columbus'
  http://www.calstatela.edu/faculty/eviau/edit557/vespucci/dan/m102.html

Maps

Take a look at the Waldseemuller map of the Americas and compare it to the map, as we know it today. Notice that what the mapmaker lacked in accuracy, he made up for in artistic embellishments.

- The Waldseemuller Portrait
  http://www.calstatela.edu/faculty/eviau/edit557/vespucci/dan/m402.html
- Las Cronicas de America
  http://web.reed.edu/academic/departments/spanish/spanish%20380/maps.html

Who Wins?

Some feel that Christopher Columbus was robbed because the land he discovered was named for another man. Compare who has more cities named for him. Go to Map Quest and key in Columbus in the city box. How many Columbus' are there in the United States? Repeat the process using America. Challenge your students to see if the results are true for other countries in North America and South America? How could they find out?

- MapQuest http://www.mapquest.com

March 9, 1822
False Teeth Patented

You might want to offer the following questions to guide the student research.

1. Who invented the 1st false teeth?
2. Did George Washington really have wooden teeth?
3. What is the false teeth timeline?
4. How are false teeth made?
   - History of False Teeth http://www.gumshield.com/history/false_teeth.html

Other 'Teeth' Projects

Because good dental hygiene is so important for children, you may want to expand your study of teeth beyond what you have the students do with the false teeth patent. There are a number of excellent lesson plans available for you to do. Many of them have experiments for classroom use. Some of my favorites are:

- Oral Health Experiments http://www.gumshield.com/experiment/index.html
- Tooth Parts and Types of Teeth http://www.gumshield.com/children/index.html
- No Cavities Clubhouse http://kids-world.colgatepalmolive.com/

Education World offers a great experiment about the importance of brushing teeth. It goes well with *Grandpa's Teeth* by Rod Clement.

For the experiment, you'll need to hard-boil a white-shelled egg. Then …

1. Put the egg in a clear glass big enough to hold it.
2. Pour enough cola in the glass to cover the egg.
3. Leave the egg in the glass overnight.
4. The next day remove the egg from the cola-filled glass.
5. Use an old toothbrush with toothpaste to brush the brown cola stain from the egg.[ix]

Dental Health Posters

Make dental health posters using the graphics at Flossies. There are many animated graphics and these can be used with programs, such as PowerPoint that support animations. I used the basic shapes to create this poster. When shown as a PowerPoint, her lips move. This is a fun way to work with animations. Record the text and insert it into the PowerPoint.

- Flossies http://www.mir.spaceports.com/~flossies/index.html

What's So Funny?

Just saying the words 'false teeth' make people smile. Have your students write their own jokes about teeth. Jokes are hard to understand for young children, even though they love them, because it really takes a fairly sophisticated language development to 'get' it. The English, What a Language site will help you explain why our language if funny.

- English: What a Language http://www.niehs.nih.gov/kids/jokeengl.htm
- False Teeth Jokes http://www.jokedictionary.com/jokes/f/falseteethjokes.html
- Kids Page Jokes and Riddles http://www.niehs.nih.gov/kids/jokes.htm

Tooth Fairy Stories

Who is the tooth fairy and where did she come from? Have students write stories the tooth fairy. Some topics might include: what she does with all of those teeth, the night she was almost caught, the tooth fairy that lost the teeth... Illustrate the stories with clip art from Flossies. Your students can join other children around the world by participating in the Tooth Tally Project sponsored by Wilburn Elementary. Record your losses!

- The Tooth Fairy Page http://www.toothfairy.org/
- Flossies http://mir.spaceports.com/~flossies/
- Tooth Tally Project http://www.kn.pacbell.com/wired/art2/choose/index.html
- The Adventures of My Dentist and the Tooth Fairy
  http://www.adventuresofmydentistandthetoothfairy.com/
- Tooth Fairy Castle http://jove.prohosting.com/~pearle/
- Tommy the Tooth Mouse http://hermes.spaceports.com/~tomtooth/
- Ginger's Place http://gingersplace.hypermart.net/

March 10, 1959
Barbie Patented

You might want to offer the following questions to guide the student research.

1. Who invented Barbie and why?
2. How has Barbie changed over the years?
3. What do Barbie's critics say?
4. How much are collectable Barbie's worth?
5. What other dolls and toys have become popular over the years? (GI Joe, hula-hoop, Cabbage Patch dolls, Beanie Babies, etc.)
   - The World of Barbie http://www.barbiecollectibles.com/about/index.asp

Note: Teachers, this is one of those sites where it is so important to use the correct prefix. www.barbie.com - good, www.barbie.org - bad! I wouldn't necessarily tell the students as they, like the rest of us will want to try it out, but, you need to be aware of it. Another example of this kind of thing is www.whitehouse.com - bad, *www.whitehouse.org* - bad, *www.whitehouse.net* - bad, but *www.whitehouse.gov* – good.

March 11, 1916
Ezra Jack Keats

Caldecott Award winner, Ezra Jack Keats, began painting as a small child. As an adult, he illustrated other author's books, but was concerned that the main character was never a black child. He vowed that when he made his own books, the hero would be a black child. With his first, *A Snowy Day*, he fulfilled that promise. Read more about this well loved children's illustrator and author.

- Biography http://www.kidstrek.com/6build/keats.html
- Author Biographies: Ezra Jack Keats
  http://www.edupaperback.org/authorbios/Keats_EzraJack.html
- Ezra Jack Keats http://coe.west.asu.edu/students/dcorley/authors/Keats.htm (students site)

His Art

Keats uses simple shapes and colors, usually with a collage technique to create his wonderful illustrations. Look at some of his outstanding illustrations.

- USM de Grummond Collection http://www.lib.usm.edu/~degrum/keats/main.html

Try to imitate his style by collecting backgrounds and pasting them on a paint program. Use paint tools to cut shapes you need for your picture. Add clip art to complete your collage.

- What is Collage? http://www.collagetown.com/history01.shtml
- A Touch of Country Backgrounds http://www.geocities.com/Heartland/Hills/7060/graphindex.htm
- Clip Art @ Kids Domain http://www.kidsdomain.com/clip/

Less is More

Keats states that his aim is simplicity – less is more.

Take a complicated story and reduce it to simple text. Choose a fairly long and complicated story or poem and have the students rewrite it using simple sentences and vocabulary. You might want to use a paragraph from Mary Shelley's *Frankenstein*. Do you think something might be lost in the process?

As the circumstances of his marriage illustrate his character, I cannot refrain from relating them. One of his most intimate friends was a merchant, who, from a flourishing state, fell, through numerous mischances, into poverty. This man, whose name was Beaufort, was of a proud and unbending disposition, and could not bear to live in poverty and oblivion in the same country where he had formerly been distinguished for his rank and magnificence. Having paid his debts, therefore, in the most honourable manner, he retreated with his daughter to the town of Lucerne, where he lived unknown and in wretchedness. My father loved Beaufort	My father had a friend named Beaufort. Due to unfortunate circumstances, he lost all of his money. Because he was ashamed of being poor Beaufort took his daughter and moved to Lucerne. This made my father very sad. He tried to find him. He wanted to help him. *Keanna, age 11*

214

with the truest friendship, and was deeply grieved by his retreat in these unfortunate circumstances. He bitterly deplored the false pride which led his friend to a conduct so little worthy of the affection that united them. He lost no time in endeavouring to seek him out, with the hope of persuading him to begin the world again through his credit and assistance. *Frankenstein - Chapter 1, paragraph 2*	

Mural Painter for WPA

During the Great Depression, President Franklin D. Roosevelt created the Works Progress Administration (WPA) to provide jobs for millions of unemployed Americans. In 1935, the Federal Art Project became part of the WPA, which resulted in jobs for hundreds of artists. Along with other artists, Ezra Jack Keats painted murals for the WPA in libraries, court houses, schools and other public buildings. Look at some of these beautful paintings that still grace our public buildings today. Do you have any WPA murals in your area? What other kinds of public art is in your town?

- About Ezra Jack Keats http://www.ezra-jack-keats.org/Top/about_keats.htm
- Norwalk's Collection of WPA Murals http://www.norwalktransit.com/mural.htm
- Lane Technical School http://www.lanehs.com/gallery4.htm
- Sweatshop Mural http://americanhistory.si.edu/sweatshops/intro/wpa.htm (see March 25, Triangle Shirtwaist Fire)
- Brockton Public Library http://www.brocktonpubliclibrary.org/building/mural.html
- Dining Hall Mural http://www.mountainsanatorium.net/wpagallery.htm
- Newark City Subway Murals http://www.nycsubway.org/us/newark/stations.html
- Post Office Mural http://www.texasescapes.com/TOWNS/SMITHVILLE/SmithvilleTexas3.htm

Books by Ezra Jack Keats
Peter's Chair
Googles!
A Snowy Day (1963 Caldecott Award)
A Letter to Amy
Louie's Search
Pet Show
Over in the Meadow
A Letter to Amy
Whistle for Willie
Regards to the Man in the Moon
Apt. 3
Hamster Chase
Two Tickets to Freedom: The True Story of Ellen and William Craft, Fugitive Slaves
John Henry: An American Legend
Hi, Cat!
My Dog Is Lost

Dreams
One Red Sun: A Counting Book

March 11, 1818
Frankenstein 1ˢᵗ **Published by Mary Shelley**
With her colorful and somewhat nontraditional views on marriage among other things, I will leave the biography of Mary Shelley up to you and will focus on her famous literary work, *Frankenstein*. But, if you need a PG rated chronology of her life, refer to Mary Wollstonecraft Shelley. For the X rated story, refer to Frankenstein Study: Anatomy of a Story.
- Mary Wollstonecraft Shelley http://www.english.udel.edu/swilson/mws/smchron1.html
- Frankenstein Study: Anatomy of a Story
  http://www.watershed.winnipeg.mb.ca/Frankenstein.html

What is it about horror stories or movies that intrigues us? If it scares us so much, why to we continue to read or to look? Are there benefits to being scared? Maybe. Not only does it force us to test our courage, but to face our fears. Whether we fear the monster on the screen, the ghost in the story or that no one will like us or we will fail the test, or we are ugly, we are learning to see them for what they are – something that can be dealt with. And that is a good thing.

The 'Cliff Notes' Version
Look at the activity for Ezra Jacks Keats Birthday on March 11 where we have the students simplify the story. To get right to the nitty-gritty, check out the AntiStudy site for 'real' notes on Frankenstein and other classics. And, for a really, really short version, your students will enjoy Disney's Last Minute Book Report.
- AntiStudy http://www.antistudy.com/
- Last Minute Book Reports http://disney.go.com/family/lastminute/index.html?clk=1012419

Frankenstein In Art and In Poetry
Enjoy looking at the Frankenstein Gallery and reading the original poetry. Encourage your students to contribute to the site.
- The Frankenstein Mail Art Exhibit http://www.cityu.edu.hk/ls/research/frankenstein/
- Frankenstein Poetry http://www.cityu.edu.hk/ls/research/frankenstein/item5.htm

For electronic texts, refer to the following sties:
- Frankenstein, 1818 by Mary Shelly http://www.sangfroid.com/frank/
- Mary Shelley's Frankenstein http://home-1.worldonline.nl/~hamberg/
- Frankenstein, by Mary Shelly http://www.dagonbytes.com/thelibrary/frankenstein/preface.htm

Frankenstein Goes To the Movies
Over the years, there has been many different movie adaptations of the Frankenstein story; some serious, some not. Have the students become a casting director. With the book they are currently reading have them select a cast. They will first have to decide if their movie will be a dramatic movie or a spoof.
- Movie Trailer http://moviefilmfest.com/html/frankenstein.htm
- Frankenstein Script http://www.geocities.com/Hollywood/Cinema/8399/frank.html
- Adaptations of Frankenstein http://www.rc.umd.edu/reference/ficrep/frankenstein.html

Frankenstein and Change

Sometimes when society is facing a change, whether in science or politics or culture, the image of Frankenstein is used to warn against experimenting with things we don't understand. People are afraid that we might be creating a monster we can't control. Using a word processor, work with the students to make a list of things from current events that might be considered a monster in the making. Some things that might be on my list today would be brain stem research, genetic engineering, computers in the classroom, giving 18 year olds the right to drink alcohol.

March 13, 1887
Earmuffs Patented

You might want to offer the following questions to guide the student research. *Note: This was a hard one. Evidently Chester Greenwood is not very well known among Internet users. I found that if I searched at the U. S. Patent and Trademark Office for earmuffs, I could find some information. Maybe your students need to make a web page for others who are looking for this information.*

1. Who invented earmuffs and why?
2. What are other ear protection devices and who wears them?
3. What sports require ear protection?
4. What other things to people wear to protect their ears?
   - U.S. Patent and Trademark Office: Earmuffs http://www.uspto.gov/
   - Chester Greenwood http://www.state.me.us/sos/kids/allabout/people/c_greenwood.htm

March 14, 1879
Albert Einstein

"Imagination is more important than knowledge."

Albert Einstein, On Science

"Only those who attempt the absurd will achieve the impossible."

Albert Einstein

Certainly one person who was not afraid scientific advancements would create a Frankenstein was Albert Einstein, Time Magazine's Person of the Century.
- Time Person of the Century
  http://www.time.com/time/time100/poc/magazine/albert_einstein5a.html

Who Was Albert Einstein?

These biographies and lesson plans will help you and your students understand this amazing man. For a real treat, listen to Einstein explain the theory of relativity; even if you don't understand the theory, his voice is amazing. For a fun activity, have your students do the Einstein Rap.
- Who Was Albert Einstein? http://www.geocities.com/CapeCanaveral/Lab/3555/einwho.html
- Einstein for Kids http://sites.huji.ac.il/jnul/einstein/.index6.html
- World Book: Albert Einstein http://www.worldbook.com/fun/tty/html/einstein.htm
- Einstein; Image and Impact http://www.aip.org/history/einstein/
  - Listen to Einstein explain E=mc^2 http://www.aip.org/history/einstein/voice1.htm
- Celebrate Pi Day and Einstein's Birthday http://www.exploratorium.edu/pi/pi99.html
  - Einstein Rap http://www.exploratorium.edu/pi/Erap.html

- Albert Einstein Home Page http://www.humboldt1.com/~gralsto/einstein/einstein.html

E=mc^2

Everything that has mass has energy. We are not only surrounded by energy; we are made out of energy. Einstein said, "Mass and energy are therefore essentially alike; they are only different expressions for the same thing." Einstein has shown that where there is mass, there is energy.[x] This quote is from Einstein Simplified, a site that does just what it says. The first E=mc^2 site is just a definition, but, if you are looking for more detail, refer to the next site.

- Einstein Simplified http://www.wildhorses.com/E=MC2.html
- E=mc^2 What Does It Stand For? http://www.physlink.com/ae3.cfm
- E=mc^2 http://www.aip.org/history/einstein/emc1.htm

Lesson Plans

Lesson Plan #1 focuses on heat and Lesson Plan #2 focuses on stars. Which one would fit into your science class today? The authors say they are geared toward middle school and high school students.

- Lesson Plan # 1
  http://www.nyu.edu/classes/murfin/microboard/microboardfall2000/messages/469.html
- Lesson Plan # 2 http://school.discovery.com/lessonplans/programs/astarisborn/

And just plain strange...send a Pi Day Card

- 123 Greetings http://www.123greetings.com/events/pi/

March 15
Ides of March

According to legend, the fortuneteller warned Julius Caesar to beware of the Ides of March. And, as we all know, the warning was not heeded, Caesar's friend, Brutus, struck him down and he was assassinated on March 15th, 44 BC. Ever since, people have feared the Ides of March as a day associated with bad luck. Actually, there was nothing sinister in the term; Ides is simply a way to refer to March, May, July and October 15th, and the 13th of all of the other months. The first two sites offer an explanation of the early Roman calendar. The last site is a reference to Shakespeare's Julius Caesar.

- Counting Down Towards the Ides of March
  http://www.latin.about.com/homework/latin/library/blides.htm
- Ides of March http://www.infoplease.com/spot/ides1.html
- Idea of March http://www.ancientsites.com/er/idusmartiae.html

Have the students search for the story behind Friday the13[th]. Use Google.com. Review the use of the + sign to refine searches and add '*superstition*' to *Friday 13*.

- Google.com http://www.google.com

March 15
Absolutely Incredible Kid Day

Absolutely Incredible Kid Day is sponsored by the Campfire Organization. Since 1997, adults have been encouraged to write letters of love, appreciation and encouragement to children. Be it a parent, teacher, neighbor or friend, children need to hear from a significant adult in their lives that they are appreciated and valued. I heard one time that a teacher had each student write on small strips of paper, something they liked about each other student in the room. The strips were given to the rightful owner. Years later, some of the students still carried one or two of the strips in their billfold. How powerful words can be.

Use a publishing program to make a small certificate to give to each one of your students telling them what you like about them. Mary Engelbreit has three very appropriate coloring pages for today: Excellent, Great Job and Terrific.

- Absolutely Incredible Kid Day http://www.campfire.org/aikd/index.html
- Mary Engelbreit Coloring Book http://www.maryengelbreit.com

Sometimes students need to see how valued who they are and what they can do are. The Kids Resume Maker does just that. Students complete an online resume listing their skills, achievements, interests and important qualities.

- Kids Resume Maker http://www.parentsoup.com/funandgames/kidsstuff/kidresume.html

March 17
St. Patrick's Day

5 Quick Things to Do

1. Visit an Irish Castle http://www.historic.irishcastles.com/
2. Play a Game http://www.kidsdomain.com/games/patrick.html
3. Learn an Irish Folksong http://www.acronet.net/~robokopp/irish.html
4. Pick up a Little Irish Lingo http://festivals.com/01-03-march/saintpatrick/lingo.cfm
5. See if you can fool Larry the Leprechaun
   http://www.ireland.com/events/st.patricks/2001/snug/games/larry/larrys-mind.htm

The Story of St. Patrick

Discover the man behind the legend. Was he really Irish? Did he remove all of the snakes from Ireland? To find the answers to these and other thought-provoking questions, check out the following Internet sites.

- Discover the Real St. Patrick http://wilstar.net/holidays/patrick.htm
- Will the Real St. Patrick Please Stand Up? http://members.nbci.com/web_lady/stpatty/
- Saint Patrick http://saints.catholic.org/saints/patrick.html

St. Patrick's Day.com is an excellent resource to begin a study of St. Patrick's Day. Whether you use it for a student assignment or just read it to add to your own background, I am sure you will find it very helpful.

- St. Patrick's Day http://www.st-patricks-day.com/

St. Patrick Day Crafts, Activities and Games

What's a holiday without crafts, activities and games? St. Patrick's Day is no different. I am sure you will find some new and interesting things on these pages. A couple of sites I really like because of their unusual suggestions is the BlackDog site and the Gaelic Games site. Have fun!

- St. Patrick's Day Crafts
- http://kidsartscrafts.about.com/library/holidays/stpatricksday/blstpatricksday_activities.htm?terms =collage
- Shape Book http://www.abcteach.com/MonthtoMonth/March/March.htm
- Preschool Activities http://www.preschoolrainbow.org/shamrock.htm
- St. Patrick's Day Activities and Crafts http://www.geocities.com/Heartland/7997/Stpatsact.htm
- Activities for Young Children http://www.nuttinbutkids.com/stpatricks.html
- Black Dog's St. Pats Fun and Games http://blackdog4kids.com/holiday/pat/
- Gaelic Games http://family.go.com/parties/holiday/feature/famf0300gaelic/famf0300gaelic.html

Stories, Songs and Legends

Of course, the Irish are great storytellers. I think you will like the ones listed here. Mr. Leahy's 4/5 grade class wrote their own Irish Blessings. What a good idea! I also like the lesson idea provided at the 5 Minute Irish Stories site.

- Stories http://spunsilk.pair.com/treasure.html
- Grandpa Tucker's St. Patrick Day Poems and Stories http://www.night.net/tucker/stpat-index.html-ssi
- Heather's Happy St. Patrick's Day Songs http://www.heathersholidaze.com/march/irish-songs.html
- What are Limericks? http://www.fi.edu/fellows/fellow7/mar99/poetry/index.shtml (with suggestions for how to write your own)
- Irish Storyteller http://www.irishstoryteller.com/contents.html
- 5 Minute Irish Stories http://www.toad.net/~sticker/blackbx.html
- Irish Proverbs http://www.daltai.com/sf_eile.htm
- Irish Blessings http://www.geocities.com/EnchantedForest/Cottage/2595/blessings.html
  - Mr. Leahy's Class Blessings http://www.beavton.k12.or.us/Greenway/leahy/98-99/irish.htm

A Wee Bit of Odds and Ends

- St. Patrick's Day http://www.geocities.com/EnchantedForest/Cottage/2595/stpad.html
- St. Patrick's Day @ Kids Domain http://www.kidsdomain.com/holiday/patrick/index.html
- Wearin' the Green http://www.kate.net/holidays/shamrock/
- Shamrock Lane http://www.fi.edu/fellows/fellow7/mar99/
- Clip art http://members.nbci.com/_XMCM/jograham/hstpat.htm
- Diane's Page @ Ireland http://home.i1.net/~theshaws/page3.htm
- Billy Bear's Top 'o the Day to You http://www.billybear4kids.com/holidays/stpatty/fun.htm

Rainbows, Lights and Prisms

I have never found a pot of gold at the end of the rainbow, but I've certainly seen some beautiful rainbows. Learn more about light and color at these sites. Finnegan's Classroom is an excellent resource for a unit on Light and Color for upper elementary to middle school.

- Finnegan's Classroom http://www.fi.edu/fellows/fellow7/mar99/light/index.shtml
- About Rainbows http://www.unidata.ucar.edu/staff/blynds/rnbw.html
- Basic Prisms http://www.explorescience.com/activities/Activity_page.cfm?ActivityID=51
- Look to the Rainbow (midi) http://www.hamienet.com/Broadway_Musical/F/Finian's_Rainbow/
- Rainbow Jello http://online-cookbook.com/goto/cook/rpage/000DD8

Note: I found I could make this faster if I poured each layer into small, clear drinking glasses, (the 3 oz. size works well for kids.) Put the glasses on a cookie sheet or tray that will fit in your freezer. Don't forget the order of the rainbow – Roy G. Biv (red, orange, yellow, green, blue, indigo, violet.) I've seen this made into finger jello, but I couldn't find the recipe on the Internet. Imagine that!

March 19
Swallows Return to San Juan Capistrano

It is so hard for us mid-westerners to think that in the same year colonists on the east coast were fighting for independence, Spanish missionaries were establishing missions on the west coast. It was going to be almost another 30 years or so before Europeans got around to even exploring our neck of the woods, or prairie as the case may be, and many more before they established churches and communities. I think it is for that reason I am so fascinated with the California missions. The Mission at San Juan Capistrano is the seventh of 21 Spanish Missions established in California by Franciscan Padres. It is considered the oldest church in California. The little church is called the "Serra Chapel" because it is the only building still standing where Fr. Serra had said Mass (1777). Tour this exquisite old mission with your students. Then, learn about the history of all 21 missions and take the grand tour. *Note: Cesar Chavez and his new bride visited all of the California missions on their honeymoon trip. See March 31.*

- Mission San Juan Capistrano http://www.missionsjc.com/historic.html
- California Mission History http://www.californiamissions.com/cahistory/index.html

To learn more about the missions of California, participate in the Missions of California ThinkQuest.

- Missions of California http://library.thinkquest.org/3615/

Legend of the Swallows

On March 19, St. Joseph's Day, thousands of little swallows return to the mission of San Juan Capistrano. There they build their summer homes. They will stay at the mission until October 23, the Day of San Juan, when they leave for the winter months. This annual migration has been the inspiration for stories and songs. Read this beautiful story.

- Legend of the Swallows http://www.sanjuancapistrano.org/the_swallows.htm
- San Juan Capistrano's Swallows http://print.factmonster.com/spot/swallows1.html

Where do these little birds go for the winter? Read the story of the Swallows of Goya to find out. Have the students draw a map retracing the fantastic flight plan.

- Swallows of Goya http://www.sjc.net/swallows/goya.html

Bird Migration Patterns

One of the most welcome signs of spring is the appearance of that first robin. To learn more about swallows and other migratory birds and when you can expect them to return to your neighborhood, refer to the following sites. The Patuxent Bird Identification Center will help you identify the birds in your locality.

- Bird Cast http://www.birdcast.org/
- Bird Migration http://north.audubon.org/facts.html
- Bird Migration http://www.birdnature.com/migration.html
- Patuxent Bird Identification Center http://www.mbr-pwrc.usgs.gov/Infocenter/infocenter.html

Have the students make a database for the different birds in your area and their migratory patterns. Sort by date so you can see if a particular bird returns to your school on a certain day. Be sure to take a picture of each new bird as it returns home for the summer. Label it with the date you first see it. The Wild Ones is a site for students and teachers with information, online newsletters and activities about all sorts of animals including birds.

- The Wild Ones http://www.thewildones.org/
  - Bird Migration Project http://www.thewildones.org/migration.html

Odds and Ends

- Birdsongs and Birding Sites Around the World
  http://www.math.sunysb.edu/~tony/birds/links.html
- Watch Bird Cams Around the World http://birding.about.com/cs/watchbirdcams/
- Watch List for Kids Trading Cards http://www.audubon.org/bird/watch/kids/cards.html

- Audubon Society http://www.audubon.org/
- Bird Clip Art http://birding.about.com/library/blalphaclipart.htm

March 20, 1954
Louis Sachar's Birthday
Newbery Award winning author, Louis Sachar, states in his autobiography that he doesn't like to talk about what he is writing while he is writing it. He didn't even tell his wife he was writing Holes until it was finished! Read more about the life of this popular children's author.
- Meet Louis Sachar http://www.cbcbooks.org/html/louissachar.html
- Teachers @ Random: Louis Sachar http://www.randomhouse.com/teachers/rc/rc_ab_lsa.html
- Meet Louis Sachar http://teacher.scholastic.com/authorsandbooks/authors/sachar/bio.htm

Lesson Plans and Reading Guides
- Eduscapes: Holes http://eduscapes.com/newbery/99a.htm
- Louis Sachar Teacher Resource Page http://falcon.jmu.edu/~ramseyil/sachar.htm
- Reading Group Guide for There's a Boy In The Girl's Bathroom http://www.randomhouse.com/teachers/rc/rc_rg_knopf1.html
- Let's Talk About Holes http://teacher.scholastic.com/bookclubs/ltab/holes_talk.asp

Safe Schools
Sachar's Holes offers us an opportunity to talk to our students about youth violence. The U.S. Department of Justice offers wonderful classroom resources and information. Have the students prepare a brochure for parents and school administration about safe schools. Use a publisher program to create your brochures. Ask the students distribute their brochures at the next PTA meeting.
- U. S. Department of Justice http://www.usdoj.gov/
  - Justice For Kids and Youth http://www.usdoj.gov/kidspage/kidspage.html
  - Youth Violence http://www.usdoj.gov/youthviolence.htm

Odds and Ends
- 1999 Newbery Medal for Holes http://www.ala.org/news/archives/v4n11/newbery.html
- Written Responses to a Novel http://www.knownet.net/users/Ackley/readnovel.html

Books by Louis Sachar
Holes – Newbery Award
There's a Boy In The Girl's Bathroom
Sideways Stories from Wayside School
Class President
Wayside School is Falling Down
Sideways Arithmetic from Wayside School
More Sideways Arithmetic from Wayside School
Wayside School Gets a Little Stranger
Sixth Grade Secrets
Super Fast, Out of Control
The Boy Who Lost His Face
Kidnapped At Birth?
Dogs Don't Tell Jokes

Magic Crystal?
Why Pick on Me?
Is He a Girl?
Alone In His Teacher's House
Flying Birthday Cake?
Someday Angeline

March 21, 1806
Benito Juarez's Birthday
The Birthday of Benito Juarez, a famous Mexican president and national hero, is an official Mexican holiday. Learn more about this famous Mexican hero by reading his biography. As it is written in Spanish, the students can use the translator service at AltaVista, Babel Fish. Simple key in the URL for the site you want translated and choose, Spanish to English translation. Some people compare him to Abraham Lincoln, not only in leadership but his life of ups and downs. What do you think?

- Biografia de Benito Juarez http://www.ticnet.com.mx/benito/benito1.htm
- Benito Juarez http://www.mexicoexporta.com.mx/esp/infor/presi/p_27.htm
- AltaVista Translations http://babelfish.altavista.com/translate.dyn
- Mexico's Lincoln http://www.mexconnect.com/mex_/history/jtuck/jtbenitojuarez.html
- Notes for His Children http://zapotec.agron.iastate.edu/juarezapuntes.html

Field Trip to Mexico
Print a map of Mexico. Attach pictures of the places on your tour with map tacks. Identify locations associated with Benito Juarez.
Map of Mexico http://plasma.nationalgeographic.com/mapmachine/
Tour Mexico http://www.earthwisdom.com/mexicomain.html

Sing Happy Birthday in Spanish
'Feliz cumpleaños a usted'
At the Babel Fish site, key in the words to Happy Birthday. Honor Benito Juarez in song.

- AltaVista Translations http://babelfish.altavista.com/translate.dyn

March 21, 1685
Johann S. Bach's Birthday
After being orphaned at 9, Bach went to live with his older brother, Johann Christoph, who was organist. Bach soon became an expert organist, but to support himself, he left his brother's home and earned his way through school singing in the choir. Bach was to become one of the most prolific and well-known composer of church music in the world. For a very extensive biography, refer to the J. S. Bach Homepage.

- J. S. Bach http://www.jsbach.org/

The true joy of celebrating Bach's birthday, however, is in the listening. From the first bell to the last, listen to these inspiring compositions. My favorite midi site is the first one listed at the Links to Midi site, but try the others. Have the students decide which ones they like best.

- Links to Midi files http://www.jsbach.org/websites.html
  - Jesu Joy of Man's Desiring
  - Toccate

Lesson Plans

The following links are for lesson plans that compare Bach's life and music to other famous composers.

- Composer Road Rally http://www.lessonplanspage.com/MusicBeethovenBachInfo.htm
- Music Appreciation http://www.remc11.k12.mi.us/~tht/385/bachless.html
- Music Masters to the Rescue http://www.learningspace.org/instruct/lplan/library/Engell.html

March 22, 1846
Randolph Caldecott's Birthday

Who was this man who lends his name to the prestigious children's book award? Randolph Caldecott was an English illustrator whose work appeared regularly in popular magazines and newspapers. Known as the father of children's picture books, Caldecott began illustrating Mother Goose rhymes for children. Children and adults alike enjoyed his clever illustrations.

- The Randolph Caldecott Society of America http://macserver.stjohns.k12.fl.us/others/rc.html

To view some of Caldecott's original masterpieces, enjoy the Animated Randolph Caldecott Books Online. These are just great!

- Animated Randolph Caldecott Books Online
  http://www.kodomo.go.jp/function/digi/Caldecott/caldecott-e.html

Randolph Caldecott Award

Since 1938, the American Library Association has awarded the Caldecott Award to the *artist of the most distinguished American Picture Book for Children published in the United States during the preceding year.*[xi] Prepared with a printout of Caldecott award-winning books, visit your library.

- The Caldecott Medal Home Page http://www.ala.org/alsc/caldecott.html

Changes Over Time

Arrange the Caldecott Books in order of publication date. Ask the students to comment on changes they see over the years. One of the things they will certainly notice is the use of more colorful pictures.

Types of Artwork

Arrange the books according to type of artwork: watercolor, collage, block printing, etc. Have the students vote on their favorite technique.

Best of the Best

Either using the criteria from the ALA site, or criteria that your students developed prior to your library visit, have the students evaluate as many Caldecott books as possible. You could put the criteria on a spreadsheet. Rank each criterion from 0-5. This would be a good opportunity to use some type of hand-held device, such as a Palm Pilot or Alphasmart. Collect the data in the library and transfer it to a computer in the classroom. What would be your classes' choice for the best of the Caldecott's book?

Field Trip: Children's Illustrators

Explore the homepages of contemporary children's illustrators.

- Children's Illustrators http://teacher.scholastic.com/fieldtrp/lanarts/illustra.htm

Mother Goose
Randolph Caldecott became famous for illustrating Mother Goose rhymes. There are some terrific Mother Goose sites on the Internet for you to enjoy with your students. For the younger child, simply reading these great pieces of our cultural heritage will be fun, plus, Mother Goose at the Enchanted Learning site has great activities.

- Mother Goose Online (narrated) http://www.ipl.org/youth/StoryHour/goose/
- Mother Goose http://www.enchantedlearning.com/Rhymes.html

For older students, test their knowledge by have them make up questions for a Who Am I Game. Example: I was a sleep while the cows were in the corn. I lost my sheep. I had way too many children.

- The Mother Goose Page http://www-personal.umich.edu/~pfa/dreamhouse/nursery/rhymes.html
- The Real Mother Goose http://www.designwest.com/Johanna/MotherGoose/

E-Book
Have your students make an e-book by using PowerPoint or another presentation tool. Have the students select a Mother Goose rhyme. Use clip art or a drawing tool to illustrate it.

And, everyone will enjoy writing new verses to Mary Had A Little Lamb.

- Bruce Lansky: Mary Had A Little Lamb
  http://www.poetryteachers.com/poetclass/lessons/maryhad.html

Books by Randolph Caldecott
Ride a Cock-Horse and Other Rhymes and Stories
Sing a Song for Sixpence
Babes in the Wood
The Queen of Hearts
Three Jovial Huntsmen
Randolph Caldecott's John Gilpin and Other Stories
The House that Jack Built

March 24, 1874
Harry Houdini's Birthday
Read about the life and times of the master magician – Harry Houdini. See if you can separate the fact from the fiction.

- And now…Houdini http://magictricks.com/houdini/
- Pictures, posters and other memorabilia http://memory.loc.gov/ammem/vshtml/vshchrn.html
- Houdini Tribute http://www.houdinitribute.com/

The American Experience at PBS has very useful information for teachers. It was developed to enhance the viewing of the PBS television show, which you can still purchase, but the teacher's guide and special features will be very helpful even without the video.

- PBS: Houdini http://www.pbs.org/wgbh/amex/houdini/

Magic Tricks
What's celebrating Houdini's birthday without learning how to do some tricks. Good luck!

- Easy Magic Tricks http://magic.about.com/library/tricks/bltrickmenu.htm
- Magic Interactive http://www.magic-interactive.com/magic/index.html
- Card Trick Central http://web.superb.net/cardtric/

- Learn2 Magic Tricks http://www.2learn-street-magic-card-tricks-get-free-video.com/
- Coin Tricks http://members.iweb.net.au/~kith/juggling/Micro/coin/coin_s.htm
- The Conjuror Magic Tricks http://conjuror.com/magictricks/

How'd You Do That?
You and your students won't believe these online magic tricks. You'll be amazed! Remember, a sucker is born everyday!
- Interactive Magic http://trendy.org/magic/interactivemagic.shtml
- Online Interactive Magic http://www.funnybone.net/showroom/
- Hocus Pocus Palace http://www.teleport.com/~jrolsen/index.shtml

March 25, 1821
Greek Independence Day
After nearly 400 years of slavery under the Ottoman Empire, the Greeks decided to rebel, taking up arms and fighting for their freedom. They began their revolution on March 25, 1821.[xii] For a detailed account of the Greek rebellion, refer to the Greek Independence site. Enjoy the pictures of contemporary Greek culture. Notice the national costumes.
- Greek Independence http://www.greece.org/ahepa/99000gid.html
- Pictures of Celebration http://home.xnet.com/~kthansen/start6.htm
- More Pictures http://home.xnet.com/~kthansen/start5.htm
- Tour Greece http://www.earthwisdom.com/greecemain.html

Olympics 2004
Athens will host the Summer Olympics in 2004. Prepare for the Olympics by staying in tune with what's going on at the developing Olympics Project 2004 site. For you virtual trip to the Olympics, you might need to learn some Greek words and phrases. You also should stop at the Greek Embassy to learn a little about Greece before you leave for the Olympics.
- Olympia Project 2004 http://www.greece.org/olympics/startup.html
- Learn Greek: Words http://www.greece.org/gr-lessons/gr-english/vocab.html
  - Phrases http://www.greece.org/gr-lessons/gr-english/phrases.html
- Greek Embassy http://www.greekembassy.org/
  - History http://www.greekembassy.org/general/history.html
- Greek Tourist Guide http://www.vacation.forthnet.gr/

History of the Games
The modern Olympics stem from Greek mythology. Make a timeline of the history of the Olympic games.
- The Games History http://www.athena2004.net/
- Summer Olympics Through the Years http://www.infoplease.com/ipsa/A0114335.html

March 25, 1911
Triangle Shirtwaist Fire
It's spring, 1911. Young women, mostly immigrants are working for $6.00 a week sewing shirtwaists (blouses.) They are crowded into a 10-story factory that has no sprinkler system and only one fire escape. To make matters worst, the supervisors lock the doors to the workplace from the outside to prevent the women and girls from taking too many breaks. For some unknown reason, about 4:45 in the afternoon a

fire broke out on the 7th floor. The fire department was quickly called, but their ladders and hoses only reached the 8th floor. Hundreds of young women were trapped. Many who could not escape, choose to jump to their death. One hundred forty-six young women died. The public outcry resulting from this tragedy resulted in the present labor laws protecting factory workers in health, disability and fire prevention. Download a short movie about the Triangle Shirtwaist Fire. Then, read accounts of this disaster.

- Movie @ Triangle Shirtwaist Fire http://tlc.discovery.com/tlcpages/newyork/1911.html
- Triangle Shirtwaist Fire
  http://www.discovery.com/guides/history/historybuff/library/refshirtwaist.html
- Triangle Shirtwaist Fire http://www.gale.com/freresrc/womenhst/trials/triangle.htm
- Triangle Shirtwaist Fire http://www.ezl.com/~fireball/Disaster11.htm

Since 1970, the Department of Labor, has been working to make the workplace safe. To learn about OSHA's projects, go to their web site. A relatively new science, ergonomics, studies the human body in the workplace. As we spend more and more time working at computer workstations, we need to be aware of the Human-Computer Interface (HCI).

- The Occupational Safety and Health (OSHA) http://www.osha.gov/
- Educational Ergonomics http://www.eduergo.com/

Note: This tragic event is related to three other events in March. See, March 8 – International Women's Day, March 31 – Cesar Chavez Day and Women's History Month.

March 26, 1874
Robert Frost's Birthday

> *"A poem begins with a lump in the throat; a home-sickness or a love-sickness. It is a reaching-out toward expression; an effort to find fulfillment. A complete poem is one where an emotion has found its thought and the thought has found the words."*
>
> Robert Frost[xiii]

Robert Frost was born in San Francisco, but soon moved to New England, where he was to spend the rest of his life. Although many of his poems are about life and sights of New England, he also expresses many others themes that are as relevant today as they were when first written. There are many Robert Frost pages on the Internet. These are some of the best.

- World Book: Robert Frost http://www.worldbook.com/fun/tty/html/frost.htm
- Robert Frost http://www.robertfrost.org/indexgood.html
- Robert Frost http://www.poets.org/poets/poets.cfm?prmID=196
- Robert Frost on the Web http://www.amherstcommon.com/walking_tour/frost.html

You may have notices that some of the sites listed above have clips of Robert Frost reading his poems. However, I think this one is too good to miss.

- Listen to Robert Frost reading his poems
  http://town.hall.org/Archives/radio/IMS/HarperAudio/012294_harp_ITH.html

One of my favorite Robert Frost poems is *Stopping By the Woods on a Snowy Evening*. Read the poem with your students and just enjoy it. Sometimes, we as teachers, feel we are not doing our job if there isn't a lesson involved. An 8th grade student expresses this so eloquently. Maybe our lesson should be – read and enjoy, you might read more!

- Stopping by the Woods on a Snowy Evening http://www.robertfrost.org/poem2.html#STOPPING BY WOODS ON A SNOWY EVENING

> After English Class
> By an 8th grade student
>
> I used to like "Stopping by the Woods on a
> Snowy Evening."
> The jingle of harness bells,
> Breaking – and – adding to the stillness,
> The gentle drift of snow…
>
> But, today, the teacher told us
> What everything stood for.
> The woods, the horse,
> The miles to go, the sleep ---
> They all have "hidden meanings."
>
> It's grown so complicated now,
> That next time I drive by,
> I don't think I'll bother to stop.

Music and Memory

How many of us learned our ABCs by singing the little ABC song? Research has shown us that music is a powerful tool in triggering our ability to remember something. Give this a try in your classroom. Choose a Robert Frost poem you would like to have the students memorize. Divide the class into two groups – the singers and the traditional 'memorizers.' Give the students a limited time to memorize the poem. See which technique was more effective. Have all of the students sing *Stopping by the Woods…* to the tunes of *Home on the Range* and *Amazing Grace*. Remember how Schoolhouse Rock on Saturday mornings helped us remember our multiplication facts, parts of speech and how a bill became a law? Share a piece of your childhood with your class.

- Schoolhouse Rock Sound Clips from Amazon
  http://www.amazon.com/exec/obidos/ASIN/B0000033TA/qid=996499649/sr=1-1/ref=sc_m_1/102-1855973-9267338
- Schoolhouse Rock
  http://www.apocalypse.org/pub/u/gilly/Schoolhouse_Rock/HTML/schoolhouse.html

A Few Lesson Plans

And now, for a few serious lesson plans.

- Discovering Robert Frost http://www.viterbo.edu/academic/ug/education/edu250/hllaurent.htm
- Robert Frost, by James Guimond http://educeth.ethz.ch/english/readinglist/frostr/
- Robert Frost: Poetry http://encarta.msn.com/alexandria/templates/lessonFull.asp?page=1287

March 29, 1919

Greatest Show On Earth – Ringling Brothers, Barnum and Bailey Circus

This date marks the first performance of the combined Ringling Brothers, Barnum and Bailey Circus in New York City's Madison Square Garden. Take you class to the Circus today. Have them learn the history of these American entrepreneurs, see some of the circus acts and play some circus games. Enjoy the day!

- Ringling Brothers, Barnum and Bailey Circus http://www.ringling.com/
- The Greatest Show On Earth http://www.library.wisc.edu/etext/WIReader/WER0434.html
- P.T. Barnum http://www.barnum-museum.org/html/barnum.html

Fact and Fiction

A lot of the circus is illusion…what is fact and what can you make people believe. Sort out some of circus facts from the fiction that surrounds it.
- There's a sucker born everyday
- http://www.discovery.com/guides/history/historybuff/library/refbarnum.html
- The Day the Clowns Cried
  http://www.discovery.com/guides/history/historybuff/library/reffire.html
- The Elephant Comes to America
  http://www.discovery.com/guides/history/historybuff/library/refelephant.html

Odds and Ends
- Circus World Museum http://www.circusworldmuseum.com/
- Circus Web http://www.circusweb.com/
- Shrine Circus http://www.shrine-circus.com/
- Big Apple Circus http://www.bigapplecircus.org/

March 30, 1858
Pencil Patented

You might want to offer the following questions to guide the student research:
1. Who invented the pencil?
2. What are different types of pencils?
3. How are pencils made?
4. Do all pencils have erasers?
5. Is there pencil museum?
6. Are pencils collectible?
   - The Pencil Page http://www.pencils.com/
   - General Pencil Company http://www.generalpencil.com/

March 31, 1927
Cesar Chavez Day

"The first collective bargaining agreement between farm workers and growers in the continental United States was signed in 1966 requiring rest periods, clean drinking water, hand-washing facilities, protective clothing against pesticide spraying while workers are in the fields and banning outright DDT." [xiv]

From an early age, Cesar Chavez learned about injustice. It became his life's passion to secure dignity and fair play for farm workers. His methods – nonviolent boycotts, pickets, and strikes. Have your students study the life of this American hero. Then, have them share their research by preparing a multimedia or PowerPoint presentation.
- Viva Cesar Chavez! http://www.sfsu.edu/%7Ececipp/cesar_chavez/chavezhome.htm
- Cesar Chavez http://www.incwell.com/Biographies/Chavez.html
- The Story of Cesar E. Chavez http://www.ufw.org/cecstory.htm

- Cesar Chavez Day http://www.nctimes.com/news/081100/aa.html
- PowerPoint Rubric http://www.uni.edu/profdev/rubrics/pptrubric.html

Labor Unions
Cesar Chavez was instrumental in the development of unions for all workers, not just Farm workers. Make a timeline of the development of labor unions in the United States. Give small groups of students a decade to research.
- 100 Years of Struggle and Success http://www.aflcio.org/gallery_hist/main_home.swf
- United Farm Workers http://www.ufw.org/
  - History http://www.ufw.org/history.htm

Cesar Chavez Posters
Chavez was a self-educated man. Even though he only completed the 8th grade of formal education, he was an avid reader of such diverse topics as history, literature, religion and philosophy. Many Chavez quotes speak to us today of culture and diversity and community. Have your students choose a quote and using a publishing program, make a poster to hang in your school's hallways.
- In His Own Words http://www.ufw.org/edofheart.htm

◆ · ◆ · ◆ · ◆ · ◆ · ◆ · ◆ ·

You are never strong enough that you don't need help!

Cesar Chavez 1967-1997

◆ · ◆ · ◆ · ◆ · ◆ · ◆ · ◆ ·

Migrant Worker Lesson Plans
To help your students understand more about migrant workers, refer to these online lesson plans.
- NYT Lesson Plan http://www.nytimes.com/learning/teachers/lessons/000807monday.html
- Print Version http://www.nytimes.com/learning/teachers/lessons/000807monday_print.html
- Where Do Migrant Farm Worker Children Live http://ucsub.colorado.edu/~fischej/socialstudieslessons.htm

- And The Earth Did Not Devour Him
  http://kancrn.kckps.k12.ks.us/read_alouds/lang/earth_not_devour.htm
- Lesson plan #2 http://www.bcs.k12.in.us/District/district%20la/CR25486.HTM
- Lesson plan # 3 http://balrog.sdsu.edu/~jolalde/project/exe1/rivera.htm
- Slide Presentation http://www.northside.isd.tenet.edu/healthww/english/waters/Rivera.htm

---

[i] 4000 Years of Women in Science http://www.astr.ua.edu/4000WS/HYPATIA.html *Hypatia*, April 8, 2001

[ii] America Quilts http://www.pbs.org/americaquilts/ March 7, 2001

[iii] Bush Proclaims Irish-American Heritage Month http://www.usembassy.ie/currentissues/irish_americanheritage.html July 31, 2001

[iv] Emily Dickinson Complete Poems http://www.bartleby.com/113/ February 9, 2002

[v] Idea Finder: The Telephone http://www.ideafinder.com/history/inventions/story078.htm April 7, 2001

[vi] Hinamatsuri http://japanese.about.com/homework/japanese/library/weekly/aa022501b.htm April 7, 2001

[vii] WebMuseum: Michelangelo http://www.ibiblio.org/wm/paint/auth/michelangelo/ July 30, 2001

[viii] Why Women's Day http://www0.un.org/cyberschoolbus/womensday/pages/why_content.asp July 30, 2001

[ix] Education World *Grandpa's Teeth* http://www.education-world.com/a_books/sr_week04.shtml July 26, 2001

[x] Einstein Simplified http://www.wildhorses.com/E=MC2.html July 28, 2001

[xi] ALSC Caldecott Award http://www.ala.org/alsc/cmedal.html July 29, 2001

[xii] Emazing: Greek Independence Day http://archives.emazing.com/archives/holiday/2000-03-24 July 29, 2001

[xiii] Robert Frost *The Man and His Work* - 1923

[xiv] Viva Cesar Chavez! http://www.sfsu.edu/%7Ececipp/cesar_chavez/chavezhome.htm March 10, 2001

5/7/2002

April

*If April showers bring Mayflowers
What do Mayflowers bring?
Pilgrims!*

Special Month

Mathematics Education Month

A Rat In The House Might Eat The Ice Cream
ARITHMETIC

April is Mathematics Education Month, a time set aside to learn, study and become more aware of how mathematics interfaces with our lives. Begun in 1995 to celebrate the National Council of Teachers of Mathematics 75th anniversary, the event has grown to have over 1 million student participants. To learn how you and your students can get involved, refer to the following sites. These sites offer many activities you can use all year long, not just during March.

- National Council of Teachers of Mathematics http://www.nctm.org
  - The World's Largest Math Event http://www.nctm.org/wlme/
  - Student Math Notes http://www.nctm.org/publications/smn/

Math and Authentic Tasks
Helping Your Child Learn Math is an online booklet that is chockfull of everyday math activities including arithmetic, geometry, measurement, money concepts and much more. It is an excellent resource for teachers as well as parents. Use it in your classroom and recommend it to your parents.

- Helping Your Child Learn Math http://www.ed.gov/pubs/parents/Math/

Online Math Resources
The following are a sample of the math resources available on the Internet.
- Education 4 Kids: Math Drill http://www.edu4kids.com/
- Plane Math http://www.planemath.com/
- Math Stumpers of the Month
  http://kidsmath.about.com/kids/kidsmath/library/weekly/blstumpers.htm
- Math Counts http://www.mathcounts.org/
- Measurement http://www.richmond.edu/~ed344/webunits/measurement/home.htm
- Alfy's Pick for Measurement
  http://www.alfy.com/teachers/teach/thematic_units/Measurement/Measurement_1.asp
- Angle Activities
  http://www.ambleside.schoolzone.co.uk/ambleweb/mentalmaths/angleshapes.html
- Do Math – and You Can Do Anything http://domath.nctm.org/
- Calculators Online http://www-sci.lib.uci.edu/HSG/RefCalculators.html
- Mega Math http://www.c3.lanl.gov/mega-math/index.html

Online Lesson Plans and Thematic Units Related to Math
These sites are the gateway to lesson plans related to math. There is something for everyone here!
- Education World: Math http://www.education-world.com/math/

- Blue Web'n: Math http://www.kn.pacbell.com/wired/bluewebn/categories.html#Mathematics
- Web Sites for Busy Teachers: Math http://www.ceismc.gatech.edu/busyt/math.html
- Teach-nology: Math http://teachers.teach-nology.com/themes/
- Discovery School: Math http://school.discovery.com/schrockguide/math.html
- Ed-helper: Math http://www.edhelper.com/cat197.htm
- SCORE: Math http://score.kings.k12.ca.us/

However you choose to celebrate Mathematics Education Month, be sure to invite the community in to visit your classroom to see how your students are using technology to strengthen their math skills.

Garden Month

A Little Seed Song
A little seed for me to sow.
A little earth to make it grow.
A little hole, a little pat,
A little wish and that is that.
A little sun, a little shower
And in a while, a little flower.[i]

- Anonymous

It's a little early at my home in South Dakota to be working in the garden, but the seed catalogs have started to arrive, so the planning, at least, has begun. The Internet provides excellent resources for all of us armchair gardeners.

Field Trips
Well, if we can't get there in person, we can do a little dreaming. These are some beautiful online gardens.
- Wave Hill, Bronx http://www.wavehill.org/
- NY Botanical Garden http://www.nybg.org/
- The Buchart Gardens http://www.butchartgardens.com/
- Claude Monet's Garden at Giverny http://giverny.org/gardens/fcm/visitgb.htm
- Australian National Botanical Garden http://www.anbg.gov.au/anbg/

Gardening in the Classroom
Even if the students can't get outside, they can do some gardening right in the classroom. The 4H Garden has lots and lots of interactive projects, games and tours. The 4 To Explore Garden is a thematic unit about gardening with links to wonderful gardening sites and suggested lessons.
- 4H Garden http://4hgarden.msu.edu/main.html
- 4 To Explore Garden http://eduscapes.com/42explore/gardening.htm

Garden in a Bag
We have all planted bean seeds in a little paper cup, but try the same thing in a sandwich bag. Place a damp, folded paper towel in the baggie with a few bean seeds on each side of the paper towel. Zip the baggie and hang it in a window. Watch what happens. Hang some of the baggies in the closet. Watch what happens. Make a spreadsheet to record the daily observations.

Plan a Pizza Garden
Have the students design a garden that will grow the ingredients for making a pizza. Use a publisher program to layout the garden. Use an online seed catalog to find out about the plants you will need to

grow. Copy and paste pictures of the plants to the location where they will be planted in the garden. You could also use clip art. Have the students use text boxes to describe the plant.

- Burpee Seeds http://www.burpee.com/
- Stokes Seed Catalog http://www.stokeseeds.com/cgi-bin/StokesSeeds.storefront (check out the teacher site)

PIZZA GARDEN

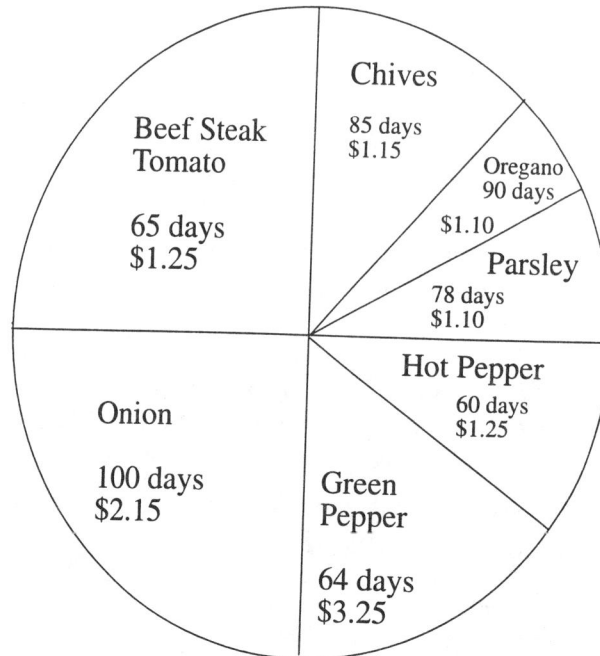

Start a School Garden

Need a little help? This site tells you everything you need to know. The National Gardening Association offers $500 grants to schools to start gardening. Get your shovels ready.

- School Gardens http://aggie-horticulture.tamu.edu/kindergarden/Child/school/sgintro.htm
- Tips for Gardening with Children http://aggie-horticulture.tamu.edu/kindergarden/pnote.htm
- National Gardening Association http://www.garden.org/

Make some compost by placing some dried leaves, some green lawn clippings and some potting soil in an empty paper box lined with plastic. Go to the cafeteria and ask the cooks for some vegetable peelings; add just a few. Stir once a week and watch what happens. Use it to fertilize your garden.

- Soil Recipe http://www.epa.gov/superfund/students/clas_act/fall/recipe.htm

Don't Have Time To Wait

Do you need some flowers right now? About.com has some neat flower crafts. Try the Easter Lily.

- About http://craftsforkids.about.com/cs/makingflowers/index.htm
  - Easter Lily Hand Flower http://craftsforkids.about.com/library/projects/blealily1.htm

Make flower pictures of your students. Go to the Kodak Playground. You will need to login. Then, upload pictures of your students. Pull down the Play menu and choose Flower Power. Have the students pick the flower they want to be. Print the pictures and paste them to a piece of card stock. Cut out the flower picture. Tape a green pipe cleaner to the back for the stem. Add construction paper leaves. Stick the flowers in a flowerpot filled with florist foam covered with moss. Set on your desk for a constant reminder that we are nurturing children and helping them bloom.

- Picture Center http://www.kodak.com

Online Activities and Games
These are some really cool sites for children about gardening.
- The Great Plant Escape http://www.urbanext.uiuc.edu/gpe/index.html
- Garden Activities in Four Seasons http://www.mnh.si.edu/garden/seasons/

Odds and Ends
- Gardening Help http://aginfo.psu.edu/PSP/01list.html
- Garden Fun http://www.bry-backmanor.org/gardenfun/springindex.html
- Gardening for Kids http://www.geocities.com/EnchantedForest/Glade/3313/
- Green and Growing From the Ground Up http://www.gatewest.net/~green/from/index.html
- Flowers http://school.discovery.com/homeworkhelp/worldbook/atozscience/f/201580.html

National Poetry Month

"When power leads man toward arrogance, poetry reminds him of his limitations. When power narrows the areas of man's concern, poetry reminds him of the richness and diversity of his existence. When power corrupts, poetry cleanses."

-- John Fitzgerald Kennedy

As April is the birthday month of some famous poets, it's a great month to celebrate poetry in our schools. Maya Angelou once said, "A poem should make you think, 'I knew that, but I didn't know anybody else knew it.'" I think that's what I like so much about poetry. It condenses our thoughts and feelings, perspectives and insights. Enjoy this month by listening to poetry, reading poetry, writing poetry and celebrating poetry.

Beginning Points

Thirty days of great writing ideas! That's what you will find at the first Internet site. Choose a different activity for each day in April. (I know, you need 31, but some are so great, you'll want to repeat them.) At the Poets.org site you will find links to all different kinds of poetry, poets and projects and resources. And, Poetry 180 is Poet Laureate, Billy Collins project – 180 poems – one for every day of school.

- 30 Days of Poetry http://members.tripod.com/the-english-room/poetry/30_days_of_poetry.htm
- Poets.org http://www.poets.org/npm/
- Poetry 180 http://www.loc.gov/poetry/180/

Listen to It
Children's poet Jack Prelutsky says poetry is as natural to children as breathing. They love the sound of it, the rhythm of it, the fun of it. Your class will have fun listening to these kids from Great Britain read some of their original poetry. Who knows, it might inspire you to write and read some of your own. The *Favorite Poem Project* is a project started by America's Poet Laureate. Listen to some famous and not-so-famous Americans read their favorite poems.
- Online Poetry http://edleston.primaryresources.co.uk/projects/poetry.htm
- Favorite Poem Project http://www.favoritepoem.org/

Read It
There is truly something for everyone when it comes to poetry. Some of us like Shakespearian sonnets, some of us like cowboy poems and some of us like just about anything. Your students are sure to find

something they like at one of these sites. Try reading poetry with a partner, in a reader's theater or as a coral reading.

For everyone
- Poet's Corner http://www.geocities.com/~spanoudi/poems/index.html

For younger students
- Poetry Aloud by Kristine O'Connell George http://64.77.108.137/poetry_aloud.htm
- Animated poems from BBC http://www.bbc.co.uk/education/wordsandpictures/longvow/poems/fpoem.shtml
- A Pocket Full of Rhymes http://members.aol.com/Bvsangl/pocket.html
- Funny Forty http://www.nesbitt.com/poetry/newpoems.html
- Grandpa Tucker's Rhymes and Tales http://www.night.net/tucker/

For older students
- Today's Poem http://www.poems.com/home.htm
- Cowboy Poetry http://www.clantongang.com/oldwest/trade.htm
- Multicultural Poetry http://curry.edschool.virginia.edu/go/multicultural/voices.html
- Borzoi Reader http://www.randomhouse.com/knopf/poetry/

Write It

I've never thought I could write poetry and most students don't think they can either. But, you and they will be surprised. With the help of some of these sites, you and your students will be poets, don't you know it! Begin by reading the article, *The Poet Within*. This is an excellent article for teachers about helping students unleash their creativity.   End by collecting all of the poems you've written for a class anthology.
- The Poet Within http://www.education-world.com/a_lesson/lesson171.shtml

Magnetic Poetry – that's right, except your computer is the refrigerator!
- Magnetic Refrigerator Poetry http://home.freeuk.net/elloughton13/scramble2.htm
- Virtual Poetry http://www.surfnetkids.com/games/funnypoems-wm.htm
- Poetry http://prominence.com/java/poetry/

Writing Instructions
- Writing with Writers: Poetry http://teacher.scholastic.com/writewit/poetry/index.htm
- How To Write Poetry http://www.poetryzone.ndirect.co.uk/howto.htm#fun
- Poetry Teachers http://www.poetryteachers.com/
- Listen and Write Home http://www.bbc.co.uk/education/listenandwrite/home.htm
- Giggle Poetry http://www.gigglepoetry.com/poetryrace.cfm
- Poetry http://www.poetry4kids.com/howto.html
- Instant Muse http://www.webcom.com/wordings/artofwrite/poetrygenerator.html (for older students)

Who I Am Poems

Each one of your students is different, with different skills, abilities, likes, dislikes, families, cultures, religions, etc. Celebrate your differences and recognize your similarities by sharing your own personal poems. The Multicultural Pavilion has a very nice format for writing simple 'Who I Am' poems. Have your students write a poem about themselves. Have each child make a flip album of their poem, with appropriate photos, illustrations and background music. Download a demo copy of Flip Album. Celebrate your individuality! Another thing you can do is to use photo program, such as Photo Studio and have the students key their poem in a text box on their picture. Then, use the crop tool to cut out puzzle shapes and print their pictures. Make a large puzzle on the bulletin board with all of the students pictures and poems.
- Who I Am Poems http://curry.edschool.virginia.edu/go/multicultural/activities/poetry.html

- Flip Album http://www.flipalbum.com/

Celebrate It

Host a poetry reading. Invite parents, community or the grandmas and grandpas from the local nursing home in for a poetry reading. Have the students read their own or someone else's poetry. Combine the poetry with a little music and light refreshment. Use one of the poetry cards from the Blue Mountain folks for your invitations. Celebrate the Day!
- Poetry Cards http://www.bluemountain.com/eng3/poetry/indexjump.html

Odds and Ends

Is it a song? Is it poetry? You decide.
- Judy and David's Song Book http://www.judyanddavid.com/Songbook/Songbookcover.html

This ThinkQuest activity will help your students write a great Bio Poem.
- BioPoem http://library.thinkquest.org/11883/data/biopoem.htm

A little writing, a little rhyming, a little reading, a lot of enjoying!
- Why Poetry What: Poetry Sampler
  http://www.kn.pacbell.com/wired/fil/pages/samwhypoetrmi.html

Still looking for more Internet links? This site will help you out.
- National Poetry Month http://www.gwc.maricopa.edu/biblio/npmonth.htm

Special Week

1st – Blue Ribbon Week

Take some time this week to learn about child abuse and what we as educators can do to help break the cycle of abuse and neglect. Make blue ribbon pins for the teachers in your building.
- National Child Abuse Hotline http://www.childhelpusa.org/child/hotline.htm
  o Major Forms of Child Abuse http://www.childhelpusa.org/child/abuse.htm
- End Child Abuse http://www.childabuse.org

Help Children Protect Themselves

Help children learn what they need to know to protect themselves. So many children think that the abuse is there fault; that they some how did something to provoke it. It is never their fault! The Child Abuse.org site has a very simple, non-threatening site for children. The Prevent Child Abuse site also has good information for children.
- Is someone hurting you? http://www.childabuse.org/forkidsnew.htm
- Resources for Kids http://www.preventchildabuse.org/family_community/kids/index.html

1-800-4-A-CHILD

- Nationwide Directory http://www.therapistfinder.net/Child-Abuse/Child-Abuse-Hotlines-Phone-Numbers.html
- What happens when you call? http://www.therapistfinder.net/help/childhelp.html

Information for Teachers

Put on the coffee pot and ask the your fellow teachers to get together to discuss child abuse. Begin the discussion by reading the article, *Impact of Child Abuse on Learning*, by Ann Rifleman. Do your experiences agree or differ from this teacher's? Then, review the Internet site from the National Clearing House. Finally, decide on a plan for your school. If you need a little advice, see what the people at Safe Child in Denver are doing.
- The Impact of Child Abuse on Learning http://www.nea.org/lac/testimon/abuse.html

- National Clearing House: Reporting Child Abuse and Neglect
  http://www.calib.com/nccanch/pubs/usermanuals/educator/section4.cfm
- Safe Child http://www.safechild.org/

And, for older students….

This is a lesson plan for older students. It is about how the courts interpret the 6th Amendment in regards to children facing their abusers. It is very provocative.
- Child Abuse and the 6th Amendment
  http://www.constitutioncenter.org/sections/teacher/lesson_plans/html/70948ag.asp
- Thinking About Violence http://www.acjnet.org/teacher/cabusum.htm

1st – Golden Rule Week

"Do unto others as you would have them do unto you."

The Golden Rule in one form or another is found in most of the world's religion. It is the ethic of reciprocity – for every action there is an equal and opposite reaction. It is considered the most concise principle of human interaction. What a lesson to teach our students! Refer to the Golden Rule and have students make posters with either a word processor or publication tool of each saying. Display them in your school's hallways.

◆◆◆◆◆◆◆◆◆◆◆◆◆◆◆◆◆◆◆◆◆◆◆◆◆◆◆◆◆◆◆◆◆◆◆◆◆◆

Hurt not others
with that which pains yourself.

Buddhist Faith

◆◆◆◆◆◆◆◆◆◆◆◆◆◆◆◆◆◆◆◆◆◆◆◆◆◆◆◆◆◆◆◆◆◆◆◆

- The Golden Rule http://www.fragrant.demon.co.uk/golden.html
- The Golden Rule http://theosophy.org/tlodocs/GoldnRul.htm
- The Golden Rule http://www.unification.net/ws/theme015.htm

Essay Punch

Have the students read the Golden Rule Essay and then write an essay of their own about a specific situation in their own school or neighborhood. Entrepreneur J. C. Penney started his well-known department store, now called Penney's, based on the principle of the Golden Rule. Ask the students to explain why the Golden Rule is a good business practice. To help students learn the basics of writing a good essay, have them work through the guided essay provided at Essay Punch.
- Golden Rule Essay http://www.jcu.edu/philosophy/gensler/goldrule.htm
- JC Penney Golden Rule Store http://www.kemmerer.org/jcp.html
- Essay Punch http://www.essaypunch.com/

Art Appreciation: Norman Rockwell

Although illustrator Norman Rockwell usually painted humorous pictures of Americana, sometimes his work reflected a more serious note. Have the students study his painting, *The Golden Rule*. Karen Andreola article on art appreciation offers some very simple suggestions for helping students look at art.

- Norman Rockwell's Golden Rule http://www.normanrockwellmuseum.org/pictures-tour/page10.html
- Another copy of Golden Rule http://www.globalgallery.com/enlarge.asp?print=slv-nr0216&x=65&y=20
- Art Appreciation the Charlotte Mason Way http://www.home-school.com/Articles/AndreolaArtAppre.html
- The Norman Rockwell Museum http://www.nrm.org/

2nd - Week of the Young Child

The National Association for the Education of Young Children sponsors the Week of the Young Child. Its purpose is to recognize that early childhood is where our future begins.[ii] For information about the week with suggested activities, go to the NAEYC site.

- NAEYC http://www.naeyc.org/woyc/default.asp

Internet Fair

Invite the kindergarten or preschool students to your class for an Internet Fair. Have your students search for Internet sites that would be appropriate for 4 and 5 year olds. Help them evaluate the site. Reinforce the concept of Internet safety. When they have selected 5 – 10 good sites, prepare invitations using a publishing program and deliver them to the preschool or kindergarten. Make table tents that have the site title and place them by the appropriate computer.   When the big day arrives, to save time, have your students upload all of the Internet sites on the computers before the guests arrive. Make sure that your students are very familiar with the Internet site. I find that it works best to have one older student paired with two younger children. Tell your students that they are the guides not the user. Their job is to help the children, not to do it for them. Play Round Robin and when you ring the bell, the group needs to move to another computer. After the students have had an opportunity to sample the Internet sites, move away from the computers for a snack.

- Learn 2: Evaluating Internet Sites http://www.2learn.ca/evaluating/evaluating.html
- Evaluating Internet Sites http://www.uic.edu/depts/lib/lhsp/resources/evaluate.shtml
- ABCs of Web Site Evaluation http://school.discovery.com/schrockguide/pdf/weval.pdf

Some fun sites for the little ones

- Alfy's Playground http://www.alfy.com/index1.asp?FlashDetect=True
- Arthur http://www.pbs.org/wgbh/arthur/
- Between the Lions http://pbskids.org/lions/
- Clifford http://www.scholastic.com/clifford/index.htm
- Crayola http://www.crayola.com/
- Seussville http://www.randomhouse.com/seussville/
- I Spy http://www.scholastic.com/ispy/
- Kratt's Creatures http://www.pbs.org/kratts/
- Sesame Street http://www.pbs.org/kids/sesame/
- Winnie the Pooh http://www.worldkids.net/pooh/
- Zoom Dinosaurs http://www.enchantedlearning.com/subjects/dinosaurs/index.html

2nd – National Science & Technology Week

The National Science Foundation sponsors National Science & Technology Week. Visit their site for information about dates and current themes.

- National Science Foundation http://www.nsf.gov/
  - National Science & Technology Week Archives http://www.nsf.gov/search97cgi/vtopic

Ways to Celebrate

1. See what's cookin'! NSF sponsors a terrific Internet site with lots of cool science projects. Try a new one everyday.
   - Find Out Why http://www.nsf.gov/od/lpa/events/fow/start.htm
2. Put it in perspective! PBS has technology lesson plans and an interactive technology timeline.
   - Lesson Plans from PBS http://www.pbs.org/teachersource/sci_tech.htm
   - Technology Timeline http://www.pbs.org/wgbh/amex/telephone/timeline/
3. Still need more? Visit Kathy Schrock's Science and Technology Internet Resource list to find just the right activity for your students.
   - Subject Access: Science and Technology http://school.discovery.com/schrockguide/sci-tech/scigs.html
4. Invite your student's parents to a Cybersurfari. Have the students be the guides as they show their parents all of the things they can do at the Discovery School Internet site. Some parents may be concerned about how computers, especially the Internet, are being used in the classroom. They are rightfully concerned about Internet safety. But also, they want to know if technology is contributing in a significant way to their child's educational experiences. Your students are the best advocates for using technology in an educational setting. Discovery School has the perfect way to introduce parents (and school board members) to the educational uses of the Internet.
   - Cybersurfari http://school.discovery.com/cybersurfari/index.html

Date Varies

Easter

At Easter, Christians celebrate the life and resurrection of Christ. It is usually celebrated on the first Sunday after the full moon following the first day of spring. To learn more about the religious significance of Easter, refer to *Easter for Kids and Teachers*. The *Easter on the Net* site has religious as well as secular information. And, the *Kids Domain* and ABC Teach sites have all sorts of games, activities, crafts and lessons.
   - Easter for Kids and Teachers http://www.kiddyhouse.com/Holidays/Easter/
   - Easter on the Net http://www.holidays.net/easter/index.htm
   - Kids Domain http://www.kidsdomain.com/holiday/easter/index.html
   - Easter Activities http://www.abcteach.com/easter/eastertoc.htm

One of the interesting ways people in Bermuda celebrate the Easter holiday is to make and fly kites. Read this interesting story and learn to make a Bermuda kite.
   - Good Friday Bermuda Kites http://cyberfair.gsn.org/gprep/kites.html#back
     - Instructions http://cyberfair.gsn.org/gprep/make.kites.html
   - Bermuda Holiday Celebrations http://bermuda-online.org/pubhols.htm

For more information about kites around the world and for very simple kite pattern refer to these two sites.
   - World on a String http://www.festivals.com/00-07-july/kite/
   - Kites http://www.earlychildhood.com/crafts/index.cfm?FuseAction=Craft&C=17

Passover

Passover is a holiday that commemorates the time in history when the Jewish people were freed from slavery and began their exodus from Egypt. The name Passover refers to the sign that the slaves put over their doors so that the Angel of Death would pass by their home, saving the life of their first-born child. Passover is celebrated today by having a Seder, this is a meal with special foods and the story of the Passover is read. Passover begins on the 15th day of the Jewish month of Nissan. To learn more about Passover, refer to the *Passover on the Net* site. These sites have stories, recipes and music. *Kids Domain* also has a very simple history of the holiday, but also contains games, stories and crafts. Hold a Seder with your students.

- Passover on the Net http://www.holidays.net/passover/
- Kids Domain http://www.kidsdomain.com/holiday/passover/index.html

Take Your Daughter to Work Day

In the early 1990s researchers were finding that girls in their early adolescence, who had earlier in their development displayed high self esteem, were now showing a significant drop in self-esteem and insecurity. In an attempt to help girls stay strong and remain confident, the people at Ms Foundation created Take Your Daughter to Work Day, a day to reinforce girls' natural strengths and focus on their abilities rather than their appearances. Learn more about the research about girls self esteem and ways to celebrate Take Your Daughter to Work Day. You will even find activities for boys.

- Take Your Daughter to Work http://www.takeourdaughterstowork.org/
- Ms Foundation http://www.ms.foundation.org

1st Sunday
Daylight Saving Time Begins

The main purpose of Daylight Saving Time is to make better use of daylight, by having more daylight in the evenings. You might be surprised that Benjamin Franklin first envisioned the idea of Daylight Saving Time. Daylight Saving Time has been used in the United States since WWI, but it wasn't until 1966 when Congress passed the Uniform Time Act, that it became the law of the land, although states may opt out. It has been revised since that time and you can read all about it at the *Daylight Saving Time* site.

- Daylight Saving Time http://webexhibits.org/daylightsaving/

Time Zones

Time zones were actually set in the United States and Canada by the railroads in 1883. Before that time cities and communities set their own local time based on the sun. Local time was usually displayed on some local focal point such as a courthouse or depot. But, the railroads needed a way to standardize time, so, they set time zones. Look at the time zones around the world as see how daylight moves from region to region and how the daylight corresponds with time zones. Have your students do a simple experiment to see how they can use their hand and the sun to tell time.

- World Time Zones http://www.worldtimezone.com/
- Sun Time Experiments http://www.kyes-world.com/suntime.htm

Clocks

The hand clock you just made is a version of one of the earliest clocks, the sundial. The following sites will teach you about the history of keeping time.

- A Walk Through Time http://physics.nist.gov/GenInt/Time/time.html
- The History of Clocks http://library.scar.utoronto.ca/ClassicsC42/Gomes/wat.html
- Clock History http://www.mystical-www.co.uk/time/clocks.htm

And, for a nice lesson plan about how clocks work, use this Newton's Apple site sponsored by PBS.

- How Do Clocks Keep Time? http://www.pbs.org/ktca/newtons/14/clocks10.html

Of course, we need to see what time it is, so go to the World Clock.

- The World Clock http://www.timeanddate.com/worldclock/

Mnemonics

One way to remember if we set the clock ahead or back an hour is to use a simple mnemonic, '*spring ahead; fall back.*' Mnemonics help us remember all kinds of things from musical notes to the names of the great lakes. Learn a little bit more about how mnemonics work and have your students develop some of their own.

- Amanda's Mnemonics Page http://www.frii.com/~geomanda/mnemonics.html
- Mnemonics http://www.happychild.org.uk/acc/tpr/mne/

Astronomy Day

Astronomy Day is a grass roots movement to share the joy of astronomy with the general population. Over the past few years, people all over the United States and Canada have celebrated Astronomy Day. There are many Internet resources to help your students get involved. Astronomy Day occurs sometime between mid April and mid May on a Saturday near or before the 1st quarter Moon.

- Astronomical League http://www.astroleague.org
  - Exact Date http://www.astroleague.org/al/astroday/astroday.html
  - Tips http://www.astroleague.org/al/astroday/adtips.html
- Astronomy Day Handbook http://www.skypub.com/resources/astroday/handbook0.html

View the night sky right in your classroom. NASA's Observatorium and the Hubble Space Telescope bring the stars and planets to you. Both have excellent teacher resource materials.

- NASA Observatorium http://observe.ivv.nasa.gov/nasa/entries/entry_5.html
  - Fun & Games http://observe.ivv.nasa.gov/nasa/fun/fun_index.shtml.html (my favorite is Earth at Night)
- Hubble Space Telescope http://hubble.stsci.edu/index.shtml
  - Tour the Cosmos http://hubble.stsci.edu/discoveries/tour_the_cosmos/

See what's playing in your night sky.

- Earth & Sky Radio Broadcast http://www.earthsky.com/
- Star Dust http://jadierose.com/midicollection.html

Get a star map from National Geographic

- Star Map http://www.nationalgeographic.com/stars/

And, read some Native American legends about the night sky.

- Starlore of Native America http://www.ac.wwu.edu/~skywise/legends.html

Arbor Day

Arbor Day was founded by J. Sterling Morton in Nebraska in 1872. National Arbor Day is celebrated each year on the last Friday in April except in Nebraska, where is it still celebrated on Morton's birthday, April 22. Arbor Day is a nationally celebrated observance that encourages tree planting and tree care. As J. Sterling Morton said, "*we will* embellish the world with plant life, trees, flowers and foliage."[iii] The *Arbor Day* site has information about tree planting, planning Arbor Day celebrations, J. Sterling Morton, including one of his Arbor Day speeches and much more. The Library of Congress site has some wonderful old posters and programs and pictures of historic trees in America. And, to help you celebrate Arbor Day and Poetry Month, read the Arbor Day poems at the Indiana Forestry site. The K-12 Teaching and Learning Center has links to lesson plans and program ideas.

- Arbor Day http://www.arborday.org/arborday/
- The 1st Arbor Day http://memory.loc.gov/ammem/today/apr10.html
- Forestry Education: Arbor Day Poems http://www.state.in.us/dnr/forestry/arborday/adpoems.html
- Teaching and Learning K-12 Center: Arbor Day http://tlc.ai.org/arborday.htm

Trees

"I think that I shall never see
A poem lovely as a tree,"

- Joyce Kilmer[iv]

Learn about the Global Releaf Program sponsored by the American Forests. You can also view and order historic trees at their site and learn about the Tree for Every Child project. What kind of tree will your class plant today, maybe one that Abraham Lincoln planted?

- American Forests Global Releaf http://www.americanforests.org/
  - A Tree for Every Child
    http://www.americanforests.org/global_releaf/earth_day_promo.html

Big Trees

What is the biggest tree in your neighborhood, playground or park? Find out how to measure the girth and height of the trees. Then, compare the size of your trees to those listed at the Big Tree Facts.

- Measuring the Height of Trees http://freeweb.pdq.net/headstrong/tree.htm
- Math lesson on estimation http://www.zip.com.au/~elanora/tmaths.html
- Big Tree Facts http://www.americanforests.org/garden/big_trees/2000_01_facts.html

Using Digital Cameras

The Lesson Plans Page has a couple of lesson plans that encourage students to use their observational skills.

- Classifying Trees http://www.lessonplanspage.com/CIScienceDigitalCamera-ShapesInNatureIdea48.htm
- Looking at Bark http://www.lessonplanspage.com/CIScienceBarkScanDigitalCameraIdea58.htm

Online Activities

These are some Internet sites that have very nice, educational activities about trees and forests to use on Arbor Day and throughout the year.

- Woodsy's Wonderful World http://www.fs.fed.us/spf/woodsy/
- Smokey the Bear http://www.smokeybear.com/cgi-bin/rbox/fr.cgi
- Forest Puzzles http://www.omsi.edu/explore/life/forestpuzzles/menu.html

Special Days

April 1
April Fools Day

Sugar in the saltshaker and telling someone the wrong time are just a couple of time honored practical jokes played on people on April Fools Day. But did you know that April Fools Day was really one of our oldest holidays, one celebrate all around the world? These sites provide fun and games for everyone. Read one version about the origin of April Fools (Fish) Day.

- April Fish Day http://www.mcphee.com/store/fishstory.html

See how April Fools Day is celebrated around the world.

- April Fools Day Around the World http://www.huddlenet.com/kilikina/fools.html
- April Fools Day http://members.aol.com/Donnpages/Holidays.html#AprilFools

And, in America…

- April Fools Day http://www.usis.usemb.se/Holidays/celebrate/april.html

Download some cool April Fools clip art.

- April Fools Day Clip Art http://www.freegraphics.com/12_FG_Specials/aprilfools.html

April 2, 1805
Hans Christian Andersen's Birthday

Born to a poor family in Denmark, Hans Christian Andersen became one of the best known, and best loved authors of all time. His stories are a combination of poetry, fantasy tale and everyday reality, with a touch of melancholy. The *Annotated Web-o-graphy* is a great resource for teachers, with links to biographies, criticisms and his stories, which are now in the public domain.

- Hans Christian Andersen Annotated Web-o-graphy http://hca.gilead.org.il/www.html
- Hans Christian Andersen Picture Page http://www.terminate.com/hc/
- Hans Christian Andersen http://www.kirjasto.sci.fi/hcanders.htm

Give Your Favorite Story a Face Lift

One of our favorite Andersen stories is the *Emperor's New Suit*; the story about a vane king who is tricked into thinking only he could see his new suit of clothes. A modern version of this story is the *Principal's New Clothes* – same story line, only the setting and time have been changed. Have the students take another Andersen tale, such as the Princess and the Pea and rewrite it, changing the setting and the time. Illustrate their story with clip art. The point we want to make here is times change, people don't.

- The Emperor's New Suit http://hca.gilead.org.il/emperor.html
- The Princess and the Pea http://hca.gilead.org.il/princess.html

The Movie v The Book

A number of Hans Christian Andersen's stories have been made into movies, most notably, the *Little Mermaid* by Walt Disney. Have the students read Andersen's story and then watch the movie. Compare and contrast Andersen's story with Disney's movie. Use the matrix graphic organizer to put the data in order.

- The Little Mermaid http://hca.gilead.org.il/li_merma.html
- Matrix Graphic Organizer http://www.graphic.org/commat.html

In A Thousand Years

Andersen wrote his the story, *In A Thousand Years*, in 1852. The story begins with these words, "Yes, in a thousand years people will fly on the wings of steam through the air, over the ocean!" Little did he know, that that prediction would come true in less than one hundred years! The story is about a trip young Americans take to see the great cities of Europe. Take that trip now, via the Internet. Place a map of Europe on your bulletin board. Title the project, "To Europe!" Follow Andersen's itinerary, locating pictures on the Internet. Print them and place on the map. Have the students write their own story, *In A Thousand Years*, about young Martians who visit the great sights of America. Have them plan the itinerary of important places the Martians should see.

- In A Thousand Years http://hca.gilead.org.il/thousand.html
- Outline Maps http://www.abcteach.com/Maps/mapsTOC.htm

Paper Cuttings

We are familiar with the wonderful storytelling ability of Hans Christian Andersen, but he was also known for his elaborate paper cutting artwork. Have the students view some of his work and make of their own paper cuttings. Both the Scherenschnitte site and the *Cutting Up with Paper* site have patterns for children. Of course, you can always start with something simple like cutting a string of paper dolls, guaranteed to delight any small child. I use adding machine paper. Just tear off a strip about 12 inches long. Fold it like a fan in about 2 inch folds, fold the fan in half and cut half a doll. Be sure to leave their hands connected. Unfold and ta da!

- Hans Christian Andersen's Paper Cuts http://www.kb.dk/kultur/expo/klenod/hca.htm
- Chinese Paper Cutting http://www.multimania.com/nguyenvanvalerie/English/Accueilx.html
- Scherenschnitte: The Art of Paper Cutting http://kidsartscrafts.about.com/library/weekly/aa020701a.htm?once=true&
- Cutting Up With Paper http://www.askasia.org/frclasrm/lessplan/puzzle.htm

April 2, 1792
U.S. Mint - Philadelphia

Congress created the United States Mint on April 2, 1792. There are a number of terrific Internet sites to help your students understand how our money is made. I suggest starting with the *U. S. Mint for Kids.*

- U.S. Mint http://www.usmint.gov/
  - For Kids http://www.usmint.gov/kids/
  - Coin Collecting http://www.usmint.gov/kids/index.cfm?FileContents=/kids/campcoin/getaclue.cfm
  - Time Traveler http://www.usmint.gov/kids/index.cfm?Filecontents=/kids/timemachine/index.cfm
  - 50 State Quarters http://www.usmint.gov/catalog/catalogb.cfm?Urlcategory=50+state+quarters

To see how our paper money is made, go to the *Bureau of Engraving and Printing.*

- The Bureau of Engraving and Printing http://www.moneyfactory.com/
  - Money Factory for Kids http://www.moneyfactory.com/kids/start.html
  - Counterfeiting http://www.moneyfactory.com/section.cfm/7

And, to see how the whole thing fits together, go right to the Department of Treasury, itself.

- Treasury Page for Kids http://www.treas.gov/kids/

The eduscapes site is an outstanding resource for teachers. It has links to all kinds of money related information, activities and projects. But, it doesn't have Dollar Bill Bow Tie.

- Money http://eduscapes.com/42explore/money.htm
- Dollar Bill Bow Tie http://www.igrandparents.com/grandTopics/articles/printables/Bowtie.asp

Money Related Slang

If a buck is a male deer and dough is what we make bread out of and bread is what we make sandwiches with, why are we talking about these words in a lesson about our monetary system? Help students explore the slang associated with money. Brainstorm a list of money related phrases, such as "phony as a $2.00 bill" and "money is the root of all evil." Have students write definitions of the phrases before you search for the actual definition.

- Word Improvisation http://www.theatlantic.com/issues/97jun/9706imp.htm
- Words and Stuff: D is for Dollar http://www.kith.org/logos/words/upper/D.html
- World Wide Words http://www.quinion.com/words/articles/money.htm

April 4, 1928
Maya Angelou's Birthday

Maya Angelou is a poet, historian, author, actress, playwright, civil-rights activist, producer and director. Little did she know, as a small child growing up in rural, segregated Arkansas that she would one day read one of her poems at a Presidential Inauguration.

- Maya Angelou http://www.mayaangelou.com/
- The Rock Cries Out To Us Today http://www.empirezine.com/spotlight/maya/maya-p2.htm#the%20rock (President Clinton's Inaugural)

Author Study

Because of her interesting and varied life, Maya Angelou would be a wonderful author study. The following sites will give you some direction on how to set up the author study and evaluate it. You will need to modify these resources to meet your classes' needs.

- Author/Illustrator Study http://www.planetesme.com/authorstudy/authorstudy.html
- Completing An Author Study http://www.sinc.sunysb.edu/Stu/tdonalds/webquest2.html
- Rubric for Evaluating an Author Study http://www.lubbock.k12.tx.us/rush/lessons/rubric.doc

Selected Poems

Maya Angelou writes for young adults and adults, but I find that younger children really enjoy listening to her poetry, even though they might not understand it. So, practice reading in your most dramatic voice and your students will eat it up!

- Poems http://www.empirezine.com/spotlight/maya/maya-p1.htm
  - Phenomenal Woman http://www.empirezine.com/spotlight/maya/maya-p1.htm#Phenomenal%20Woman
- African American Poets http://web.reed.edu/academic/departments/english/courses/english213/African_American_.html

And for the teacher.....

- Teacher Resource File: Maya Angelou http://falcon.jmu.edu/~ramseyil/angelou.htm

Selected Books by Maya Angelou
I Know Why the Caged Bird Sings
The Complete Collected Poems of Maya Angelou
The Heart of a Woman
Life Doesn't Frighten Me
Still I Rise
All God's Children Need Traveling Shoes
Phenomenal Woman

April 6, 1909
North Pole – Robert E. Peary

Was he or wasn't he the first man to discover the North Pole? It seems Captain Cook also claims this accolade. Read about this dispute and decide for yourself. You can also read excerpts from Peary's book, *The North Pole* plus view many old photos and maps at the Matthew Henson site.

- The Cook – Peary North Pole Dispute http://members.tripod.com/PolarFlight/controversy1.htm
- The North Pole http://www.matthewhenson.com/1910.htm
  - Map Room: Where is the North Pole? http://www.matthewhenson.com/maproom.htm
- Robert Peary http://www.pbs.org/wgbh/amex/ice/sfeature/peary.html
- The North Pole Race http://www.the-north-pole.com/visit.html (I'll let you be the judge.)

Where is the North Pole?

This sounds like an easy question, but it keeps moving. Get out your map and check it out!

- Tracking the North Magnetic Pole http://www.geolab.nrcan.gc.ca/geomag/e_nmpole.html
- North Pole http://geography.about.com/science/geography/library/weekly/aa090800a.htm

This isn't a problem for children. They know the North Pole is where Santa Clause lives.

- Welcome to the North Pole http://northpole.net/

April 7
World Health Day

World Health Day is held to heighten awareness to the health needs of the peoples of the world. To find information about World Health Day and teaching materials, go to either one of these sites.

- World Health Organization http://www.who.int/home-page/
- American Association of World Health http://www.aawhworldhealth.org/

The United Nations' Cyberschool Bus site has an excellent curriculum guide about world health issues.

- Health Curriculum http://www.un.org/Pubs/CyberSchoolBus/special/health/index.html

April 14 is designated Healthy Kids Day. I suggest you use the week between the two to discuss health issues with your students, including the DARE Day materials. The YMCA has many resources for you and your students to use.

- YMCA http://www.ymca.net
- HealthyKids http://www.ymca.net/programs/hkd/hkd.htm

UNICEF's mission is to advocate for the protection of children's rights, to help meet their basic needs and to expand their opportunities to reach their full potential.[v] There are many ways your students can support UNICEF programs around the world. Go to their site to see how you can get involved.

- UNICEF http://www.unicef.org/
- "Say Yes for Children" http://unicefusa.org/say_yes/actions/index.html

April 8
Kambutsu-e
Buddha's Birthday Festival

> *"We are shaped by our thoughts;*
> *we become what we think.*
> *When the mind is pure,*
> *joy follows like a shadow that never leaves."*
>
> Buddha

2,500 years ago, a young man, Siddhattha Gotama, left his father's palace to live the life of a spiritual seeker; searching for the answers to life. Buddha is the title given to this man. Read more about Kambutse-e and about the life of Buddha.

- Kambutsu-e http://www.jinjapan.org/kidsweb/calendar/april/kambutsue.html
- Buddha's Life (in pictures) http://www.abm.ndirect.co.uk/leftside/arty/his-life/lanka/life-1.htm
- The Life Story (brief) http://www.abm.ndirect.co.uk/leftside/arty/his-life/life-intro.htm
- What is a Buddha? http://www.abm.ndirect.co.uk/riteside/moondogs/moondogs.htm

Japanese Tea Ceremony

Part of the Kambutsu-e celebration is drinking a sweet tea. Learn about a Japanese Tea Ceremony. Make some sweet tea to drink while you tour the Japanese Buddhist Temples. Most children will drink a Jasmine tea with a little sugar.

- Tea http://www.teahyakka.com/

Visit a Japanese Temple

- Japanese Temple Gazing http://www.foutz.net/japan/ryoanji.htm
- Japanese Buddhist Temples http://faculty-web.at.nwu.edu/art-history/fraser/b40/test2-japanese-bud-tmp.html

Haiku Poetry

In recognition of Poetry Month, read some Haiku poems, and then try writing some of your own.

- In Buddha's Temple: Haiku Poems
  http://haibun.tripod.com/sanders_publishing/BUDDHA/BUDDHA.html
- Haiku Format http://www.geocities.com/EnchantedForest/5165/pages/poetry_samples.html#haiku

April 12
National D.A.R.E. Day

The DARE program was founded in 1983 in Los Angeles, CA. It is now being implemented in 80 percent of our nation's school districts and in more than 52 countries around the world. DARE is a collaborative program between schools, parents and law enforcement agencies to help educate our students about the dangers of drug abuse and violence and give them tools to resist peer pressure. The DARE Homepage is the portal for kids, parents, educators and police officers. There is a wealth of information at all of these sites. Have your students use a publishing program to make posters to hang in the businesses in your community. You can download official DARE clip art and logos.

- Drug Abuse Resistance Education (DARE) http://www.dare.com/index_3.htm

Odds and Ends

Looking for interactive quizzes, activities, experiments and movies about drug abuse? This is it!

- BrainPOP: Drug Abuse http://www.brainpop.com/health/nervous/drugabuse/index.weml

These are a couple of really good sites about the warning signs of abuse.

- Do you have a problem with alcohol or drugs? http://www.aafp.org/afp/990915ap/990915e.html
- Tips for Teens http://www.soundvision.com/teens/drug.shtml

In recognition of Poetry Month, write an Acrostic poem using the letters DARE.

- Acrostic Format
  http://www.geocities.com/EnchantedForest/5165/pages/poetry_samples.html#acrostic

April 13, 1938
Lee Bennett Hopkins' Birthday

Lee Bennett Hopkins grew up in a poor, single parent home. Because he had to go to work to help support his younger brothers and sisters, his school attendance was poor as was his schoolwork. It wasn't until a teacher inspired in him a love of the theatre and, subsequently, of reading, that his attendance and work improved. He was so grateful to this teacher that after graduation, he went to college and became a teacher himself. As a teacher, he taught 6th grade and found that poetry could help children with reading problems. He went on to write poetry and books for children and also to compile and edit many anthologies of children's poetry. It is very appropriate that we celebrate his April-Poetry-Month birthday. Read a little more about this favorite author.

- Lee Bennett Hopkins http://www.cbcbooks.org/html/lbhopkins.html
- Lee Bennett Hopkins
  http://www.simonsays.com/subs/183/Kids_Author_Bio.cfm?AUTHOR_KEY=706601&areaid=18 3

Personal Anthology

When Hopkins was teaching he used poetry in every area of the curriculum. He began collecting his favorite poems and eventually published them so other teachers could use poetry in their classrooms as well. Throughout the month, have your students collect the poems they like best. Copy and paste them into a word processor. At the end of the month, have the students arrange the poems in their book using some identifiable scheme, such as alphabetical by title or author, theme, date of publication or some other grouping. Use a publishing program to make a cover and be sure to make a bibliography. Print the books and place them in your classroom or school library for students to check out.

For the teacher....

- Teacher Resource File: Lee Bennett Hopkins http://falcon.jmu.edu/~ramseyil/hopkins.htm

Selected Books by Lee Bennett Hopkins
Hand in Hand: An American History Through Poetry
Lives: Poems About Famous Americans
Good rhymes, Good times: Original Poems
Marvelous Math: A Book of Poems
Extra Innings: Baseball Poems
School Supplies: A Book of Poems
My America: A Poetry Atlas of the United States
Yummy! Eating Through a Day

April 15
Income Tax Day

In 1913, the 16th Amendment of the Constitution was ratified. It allowed the Federal Government to levy an income tax law based on ability to pay. Tax money provides public goods and services for the community as a whole. The U. S. Treasury provides an excellent history of taxes in the United States. It is written in a dialog format. Choose two students to read it to your class.

- TAXi History http://www.irs.ustreas.gov/taxi/learninglab/history/index.html

Besides the history of income tax, the *TAXinteractive* site has an excellent resource to help students understand what taxes are and how taxes are figured. It is based on the weekly salary of a clerk and waitress. Use the calculator on your computer to figure how much income tax students will pay based on various salary levels. Have your students make a spreadsheet with the formulas built in so students could see how their take-home pay will change if the tax rate changes or their hourly wage change. You can also add state taxes and tips to your hourly wage.

Taxes

hourly	weekly	tax	take home
$6.75	$101.25	$30.38	$70.88

hourly	weekly	tax	take home
$5.00	$75.00	$22.50	$52.50

- It's Payday – Money In Your Pocket
  http://www.irs.ustreas.gov/taxi/learninglab/payday/index.html
- TAXinteractive http://www.irs.ustreas.gov/taxi/index.html

For more information....

- U. S. Treasury http://www.treas.gov/

April 15, 1912
Titanic Sinks
During the night of April 14-15, 1912, the unsinkable luxury passenger liner Titanic sunk. The great ship was on her maiden voyage from Southampton, England to New York City. About 1,500 lives were lost. Since then, the mystery and majesty of the Titanic intrigued historians, scientists, and just plain folks. Learn more about this great ship and the tragedy of what happened to her and her passengers.
- Titanic http://titanic.eb.com/
- The Titanic Online http://www.titanic-online.com/
- Titanic's Final Hours http://www.discovery.com/stories/science/sciencetitanic/sciencetitanic.html

Raising the Titanic
Travel with the crew of the manned submarine Nautile as they search for the Titanic. These sites have lots of multimedia. You can even take a tour of a virtual Titanic.
- Raising a Legend http://www.discovery.com/area/science/titanic/titanicopener.html
- Live from the Titanic http://www.discovery.com/stories/science/titanic/titanic.html
- The Final Resting Place http://seawifs.gsfc.nasa.gov/OCEAN_PLANET/HTML/titanic.html

April 15, 1955
1ˢᵗ McDonald's Opens
Ray Kroc opened the first McDonalds Hamburger Drive-in in Des Plaines, Illinois. Today, there are over 28,000 McDonalds in 121 countries. At the McDonalds Homepage, you can find links to the McDonalds around the world. Have the students research a country to see how their McDonalds is different from ours. Some of them have different sandwiches, some have different décor, but they all have the same quality, service, cleanliness and value that Ray Kroc insisted upon. In the early 1950's Kroc felt that Americans were changing; he sensed that they were becoming a people on the move who no longer could eat at home, but wanted quick meals on the run. Read about the life one of Time Magazine 100: Builders and Titans – Ray Kroc.
- McDonalds http://www.mcdonalds.com/
  - The History of McDonalds http://www.mcdonalds.com/corporate/info/history/index.html
- Ray Kroc http://www.time.com/time/time100/builder/profile/kroc.html
Stop by and play with Ronald McDonald and his friends at the McDonald Homepage.
- Ronald and Friends http://www.mcdonalds.com/mcdonaldland/index.html
Ray Kroc saw what people needed and set out to fill that need. Have your students develop a new business that meets the needs of people in your community. Have them prepare a vision statement for their new business.
- McDonald's Vision Statement http://www.mcdonalds.com/corporate/index.html

Nutritional Comparison
How does McDonald's hamburger compare in nutritional value to Burger King, or White Castle or Wendy's? Check it out by making a spreadsheet. Go to the homepage and search for nutrition. Be sure the students are comparing 'apples to apples' not 'apples to oranges.'
- McDonalds http://www.mcdonalds.com/
- Burger King http://www.burgerking.com/flash.htm
- White Castle http://www.whitecastle.com/
- Wendy's http://www.wendys.com/index0.html

April 18, 1906
San Francisco Earthquake
Another disaster that occurred in April was the great San Francisco Earthquake. The San Francisco Earthquake occurred shortly after 5 o'clock in the morning, causing major damage to the city and

surrounding area and taking the lives of over 3000 people. The earthquake and the resulting fire destroyed 28,188 buildings. Read an account of this devastating earthquake and view the shocking pictures. Some of the sites have eyewitness accounts.

- The Great San Francisco Earthquake http://quake.usgs.gov/info/1906/
- Museum of San Francisco: Earthquake and Fire http://www.sfmuseum.org/1906/06.html

Helping Students Understand Earthquakes
- KidZone http://www.abag.ca.gov/bayarea/eqmaps/kids.html
- On the Road with the Faultline Project http://www.exploratorium.edu/faultline/project/start.html
- The Disaster Area: Earthquakes http://www.fema.gov/kids/quake.htm
- Earthquake ABCs for Children (with guides for adults) http://home.earthlink.net/~torg/eqindex.html
- Earthquakes http://scign.jpl.nasa.gov/learn/eq.htm
- Geosphere http://www.ldeo.columbia.edu/EV/GEO/geo_main.html

Go to Ask Jeeves for Teachers for an excellent research project for your students.
- Earthquakes – A Lesson Plan http://ajkids.com/teachers/TeachersplansMR.asp
  - Ask Jeeves Earthquake Tour http://ajkids.com/tours/earthquaketour.asp

Odds and Ends
- ABAG Earthquake Maps and Information http://www.abag.ca.gov/bayarea/eqmaps/eqmaps.html
- Global Seismic Hazard Assessment Program http://seismo.ethz.ch/GSHAP/
- Science Fair Earthquake Project Ideas http://earthquake.usgs.gov/4kids/sciencefair.html

April 19
Patriots Day
Patriots Day is celebrated in remembrance of the Battle of Lexington & Concord. It is the day after Paul Revere's famous ride. Start your field trip at the Old North Church. Then, learn more about Patriots Day by touring the Boston, Lexington and Concord area. Visit the Battlefield National Park for a brief history of the 1st battle of the American Revolution.

- Old North Church http://www.oldnorth.com/
- Patriots Day http://www.world.std.com/~adamg/patriotsday.html
- Patriots Day http://www.nps.gov/mima/index.htm
- Coloring Pages http://www.childlight.com/revere/html_pages/coloring.htm
- Revolutionary Tea http://www.acronet.net/~robokopp/usa/revoltea.htm (lyrics to an old song)

Paul Revere's Ride
Look at Grant Wood's painting, Paul Revere's Ride and read as a reader's theater, Longfellow's poem, *The Midnight Ride of Paul Revere* or Emerson's *Concord Hymn*.

- Paul Revere's Ride by Grant Wood http://zeus.ia.net/~kwradio/revere.html
- Longfellow Poem http://www.noblenet.org/year/paul.htm
- Concord Hymn http://www.noblenet.org/year/concord.htm

Learn more about Paul Revere, patriot and silversmith.
- Paul Revere http://gonewengland.about.com/travel/gonewengland/cs/paulrevere/index.htm

April 20
Holocaust Day

"to ensure that such suffering will never be repeated..."

Holocaust Day helps students develop an understanding and respect for those who went through the Holocaust. The *Don't Let the Light Go Out* is a wonderful way to begin your discussion of the Holocaust. It is treasure trove of multimedia resources such as video and audio files.

- Don't Let the Light Go Out http://www.jewishpost.com/holocaust/

Use the PBS site to focus on the historical aspects of the Holocaust. I've also listed a couple of other teacher guides and projects. Follow up your discussion with a field trip to the Holocaust Museum.

- Remembering the Holocaust http://www.pbs.org/holocaust/
  - Classroom activities http://www.pbs.org/holocaust/classroom.html
- A Teacher's Guide to the Holocaust http://fcit.coedu.usf.edu/holocaust/
- Holocaust History Project http://www.holocaust-history.org/
- The Holocaust: A Tragic Legacy http://library.thinkquest.org/12663/
- United States Holocaust Museum http://www.ushmm.org/

Anne Frank

> *"It's a wonder I haven't abandoned all my ideals, they seem so absurd and impractical. Yet I cling to them because I still believe, in spite of everything, that people are truly good at heart."*
>
> - Anne Frank[vi]

One of the ways to personalize this story is to look at it from the viewpoint of a real child. Anne Frank was just a child when she and her family were forced to go into hiding. They spent 25 months in small rooms located above her father's shop until they were betrayed and sent to Nazi concentration camps. Anne, age 15, died of typhus in the camp. The Internet has many excellent resources to bring her story to life for your students. The first site listed provides an overview of her life and a timetable of WWII and the Holocaust. I've listed web quests and lesson plans last.

- Anne Frank Online http://www.annefrank.com/
- The Anne Frank Internet Guide http://www-th.phys.rug.nl/~ma/annefrank.html
- Anne Frank http://www.time.com/time/time100/heroes/profile/frank01.html

These sites have lesson plans and activities.

- Anne Frank Lesson Plans http://www.uen.org/utahlink/lp_res/AnneFrank.html
- Anne Frank Lesson Plan – Timeline Quote Project http://fcit.coedu.usf.edu/holocaust/activity/68plan/afcntr1.htm
- Anne Frank and the Holocaust Web Quest http://www.plainfield.k12.in.us/hschool/webq/webq11/afrank.htm

Take a field trip to the Anne Frank House in Amsterdam.

- Anne Frank House http://www.annefrank.nl/eng/default2.html

April 22
Earth Day

In her Earth Day speech to the United Nations, March 20, 1977, Margaret Mead said, "Earth Day is to be the first completely international and universal holiday that the world has ever known. Every other holiday was tied to one place, or some political or special event. This Day is tied to Earth itself, and to the place of Earth in the whole solar system."[vii] She went on to say that when we looked at Earth from space we realized how precious and fragile Earth is. She called on us to be custodians of Earth. Read her complete address at the International Earth Day site. You will also find additional information and resources at the following Internet sites.

- International Earth Day http://www.earthsite.org/
- Earth Day http://www.earthday.net/
- All About Earth Day http://www.earthday.wilderness.org/history/

Planet Earth

On this Earth Day, take a look at our wonderful planet. Make a music video of our planet. Use a presentation tool, such as PowerPoint. Combine pictures, music and text to celebrate our beautiful planet.

- Look at the Earth: Globes http://www.educationplanet.com/search/redirect/redirect?id=418&mfcat=/maps/socialstudiesplanet/search/Geography_and_Countries/Cartography/&mfcount=35
- NASA Images of Earth for Earth Day http://www.space.com/scienceastronomy/planetearth/landsat_zoom_010420.html
- The Internet Piano Page http://www.geocities.com/Paris/3486/index.htm
- Chief Seattle's Thoughts http://www.webcom.com/duane/seattle.html

Earth Day Activities

"Unless someone like you cares a whole awful lot...
nothing's going to get better... it's not."

- The Lorax by Dr. Suess

There are many helpful resources on the Internet to help you and your students celebrate Earth Day. I hope you enjoy using some of these.

- The Lorax's Save the Tree Game http://www.randomhouse.com/seussville/games/lorax/
- Earth Day Activities http://www.eduplace.com/monthlytheme/april/earth.html
- A is for Air http://www.epa.gov/superfund/kids/alphabet/a.htm
- Environmental Explorer (lesson plan) http://www.nationalgeographic.com/resources/ngo/education/ideask4/k4environ.html
- Recycle Games http://www.eduplace.com/hac/acts/recycle/passon.html
- Garbage: Shrinking a Landfill (game) http://www.learner.org/exhibits/garbage/landfill/
- Earth Day Riddles http://www.mamamedia.com/activities/riddle_machine/earth/right.html?startAt=&difficulty=
- Amazing Moms Earth Day Activities http://amazingmoms.com/htm/Earthday.htm
- The Happy Earth Day Coloring Book http://www.epa.gov/docs/Region5/happy.htm
- Earth Day Groceries Project http://www.earthdaybags.org/
- Earth Day Activities http://www.abcteach.com/earthday/earthtoc.htm
- Happy Earth Day from Whales Times http://www.whaletimes.org/earthday.htm

Odds and Ends

These are just a couple of sites to use throughout the month. I would set these up on your classroom computer and have students cycle through as time permits.

- Test Your Earth IQ http://www.earth2kids.org/Games/earthiq_quiz.html
- Turn Trash Into Art http://www.eduplace.com/hac/acts/recycle/whatsit.html
- The Dirt On Soil http://school.discovery.com/schooladventures/soil/index.html
- Virtual House (biodiversity) http://www.virtualhouse.org/game.cgi
- Miss Maggie's Earth Adventures http://www.missmaggie.org

And, two plays for your class to perform.

- Down in the Dumps http://www.allspecies.org/edu/downnthedu.htm
- It's All About Connections http://www.allspecies.org/ecokids/connectplay.htm

April 22, 1889
Oklahoma Land Rush

This day commemorates one of the most exciting days in the history of the old west. A large area of land, called No Man's Land had been restricted to settlers. But, cattle ranchers and homesteaders wanted to settle there. The United States government kept refusing permission. Finally, after many years of petitioning and struggle, the land was finally opened up. On April 22, 1889 men and women on horseback and in wagons of all kinds were lined up on the border, ready to claim their land. When the signal was given they rushed to lay their claim. By nightfall, whole towns had been plotted and thousands of people had claimed their homestead. Oklahoma gets its nickname, the Sooner State, from those people who couldn't wait and jumped the lines to get to their land *sooner* than anyone else.

- Brief History of Oklahoma http://users.rootsweb.com/~oknowata/OklaHist.htm
    o No Man's Land http://users.rootsweb.com/~oknowata/GCNML.htm

Learn more about the early pioneers of Oklahoma and other parts of the west with this unit plan from eduscapes.

- Pioneers http://eduscapes.com/42explore/pioneer.htm

Indian Territory

Earlier, during 1838-1839, one of the most disgraceful events in American history took place. The Government forced Native Americans living in the land between the east coast and the Mississippi to move to Indian Territory, today known as Oklahoma. Thousands of Indians died on that long and arduous journey.

- Indian Territory http://www.historychannel.com/cgi-bin/frameit.cgi?p=http%3A//www.historychannel.com/perl/print_book.pl%3FID%3D21687
- Trail of Tears http://rosecity.net/tears/trail/map.html
- National Historic Trail http://rosecity.net/tears/trail/tearsnht.html
- Trail of Tears – Dedicated to the Choctaw Nation of Oklahoma http://www.peaknet.net/~aardvark/

A number of Indian tribes lived in what is now known as Oklahoma. They included, among others, the Osage, the Comanche and the Ute. Visit these sites to learn more about the Native Americans of Oklahoma.

- The Native Tribes http://users.rootsweb.com/~oknowata/NatTri.htm
- The Chickasaw Nation http://www.chickasaw.net/
- The Choctaw Nation of Oklahoma http://www.chickasaw.net/
- The Cherokee Nation http://www.cherokee.org/

April 23, 1564
William Shakespeare's Birthday

> *"This above all: to thine own self be true;*
> *And it must follow, as the night the day;*
> *Thou canst not then be false to any man.*
> William Shakespeare, *Hamlet* Act I, Scene iii

The greatest writer of all times (at least in English) William Shakespeare was born in Stratford-On-Avon, 94 miles from London, England. The Internet has so much information about him, his life, his work, and his times that it's almost impossible to sift through it. I've listed some of my favorites that I feel should be in every teacher's bookmarks.

- Life and Times of William Shakespeare
  http://www.gprc.ab.ca/courses_and_programs/en1010/shakespeare/

- William Shakespeare @ the Web English Teacher
  http://www.webenglishteacher.com/shakespeare.html
- Mr. William Shakespeare http://shakespeare.palomar.edu/ one of the best on the web

About his works
- The Complete Works of William Shakespeare http://tech-two.mit.edu/Shakespeare/works.html
- The Shakespeare Bookshelf http://www.ipl.org/reading/shakespeare/shakespeare.html

Shakespeare for the Younger Students
- Between the Lions: Dreaming Shakespeare http://pbskids.org/lions/dreaming/index.html
- Shakespeare is Elementary http://www.cps.ednet.ns.ca/pageone.htm

Interactive and Multimedia Shakespeare
- Hunt for Shakespeare: Internet Treasure Hunt
  http://www.kn.pacbell.com/wired/fil/pages/huntshakespebr1.html
- ThinkQuest: Globe Theater http://library.thinkquest.org/10502/
- ThinkQuest: On Your Toes With Odes
  http://tqjunior.thinkquest.org/4382/odes.html#Top%20of%20Page
- Poetry Machine http://www.shakespeare.com/Poetry/ieindex.html

If you lived in the days of Shakespeare
Based on the popular children series, have the students write a book about life in Shakespeare's time. Children are very concrete people. They want to know what they ate, where they lived, what they wore, what games they played and so forth. With the students, make a list of these and other things they want to know. Give each student or group of students one of the things on the list to research. They will write that page for the book. Use a presentation tool to publish the book.

If You Lived in the Days
Of Shakespeare

By Our Class

THE ALPHABET

Shakespeare's alphabet had 24 letters instead of 26 letters. The **I** and **J** are the same and so are the **U** and **V**. "I have an uncle" is written as
"J haue an vncle."

The letter **y** is used to represent the **th** Sound. So "Ye Olde Tea Shoppe" is read **The old tea shop**.

- Life in Elizabethan England http://renaissance.dm.net/compendium/
- Elizabethan England
  http://www.springfield.k12.il.us/schools/springfield/eliz/elizabethanengland.html
- The Shakespeare Resource Center: Elizabethan England http://www.bardweb.net/england.html
- Modern History Sourcebook: Description of Elizabethan England
  http://www.fordham.edu/halsall/mod/1577harrison-england.html
- The Life of a Child in Elizabethan England
  http://library.thinkquest.org/3588/Renaissance/Town/Children.html

April 25
Anzac Day – Australia and New Zealand

"They shall grow not old, as we that are left grow old:
Age shall not weary them, nor the years condemn.
At the going down of the sun and in the morning
We will remember them.
We will remember them."[viii]

- Laurence Binyon, *For the Fallen*

Anzac Day is a day when Australian and New Zealand soldiers are honored and remembered for their bravery and heroism. Anzac is an acronym for Australian and New Zealand Army Corps. During WWI, on April 25, 1915, the Anzacs led the Gallipoli Campaign. 7000 Australians and 8000 New Zealanders were killed during the campaign. Today, Anzac Day honors all war veterans. These sites explain the meaning of the day and provide links to pictures, paintings and diaries of those WWI soldiers. There is also an Anzac Day Program with pictures.

- The Anzacs http://www.lzs.com.au/~lmutimer/oz_history/oz_history.html
- Anzac Day http://www.nzhistory.net.nz/Gallery/Anzac/Anzac.htm
- Anzac Day Celebration http://www.dva.gov.au/commem/anzac/france.htm

Learn more about WWI and the Gallipoli Campaign.
- The Great War http://www.pbs.org/greatwar/ (nice overview)
- The First World War http://www.spartacus.schoolnet.co.uk/FWW.htm (much more depth)
- The Gallipoli Campaign http://www.nzhistory.net.nz/Gallery/Anzac/galli-poli/index.htm

Anzac Biscuits
During the war, many foodstuffs were rationed or not available. These cookies or as they are called in Australia, biscuits were made by the families and sent thousands of miles to the soldiers fighting in Egypt and Turkey. Make some with your class and enjoy them while you listen to Waltzing Matilda.

- Anzac Biscuits http://www.lzs.com.au/~lmutimer/oz_history/anzac_7.html
- Anzac Biscuits http://www.anzac.com/nzld/misc/anzbis.htm
- Waltzing Matilda (lyrics) http://www.ozramp.net.au/~senani/waltz.htm
- Waltzing Matilda (midi) http://www.hamilton.net.au/matilda.html

Odds and Ends
- Guide to Australia http://www.csu.edu.au/australia/
- New Zealand http://nz.com/guide/
- Australia Crafts http://www.dltk-kids.com/world/australia/index.htm
- Aussie Slang http://goaustralia.about.com/library/weekly/blstrine.htm

April 27, 1898
Ludwig Bemelmans' Birthday

"In an old house in Paris
all covered with vines
lived twelve little girls
in two straight lines."

- Ludwig Bemelmans

Two-time Caldecott Award winning author/illustrator Ludwig Bemelmans was born in Austria, but immigrated to the United States in 1914. Read his biography to find out why! He has written more than 40 books for children, but is best known for his Madeline books. Read the story, in his own words, of how he got the idea for writing his first Madeline book.

- Ludwig Bemelmans
  http://www.penguinputnam.com/static/packages/us/yreaders/madeline/bio.htm
  - The Isle of God
    http://www.penguinputnam.com/static/packages/us/yreaders/madeline/history.htm
- Ludwig Bemelmans http://www.penguinputnam.com/Author/AuthorFrame?0000001870
- Ludwig Bemelmans http://www.edupaperback.org/authorbios/Bemelmans_Ludwig.html

Read an online version of Madeline.

- Madeline, by Ludwig Bemelmans http://www.duke.edu/~icheese/madeline.html

Visit Madeline's Homepage for some fun and games. While there, meet Madeline's friends. This is a site with characters, plots and unfinished stories just waiting for your students to finish.

- Madeline's Homepage http://www.madeline.com/
  - Meet Madeline's Friends http://www.madeline.com/charindx.htm

Have some more fun with Madeline.

- Game: Go, Madeline, Go! http://www.spe.sony.com/movies/madeline/game1.html
- Multimedia from the Movie http://www.spe.sony.com/movies/madeline/movie/multimedia.html
- Madeline Fun and Games
  http://www.penguinputnam.com/static/packages/us/yreaders/madeline/fun.htm

Lesson Plans for Madeline

- Education World: A Month of Mapping Literature http://www.education-world.com/a_lesson/00-2/lp2232.shtml
- Madeline and the Magnificent Puppet Show http://teachers.net/lessons/posts/1102.html

Books by Ludwig Bemelmans
Madeline – Caldecott Honor
Madeline's Rescue – Caldecott Award
Mad About Madeline
Madeline and the Bad Hat
Madeline in America
Madeline in London
Madeline and the Gypsies
Madeline's Christmas

April 28
Puppet Day
Learn about puppets and puppeteering. *Legends and Lore* has lots of information for teachers and students about puppets plus puppet patterns and scripts. Have fun!

- Legends and Lore http://www.legendsandlore.com/index.html
- Puppeteers of America http://www.puppeteers.org

Use one of Ludwig Bemelmans' books to make a puppet show. Have one group of students write the script. Have another group of students make the scenes by using PowerPoint slides for the backgrounds and sound effects. Have another group of students make the puppets by making silhouettes of the characters. Attach the puppets to a clear strip of transparency film by taping it to the back of the puppet's head. Use the computer screen as the puppet theater. Have the puppeteers stand behind the computer and dangle the puppets over the top of the screen. Have one person be the computer operator who changes the scenes. You might want to have readers read the script while the puppeteers operate the puppets.

April 30
National Honesty Day
According to the USA Report, dishonesty is on the increase among teens in America. One survey reports that 92 percent of the teenagers surveyed say they have lied to a parent (up from 85 percent in 1996).[ix] This is perhaps the day you will want to survey the students in your school. Have your class develop survey questions, such as 'have you ever lied to your parents, to a friend, to a teacher, have you ever cheated on a test, have you ever shoplifted, etc.' Distribute your survey to students in your school. Record the results on a spreadsheet. Use the spreadsheet to compute the percentages. How do the students in your school compare with those in this national survey? Make a graph of the results and give to each class.

```
USA Today Survey

Lied to Parent................92%

Cheated on Test..........70%

Shoplifted.................46%
```

- America's Escalating Honesty Crisis
  http://www.usaweekend.com/98_issues/981018/981018nationalforum.html

Many schools are involved in a program such as Character Counts. Visit the Evergreen Elementary School to see what they are doing. This site gives a number of scenarios where students are asked what they would do. You might want to ask your students if they think there are degrees of lying and if they think it is ever OK to lie.

- Evergreen Elementary School: Character Counts – Honesty
  http://www.mead.k12.wa.us/EVER/Honesty.htm

PBS offers an excellent resource for teaching and discussing honesty. It uses three classic stories: the Frog Prince, George Washington and The Indian Cinderella.

- Honesty http://www.pbs.org/adventures/PTMenu/honesty.htm

As a reminder, send your students an Honesty Day card.

- Honesty Day Cards http://www.cyberkisses.com/platinum/html2/HonestyDay.shtml

April 30
Feast of Valborg – Sweden

> "The Witches' excursion takes place on the first night in May...they ride up
> Blocksberg on the first of May, and in 12 days must dance the snow away;
> then Spring begins... Here they appear as elflike, godlike maids."
>
> — Grimm Brothers

On Walpurgis Eve, Swedes gather around bon fire to celebrate the end of winter and the beginning of spring. Songs and sung, dances are danced. This is a very old custom throughout the Scandinavian countries and Germany held the night before May Day. It is steeped in legend and lore. It has been six months since Halloween Eve and at midnight the evil spirits, hobgoblins, will-o-the-wisps, imps, and the ilk emerge from the bowels of the Earth.[x] *Note: The Walpurgisnacht site has excerpts from Goethe's Faust – Walpurgis Night. After reading the history and customs related to this holiday ask the students to recall other festivities involving bonfires and/or the seasons.*

- Walpurgis Night http://home.swipnet.se/~w-45311/beowulf/walpurgis.html
- Walpurgisnacht http://www.serve.com/shea/germusa/walpurgi.htm
- Walpurgis Night: Personal Rememberances http://www.inv.se/svefa/tradition/engtrad/valborgeng.html
- KidPro: Walpurgis Night http://www.kidlink.org/KIDPROJ/MCC/mcc0404.html
- Waelburga and the Rites of May http://members.tripod.com/~InFrith/walburga.htm

[i] About Family Crafts http://craftsforkids.about.com/parenting/familycrafts/library/misc/blseedsong1.htm May 26, 2001

[ii] Week of the Young Child http://www.naeyc.org/woyc/default.asp August 16, 2001

[iii] J. Sterling Morton http://www.arborday.org/arborday/morton1887.html August 18, 2001

[iv] Joyce Kilmer, Trees http://www.state.in.us/dnr/forestry/arborday/adpoems.html#anchor572292 August 18, 2001

[v] UNICEF http://www.unicef.org/mission.htm August 18, 2001

[vi] Anne Frank. On still believing http://www.annefrank.com/site/af_life/2_life_exrpt/2_life_diary.htm August 17, 2001

[vii] Margaret Mead, Earth Day Ceremony http://www.earthsite.org/mead77.htm August 17, 2001

[viii] Anzac Day Celebration http://www.dva.gov.au/commem/commac/studies/anzacsk/eduact1.htm#Ode August 15, 2001

[ix] Patricia Edmonds. America's Escalating Honesty Crisis http://www.usaweekend.com/98_issues/981018/981018nationalforum.html August 17, 2001

[x] Halloween / Walpurgis Eve http://www.cns.uni.edu/~campbell/gened/hallow.html August 17, 2001

5/7/2002

May

"O beautiful for heroes proved in liberating strife,
Who more than self their country loved, and mercy more than life!"

America the Beautiful - Katherine Lee Bates

Special Month

Bike Safety Month

Bike Safety Month comes just in time to get those bikes in shape for spring and summer riding and to refresh bike safety rules. To get started, read about Bike Safety Month and plan to use Disney's lesson plan.

- May is Bike Safety Month
  http://www.nhtsa.dot.gov/people/injury/pedbimot/bikemonth/Nbsnann.html
- Disney Bike Safety Lesson Plan http://disney.go.com/educational/feature_may.html

Get Those Bikes in Shape

- Learn2 Adjust A Bicycle To Fit You http://www.learn2.com/04/0429/0429.asp
- Equipment Check http://www.nhtsa.dot.gov/kids/biketour/equipment/index.html

Bike Safety Posters

Use a publishing program to make posters about bike safety. Display them in the school lunchroom.

- Bike Safely Tour http://www.nhtsa.dot.gov/kids/biketour/index.html
- Sparky's Bike Safety Tips http://www.sparky.org/cool/cool-bike_safety_tips/cool-bike_safety_tips.html

Bike Races

One of the most famous and prestigious bike races is the Tour de France. This annual bike race is 3,454 kilometers, making a circular tour from Dunkerque to Paris. American cyclist, Lance Armstrong is not only a three time Tour de France winner, but also a cancer survivor. Read about this famous race and Armstrong's' amazing life story. To get a feel for the race terrain, copy the map of France. Have different groups of students research cities and regions on the map. Attach pictures and information about the various locations to the map using map tacks.

- Tour de France http://www.letour.fr/
- Lance Armstrong http://www.lancearmstrong.com/
- Tortoise Tango Bike Race Game
  http://family2.go.com/games/famf/famfgam_tangobike/famfgam_tangobike.html

Odds and Ends

Did you know the first bicycle was called a swift walker. It was imported from England to the United States in 1819. My great grandfather rode across his bicycle across the prairie from Ohio to Dakota Territory to claim his homestead in the late 1880s.

- Timeline http://www.exploratorium.edu/cycling/timeline.html

PBS Teacher Source has a great math lesson plan about bicycle design.

- Geometry of Bicycle Design
  http://www.pbs.org/teachersource/mathline/concepts/designandmath/activity1.shtm

For an excellent resource about bicycles and related subjects, check out the American Bicyclists League.

- American Bicyclists http://www.bikeleague.org/

The Schwinn Bicycle Company is one of America's oldest manufacturers of bicycles. Read about the history of Schwinn bicycles as well as the latest in bicycles.

- Schwinn http://www.schwinn.com/

Learn about the Olympic sport of bicycle racing.

- United States Olympic Committee: Bicycle http://www.usoc.org/usoc/sports_az/cy/az_over.html

Asian Pacific American Heritage Month

Asian Pacific American Heritage Month began as a weeklong celebration in 1979. It grew to be a month long celebration. Finally, Public Law 102-450 approved in October 23, 1992, designated May of each year Asian Pacific American Heritage Month. The purpose of the celebration is to recognize and honor the Asian Americans who have so greatly contributed to the history and culture of America.

- Asian Pacific American Heritage Month http://www.apaha.org/
- Asian Pacific Heritage Month http://www.familyculture.com/apamonth.htm

History

The history of the Asian Pacific people in America has been an important part of American history in general. From the early gold rush days in California and the building of the Transcontinental Railroad to the World War II and beyond, Asian Pacific Americans have been part of the American mosaic.

- Asian Pacific Resources at the Smithsonian http://www.si.edu/opa/asian/start.htm
- Asian American Resources http://www.si.edu/resource/faq/nmah/asianam.htm
- Japanese American National Museum http://www.janm.org/main.htm

1. Make a timeline for your classroom that highlights Asian Pacific American history. Use Tom Snyder's Timeliner.

- Chronology of Asian American History http://web.mit.edu/21h.153j/www/chrono.html
- Timeline http://www.itp.berkeley.edu/~asam121/timeline.html
- The History of Chinese in California
  http://www.cr.nps.gov/history/online_books/5views/5views3.htm
- The Timeliner http://www.tomsnyder.com/classroom/timelineronline/

2. One of the reasons Asian Pacific American Month is held in May is to recognize the contributions the Chinese made to the completion of the Transcontinental Railroad, May 10, 1869. Read about their historic feats.

- Chinese American Contribution to the Transcontinental Railroad
  http://cprr.org/Museum/Chinese.html
- Fusang - The Chinese Who Build America http://cprr.org/Museum/Fusang.html

3. From authors and artists to athletes to scientists to business people, Asian Americans have contributed to our American landscape. Have the students research one of these famous Asian Americans for an Asian American Hall of Fame. Using a publishing program, have students make posters to display throughout the community.

- Asian Pacific Americans http://falcon.jmu.edu/~ramseyil/asiabio.htm

Art, Music and Literature

Use a presentation tool to combine Asian art and music with original haiku by having the students select an art print from the one of the galleries and a midi from the midi file. Then, have the students write an original haiku to go with it. Use your slides for a Multimedia Art Museum performance. *Note: Be very careful to observe copyright laws and use only for your classroom. Do not publish these electronically or by printing.*

- Stuart Jackson Gallery http://jacksonarts.com/Pages/Prints.htm
- Japan Gallery http://www.japangalleryprints.com/
- Hara Shobo Online Gallery http://www.harashobo.com/english/index.html

- Haiku http://www.abcteach.com/Contributions/HaikuInfo.htm
- Asian Midi Files http://www.geocities.com/MotorCity/Downs/5676/main.html
- International Midi Music http://www.ultimatemidi.com/midi4.html

Additional Art Activities
- Areas of Tangrams http://forum.swarthmore.edu/trscavo/tangrams/area.html
- Origami Crane http://www.csi.ad.jp/suzuhari-es/1000cranes/paperc/index.html
- Paper Cuts http://www.isaacnet.com/culture/papercut.htm
- Sing in Chinese http://www.familyculture.com/singnlearn.htm
- Asian American Images in Children's Picture Books http://scils.rutgers.edu/%7Ekvander/ChildrenLit/asian.html

Teaching Asian Pacific American Children

With a growing number of Asian Pacific American children enrolled in our schools, it becomes even more important for us as teachers to understand the culture of the students in our care. These sites give us information about the culture and families of this increasing student population.
- Asian American Children – What Teachers Should Know http://www.cacf.org/
- Beyond Culture – Communicating with Asian American Children and Families http://eric-web.tc.columbia.edu/digests/dig94.html

Odds and Ends
- Asia Society http://www.asiasociety.org/
- WWW Hmong Homepage http://www.hmongnet.org/
- National Anthems of Asia http://www.hamienet.com/National_Anthem/Asia/

Get Caught Reading Month

Get Caught Reading is a nationwide campaign to remind people of all ages how much fun it is to read. Go to the *Get Caught Reading* homepage to see all of the celebrities who were 'caught reading.' Then, take pictures of your students reading their favorite book for your bulletin board. Have the students walk through the school to 'catch' others reading to add to your bulletin board. You could also have the students make a self-portrait of themselves with their favorite book.
- Get Caught Reading http://www.getcaughtreading.org
- Self-portrait http://crayola.com/educators/lessons/display.cfm?id=124

Favorite Book Survey

Have the students interview people of different ages to find their favorite book. Decide on the questions you will have the students ask, such as favorite book, favorite author, favorite illustrator, and so forth plus the age (use categories, like K-2, 3-5, middle school, high school moms and dads, grandmas and grandpas). Record the responses on a spreadsheet. Analyze the data to see what conclusions students will draw. Have the students write an article for the local newspaper about the project. Include charts of your data.
- Celebrity Book Picks http://www.nea.org/readacross/press/celebooks.html

Join an Online Book Club

Everyone enjoys talking about his or her favorite books. Join an online book club that encourages and supports reading.

For Students
- Book Adventure http://www.bookadventure.com/
- The Audrey Woods Clubhouse http://www.audreywood.com/
- EPals Online Book Club http://www.epals.com/projects/class/book_club/pi_bookclub_en.html
- Kids @ Scholastic http://www.scholastic.com/kids/index.htm

- Girl Zone http://www.girlzone.com/
- Book Discussion Guide http://www.bookspot.com/discussion/

For Adults – It means so much for students to see us doing what we tell them to do. Talk to your students about the books you read.

- Oprah's Book Club http://www.oprah.com/obc/obc_landing.html
- Bookworms http://www.geocities.com/Athens/Styx/3544/
- Book Chatter http://www.bookchatter.tierranet.com/
- Virtual Book Club http://www.achievement.org/library/bookclub.html
- Online Book Discussions http://www.his.com/~allegria/online.html

Prepare a Summer Reading List

Have the students make a bookmark of books they would like to read during the summer. There are lots of lists available on the Internet to help the students select their personal choice. These are some of the best. Be sure to make a bookmark for yourself, also. As you know, it is so important to model for our students.

- Oprah's Book Club: Kids Reading List http://www.oprah.com/obc/kids/obc_kids_20000803.html
- Wetlands Reading List http://www.epa.gov/OWOW/wetlands/science/readlist.html
- Best Children's Books of the Century http://www.amazon.com/exec/obidos/ts/feature/11295/002-2059317-6240828
- Caldecott Award Books http://www.ala.org/alsc/caldpast.html
- Newbery Award Books http://www.ala.org/alsc/nquick.html
- Coretta Scott King Award http://www.ala.org/srrt/csking/cskawin.html
- Children's Choice Awards http://www.reading.org/choices/cc2001.html

Special Week

1st Week
Postcard Week

"HGTWYWH."
(Having a Great Time, Wish You Were Here)

The Continental Congress created the United States Postal Service in 1776 with Benjamin Franklin serving as the first postmaster general. But, there has always been a need for a communication system. From Richard Fairbanks' tavern in Boston in 1639 to the old post roads to the pony express, the postal service has had an exciting and colorful history. Today, the U. S. Postal Service office provides mail delivery to over 250,000,000 people and 8 million businesses. Read about the history of the postal service and tour the National Postal Museum. The Museum has online exhibits and games, videos and resources for teachers. One of the programs outlined is *Pen Pals Across the Nation*, an intergenerational writing activity.

- History of the U.S. Postal Service http://www.usps.gov/history/his1.htm
- National Postal Museum http://www.si.edu/postal/
  - Pen Pals Across the Nation
    http://www.si.edu/postal/education/educationmaterials/pfedu.html

Postcards were first issued in Europe around the middle of the 1800s but did not appear in the United States until later. They were meant for short communications and had the added benefit of being cheaper to mail. Postcards have been made out of linen, wood and metal; they have been used for advertisements and personal greetings. The following Internet sites provide a brief history of the postcard and also have wonderful pictures of old and different postcards.

- Postcard History http://www.soultones.com/pc_history.html

- Brief History of Postcards http://www.ecollectmall.com/articles/pchistory.html
- A Brief History and Timeline of Postcards http://members.aol.com/rrpstcrd/pchistory.html

Collecting Postcards

Vintage and unusual postcards are very collectable. Collecting postcards is a good way for students to learn about collecting, as many postcards are very affordable. These sites have great examples of different types of postcards and what to look for when collecting. *Note: these are commercial sites.*
- Memory Lane Postcards http://www.memorylanepostcards.org/
- Vintage Collectables http://www.marknliz.com/
- Postcard History of Motels http://www.sjsu.edu/faculty/wooda/card.html
- Pricing A Postcard http://www.ecollectmall.com/articles/pricing.html

Postcards to Send via the Internet

It is always fun for students to send a card or postcard online. Have them bring an e-mail address of a friend or relative. Choose a postcard from the following list. Ask the students to write about something they've learned about postcards or the postal system on their postcard. Have the students send a postcard to the principal or librarian if they do not know someone with an e-mail address.
- 1001 Postcards to Send http://www.postcards.org/postcards/
- 1001 Postcards http://www.1001.com/postcards/
- Postcards.com http://www.postcards.com
- 1000+ Postcards http://12all4you.com/

Postcard Activities

1. There are some really super postcard activities on the Internet for your students to become involved with. *Postcards from America* send a different postcard almost every day to your classroom from some place in the United States. The postcards describe the location or historical site. *Postcard Geography* links your classroom up with another classroom and you exchange postcards for a year. Both will get your students excited about map skills.
    - Postcards From America http://www.postcardsfrom.com
    - Postcard Geography http://www.cyberbee.com/pcg/
2. Postcards are fun ways to have students do book reports. Have the students pretend to be a character from a book they are currently reading. Design a postcard based on the setting of the story using a publishing program. Have the students write about something that has just happened in the story. This is a good way to summarize the chapters for chapter books.

2nd Week
Be Kind to Animals Week

The Humane Society has been protecting children and animals since 1877. Take this week to learn about the pets we share our lives with and the people who care for them. The AHA has a terrific Internet site with lots of information about caring for our pets. There are games and educational resources available also. The *Pet Care* page has information about caring for family pets. For information about the medical needs of pets, refer to *Care for Animals*. Using a publishing program, have the students make separate brochures for cats and dogs. Display their brochures in local veterinarian's offices.
- American Humane Association http://www.americanhumane.org
    - Pet Care http://www.americanhumane.org/animals/tips/care.htm
- Care For Animals http://www.avma.org/careforanimals/pawsforpets/default.asp

The American Veterinary Medical Association also has a great website for students. There is information about veterinarians as well as pet care. Be sure to check out the activities at the Kids Corner. I especially like the projects at *Petpourri*.

- AVMA http://www.avma.org

Pet Stories

Have your students write a story about their pet or a pet they know. Use the story grammar chart to outline the story. Writing about pets provides a great opportunity to use onomatopoeia. This is really fun if you have the opportunity to have the computer 'read' the story as 'woof' will really sound like a dog's bark. Illustrate the story with a digital picture of the animal. Submit the best to *Pet Stories*. Use all of the stories and pictures for your bulletin board.

- Story Grammar http://www.abcteach.com/Elections/storygram1.htm
- Onomatopoeia http://www.abcteach.com/Writing/onomatopoeia.htm
- Pet Stories http://www.avma.org/careforanimals/petstories/default.asp

Safety Posters

Have the students make posters about being safe around dogs. Ask the Human Society if you can display them at the shelter. Use either a word processor or a publishing program. Illustrate the poster with clip art.

- Keep Yourself Safe Around Dogs http://www.americanhumane.org/kids/dogs.htm
- Dog Clip Art http://www.dogclipart.com/

Favorite Pet Survey

Use a spreadsheet to record the responses on a favorite pet survey. Make a chart to display the results.

Last Week
Backyard Games Week

Backyard Games Week is just in time to get ready for summer fun plus, we know how important it is for young people to be involved in physical activity. Research is showing that physical activity declines dramatically during adolescence especially for girls. Therefore, childhood is a critical time to lay the foundation for lifelong physical activity, and, what can be a better way than by playing some really fun and challenging games. Remember, physical fitness is the key to a happier, healthier, and more productive life. Refer to the *Presidents Council on Physical Fitness and Sports* site for more information about our student's physical fitness. You will find additional information at the last two sites.

- Presidents Council on Physical Fitness and Sports http://www.fitness.gov/
- National Association for Health and Fitness http://www.physicalfitness.org/aboutus.html
- American Alliance for Health, Physical Education, Recreation and Dance http://www.aahperd.org/

Get In Shape

You know the facts: heart disease is this nation's No. 1 killer, 1/3 of our youngsters are overweight, only 1 out of every 10 Americans participates in 30 minutes of physical activity daily, and the list goes on. The American Heart Association and AAHPERD cosponsor Jump Rope and Hoops for Heart to get your heart pumping. Get your kids involved!

- Jump Rope for Heart http://www.americanheart.org/jump/
- Hoops for Heart http://www.americanheart.org/hoops/

Let's Play

Are you and the students ready for some new games or maybe just a new twist on some old ones? Check out these sites. Divide the class into small groups. Have each group go to a different site and find a game to teach the rest of the class. As these sites have more than one game, in fact, usually lots of games, you might want to choose one main site, for instance, the *Tag Games* has many different versions of tag; each group could take a different version to teach the class. You can even learn to play some games from Australia. Have fun!

- Game Finder http://family.go.com/parties/birthday/tool/gamefinder_tlp/?clk=1012156
- Eldrbarry's Group Game Guide http://www.seanet.com/~eldrbarry/mous/games.htm
- Every Rule Kids Games http://www.everyrule.com/kids_azlist.html
- Games Kids Play http://www.gameskidsplay.net/index.html
- Tag Games http://www.funattic.com/game_tag.htm
- Relay Games http://www.funattic.com/game_relay.htm
- Streetplay: Games http://streetplay.com/thegames/
- Best Games in a Small World: Playground Games from Richardson Primary School, Australia http://www.richardsonps.act.edu.au/index.htm

Writing Directions

Writing directions for a game provides students an opportunity to practice writing non-fiction and to work on logical and sequential order. Have the students think of a game (keep it simple) that they know how to play really well. Begin by having the students complete a Chain of Events graphic organizer. When they are satisfied they have not left out any steps, have them use a word processor to write their directions. If students haven't used bullet lists before, this is an excellent activity for teaching that concept. Of course, the proof of the pudding is in the playing.

- Chain of Events http://www.sdcoe.k12.ca.us/score/actbank/tchain.htm

Date Varies

1st Saturday
Kentucky Derby

The Kentucky Derby is one of the most prestigious horse races in the world. It is the first leg of the Triple Crown. Since 1875, the Kentucky Derby has been the highlight of the racing world. Learn more about the men and women, the historic racetrack, and most importantly, the horses themselves.

- Chruchill Downs http://www.churchilldowns.com/
  - Derby History http://www.churchilldowns.com/kderby/history/
- Kentucky Derby Museum http://www.derbymuseum.org/
- Kentucky Derby Festival http://www.kdf.org/

The History of the Horse

Visit the *Online History Exhibit* at the International Museum of the Horse to learn about the relationship between man and horse from Attila the Hun to the pony express to the modern day racehorse. Then research the different breeds of horses. Have the students contribute to a horse database. Each student researches a different breed of horse and records the horse's vital statistics. Combine all of the research on one database and perform different queries, such as the oldest breed, the biggest horse, and the horse used for sport, etc. When you set up a database, it is important that everyone collects the same type of data and uses the same terminology. Before you begin, identify the fields you will be researching.

- Online History Exhibit http://www.imh.org/imh/exh1.html
- Breeds of Livestock - Horses http://www.ansi.okstate.edu/breeds/HORSES/
- Listen to *My Old Kentucky Home* http://www.50states.com/songs/kentucky.htm

2nd Saturday
Windmill Day

Windmill Day is celebrated in the Netherlands as a day to remember the dependence the Dutch have on windmills. Because much of the land is below sea level, windmills were used to drain rainwater off of the land and to the sea. Since 1950, pumping stations, some of the largest in the world, have been used. Windmills, however, are still used as back up. Tour Kinderkijk, one of the most popular windmills in the

Netherlands. While there, you might want to travel through the rest of Holland to see the historic cities and the beautiful gardens. Crayola has a very nice picture of a windmill to color.

- Kinderdijk http://www.kinderdijk.org/home.shtml
- Welcome to Holland http://www.visitholland.com/
- Windmill http://crayola.com/activitybook/display.cfm?id=699

The Leak in the Dike

Read the famous story of courage and faithfulness, *The Boy and the Dike*. Then, have the students rewrite the story in poetry form using the story pyramid.

- The Boy Who Saved Holland http://www.zip.com.au/~elanora/dike.html
- The Leak in the Dike http://www.geocities.com/~spanoudi/poems/cary01.html#1
- Story Pyramid http://www.courses.dsu.edu/libm205/Poems.doc

Everything Old Is New Again

Need more electricity? As Americans are facing an energy crisis, learn how modern windmills are being used as a source of electricity.

- Need more electricity? http://www.mindfully.org/Energy/Windmills-Electricity-Answer.htm
- How do windmills generate electricity?
  http://www.education.eth.net/mysteries/framepages/ccorner_mysteries21.htm
- Electricity from Windmills http://www.energyadvocate.com/fw67.htm

2ⁿᵈ Sunday
Mother's Day

"God could not be everywhere, therefore, He made mothers."

- Jewish Proverb

Mother's Day, or a day set aside to honor mothers, is one of the oldest holidays in the world. The roots can be traced back to the Greek Goddess Rhea, Mother of the Gods. In England, Mothering Sunday was a day when the servants were encouraged to visit their mothers. But, in the United States, it was Julia Ward Howe in 1872 who first suggested a Mother's Day. Ana Jarvis took up the cry and lobbied to have it declared a national holiday. And, finally in 1914, President Woodrow Wilson made the official announcement proclaiming Mother's Day a national holiday. Read more about the history of Mother's Day at the following sites. Have the students use a search engine to find the most recent Executive Order for Mother's Day.

- The Story of Mother's Day http://www.holidays.net/mother/
- Mother's Day http://www.21stcenturyplaza.com/taste/mothers.html
- Celebrate Holidays in America: Mother's Day
  http://www.usis.usemb.se/Holidays/celebrate/mothers.html
- Annie's Mother's Day http://annieshomepage.com/mothersday.html
- Mother's Day Language Games
  http://www.geocities.com/Athens/Troy/9087/mother/mlanguage.html

Simple Gifts to Make

- Celebrating Moms http://www.familyeducation.com/topic/front/0,1156,22-6251,00.html
- Kid's Domain: Mother's Day http://www.kidsdomain.com/holiday/mom/index.html
- Billy Bear's Mother's Day http://www.billybear4kids.com/holidays/mother/mom.htm
- A Girl's World: Mother's Day http://www.agirlsworld.com/amy/pajama/mothersday/index.html

The Most Beautiful Woman in the World

This is one of the most beautiful stories in the world. *My Mother is the Most Beautiful Woman In The World* is a folktale about a little lost child. When asked to describe her mother, the child says she is the most beautiful woman in the world. Of course, the authorities look for – you guessed it. This story lends itself very well to either a puppet play or a class play as it requires very simple props and can have as many or few actors as needed. It also has a very nice moral – beauty is in the eye of the beholder, and don't we all think our mother is beautiful. For older students, it provides an opportunity to talk about inner beauty; beauty is skin deep, etc. Here are a couple of versions of the story.

- My Mother is the Most Beautiful Woman In The World
  http://achilles.mitra.net.id/family/kid/reading/mom.htm
- Varya's Mother http://www.interlog.com/~kms/Laadan/varya-e.html

Family History

"All that I am or ever hope to be I owe to my mother."

- Abraham Lincoln

In today's society, it is especially important for students to have a sense of family, of who they are and where they come from. Mother's Day offers an excellent opportunity to learn about their families. Have the students do the research first, and then choose how they wish to share it.

- Interview Oral History
  http://www.genealogy.about.com/hobbies/genealogy/library/howto/htinterview.htm
- Family History Center: Ellis Island http://www.ellisislandrecords.org/default.asp
- Discussion Questions http://www.geocities.com/Athens/Troy/9087/mother/mdiscuss.html

Make a Family Tree

- Just for Fun Family Trees
  http://genealogy.about.com/hobbies/genealogy/cs/famousandfun/index.htm

Mom's Biography

- 100 Moms http://www.biography.com/features/mother/100.html
- Autobiographical Poem
  http://www.geocities.com/EnchantedForest/5165/pages/poetry_samples.html#autobiographical

Another Poem

This one is almost too easy…use the pattern from the old song, MOTHER and have the students write another acrostic poem. Can you sing the new poem to the original melody?

- Acrostic Poem
  http://www.geocities.com/EnchantedForest/5165/pages/poetry_samples.html#acrostic
- Mother (midi and lyrics) http://www.smickandsmodoo.com/aaa/lyrics/mother.htm

Around the World

"The hand that rocks the cradle, rules the world."

- South African Proverb

From Canada to Mexico to Italy to Australia, mothers are honored for the special place they have in our hearts. Learn how these countries celebrate their Mother's Day.

- Mother's Day Around the World
  http://pressroom.hallmark.com/mother_s_day_around_the_world.html
- How Mother's Day Is Celebrated Around The World http://www.mothers.net/aroundtheworld.htm
- Dia de las Madres http://www.floramex.com/li-momsday.htm#La%20Historia%20y%20Leyendas%20del%20Dia%20de%20Las%20Madres

- Mothering Day UK http://www.shoptheplaza.com/taste/mothers.html
- Mothering Day http://www.floramex.com/li-momsday.htm#ENGLAND'S%20MOTHERING%20SUNDAY
- India Mother's Day http://www.feminaindia.com/mothersday/calledmom.html
- La Festa della Mamma http://www.pubblinet.com/fioristi/mamma-it.htm (need to translate)

Mary Cassatt's Mother and Child Paintings

Mary Cassatt was an American impressionist artist. One of her favorite subjects was 'mother and child.' Look at some of her work. Have the students choose a 'mother and child' painting and copy it to a word processor. Have the students write a dialog of what the subjects are saying. You could have the students use a 'first – then' scenario by writing about what is happening now in the picture and what will happen next.

- Mary Cassatt http://www.ibiblio.org/wm/paint/auth/cassatt/
- Mary Cassatt http://www.artcyclopedia.com/artists/cassatt_mary.html

Last Monday
Memorial Day

Memorial Day is a national day of mourning when we honoring our nation's war dead by remembering their service and sacrifice. Originally called Decoration Day, it was first celebrated soon after the Civil War. It was made a national holiday in 1971. *Note: Some southern states celebrate Memorial Day on other dates.* Read about the meaning and history of Memorial Day.

- History http://www.usis.usemb.se/Holidays/celebrate/memorial.html
- The Meaning of Memorial Day http://www.vfw.com/amesm/memorialday.shtml

To learn more about America's wars and the soldiers who fought them, refer to the Fact Monster site.

- Memorial Day http://www.factmonster.com/spot/memorialday1.html

Memorial Day Program

Help your students plan a Memorial Day Program for family and friends. Assign students letters to read from the different wars. As some are long, you might want to help them edit the letter. Prepare a PowerPoint to use for the background with the name of the war and a graphic; use music from the Memorial Day Concert as background.

- War Letters http://www.warletters.com/
- National Memorial Day Concert http://www.pbs.org/kaze/memorialdayconcert/memhtml/

Arlington National Cemetery

Arlington National Cemetery, just outside Washington, DC, is America's most revered burial ground. Soldiers from the Civil War to the Gulf War have been buried there. Originally the home of Robert E. Lee, today, it is the final resting place of over 220,000 people who have served their country in war and in peace. Take a field trip to Arlington National Cemetery to visit the Tomb of the Unknown Soldier and the burial site of President John F. Kennedy.

- Arlington National Cemetery http://www.arlingtoncemetery.com/homepage.htm
- Arlington National Cemetery http://www.arlingtoncemetery.org/
- Think Quest http://library.thinkquest.org/2901/

Visit other famous military cemeteries including Flanders Field in Waregem, Belgium. Read the famous poem, *In Flanders Field* and visit the author's home.

- American Battle Cemeteries http://www.abmc.gov/abmc2.htm
- Flanders Field American Cemetery and Memorial http://www.abmc.gov/ff.htm
- In Flanders Field http://www.noblenet.org/year/fland.htm
- The McCrae House http://www.museum.guelph.on.ca/mccraenew.htm

Odds and Ends
- Activities http://www.umkc.edu/imc/memorial.htm
- Oliver Wendell Homes' Famous 1884 Memorial Day Speech
  http://www.people.virginia.edu/~mmd5f/memintro.htm
- Fly Girls http://www.pbs.org/wgbh/amex/flygirls/ WWII

Tuesday of 1st full week
National Teacher's Day

"I touch the future, I teach"

- Christa Corrigan McAuliffe

No matter what we call it, Dia del Profesor, Dia del Maestro, or just plain Teacher's Day, this is a day to pay tribute to all of those teachers who guided us, encouraged us and helped shape who we are today. All of us can look back and see a teacher who was special in our lives. Take this day to say thank you to those dedicated men and women who touch the future. Write a thank you note to a special teacher. You need to model this by writing to one of your past teachers also. Tell your students about that teacher and why he or she was important to you. A number of authors credit one of their teachers with turning their life around. One of these is Patricia Polacco. She writes about teachers in a number of her books. Have the students use the clip art to design a thank you card for the teacher.
- Coloring http://www.janbrett.com/welcome_back_to_school.htm
- I love my teacher http://www.janbrett.com/i_love_my_teacher.htm
- School clip art http://www.kidsdomain.com/holiday/school/clip.html
- Educational Web Graphics http://www.chibicreations.com/freesets/educational.shtml
- Educational Clip Art http://www.ametro.net/~teachers/school_clipart.html
- Crafts http://www.dltk-kids.com/school/teacher.htm

Christa Corrigan McAuliffe
Read about the 1st Teacher in Space and the tragic accident of the Challenger. In 1986, Christa McAuliffe, a social studies teacher from Concord, New Hampshire stepped from the classroom into history[i]. Chosen by NASA to be the first civilian in space, Christa said she was going to keep a journal of her 'ultimate field trip' because she had been inspired by the journals of the pioneer women who left their homes in search of a new frontier. Just 73 seconds after lift-off, the space shuttle Challenger exploded, killing all seven astronauts aboard. Christa's motto was "I touch the future, I teach." Have your students keep a journal. I like to give the students a few minutes just before the end of class to think about what they've learned and how they felt about it. Sometimes I give them a started line, such as "Today, we read about Christa McAuliffe, the 1st teacher in space…." It is important to tell the students if you will be reading their journals or not and if they will ever be required to share them with others in the class. They like us, write differently for different audiences.
- Christa Corrigan McAuliffe http://www.jsc.nasa.gov/Bios/htmlbios/mcauliffe.html
- Christa McAuliffe http://www.starhop.com/cm_bio.htm
- NASA Explores Lesson Plans http://www.nasaexplores.com

Space Day
1st Thursday in May
Space Day was created to advance science, math, and technology education and to inspire young people to realize the vision of our space pioneers. Celebrate the day by learning more about the history of our space program and the men and women of our space mission.
- Space Day http://www.spaceday.com/
- Alan Shepard http://www.achievement.org/autodoc/page/she0int-1

- John Glenn http://www.pbs.org/kcet/johnglenn/
- Sally Ride http://starchild.gsfc.nasa.gov/docs/StarChild/whos_who_level2/ride.html
- Donna Shirley http://www.achievement.org/frames.html
- NASA's Gallery: Neil Armstrong http://spaceflight.nasa.gov/gallery/search.cgi
- Discover the Heroes http://www.astronauts.org/discover_heroes/default.htm

Timeline

To gain a historical perspective, have the students make a timeline of space history. To begin, work with the students to complete a KWLH chart. Use a demo copy of the Timeliner by Tom Snyder or use a simple timeline format to record your research.
- NASA http://www.nasa.gov/
  - NASA History http://www.hq.nasa.gov/office/pao/History/factsheet.htm
  - NASA for Kids http://www.nasa.gov/kids.html
- KWLH Technique http://www.ncrel.org/sdrs/areas/issues/students/learning/lr1kwlh.htm
- Timeliner http://www.tomsnyder.com/classroom/timelineonline/
- Timeline Format http://w3.nai.net/~chewie/mapi.gif

Field Trip to the International Space Station

What an exciting field trip for you students – the International Space Station! After the field trip, use a word processor to make a Language Experience Chart by asking the students to recall what they saw and did on the field trip. Write in 1st person plural. Make a disk copy for each student. Then have them use the find and replace function of the word processor to change the 'we' to 'I' or their first name. You can also look at the space station from your home. Sky Watch will tell you when the space station will be visible from your hometown.
- International Space Station http://spaceflight.nasa.gov/station/
- Looking@Earth http://www.nasm.si.edu/galleries/lae/css_gal110.htm
- Sky Watch http://spaceflight.nasa.gov/realdata/sightings/index.html

Odds and Ends
- NASA Quest http://quest.arc.nasa.gov/
- Smithsonian National Air and Space Museum http://www.nasm.edu/
- Be A Spacecraft Engineer http://stardust.jpl.nasa.gov/education/jason/a1.html
- Modeling the Solar System
  http://www.pbs.org/teachersource/mathline/concepts/space/activity3.shtm

Shavou'ot

Shavou'ot is known as the Festival of Weeks. It marks the period from Passover to Shavou'ot - 7 weeks or a week of weeks. It has both an agricultural and historical meaning. Agriculturally speaking, it is the time when the first fruits of the harvest are given to the temple and historically speaking, it is the time when the Torah and the 10 Commandments were given at Mount Sinai. Read more about the significance of this holiday and the customs associated with it at the following sites. There are many games and activities for children at the Torah Tots page.
- Annie's Shavou'ot Page http://annieshomepage.com/shavuot.html
- Shavout Is Here! http://www.torahtots.com/holidays/shavuos/shavuot.htm
- Shavou'ot http://207.168.91.4/vjholidays/shavuot/
- Shavuot on the Net http://www.holidays.net/shavuot/

10 Commandments Poll

Recently, there has been a lot of discussion and debate about displaying the 10 Commandments in public schools. On one hand, our country's tradition and law separates church and state, on the other hand, due to or perhaps in reaction to the recent violence in public schools, some people feel students need a constant reminder of the 10 Commandments. What do your students think? Have them take a poll and record the results on a spreadsheet. Publish the results in your school or classroom newspaper.

- 10 Commandments http://our-father-who-art-in-heaven.com/exodus/ten-commandments.htm

Special Days

May 1
May Day
Another ancient holiday is May Day. This day celebrates the end of winter and coming of summer. Flowers are given, dances are danced and songs are sung. Enjoy adding some of these traditional customs to your May Day celebration.

- May Day Celebrations Around the World http://www.umkc.edu/imc/mayday.htm
- May Day http://www.cstone.net/~bry-back/holidayfun/mayday.html
- Lei Day in Hawaii http://members.home.net/starview/beenthr7.htm
- Beltaine – Ireland http://www.whitemtns.com/~tarna/beltaine.html
- May Songs http://www.stonecreed.org/songbook/beltaine/

Robin Hood and Maid Marian
An old English custom is to select a May Day king and queen called Robin Hood and Maid Marian. These names stem from the popular Robin Hood legends. The Robin Hood ballads are some of the oldest stories in the English language. They tell a story of the brave and dashing Robin Hood and his merry men who robbed from the rich and gave to the poor. Use some of the original artwork and make your own Robin Hood book with a publishing program.

- Robin Hood Tales and Ballads http://www.geocities.com/puckrobin/rh/rhbal.html
  - Images of Robin Hood http://www.geocities.com/puckrobin/rh/robpics.html#rhages
- Legends http://www.legends.dm.net/robinhood/
- Robin Hood and the Monk http://www.robinhood.ltd.uk/robinhood/monkstory.html

A Play
Have your students perform Tennyson's Robin Hood and Maid Marian. If you don't have time for a full play, do it as a reader's theater.

- Robin Hood and Maid Marian, by Alfred, Lord Tennyson http://www.lib.rochester.edu/camelot/rh/forest.htm

Labor Day
In many countries, the 1st of May is known as Labor Day or Worker's Day, a day to recognize the workingmen and women in our factories and shops. In our own country, May 1,1886 was the day designated by the Federation of Organized Trades and Labor Unions as the day that "eight hours shall constitute a legal day's work" and workers would strike at companies that did not recognize the eight-hour day.[ii]

- The Real Labor Day http://uts.cc.utexas.edu/~rjensen/vol2no4/labor10124.htm

May 2, 1837
Robert's Rules Day
May 2, 1837 is General Henry M. Robert's birthday. He is the author of *Pocket Manual of Rules of Order* first published in 1876. The publication was intended to bring the rules of the American Congress to members of ordinary societies.[iii] Learn more about parliamentary procedure at the following sites.

- Rules of Order http://www.bartleby.com/176/

- Official Robert's Rules of Order http://www.robertsrules.com/

These rules might be a little hard for students to understand. Have students make a list of rules for conducting a classroom meeting. Publish their rules in a *Pocket Manual of Classroom Rules of Order*. The following sites have a nice, easy to understand list of rules your class might want to modify.
- Missouri 4-H: Parliamentary Procedure http://4h.missouri.edu/volunteer/PProcedure.stm
- The Unofficial parliamentary procedure Cheat Sheet http://www-personal.umich.edu/~juip/unofficial.html

Odds and Ends
- Activities http://crayola.com/eventcalendar/mark_cal/event.cfm?evnt_id=1261&Set_subdir=mark_cal&cal_main=%
- Survival Tips http://www.calweb.com/~laredo/cuesta5.htm
- Basic Parliamentary Procedure http://www.abqyellowpages.com/district23/parliamentary.htm

May 3, 1904
1st Automobile Speed Law
It's hard to realize that four years before Henry Ford sold his first Model T, speed laws were already in effect. The state of New York passed the first automobile speed law. Research other traffic safety laws at the NHTSA site. They also have an excellent interactive site called *Safety City*.
- National Highway Traffic Safety Administration http://www.nhtsa.dot.gov/
  - Safety City http://www.nhtsa.dot.gov/kids/

The following sites have excellent information about current car safety and speed law enforcement. Check out the laws in your state.
- Speed Law Enforcement http://www.hwysafety.org/safety_facts/qanda/speed_lawenf.htm
- Speed Trap Exchange http://www.speedtrap.org/
- Summary of State Speed Laws http://www.nhtsa.dot.gov/people/injury/enforce/stlaw2000/

Henry Ford

"Nothing is particularly hard if you divide it into small jobs."

Henry Ford

Henry Ford was born on a farm on July 30, 1863. As a young man, he left the farm to apprentice as a machinist in nearby Detroit, Michigan. Later, he worked for Thomas Edison but he always focused on developing an affordable automobile. Henry Ford realized his dream by producing the Model T in 1908. This automobile was reliable and efficient and with the introduction of the moving assembly line he revolutionized automobile production by significantly reducing assembly time per vehicle, making it reasonably priced. Take a field trip and visit the Henry Ford Museum and home to learn more about this giant of American industry.
- Museum http://www.hfmgv.org/histories/index.html
- Edison – Ford Tour http://www.edison-ford-estate.com/

Assembly Line
The movable assembly line revolutionized the automobile industry by reducing the time it takes to produce an automobile. Learn more about the assembly line and then make one in your classroom so the students can experience working on one. Use the airplane template that comes with MS Publisher. Have one student print the pattern, one cut it out, one make one fold, etc. Divide the class into teams and have them race against each other to see who can produce the most airplanes in a given period of time. Stop

half way through to ask the students how they can make adjustments to speed up the time. Be sure to have a quality control person who must discard airplanes that don't come up to snuff. The proof is in the pudding so have the students try out their products. This activity produces lots of discussion. If you don't have Publisher, try the template at the *Paper Airplane* site.

- Movable Assembly Line http://www.pbs.org/wgbh/aso/databank/entries/dt13as.html
- Paper Airplane http://www.esdtoolkit.org/exer/airplane.htm

Odds and Ends
- BrainPOP: Cars http://www.brainpop.com/tech/transportation/cars/index.weml
- History of the Auto Industry http://detnews.com/joyrides/laramie/

May 5, 1862
Cinco De Mayo
Cinco De Mayo commemorates the Mexican victory over the French at the "Batalla de Puebla" outside of Mexico City in 1862. Learn more about this battle and the place it has in Mexican history.
- History http://www.vivacincodemayo.org/history.htm
- History http://latino.sscnet.ucla.edu/cinco.html
- Mexican Holidays: Cinco De Mayo http://www.mexonline.com/cinco.htm
- Cinco De Mayo Web Quest http://coe.west.asu.edu/students/jmendez/cmwebqst/WQ.htm
- Cinco De Mayo Web Quest (grades 2 and 3) http://www.zianet.com/cjcox/edutech4learning/cinco.html

Cinco De Mayo Celebrations
In the United States, various communities have adopted this national holiday as an opportunity for celebrating Hispanic customs and the richness of their culture. Fiestas are held with food, music, dancing, and art. Use these resources to help plan your Cinco de Mayo celebration.
- Family Celebrations http://intergate.bcsd.k12.ca.us/fremont/h5mayo.htm
- Cinco de mayo Celebration
- Fun and Games http://www.kidsdomain.com/holiday/cinco/print.html
- Learn about Mexico Traditions http://www.elbalero.gob.mx/kids/about/html/holidays/home.html
- Holiday Zone http://www.geocities.com/Athens/Troy/9087/cinco/cinco.html
- Make a Piñata http://www.hpl.lib.tx.us/youth/cinco_pinata.html
- How to Make Piñatas http://star.ucc.nau.edu/ES/Pinata2.html
- Mexican Food http://www.geocities.com/Heartland/Woods/9662/mexican.html
- Rick Bayless – Mexico, One Plate At A Time http://www.fronteracooking.com/mexico_main.htm
- El Mariachi http://www.elmariachi.com/realaudio/default.asp
- Music http://www.elbalero.gob.mx/kids/about/html/music/index.htm

A Day in the Life
Use the following resources to compare life in your hometown with a typical child's life in Mexico. Use a presentation tool and divide the slide in half with one half representing your student's life and the other side representing a Mexican student's life. After the students have created their background, use the duplicate slide feature to make additional slides.

I live in South Dakota. The land is flat farm land. The winters are very cold with lots of snow and summers are hot.	*In the central part of Mexcio, the land can be dry desert in the north, or towering mountain ranges, and peaceful valleys. Some people say the climate of the central highlands is 'eternal spring.'*
WE BOTH LIVE WHERE AGRICULTURE PLAYS A BIG ROLE.	

- Mexico the Country http://virtualmex.com/general.htm
- Talking About Mexico http://www.elbalero.gob.mx/kids/about/html/home.html

De Colores

A popular folk song in Mexico is *De Colores* or *The Colors*. Learn to sing this song in both Spanish and English.

- De Colores http://www.coloradovdc.org/audio/decolores.html
- http://www.coloradovdc.org/audio/decolores.mid (midi and lyrics)
- De Colores http://www.olympia.anglican.org/min/Cursillo/decolores.htm (lyrics and story)
- Midi file http://texasmidi.tripod.com/MIDI/De_Colores.mid
- Music http://www.xtec.es/rtee/europa/164es/lletra_eng.htm

Make a book of colors to go with the song. You could use either a presentation software or KeeBoo. Download a demo copy of KeeBoo.

- KeeBoo http://www.keeboo.com/enu/index.asp
- Learn Some Spanish Words http://star.ucc.nau.edu/ES/g1voc.html

May 5
Children's Day – Japan
Kodomo no Hi

The 5th of May is Children's Day in Japan. Traditionally, it was known as Boy's Day and is still primarily celebrated by families with sons. *Note: Girls Day is celebrated in March.* On this day, kites in the shape of carp are displayed. Family traditions such as baths and special foods are a part of the celebrations. Use these sites to help you plan your celebration.

- Children's Day http://www.jinjapan.org/kidsweb/calendar/may/children.html
- Kodomo no Hi http://www-japan.mit.edu/mit/culture-notes/May/kodomonohi.html
- Growing Up Strong http://www.embjapan.dk/spotlight/koinobori.htm
- Children's Day (Kodomo no Hi)- http://leahi.kcc.hawaii.edu/~jclub/festival/children.htm
- Children's Day – Japan http://www.watanabegumi.co.jp/jpculture/gogatsu/gogatsu.html

Carp Streamer Kites

Look at some beautiful kites from around the world, and then make your own.

- World on a String http://www.festivals.com/07-july/kite/
- International Kite Festival http://www.ahmedabad.com/travel/fairfest/kitefes.htm

Simple Kite Patterns

While the students are working on their kite, listen to the Carp Streamers Song.

- Carp Streamer http://crayola.com/educators/lessons/display.cfm?id=302
- Make a Kite http://www.festivals.com/~kids/pentewa/01-05/
- Make a kite http://www.dltk-kids.com/crafts/summer/mkite.html
- Carp Streamers Song http://www-japan.mit.edu/mit/culture-notes/May/song-koinobori.html

May 5, 1910
Leo Lionni's Birthday
Award winning children's author and illustrator Leo Lionni was born in Holland. He never had an art lesson, in fact he earned a doctorate degree in economics. But, he did spend a lot of time in museums teaching himself to draw. He eventually moved to Philadelphia and became an art director for a magazine. His first book, *Little Blue and Little Yellow* was written for his grandchildren. His books have won four Caldecott Honor Awards.
- Leo Lionni Biography http://www.randomhouse.com/teachers/rc/rc_ab_lli.html
- Author Study
  http://www.ci.shrewsbury.ma.us/Sps/Schools/Beal/Curriculum/media/Lionni/leolionni.html
  o Make Your Own Mouse
    http://www.ci.shrewsbury.ma.us/Sps/Schools/Beal/Curriculum/media/Lionni/makeamouse.html

Little Blue and Little Yellow
As a first year teacher, this was one of the first stories I ever read to children. It's simplicity and lesson about friendship is as beautiful today as it was hmmm years ago. Lionni was traveling with his young grandchildren and needed to keep them entertained. The story goes that he didn't have any drawing materials with him, so he tore circles (blue, yellow and green) out of a magazine to use for the storytelling. This story just begs us to tell our own story of little red and little blue or little yellow and little red and, why not tell it in Spanish? This is where you want to pull out the overhead projector. Use colored cellophane and let the students make up their own stories. Of course you can use a paint program to make slides for a digital story.
- Story about Little Blue and Little Yellow
  http://smithsonianmag.com/smithsonian/issues97/nov97/books_nov97.html
- Little Blue and Little Yellow http://www.carolhurst.com/titles/littleblue.html

Lesson Plans for Leo Lionni's Books
- Teacher Resource File http://falcon.jmu.edu/~ramseyil/lionni.htm
- Lesson Plans http://www.kiddyhouse.com/Teachers/Literature/LeoL.html
- Swimmy Lesson Plan www.bconnex.net/~jarea/across/swimmy.htm

Books by Leo Lionni
Frederick – Caldecott Honor
Inch by Inch – Caldecott Honor
Alexander and the Wind-up Mouse – Caldecott Honor
Swimmy – Caldecott Honor
It's Mine
The Alphabet Tree
A Color of His Own
A Flea Story
Fish is Fish
Extraordinary Egg
Little Blue and Little Yellow
Matthew's Dream

May 7, 1840
Peter Tchaikovsky's Birthday
Peter Ilyich Tchaikovsky was born in Russia. He studied music while growing up, but went to work as a government clerk and hated it. He continued his music lessons in St. Petersburg and became one of the world's best-known composers of the late romantic period. Although his teachers criticized his compositions, they were always very popular among the concertgoers. Because the criticisms made him doubt his work, he often backed it up with full orchestration. He visited America one time - to play for the opening of Carnegie Hall in New York in 1891. Tchaikovsky died in St. Petersburg, November 6, 1893.
- Biography http://www.ipl.org/exhibit/mushist/rom/tchaikovsky.htm
- Peter Ilyich Tchaikovsky http://www.geocities.com/Vienna/5648/Tchaikovsky.htm
- Carnegie Hall http://www.carnegiehall.org/intro.jsp

The Nutcracker
The Nutcracker is one of Tchaikovsky's the most popular ballets, especially at Christmas time. Have the students make a multimedia book to share with younger students. This is an excellent opportunity to work with custom animation and timing to get the 'ballet' just right. Use a presentation tool and Christmas clip art.
- The Nutcracker On the Net http://www.nutcrackerballet.net/
  - The Story http://www.nutcrackerballet.net/html/nutcracker_story.html
  - The Music http://www.nutcrackerballet.net/html/nutcracker_music.html
- History of the Nutcracker Ballet http://www.webcom.com/shownet/kirov/nuthist.html
  - The Nutcracker Story http://www.webcom.com/shownet/kirov/story.html
- The Bolshoi Theater's Nutcracker Ballet http://www.alincom.com/bolshoi/nut/nut.htm
- The Nutcracker http://www.kidsdomain.com/holiday/xmas/music1/nutcracker.html
- Midi http://www.sciortino.net/music/pit.html
- Christmas Clip Art http://www.kidsdomain.com/holiday/xmas/clip.html

Odds and Ends
- Lesson Plan http://www.davis.k12.ut.us/etc/tcip/TCIP295.htm
- 2nd Grade Goes to the Nutcracker http://www.bpcweb.net/class/2nd/2nutcr/
- Tchaikovsky's Nutcracker http://victorian.fortunecity.com/bacon/1104/
- Who's Dancing Now? http://www.pbs.org/wnet/dancin/resources/lesson_plan-m1.html
- Dance for Children http://www.susankramer.com/DanceSeries.html#Rhythmic%20Dances%20for

May 8, 1886
Coca-Cola Introduced
Coca-Cola was not the first soft drink invented. Indeed, soda water was available as early as 1789. Then came ginger ale, root beer and Dr. Pepper. And finally, in 1886 Dr. John S. Pemberton invented Coca-Cola. Make a timeline of soft drinks.
- History of Soft Drink Timeline http://inventors.about.com/library/weekly/aa091699.htm
- Coca-Cola http://www.cocacola.com/gateway.html
- A Little Coca-Cola History http://www.icubed.com/~colagrrl/history.htm
- Coca Cola and It's Evolution http://users.ntplx.net/~pfarris/essays/history/cocacola.txt
- Some Coca-Cola History http://members.aol.com/rcrown/Coke/CokeHist.htm
- Coca-Cola Goes To War http://xroads.virginia.edu/~class/coke/coke.html

Of course, the Coca-Cola of 1886 was very different from the Coca-Cola of today.
- Cocaine and Coca-Cola http://www.snopes2.com/cokelore/cocaine.htm

Collectibles And Advertising

"I'd like to teach the world to sing...."
"It's the real thing.."

These are just a couple of slogans that have become a part of our cultural lexicon. Have the students design an advertisement for Coca-Cola. Use a publisher tool for a print ad or a presentation tool for a multimedia ad. *Note: The last link is a very nice tutorial on how to download and save midi files.*
- Coca-Cola History and Collecting http://www2.netdoor.com/~davidroy/cocacola.html
- Coca-Cola Advertising and Slogans http://www2.netdoor.com/~davidroy/cocacola.html
- Images http://xenon.stanford.edu/~liao/cokewww.html#IMAGE
- Coca-Cola Clip Art, Music and Fonts http://members.tripod.com/ambirz2/coke2/downloads.htm
- I'd Like to Teach the World To Sing http://www.crosswinds.net/~psplisa/jukebox.html

Spreadsheets
1. What's Your Favorite?
Do a survey of parents, teachers and other students to determine the favorite soft drink. Record the data on a spreadsheet. Make a chart to display the results.
2. Nutrition Facts
Make spreadsheet comparing the nutrition facts of various sodas. Be sure to include diet, regular and no caffeine drinks. Publish the results in your school newspaper.

Soda Fountain
The first soda fountain patent was granted to Samuel Fahnestock, in 1819[iv] and we've been eating it up ever since! Ice Cream parlors and soda fountains were really popular in the first half of the last century. The soda jerks of course were the people responsible for those great drinks. Invite family and friends to an old fashioned soda fountain. Decorate the room with posters displaying what the students have learned about soft drinks. Make some great sodas. Give the proceeds to a women and children's shelter.
- History of the Soda Fountain
  http://www.inventors.about.com/science/inventors/library/inventors/blsodafountain.htm
- Soda Fountain Recipes http://www.masterstech-home.com/The_Kitchen/Recipes/Reminiscent_Recipes/SodaFountainRecipes.html

Odds and Ends
- Coca-Cola Games http://www.coca-colastore.com/proddata.world/SilverStream/Pages/pgGames.html
- Coca-Cola Links http://www.americancola.com/links.htm

May 8, 1945
VE Day
VE Day (Victory in Europe) marks the date the allied forces defeated the Nazis and Germany surrendered unconditionally. Certainly a day to celebrate! England's Prime Minister Winston Churchill said it best, "This is your victory…" Nothing is more powerful for students than a first hand account from a real person. Read Tom Fletcher's story.
- "This is your victory…" http://www.winstonchurchill.org/veday.htm
- VE Day – USAF http://www.wpafb.af.mil/museum/history/wwii/veday.htm
- VE Day http://ebooks.whsmithonline.co.uk/encyclopedia/80/M0047980.htm

- Tom Fletcher's True Story http://www.macksites.com/PART8.htm

For a brief history of WWII, refer to the Info Please site.
- WWII http://www.infoplease.com/ce6/history/A0852743.html

May 9, 1860
Sir James Barrie's Birthday

> *"When the first baby laughed for the first time,*
> *the laugh broke into a thousand pieces and they all went skipping about,*
> *and that was the beginning of fairies."[iv]*

James Barrie - Peter Pan

James Barrie was born in Kirriemuir, Scotland, the ninth of ten children. After receiving his degree from the University of Edinburgh, he worked as a journalist for the *Nottingham Journal* and moved to London as a freelance writer in 1885. His most well known work, *Peter Pan* evolved from the stories that Barrie told the young sons of his friends Arthur and Sylvia Davies. Learn more about the life and times of this renowned author at the following Internet sites and take a tour of his hometown.
- Sir James Barrie http://www.kirjasto.sci.fi/jmbarrie.htm
- Short Biography http://www.pbs.org/wgbh/masterpiece/railway/age/barrie_bio.html
- Great Scots: Sir James Barrie http://www.greatscots.webscot.com/jmbarrie.htm
- Barrie and Peter Pan http://www.kirriemuir.co.uk/JMBarrie.htm
- Kirriemuir, Scotland http://www.angusanddundee.co.uk/guide/towns/kirriemr/indx_frm.htm

Peter Pan
Peter Pan is one of the best-loved stories of all time. Who wouldn't love a story where people can fly to a land where there is no responsibility and you don't have to grow up? Enjoy reading this story with your students. For a complete e-text version refer to the first site. I've also included additional links and study guides.
- Peter Pan http://www.siscom.net/~john2101/peter.htm
- Peter Pan Links http://www.bowernorth.com/greenroom/links/linkspeterpan.htm
- Peter Pan Study Guide http://www.chebucto.ns.ca/~alf/NYPCO/peterstu.htm
- Study Guide http://www.depaul.edu/~sleigh1/study.html

Neverland
Peter Pan and friends lived in Neverland, a perfect place where you never had to grow up, but yet, there was danger and scary things and Captain Hook. Ask the students to discuss why Barrie created a perfect place but yet, included dangers. Ask them to write a paragraph describing a perfect place that they would like to live in. Are they going to put scary things in their perfect place?

Growing Up
1. Unlike most children, Peter Pan didn't want to grow up. Have the students brainstorm a list of the good and bad things about growing up. Have them do a survey of grownups asking them what they think the perfect age is and why. Record their answers on a spreadsheet. What conclusions can they draw?
2. Almost the worst insult one child can bestow upon another is to say they are being a baby. What does that mean? Again, brainstorm a list of things that are *babyish*.

> *"Backward, turn backward, O Time, in your flight*
> *Make me a child again just for tonight! "*

- Elizabeth Akers

The other day, after a long and busy family reunion, my granddaughter said she was so tired she wished someone would just put her to bed. I've also wished for one reason or another that I could go back to a simpler time when a grownup would just take care of things for me. Humorist Garrison Keillor said childhood was a time when someone else was concerned about your happiness. It's hard for children to realize that adults sometimes get tired of being adults. Have them read and discuss Elizabeth Akers's poem.

- Make Me a Child Again Just for Tonight
  http://www.cathieryan.com/songs_Rock_Me_to_Sleep_Mother.html

In Art and Theater
Most of us know the Peter Pan story through the stage and movie versions. Today, we are familiar with the stage version by Kathy Rigby and of course the Disney version, but my favorite is the Mary Martin version. How did they make her fly? As someone once said, "There is magic in the theater." But, if you want to know how the magic works, read the article *Flying by Foy*. Also, look at the classic illustrations.

- Mary Martin as Peter Pan http://kennedy-center.org/honors/history/honoree/martin.html
- Flying by Foy http://www.depaul.edu/~sleigh1/study.html#foy
- Rackham Art Images: Peter Pan http://www.artpassions.net/rackham/rackham.html

Elements of Fantasy
Unfortunately, Peter Pan's world is a fantasy. What elements of a story make it a fantasy? Read the article Elements of Fantasy. This month, we celebrate the birthday of another fantasy writer, L. Frank Baum, the author of the *Wizard of Oz*. After the students read these two books, have them record the elements of fantasy they recall to see if the two authors used the same techniques. Record their responses using a graphic organizer.

- Elements of Fantasy http://www.d118.s-cook.k12.il.us/east/media/fantasies.htm
- Wizard of Oz http://www.cs.cmu.edu/People/rgs/wizoz10.html
- Expanded Venn Graphic Organizer http://www.graphic.org/venexp.html

May 10, 1869
Golden Spike – Promontory Point, UT
In 1862 Congress passed the Pacific Railway Act which authorized the building of the transcontinental railroad with the Union Pacific Railroad building west from Omaha, Nebraska and the Central Pacific Railroad building east from Sacramento, California. On May 10, 1869, at Promontory Summit in Utah territory, a golden spike was driven in the last tie plat to commemorate the completion of the first transcontinental railroad. The golden spike symbolized the nation was now joined with 3500 miles of transcontinental railroad, a railroad from New York to California.

- Transcontinental Railroad
  http://www.linecamp.com/museums/americanwest/western_clubs/transcontinental_railroad/transcontinental_railroad.html
- Union Pacific Railroad http://www.uprr.com/aboutup/history/
- Central Pacific Railroad Museum http://cprr.org/

How Did They Do It?
It took bigger than life men of vision and the hard labor of thousands of recent immigrants to the United States to complete this massive feat. Read their stories. Have the students choose one of these men either real, like Leland Stanford or a composite person, like an Irish immigrant and write their eyewitness account of building the railroad.

- The American Experience: The Iron Road http://www.pbs.org/wgbh/amex/iron/
- Transcontinental Railroad http://www.mindspring.com/~jjlanham/trcc1.htm
- Driving the Last Spike http://www.sfmuseum.org/hist1/rail.html

- Steal Rails and Iron Horses http://www.blm.gov/education/railroads/trans.html

This feat was a massive endeavor that could not have been accomplished without the workers from China. Refer to additional information about these men at the Asian Pacific American Heritage Month section.

The Railroads Continue to Grow
Transcontinental railroads continued to grow throughout the remaining years of the 19th Century. This site has a map of later routes. It also has pictures and primary research.
- Transcontinental Railroad Lines 1880's http://www.wwnorton.com/college/history/tindall/timelinf/tranrail.htm

Field Trip
Take a field trip to Promontory Point to see what it looks like today. Is there really a golden spike? Inquiring minds want to know.
- National Park http://www.nps.gov/gosp/
- Road Side America http://www.roadsideamerica.com/set/HISTspike.html
- Rails to Promontory Project http://www.goldenspikerails.com/

May 12, 1812
Edward Lear's Birthday

There was an Old Man with a beard,
who said, 'It is just as I feared!
Two Owls and a Hen,
Four Larks and a Wren,
Have all built their nests in my beard![vi]

- Edward Lear

Edward Lear was the twentieth child of Jeremiah Lear, a London stockbroker, and his wife Ann. When he was a very young child, his father's business failed and he went to live with his older sister also named Ann. Ann became his guardian and teacher, teaching the classics and drawing. As a young man, he earned his living as an artist. Although throughout his life, he was an avid traveler, writer and artist, we remember him most for his limericks and Book of Nonsense. Fortunately for us, his limericks, alphabets, stories, songs and artwork are all available on the Internet.
- Official Homepage http://edwardlear.tripod.com/
- Teacher Resource File http://falcon.jmu.edu/~ramseyil/lear.htm

The Limerick
Edward Lear's limericks have made us laugh for over a century. They are not only fun to read, but also fun to write. Enjoy them with your students.
- A Book of Nonsense http://edwardlear.tripod.com/BoN/index.html
- Limerick Form http://www.geocities.com/EnchantedForest/5165/pages/poetry_samples.html#limerick

Make a Book
- Table and Chair http://edwardlear.tripod.com/ns/table.html
- Flip Album http://www.flipalbum.com

Nonsense Botany
Lear's wonderful illustrations of fantasy plants make a great starter for writing scientific description. Copy the picture to a word processor. Have the students describe the plant – where it grows and what it's used for. Depending on the age of the students, the descriptions could get quite detailed.

MANYPEEPLIA UPSIDEONIA

The Manypeeplia Upsideonia, commonly called the people plant, is often found in the back of playgrounds. It is a member of the Peeplia Family. The mature plant will be 4-6 feet tall. It blooms from September to June.

- Nonsense Botany http://edwardlear.tripod.com/ns/nb.html

Alphabet Frieze
Edward Lear's wonderful alphabet would make a great frieze for your room. Simple copy and paste the pictures and text to a presentation tool or publisher program. It would be great to have the students illustrate the second alphabet. Make one slide for each letter. *Note: The text may not be appropriate for today's classroom.*

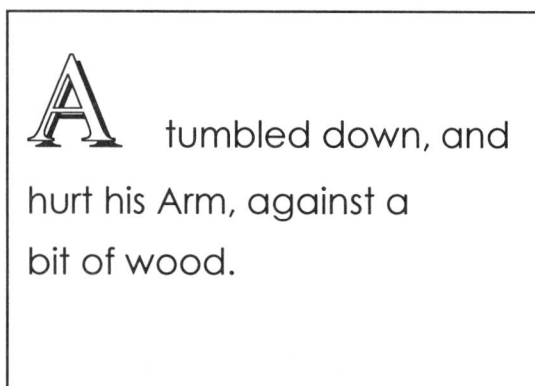

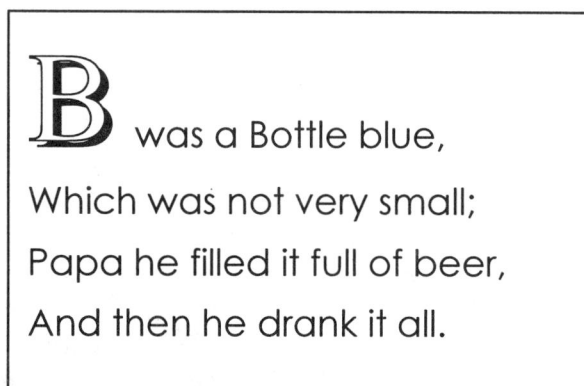

A tumbled down, and hurt his Arm, against a bit of wood.	B was a Bottle blue, Which was not very small; Papa he filled it full of beer, And then he drank it all.

- Alphabet http://edwardlear.tripod.com/ll/na1al.html
- Another Alphabet http://edwardlear.tripod.com/ll/na2.html

May 14, 1804
Lewis and Clark Expedition

"...all in health and readiness to set out. Boats and everything Complete, with the necessary stores of provisions & such articles of merchandize as we thought ourselves authorised to procure..."
William Clark, May 13, 1804

In my mind, the Lewis and Clark expedition was the greatest adventure in American history. This small band of men and one woman, using little but their own skills, heading out into completely unknown territory, is a great story. In 1803 President Thomas Jefferson gained approval from the Congress to send a group of people he called the Corps of Discovery to explore the uncharted West and find a route to the Pacific Ocean. Jefferson's secretary, Meriwether Lewis, and Lewis' friend, William Clark, led 33 people and one dog to Fort Clatsop and back. The adventures they had, the people they met, the new animals and plants they recorded only add to this amazing story. As we approach the bicentennial of there expedition, more and more web sites are being developed. Continue to search for new ones. These are just a few that will get you and your students started on your expedition. The University of Montana L&C site has the original journals with hyperlinks for additional information.

- Lewis and Clark Education Center http://www.lewisandclarkeducationcenter.com/
PBS has created an interactive journey for your students along with descriptions and stories about all of the corps members.

- Lewis and Clark http://www.pbs.org/lewisandclark/

This is a site by Enchanted Learning that has information about lots of different explorers created especially for the younger learners.

- Lewis and Clark http://www.enchantedlearning.com/explorers/page/l/lewisandclark.shtml

President Jefferson wanted the L&C Expedition to find a direct route to the Pacific Ocean, and to record and document the wild life and plants they encountered. Take a look!

- The Science of the Lewis and Clark Expedition
  http://www.scsc.k12.ar.us/1999outwest/members/WarnockJ/lesson_plan.htm

Captain Clark's manservant, York, was the first black man to travel through the American west. Download an e-book of his story.

- 3D Publishing: York http://www.3dpublishing.com/download/york.exe

Sacagawea was the young Native American woman who guided Lewis and Clark through the mountains. As William Clark said, "…she deserved a greater reward for her attention and services on that rout than we had in our power to give."

- Sacqgawea
  http://www.riverdeep.net/teaching_the_news/news_2000/march/front.100300.sacagawea.jhtml

May 15, 1856
L. Frank Baum's Birthday

Baum was born in Chittenango, New York to wealthy family. Although he tried many professions including businessman, moviemaker and writer, he was to spend most of his life writing for and publishing and editing newspapers. He moved his family to Aberdeen, South Dakota and started a general store, Baum's Bazaar and the Aberdeen Saturday Pioneer newspaper. After both ventures failed, he moved his family to Chicago where he worked as a traveling salesman and also wrote for the Chicago Evening Post. He began writing a fantasy for children he called the *Wizard of Oz*. He wrote many sequels to the original book, but it was after his death and the movie version, that the original story became the classic it is today. Read his biography and compare his life to that of James Barrie.

- Literary Traveler http://www.literarytraveler.com/spring/west/baum.htm
- Baum Portal http://www.teach-nology.com/teachers/child_lit/authors/baum/
- Baum Timeline http://www.geocities.com/Hollywood/Hills/6396/baum.htm

Wizard of Oz

Everyone enjoys this story of Dorothy and her dog Toto who lost during a terrible storm, find their way home with the help of the Tin Man, the Scarecrow and the Lion. The following Internet sites include the full text plus lesson plans and other activities.

- Text http://www.cs.cmu.edu/People/rgs/wizoz10.html
- Wizard of Oz http://www.literature.org/authors/baum-l-frank/ (includes other Oz books)
- Wizard of Oz http://www.eskimo.com/~tiktok/index.html
- Teacher Resource Guide http://falcon.jmu.edu/~ramseyil/baum.htm
- Crafts http://www.dltk-kids.com/crafts/cartoons/oz.html

The Movie

The classic *Wizard of Oz* movie with Judy Garland was made in 1939. Over sixty years later, it is still a favorite of children and adults. After reading the story watch the movie and compare the two versions. What was changed in the movie? What was added or left out? Which one do the students like better?

- The Movie http://us.imdb.com/Title?0032138
- The Wizard of Oz http://www.geocities.com/Hollywood/Land/4241/index.html

Tornados

*"There's a cyclone coming, Em," he called to his wife. "I'll go look after
the stock." Then he ran toward the sheds where the cows and horses were
kept. Aunt Em dropped her work and came to the door. One glance told
her of the danger close at hand. "Quick, Dorothy!" she screamed. "Run
for the cellar!"[xvii]*

- L. Frank Baum, The Wizard of Oz, Chapter One

Dorothy, Aunt Em and Uncle Henry lived in Kansas, part of the Great Plains states known as Tornado Alley.   The following sites have great pictures, facts, trivia and other information about tornados. You can also make a tornado in a box for a terrific science project and make a brochure about tornado safety using the information from FEMA. Take your safety brochure to your local TV station.
- Where is Tornado Alley? http://www.tornadochaser.net/tornalley.html
  o Tornado Chaser http://www.tornadochaser.net/
- Tornado Project Online http://www.tornadoproject.com/
  o Tornado Simulator http://www.tornadoproject.com/cellar/workshop.htm
- FEMA Fact Sheet http://www.fema.gov/library/tornadof.htm

May 15
Peace Officer Memorial Day
Today we honor and celebrate the men and women who have sworn to serve and protect their fellow citizens. It is a date set aside by the President John. F. Kennedy as a day to remember the police officers who gave their lives in the line of duty. Read the stories of these brave civil servants.
- American Police Hall of Fame http://www.aphf.org/memday.html
- Police Officers Memorial Foundation http://www.pomf.org/
- Behind the Badge http://www.behindthebadge.net/pmemorial/pmemorial.html

Thank You Card
Use a publishing program to make a thank you card. I used the Wizard that is part of MS Publisher and changed the color scheme. I also choose the text from a pre-selected list. You could have students write their own saying. Send or take your cards to your local police station.
- Police Clip Art http://www.texaspolicecentral.com/clipart.html
- More Police Clip Art http://www.clipsahoy.com/occupations/police.htm
Note: Some of these clips show guns and some violence.

Most Wanted Posters
We usually think of Wanted Posters for master criminals, but, why not have your students make posters of themselves for your bulletin board and title it: **The Most Wanted Students**. Take a digital picture of each student. Have them import their picture to a word processor. Have the students key in their vital statistics and description. Their description should list all of their positive attributes, such as great runner, excellent in math, super big brother. Hopefully, this will be the only time their face appears on a wanted poster.
- 10 Most Wanted http://www.fbi.gov/mostwant/topten/tenlist.htm

Odds and Ends
- FBI Homepage http://www.fbi.gov/homepage.htm
- Office of Juvenal Justice and Delinquency Prevention http://ojjdp.ncjrs.org/

- Police Headquarters http://www.rescue1.com/police.htm
- National Law Enforcement Officers Memorial http://www.nleomf.com/

May 17, 1939
Gary Paulsen's Birthday

Gary Paulsen was born in Minneapolis, Minnesota and lived most of his early life in a small town in northern Minnesota. His childhood was not happy as his parents were alcoholics and he was left to his own devices much of the time. One evening wanting to warm himself, he took refuge in the city library where the librarian offered him a library card and encouraged him to read. He took comfort in books and read constantly, even as much as a book a day. He says that he owes his success to that librarian. His life story is as much a survival story as the ones he writes and is just as inspiring. He is one of the most popular writers of children's literature today. Three of his novels, *Hatchet, Dogsong,* and *The Winter Room* were Newbery Honor Books.
- Gary Paulsen http://www.randomhouse.com/features/garypaulsen/
- Gary Paulsen http://falcon.jmu.edu/~ramseyil/paulsen.htm

Lesson Plans
There are many lesson plans on the Internet based on Paulsen's books. These are a few of the best, but if you don't find what you're looking for, search for *'Gary Paulsen'+lesson plan*.
- Woodsong Integration Unit http://www.ticon.net/~rziol/
- CyberGuide: Hatchet http://www.sdcoe.k12.ca.us/score/hatch/hatchettg.htm
- Hatchet KidReach http://www.westga.edu/~kidreach/hatchet.html

Survival
Many of Gary Paulsen's books have a survival theme where the protagonist has to use his wits to stay alive. Students of all ages love this! The South Dakota Reading Council recently surveyed students in grades 3-12 and found their all time favorite book to be *Hatchet*. Maybe our students won't be lost in the Canadian woods, like Brian was, but being lost in the mall or the park might happen. Have students write a survival manual. These sites will help them get started.
- Survival For Kids http://www.dsaweb.com/kidsrvl.htm
- Would you be the last one to survive? http://www.gorp.com/gorp/pr061200.htm
- Top Ten Maxims for Outdoor Survival http://www.gorp.com/gorp/interact/topten/survive.htm

The Brian Novels
After the success of *Hatchet*, the first Brian novel, Paulsen received thousands of letters asking what happened next. So, we wrote a sequel, *The River*. Again, readers wrote to say it was too easy; what if Brian had had to spend the winter alone and lost. So, Paulsen wrote *Brian's Winter*. Ask the students to write two endings for same story. Begin with a familiar story, such as Cinderella. Ask the students to respond to the following question: which one is the most satisfying and why?
- Brian's Books http://www.randomhouse.com/teachers/guides/bria.html

Some books by Gary Paulsen
Hatchet – Newbery Honor
Dogsong – Newbery Honor
The Winter Room – Newbery Honor
The River
Brian's Winter
Brian's Return
Alida's Song
Nightjohn

Mr. Tucket
Tucket's Ride
Escape from Fire Mountain
Canoe Days
The Christmas Sonata
The Boy Who Owned the School
For a full list with synopses
- The Library http://www.randomhouse.com/features/garypaulsen/library/

May 18, 1980
Mount St. Helens Erupted
When Mt. St. Helens erupted, we in South Dakota could feel the impact or at least see the ash as well as people in other states in the northwestern part of the United States. This beautiful mountain, known as the Mount Fuji of America stood over 9,677 feet. It is part of the Cascade Range in Oregon and Washington. Mount St. Helens was recognized as a volcano as early as 1835 when Northwest Indians told early explorers about the fiery Mount St. Helens. The Indian name for the mountain, Louwala-Clough, actually means, "smoking mountain"[viii]. On May 18, 1980 the mountain suddenly began a major explosive eruption that would last nine hours. At the end, more than 150 square miles of forest and recreation area would be devastated, countless animals would be killed and about 60 persons would be dead or missing. Refer to the following Internet sites to learn more about Mount St. Helens and other volcanoes in the Pacific Ring of Fire.
- Mount St. Helens, Washington http://vulcan.wr.usgs.gov/Volcanoes/MSH/framework.html
- Live Volcano Cam http://www.fs.fed.us/gpnf/mshnvm/volcanocam/
- Mount St. Helens Seismicity Information http://www.geophys.washington.edu/SEIS/PNSN/HELENS/
- Pacific Ring of Fire http://hum.amu.edu.pl/~zbzw/glob/glob28d.htm
- Mount Krakatoa; Ring of Fire http://www.geocities.com/RainForest/3678/krakatau1.html

About Volcanoes
Whether you are studying and learning about Mt. St. Helens or volcanoes in general the following sites have information, activities, resources and online projects to explore. Many of the sites have excellent lesson and curriculum plans.
- Volcano World http://volcano.und.nodak.edu/vw.html
  - Volcano World Lesson Plans http://volcano.und.nodak.edu/learning.html
- Volcano Simulations http://davem2.cotf.edu/ete/modules/volcanoes/volcano.html
- Exploring Volcanoes http://www.cotf.edu/ete/modules/volcanoes/vmtvesuvius.html
- Volcano Observatories and Facilities http://volcanoes.usgs.gov/About/Where/WhereWeWork.html
- Build a Volcano http://www.teachervision.com/lesson-plans/lesson-335.html

Field Trip
Take a field trip with a class of 5th graders to Mount St. Helens and tour the Mount St. Helens National Monument.
- Virtual Tour of Mt. St. Helens http://www.riverdale.k12.or.us/~pnelson/56team/sthelens/tour.html
- Mount St. Helens National Monument http://www.fs.fed.us/gpnf/mshnvm/

May 20
Midnight Sun
As the earth rotates on it's axis, there is a period of time in the extreme northern countries where the sun never sets in the summer and never rises in the winter. The period of time between May 20 and July 22 is known as the Midnight Sun. Take a field trip to Norway to see this beautiful scene.
- North Cape, Norway http://www.norway.com/north_cape/
- Picture of the midnight sun http://www.kingoftheroad.com/Norway/dag1/dag1-3-4.JPG
- Visit Norway – Land of the Midnight Sun
  http://odin.dep.no/ud/html/brosjyrer/norway/geography3.html
You can enjoy the Midnight Sun everyday on your computer by downloading the Midnight Sun screensavers.
- Midnight Sun
  http://www.saveourscreen.com/TNV/Europe/Norway_Midnight_Sun/Midnight%20Sun%20SS1.htm

May 20, 1862
Homestead Act
When the Homestead Act became law on January 1, 1863, anyone could file a claim for a quarter section, 160 acres, of free land. All a person had to do to "prove up" was to built a house, dig a well, plow 10 acres, fence a specified amount, and actually live there for five years. As there were so few trees on the prairie, the pioneer could actually claim another section of land if he or she planted at least 10 acres of timber. This was called a "tree claim." There are a number of remnants of these tree claims left, with the now tall trees standing stately in rows. Both of my great-grandfathers were homesteaders in Dakota Territory and I live just a few miles from one of their original claims. Thousands of men and women (yes women) took advantage of this free land. Learn more about the Homestead Act at the following site.
- Homestead Act of 1862 http://www.ultranet.com/~deeds/homestead.htm
Read some first hand accounts of these early pioneers who settled the west.
- Adeline Hornbek: Colorado Success Story
  http://www.cr.nps.gov/nr/twhp/wwwlps/lessons/67hornbek/67hornbek.htm
- Time Passages http://www.time-passages.com/homestead-act.html

The Prairie is My Garden
Pioneer and painter Harvey Dunn recorded the lives of early Dakota Territory pioneers in his paintings. Read his biography and view some of his paintings of pioneer life. Have the students choose one of his paintings for a story starter. Harvey Dunn was a contemporary of another famous South Dakota homesteader, Laura Ingalls Wilder.
- Harvey Dunn http://www.bpib.com/illustrat/dunn.htm
- The Harvey Dunn Collection http://web.sdstate.edu/sites/artmuseum/harvey.html
- Harvey Dunn http://askart.com/artist/D/harvey_t_dunn.asp
- Biggs Museum of American Art http://www.tfaoi.com/aa/2aa/2aa633.htm
- The Laura Ingalls Wilder Memorial Society http://www.liwms.com/index.htm
Of course when the homesteaders claimed their land, they found native people already living there. Dr. Sally Roesch Wagner has transcribed hundreds of diaries written by the women pioneers of Dakota Territory. Their first hand accounts of those early days in Dakota Territory tell of courage and strength and surprisingly, friendship between the whites and native peoples. One of those stories is about Sitting Bull, the famous Sioux leader.
- Sitting Bull http://www.dickshovel.com/sittingbull.html

Modern Day Homesteaders

From time to time, the Alaska opens up parcels of public land for homesteading. Have your students write a letter to the Division of Mining, Land and Water requesting a homestead claim. Have them tell why they want to be a homesteader and how they will use and care for the land.

- Division of Mining, Land and Water, Remote Recreation Cabins Staking Program http://www.dnr.state.ak.us/land/disp01/remote_recsites.htm
- Thinking About Relocating to Alaska http://www.labor.state.ak.us/research/relocate/relocmap.htm

May 20
Famous Flights

Two of the most famous flights in American history occurred on the twentieth of May. The first was on May 20, 1927. Aviator Charles Lindbergh made the first solo flight from New York to Paris. The second occurred five years later, May 20, 1932, when Amelia Earhart became the 1st woman to fly solo over the Atlantic.

Lindbergh Flight

When Charles Lindbergh was only 25, he became an overnight celebrity when he flew the Spirit of St. Louis from New York to Paris. This however, was only the beginning of his career as aviator, inventor, and writer. Learn more about this American hero.

- Charles Lindbergh Web Resources for Children http://www.stemnet.nf.ca/CITE/lindy.htm
- Time 100 Heroes & Icons http://www.time.com/time/time100/heroes/profile/lindbergh01.html
- The American Experience: Lindbergh http://www.pbs.org/wgbh/amex/lindbergh/
- Charles Lindbergh http://www.charleslindbergh.com/
  o The Spirit of St. Louis http://www.charleslindbergh.com/plane/index.asp

Earhart Flight

Amelia Earhart served as a nurse in WWI, but when she went with her father to an "aerial meet" in Long Beach, California, she knew that she had found her true calling. After taking flying lessons she purchased her first plane, the Canary, and began breaking records. But she came into her own, when she became the 1st woman to fly solo across the Atlantic, on May 20, 1932. Of course, her last fight and disappearance remain a mystery but her leadership as a woman aviator is still felt today.

- Amelia Earhart http://www.ellensplace.net/eae_intr.html
- Official Amelia Earhart Website http://www.ameliaearhart.com/
- Amelia Earhart Museum http://www.ameliaearhartmuseum.org/
- The Tighar Hypothesis http://www.tighar.org/Projects/Earhart/AEhypothesis.html

Timeline

Compare the lives of these two great aviators. Divide the students into two groups. Have each group research the life and contributions of either Lindbergh or Earhart. After each group has prepared a timeline, combine the two timelines and compare their biographies and history. Ask students to respond to the following questions. Record their responses on a Venn Organizer.

1. What similarities do you see?
2. What differences do you see?
3. Which one made a greater contribution to aviation? Why?
4. Which one had a happier life? Why?
5. Which one was more tragic? Why?
6. If you could meet just one of the aviators, which one would you like to meet? Why?

- Milestones of Flight http://www.nasm.si.edu/galleries/gal100/gal100.html
- Graphic Organizers http://home.earthlink.net/~tsdobbs/go/go.html

May 24
Victoria Day

"The twenty-fourth of May
Is the Queen's birthday.
If we don't get a holiday,
We'll all run away!"[ix]

- Old Rhyme

Victoria Day is celebrated in Canada to commemorate the birthday of Queen Victoria, May 24, 1819. She became Queen of England in 1837 and reigned until her death in1901, sixty-four years later. Her birthday is celebrated with picnics, fireworks and balls where people dress in period costume. Read about the life and times of this famous English monarch.

- Queen Victoria http://www.royal.gov.uk/history/victoria.htm
- The Victorians http://65.107.211.206/

Plan a Picnic

Plan a picnic to celebrate Queen Victoria's birthday. Make cucumber sandwiches and dress in period costume. Play the midi, *God Save the Queen*.

- Victoria Day http://www.craigmarlatt.com/craig/canada/symbols_facts&lists/victoria_day.html
- Victoria Day http://www.pch.gc.ca/ceremonial-symb/english/day_vic.html
- Queen Victoria's Birthday http://cbc4kids.ca/general/time/cultural-calendar/may/calendar-5-24.html
- God Save the Queen http://www.chrisuk.com/british/anthem.htm

Field Trip

Take a virtual field trip of Canada to learn the provinces and territories. Use a presentation tool with the Canadian National Anthem for a background.

- PhotoTour http://www.phototour.ca/
- Canadian Postcards http://www.netcards.ca/
- What Does Canada Look Like? http://www.ualberta.ca/~bleeck/canada/canada1.html#photos
- Virtual Tours http://canada.gc.ca/canadiana/interactive_zone_e.html#vir
- Mr. Dowling's Electronic Passport http://www.mrdowling.com/709canada.html
- Celebrate Canada http://www.craigmarlatt.com/craig/canada/provinces&territories/provinces&territories.html
- Victoria, BC http://www.city.victoria.bc.ca/

May 24, 1883
Brooklyn Bridge

John A. Roebling, who unfortunately died before construction could begin, designed the Brooklyn Bridge, using his patented wire cable for this 'modern suspension bridge'. His son, Washington Roebling, however, continued and completed the project in 1883, eighty years after it was first proposed. The bridge spans the East River, from New York to Brooklyn.

- The Brooklyn Bridge http://www.greatbuildings.com/buildings/Brooklyn_Bridge.html
- Brooklyn Bridge Web Site http://www.endex.com/gf/buildings/bbridge/bbridge.html
- Web Cam http://romdog.com/bridge/brooklyn2.html
- Photos http://www.endex.com/gf/buildings/bbridge/bbgallery/bbgallery.htm
- Photo Tour http://www.nyctourist.com/bridge1.htm

May 27, 1937
Golden Gate Bridge
On the other side of the United States, another suspension bridge, the Golden Gate Bridge in San Francisco, was begun in 1933 and completed in 1937. Joseph B. Strauss was the chief engineer. The Golden Gate Bridges connects San Francisco with the surrounding northern counties.
- Golden Gate Bridge http://www.greatbuildings.com/buildings/Golden_Gate_Bridge.html
- Sightseers Guide http://www.engineeringsights.org/SightDetail.asp?Sightid=541&id=CA&view=s&name=California&page=1
- Golden Gate Bridge http://www.goldengatebridge.org/

Guided Internet Activities
There are a couple of excellent Internet sites that help teachers make guided Internet activities for their students. First, decide what it is you want the students to learn about these bridges or bridges in general. Then, identify the sites you want the students to use. Write guided inquiry questions for each site. Using one of these tools allows the teacher to customize the learning activity for a specific group of young people that meets his or her specific learning outcomes and standards, rather than relying on a pre-made activity. You will need to register for both of these sites, but there is no cost.
- Discovery School Lesson Planner http://school.discovery.com/teachingtools/lessonplanner/index.html
- Track Star http://trackstar.hprtec.org/
If you have your students develop a presentation based on their research, you might want to make a rubric to evaluate their projects.
- Rubric Generator http://teachers.teach-nology.com/web_tools/rubrics/presentation/

May 31, 1790
Copyright Law Passed
On May 31, 1790, President George Washington signed the first copyright law. It was designed to protect books published in the United States for 14 years. In brief, today's law protects a work created on or after January 1, 1978, for a term consisting of the life of the author plus 70 years after the author's death. Because the Internet makes it so easy to copy and paste information, it is particularly important for educators to help students understand and comply with copyright laws. These sites will help students understand the intent of the copyright law.
- US Copyright Office http://www.loc.gov/copyright/
  - Copyright Law of the United States http://www.loc.gov/copyright/title17/
- 10 Big Myths about Copyright http://www.templetons.com/brad/copymyths.html

Compile a Bibliography
First of all, read the online article from *Copyright Central*. Then, have your students open a word processor and practice creating a bibliography. *NoodleBib* creates citations for you. Check it out!
- Copyright Central http://www.copyrightcentral.org
- How to Compile a Bibliography http://www.intac.com/~aroldi/biblio.html
- NoodleBib http://www.noodletools.com/noodlebib/

[i] Christa McAuliffe http://www.starhop.com/cm_bio.htm August 31, 2001

[ii] Jackie Dana *May Day, the Real Labor Day* The Working Stiff Journal Volume 2 #4 May – June 1999 http://uts.cc.utexas.edu/~rjensen/vol2no4/labor10124.htm August 31, 2001

[iii] Robert's Rules of Order http://www.bartleby.com/176/ August 25, 2001

[iv] Who Invented the Soda Fountain http://inventors.about.com/library/inventors/blsodafountain.htm?once=true& September 7, 2001

[v] J.M. Barrie http://www.kirjasto.sci.fi/jmbarrie.htm September 1, 2001

[vi] Edward Lear *A Book of Nonsense* http://edwardlear.tripod.com/BoN/bon010.html September 2, 2001

[vii] L. Frank Baum *The Wizard of Oz*, Chapter One http://www.literature.org/authors/baum-l-frank/the-wonderful-wizard-of-oz/chapter-01.html September 2, 2001

[viii] USGS *Northwest Legends* http://vulcan.wr.usgs.gov/Volcanoes/MSH/description_msh.html#msh_northwest_legends September 9, 2001

[ix] CBC 4 Kids Cultural Calendar *Victoria Day* http://cbc4kids.ca/general/time/cultural-calendar/may/calendar-5-24.html September 9, 2001

5/7/2002

June

"What is so rare as a day in June? "

James Russell

Special Month

Dairy Month

Got milk? What do we really know about that most wholesome drink? Start at MooMilk. Take the online quiz to test you knowledge and then take the virtual tour of MILK. Visit the famous milk faces at Got Milk and then, take your own. Have the students insert their picture on a word processor and write a testimonial about how much they like milk. CoolWhip makes a good milk mustache.

- MooMilk http://www.moomilk.com/
- Got Milk? http://www.whymilk.com/

Family Farm Field Trip

Nothing is more fun than a field trip to your local dairy farm, but, it you don't have one handy, you can visit one online. Before you start, go to the Dairy Day Planning Guide and check out some of the online activities.   This will help your students gain a holistic view of farming and learn related vocabulary. For younger children, you might want to go directly to the Kids Farm.

- Dairy Day Planning Guide http://www.dasc.vt.edu/youth/dairyday.html
- Kids Farm http://www.kidsfarm.com/

Now, choose where in the world you want to go next.   This would be a good time to use a webbing technique. Put *FARM* in the middle of your web and the different countries stem from that with the descriptors going out from each country. If you don't have Inspiration, a webbing tool, you can download a trial copy.

- Family Farms Around the World http://www.disknet.com/indiana_biolab/farms.htm
- The Cannons http://www.loughries.demon.co.uk/
- Dairy Farm in New Zealand http://ps.gen.nz/~windy/
- Dairy Australia http://www.dairy.com.au/
- Dairy Council of Great Britain http://www.milk.co.uk/ (look at the adverts and compare their advertising techniques to our Got Milk campaign)
- Canadian Dairy Farms http://www.rkde.com/candairydir/
- Inspiration http://www.inspiration.com

Nutrition

Did you notice the nutrition activities at the Dairy Day Planning Guide site? Use those now and also explore the games and lesson ideas at Nutrition Explorations. That site has a link to Chef Combo. For older students, you might want to skip directly to the Nutrition Quiz at the National Dairy Council. Have students bring in the nutrition labels from various dairy products. Use the information on the labels to create a spreadsheet. Have the students graph various elements such as calcium, fat, calories, etc.

- Nutrition Explorations http://www.nutritionexplorations.org
- Nutrition Quiz http://www.nationaldairycouncil.org/news/nwindex.html

Milk Builds Strong Bones

Does milk really make strong bones? How much calcium does the body need? Read the article, Major Function of Calcium in the Body to find out. Then, learn a little more about the skeletal system.

Yucky.com is a good introductory site or would be good for younger children; the Emuseum site is a bit more complex. The Interactive Skeleton allows the viewer to click on a bone to learn more about it. Of course, click on the bones as you sing, "Dem Bones…"

- Major Function of Calcium in the Body
  http://www.nationaldairycouncil.org/medcent/calcium/htmls/cal9.html
- Skeletal System http://yucky.kids.discovery.com/flash/body/pg000124.html
- The Skeletal System
  http://emuseum.mnsu.edu/biology/humananatomy/skeletal/skeletalsystem.html
- An Interactive Skeleton http://www.innerbody.com/image/skelfov.html

Dem Bones, Dem Bones, Dem Dry Bones
- Good midi http://www.fortunecity.com/millenium/quarrybank/194/music2.htm
- The lyrics http://ingeb.org/spiritua/demdrybo.html

Cooking
You couldn't complete your Dairy Month investigation without enjoying some great dairy treats. Check out the Quick Fix Cheese Snacks at Ahh! The Power of Cheese and the wonderful Smoothies at Taste Buds. But, my favorite is Berry Cream Pops from the Dairy Council.

- Berry Cream Pops http://www.dairycouncilofca.org/kids/kids_cook_rcp14.htm
- Ahh! The Power of Cheese http://www.ilovecheese.com/
- Taste Buds http://www.whymilk.com/tastebuds/blenders/index.html

Odds and Ends
The poor king just wants a little bit of butter for his bread in A.A. Milne's poem *The King's Breakfast*. Act out the poem and take digital pictures to make a Flip Book.

- The King's Breakfast http://ingeb.org/songs/thekingb.html
- National Dairy Council http://www.nationaldairycouncil.org/
  - Great pictures of milk and dairy products http://www.nationaldairycouncil.org/
- Breeds of Livestock http://www.ansi.okstate.edu/breeds/cattle/
- USDA for Kids http://www.usda.gov/news/usdakids/index.html this is a terrific site with many links to things related farming and agriculture

Safety Month
With summer just beginning, now is a great time to remind students of summer safety rules. Begin your discussion of Summer Safety by having the class take the Summer Safety Quiz. Kidsource also has a summer safety calendar with thirty different safety tips ranging from bike safety to gun safety.

- Safety Quiz http://kidexchange.about.com/kids/kidexchange/library/weekly/aa053101a.htm
- Summer Safety Calendar http://www.kidsource.com/safety/calendar.summer.safety.html

Write Letters to the Editor
101 Summer Safety Sites is just that, a comprehensive list of Internet sites about safety. It has information on everything from boating to wildfires. Have each student take a different safety concern to research. To share their knowledge, have them use a word processor to write letters to the editor reminding readers of the safety concerns and tips.

- 101 Summer Safety Sites http://www.gordon.army.mil/dps/safety/newpage12.htm

Make Summer Safety Posters
Use a publishing program, like MS Publisher, and have the students design a summer safety poster. If you are using MS Publisher, this is a good time to introduce using wizards. If you do not have a publishing program, you can use a word processor. Ask local business to hang them in the windows.

- Safety Poster http://www.education-world.com/a_lesson/00-2/lp2029.shtml

- 0Summer Safety
  http://www.nfpa.org/Research/NFPA_Fact_Sheets/Summer_safety/summer_safety.html
- Beat the Heat http://www.srh.noaa.gov/fwd/heatindex/heat3.html
- Summer Safety http://www.ynhh.org/pediatrics/prevention/summer_safety.html
- Tips for Kids http://www.atlantichealth.org/services/emergency/safetymain.asp
- Safe Kids http://www.llu.edu/lluch/safekids/

Officer Buckle and Gloria Online Lesson Plans

This is a great book, (Caldecott winner) to use with any group of students. The Internet offers many lesson plans to go along with it. Here are just a few.
- Caldecott Winner: Officer Buckle and Gloria http://eduscapes.com/caldecott/96a.html
- Laws Within the Community http://www.chrisplummer.homestead.com/worksample.html
- Careers: Police Officer http://www.becon-itv.org/dimensions/programs/rr/lesson21.htm
- Community Safety With Officer Buckle and Gloria
  http://cohort.csus.edu/sanjuan1/communitysafety/socialstudies.html
  - Emergency Words and Signs in Different Languages
    http://cohort.csus.edu/sanjuan1/communitysafety/safetywords.html
- A Book A Week Lesson Plans: Officer Buckle and Gloria
  http://curry.edschool.virginia.edu/go/wil/classroom_instruction.htm#Weekly%20Instruction
- Fire Safety and Science http://www.sanjuan.edu/select/etma/communitysafety/science.html

Mouse Pad Safety Rules

Have the class develop a list of Internet Safety Rules. Use a word processor to record the rules. Be sure to measure the size of your mouse pad to insure that your safety rules will fit. Print them on the Mouse Pad paper available at office supply or computer stores. Print the design a little bigger than the mouse pad. You can trim it later. *(Reverse your list to print it backwards – when you iron it on, it will be correct.)* If you cannot find the Mouse Pad paper, use T-Shirt transfer paper and iron them on blank mouse pads. Make one for each computer in your classroom or lab.
- America Links Up http://www.getnetwise.org/americalinksup/
- Safe Surfin' http://www.safesurfin.com/kids.htm
- Staying Street Smart on the Internet http://www.yahooligans.com/docs/safety/
- Internet Safety Game http://www.kidscom.com/orakc/Games/newSafe/indexright.html
- Disney's Internet Safety http://www.disney.go.com/cybersafety/
- Operation Blue Ridge Thunder http://www.blueridgethunder.com/

Supplies and Instructions
- Make A Mouse Pad
  http://desktoppub.about.com/compute/desktoppub/library/weekly/aa120100a.htm
- Office Max http://www.officemax.com
- BlanxEtc http://www.blanxetc.com/ 1-800-662-5269
- Tips for Printing Mouse Pads http://www.edps-nj.com/blmoco.htm

Odds and Ends
- Safety Always http://library.thinkquest.org/J002337/index.shtml (another great think quest activity)
- Red Cross: Health and Safety http://www.redcross.org/services/hss/
  - Anatomy of a First Aid Kit http://www.redcross.org/services/hss/lifeline/fakit.html (make one for your classroom)
- Canine Summer Safety Tips http://www.akc.org/love/dah/candt/sumtips.cfm
- Food Safety Lesson Plan http://www.education-world.com/a_lesson/00-2/lp2031.shtml
- Gun Safety http://filebox.vt.edu/org/rsvt/safety.html (you never can be too cautious)

Rose Month

"The rose is a rose,
And was always a rose."

Robert Frost

The rose is the official National Floral Emblem of the United States. President Ronald Reagan signed this legislation into law on November 20, 1986. June has been the National Rose Month since 1969. To learn more about the history of roses and some interesting tid-bits, read Rose Vignettes at the Roses Incorporated site. This site also has good lists of International and State Flowers.

- Roses Incorporated http://www.rosesinc.org/
  - Rose Vignettes http://www.rosesinc.org/vignettes.htm
  - International Flowers http://www.rosesinc.org/flower_facts.html#NATIONAL%20FLOWERS
  - State Flowers http://www.rosesinc.org/flower_facts.html#STATE%20FLOWERS
- Rose History http://www.rose.org/public/connect/home.html?c=9035191&pageid=33685

The Rose Show

Take your students and your digital camera on a field trip to a rose garden or flower shop. Take pictures of the roses. Have the students take notes on the size, color, foliage and fragrance of each rose. When you return to the classroom, search one of the online rose databases to identify each rose.

- Types of Roses http://www.rose.org/public/connect/home.html?c=9035477&pageid=108451
- Classification http://www.vintagegardens.com/cgi-bin/newclass.pl
- EveryRose http://www.everyrose.com/everyrose/index.lasso
- Rose Encyclopedia http://www.marthastewart.com/gardening/encyclopedia/searchresult.asp?Returning=TRUE&2&3

Use your pictures to create a 'virtual' rose show. Use the flip album (see June 25 – Eric Carle) to display your roses and the descriptions, classifications and history the students discovered. You might want to use the Yellow Rose of Texas for the background; or for a more traditional sound, choose one from Music Inspired by the Rose.

- Flip Album http://www.flipalbum.com
- Songs of Texas http://www.lsjunction.com/midi/songs.htm
  - Yellow Rose of Texas
  - San Antonio Rose
- Music Inspired by the Rose http://www.geocities.com/Heartland/Flats/8076/rosemusic.html
- To A Wild Rose http://www.tvkmusic.com/songlist/ceremony.htm

Flower Arranging Still Life

Ikebana is the exquisite art of Japanese flower arranging. Help your students explore this art form. Have the students locate pictures the flowers and greenery they will need. Use a paint program to create the background (black fill is always good.) Make a vase or base for the arrangement. Copy and paste your flowers and greenery in a pleasing fashion. You may need to use a program that allows you to free-form select to cut out the flowers. You may wish to stop here, or take a look at some still life paintings and then use a filter on a photo program to create a painting-life effect. You can download a free copy of PhotoStudio if you do not have a photo program.

- Japanese Flower Arranging http://www.psigroup.co.uk/lifestyle/family_and_friends/ikebana.html
- Say It With Roses http://www.ars.org/experts/bunny.html
- Artists
  - Van Gogh http://www.theartcanvas.com/gogh.htm
  - Monet http://www.getty.edu/art/collections/objects/o828.html

- o Picasso http://www.buehrle.ch/index.asp?lang=e&id_pic=139
- PhotoIsland http://www.photoisland.com (download a free copy of PhotoStudio)

Original picture of roses	Roses cut, copied and arranged	Rose picture after using a fine art effect

Special Week

1st Week
Fishing Week
Web Cams of Fishing/Water Locations
At the beginning of the month, have each student choose a web cam location. Then, each day a different student starts the day by sharing with the class his or her location and telling a little bit about it.
- Web Cams http://www.fishingworks.com/web_cams/

Fish Identification
Make a fish database. Have each student research a fish for the class database. Excel or another spreadsheet with a filter makes a good database for this activity. With the students, agree upon the basic field headings. Most spreadsheets will also let you insert pictures. After your database is completed, search for the largest and smallest fish. Use your data to make a graph. Query any of the fields. Challenge the students to think of a question that only their fish data can answer.
- Field & Stream: Fishing Guide http://www.fieldandstream.com/fishing/index.html
- Fish Species http://www.dnr.state.mn.us/fishing.html
- Fish Facts http://www.nefsc.nmfs.gov/faq/

Fishing Crafts
Fishing is associated with a couple of crafts that have been elevated to an art form, if done correctly. They are knot tying and fly tying. The following sites will help you and the students learn to do these basic fishing crafts.
- Learn to tie a knot @ Kids Corner http://www.texasgulfcoastfishing.com/kids.htm
- Fly Tier's Bench http://www.flyshop.com/Bench/ (the carrot is an easy one to begin with)
- A Gray Knight's Tale (a poem about fishing flies)
  http://www.flyshop.com/Marketplace/anglersroost/Images/poem.html

Tell a Whopper
Fishermen have been telling stories about the big one that got away since the beginning of time. Have students write stories about catching the biggest fish or the one that got away. See who can make up the biggest whopper! I've included some sites with photographs of kids fishing and some clip art sites that they might want to use to illustrate their stories.
- Fishing Kids: Pictures of the Month http://www.fishingkids.net/kidspic.htm
- Read Kids Fishing Adventures http://www.fishnews.com/realkids.htm

- Fish Art http://www.psykho.com/fishart/
- Fishing Art http://www.fishingworks.com/fishing_art/
- Historical Drawings of Fish http://www.photolib.noaa.gov/historic/nmfs/fish1.html
- The Fisherman and His Wife http://www.ipl.org/youth/StoryHour/Fisherman/fishstory/fish1.html

Rivers

National Geographic offers an outstanding unit about river geography that includes basic river terminology and conservation issues.

- Geography: Rivers http://www.nationalgeographic.com/geographyaction/
- Aquaculture http://www.tommytrout.com/schools/lesson_aquaculture.asp
- Fish Hatcheries http://fisheries.fws.gov/FWSFH/NFHSmain.htm check out your state

Additional Web Sites

- Fishing Kids http://www.fishingkids.com/
- Fish Cam http://home.netscape.com/fishcam/fishcam.html
- Electronic Zoo: Fish http://netvet.wustl.edu/fish.htm
- Fishing Fun http://kidsdomain.funschool.com/current/games/arcade/arcade_fishing1.a

2nd Week

Little League Baseball

Carl Stotz founded little League Baseball in 1939. From that first league with three teams, little league has grown to include close to 3,000,000 participants in 100 different countries. Visit the Little League Baseball site to check out the history of Little League Baseball. Read the Sporting News to learn about the major league players who used to be little league players and test your knowledge about Little League Baseball.

- Welcome to Little League Baseball http://www.littleleague.org/
- History of the Little League World Series http://tsn.sportingnews.com/archives/littleleague/

Casey at the Bat[1] first appeared in *The San Francisco Examiner* on June 3, 1888. This tragic story of the Mudville nine and the mighty Casey makes a wonderful reader's theater and an interesting math lesson. Your students might also enjoy reading about the controversy about the poem over the years.

- Perform it as a Reader's Theater http://www.aaronshep.com/rt/RTE23.html
- Casey At the Bat http://www.baseballscorecard.com/casey1.htm
- The Sporting News Archive http://tsn.sportingnews.com/archives/baseball/94640.html

Joyce Mealo provides a very nice lesson plan based on the characters in the poem. Additional poems and songs about baseball are located at the Baseball Almanac.

- Lesson Plan http://www.mcps.k12.md.us/curriculum/socialstd/FT/Casey_Act.html
- Baseball Almanac http://baseball-almanac.com/poems.shtml

So, invite the parents, sing "Take Me Out To the Ball Game", pass out the Cracker Jacks and have your students perform "Casey At The Bat".

- Take Me Out To The Ball Game http://www.melodylane.net/ballgame.html (Yes, all three verses.) Be sure to listen to the vintage recording found at the same site.
- Cracker Jacks http://www.crackerjack.com/index-fl.html Play the baseball games.

4th Week

Camping Week

---

[1] For a great new edition, look at Casey at the Bat : A Ballad of the Republic Sung in the Year 1888, Ernest Lawerence Thayer, Handprint Books; ISBN: 1929766009. This is a Caldecott Honor Book.

Start by planning your camping trip at GORP, the Internet site, not the snack. Be sure to check out the videos of camping destinations. You can even see camping sites around the world!

- Camping Destinations http://www.gorp.com/gorp/activity/Camping/cam_place.htm

CyberCamp and Black Dogs Summer Camp offer some fun camping activities, as does Kids Camping Corner. If it's hard to get away, try the camping ideas by Family.com, backyard campout.

- CyberCamp http://www.worldbook.com/fun/wbla/camp/index.html
- Black Dogs Summer Camp http://blackdog4kids.com/holiday/summer/do/index.html
- Kids Camping Corner http://www.woodalls.com/kidscamp/kidscamp.html
- Backyard Camp-Out
  http://family.go.com/features/family_2000_07/dony/dony0700aaback_camp/?clk=5

Nothing is more fun than sitting around a campfire, eating s'mores and singing camp songs. Michigan Campgrounds offers an easy kids camp cookbook and songbook. If you're feeling brave, there is also a section on building a campfire, and if necessary, a great first aid book. But, for some really great s'mores, go to S'more the Merrier.

- Michigan Camping http://www.michcampgrounds.com/
  - Campfire Cookinghttp://www.michcampgrounds.com/cooking_kids.html
  - Camp Songbook http://www.michcampgrounds.com/songs.html
- S'more the Merrier http://www.epicurious.com/e_eating/e07_smores/smoreintro.html

While you are sitting around the campfire, read *Toasting Marshmallows* by Kristine O'Connell George. Her web site offers samples of her poetry and curriculum ideas based on the camping theme. There is also a wonderful rendition of She'll Be Coming Round the Mountain, Kumbayah and Taps. She offers an excellent teacher's guide. Enjoy!

- Toasting Marshmallows http://64.77.108.137/toasting_marshmallows.htm

National Park Brochure

Ask each student to choose a National Park to research. Have them design a brochure highlighting the major features of their park. Use either a publishing program like MS Publisher or just a word processor. You might want to introduce the students to this site first as there is so much information about historical preservation, science and statistical data about park usage.

- National Park Service http://www.nps.gov/
- Lesson Plan: National Parks
  http://www.nationalgeographic.com/xpeditions/lessons/14/gk2/parks.html

Multimedia Poetry Book

After learning about some of the Creatures of the Night, ask the students to use the Puzzlers poetry form to write riddles about nocturnal animals. Have the students select a night sky background from Catching the Light for a PowerPoint page and publish their poems in a multimedia book. Use one of the nighttime midis for a background. Creatures of the Night http://eduscapes.com/42explore/night.htm

- Puzzlers http://www.geocities.com/EnchantedForest/5165/pages/poetry_samples.html#puzzlers
- Catching the Light http://www.astropix.com/INDEX.HTM
- Midi Collection http://jadierose.com/midicollection.html
  - Clare de Lune
  - Midnight Sonata
  - Stardust
  - Blues at Night
- Deep In the Heart of Texas http://www.lsjunction.com/midi/songs.htm

Odds and Ends

- Visit Camp Yucky @ http://www.nj.com/yuckykids/
- Listen to Earth and Sky to see what's happening in the night sky @ http://www.earthsky.com/

- View Van Gogh's Starry Night @ http://www.artprintcollection.com/html/vincent_van_gogh_-_starry_nigh1.html
- Read about how camping used to be @ Camping – The Way It Was http://www.scouting.org/mags/scouting/0009/d-wwas.html
- Learn about wood ticks @ The Wood Tick http://balarat.dpsk12.org/stories/storyReader$472

Additional Sites
- Camping Links by the Girl Scouts http://jfg.girlscouts.org/LINKS/linksod.htm#Links to Camping and Outdoor Recreation
- American Camping Association http://www.acacamps.org/
- Camping and Picnic Clip Art http://www.bry-backmanor.org/campclips.html
- Rick Rambo's Wood Badge Songbook http://www.geocities.com/rickram.geo/songbook/songbook.html#TableOfContents
- Backyard Camping Crafts http://family.go.com/crafts/season/hottopic/camp_crafts_ip/?clk=1012971

Date Varies

June, July and August can sometimes seem very long to children. *Activities for Kids* is an Internet site that offers an interactive calendar featuring interesting Internet sites for each day. They say it is 15-minute daily activities to help children learn about the Internet. In a school setting, this would be a great way to start your day or to use in your computer center.
- Activities for Kids http://www.activitiesforkids.com/summer/calendar.htm

Father's Day, 3ʳᵈ Sunday
PL 92-278
In1924, President Calvin Coolidge made Father's Day a national event to "establish more intimate relations between fathers and their children and to impress upon fathers the full measure of their obligations." Here are a few ideas to help you honor dad.

5 Quick Things To Do
1. Make a card
   Tie card http://www.kidsdomain.com/craft/tiecard.html
2. Learn a song to sing to dad
   Yea, Dad! http://www.night.net/tucker/sg-yeadad.html-ssi
3. Research the history of Father's Day
   Celebrate Holidays in the USA: Father's Day
   http://www.usis.usemb.se/Holidays/celebrate/fathers.html
4. Test your Father's Day knowledge with this trivia game
   http://www.aristotle.net/fathersday/trivia.html
5. Make a "check" for dad http://www.agirlsworld.com/amy/pajama/fathersday/dad-craft.html

Famous Last Words
Dads love to tell about the 'good old days' or give lots of advice, which is sometimes hard for kids to understand. Have the students read some quotes about fathers. These are probably just as hard to understand. Ask them to translate their favorite quote into 'today's' English.
- Quotes about Dad http://wilstar.com/holidays/fathers.htm#QUOTES

Poetry

Edgar A. Guest started work at the age of 13 for the Detroit Free Press as a copy boy. He became known as the 'Poet of the People' as his folksy verses were published in over 300 newspapers. My dad cut Guest's poems out of the paper every evening. So I thought Father's Day was a perfect time to read some of Guest's poems and try writing poems about dads in the 'Guest' style. After reading *Home (It Takes a Heap O' Livin')*, have the students list what they see and hear in his poetry. A couple of things that readily stand out are the use of couplets, contractions and dialect. Have the student's brainstorm a list of words about their dad, then think of a rhyming word for each word in the list. Use these words to write couplets. Most of Guest's verses are six lines or three sets of couplets.

- Edgar Guest's Biography http://www.freep.com/jobspage/club/guest.htm
- Home http://www.dnc.net/users/garrenmg/quotes/heapoliv.htm
- Only a Dad http://www.library.utoronto.ca/utel/rp/poems/guest12.html
- A Boy and His Dad http://www.dnc.net/users/garrenmg/quotes/boyndad.htm
- Sermons We See http://www.dnc.net/users/garrenmg/quotes/sermon.htm

Gifts for Dad

Get out those digital cameras and take some pictures. Have the students print out three of their favorites to use in their card for dad. Both of the DAD frame sites have good patterns plus some other fun crafts. The Photo House is a larger version if you're looking for something more involved.

- DAD Frame http://www.enchantedlearning.com/crafts/fathersday/dadcard/
  - Family Tree http://www.enchantedlearning.com/crafts/familytree/tree/
- DAD Photo Frame http://www.sesameworkshop.org/parents/activity/article/0,4117,54280,00.html
  - Sesame Street http://www.sesameworkshop.org/celebrate/holiday/fathersday/
- Photo House http://www.billybear4kids.com/holidays/father/photo-house/instructions.html

Coloring Pages and Clip Art

Have the students use a coloring page or piece of clip art as a story starter. Copy the picture into a word processor and write a story about what's happening in the picture. Don't forget that the pictures can first be brought into a Paint program and 'colored' before being copied again into the word processor.

- @ Kids Domain http://www.kidsdomain.com/holiday/dad/color.html
- @ About http://www.dltk-kids.com/crafts/dad/color/index.htm
- Clip Art http://www.kidsdomain.com/holiday/dad/clip.html

Just for Fun

There are lots of online games, mazes, word finds and puzzles available, but some of the best are at the following sites. I particularly like the off-line games found at Language Games and Searching for Dad.

- Black Dog: Father's Day http://www.blackdog.net/holiday/dad/
- Father's Day Language Games http://www.geocities.com/Athens/Troy/9087/father/fgames.html
- Searching For Dad http://www.geocities.com/Athens/Troy/9087/father/flanguage.html

General Father's Day Internet Sites

- Father's Day @ Web Holidays http://www.web-holidays.com/dadsday/
- Father's Day @ Alphabet Soup http://www.marvelicious.com/fathersday.html
- Father's Day @ Perpetual Preschool http://www.perpetualpreschool.com/fathers_day.html
- Billy Bear's Father's Day http://www.billybear4kids.com/holidays/father/dad.htm
- Kid's Domain http://www.kidsdomain.com/holiday/dad/

Summer Solstice

> *"Wherever you go, no matter what the weather, always bring your own sunshine."*
> Anthony J. D'Angelo, The College Blue Book

> *"A good laugh is sunshine in a house."*
> Author Unknown

- *Here Comes the Sun* http://www.christianteens.net/amp/audio/m.htm

In the northern hemisphere, the longest day of the year (near June 22) is when the sun is farthest north. This is the shortest day of the year in the southern hemisphere. For an excellent explanation of the summer solstice, refer to Eric Weisstein's article @ http://www.treasure-troves.com/astro/SummerSolstice.html Be sure to look at the QuickTime movie to watch how the daylight pattern moves throughout the year and try the egg experiment.

Learn more about Summer Solstice Celebrations
Teachnet offers an excellent lesson plan about the Summer Solstice. You might also want to visit Finland, Norway and Alaska to view their midsummer celebrations. For an overview of different midsummer celebrations, go to the Religious Tolerance site.
- Solstice http://school.discovery.com/homeworkhelp/worldbook/atozscience/s/519440.html
- Lesson Plan @ Stonehenge http://www.teachnet.com/lesson/seasonal/solstice061899.html
- Summer Solstice Celebrations http://www.religioustolerance.org/summer_solstice.htm
- Midsummer – Finland http://virtual.finland.fi/finfo/english/juhannus.html
- The Midnight Sun - Alaska
  http://www.micronet.net/users/~callingaliens/solstice%20folder/solstice.html
- Celebrate the Midnight Sun – Alaska http://fairbanks-alaska.com/midnight-sun-events.htm#top
- Norway – Land of the Midnight Sun
  http://www.saveourscreen.com/TNV/Europe/Norway_Midnight_Sun/Midnight%20Sun%20SS1.htm (change your screensaver)

Tour of the Sun
Yes, the ultimate field trip – the sun! Visit the Multimedia Tour of the Sun, but before you go, start some sun music. The visit the Sun, Man's Friend or Foe and explore the art, music and stories related to the sun. For more information, check out Solar Max.
- Here Comes the Sun http://www2s.biglobe.ne.jp/~syuLove/sunsun.htm
- Multimedia Tour of the Sun http://www.michielb.nl/od95/
- Solar Max http://www.exploratorium.edu/solarmax/index.html
- The Sun, Man's Friend or Foe http://library.thinkquest.org/15215/

Protect Yourself From UV Rays
As this is National Safety Month, start right by learning about proper skin care in the sun. Both of the following sites offer good advice. Have the students take the Sun Care Quiz at Coppertone. Also, Scholastic and teamed up with Coppertone to offer an in-depth lesson on Science Under the Sun – Block the Sun, Not the Fun. Help your students understand what ultraviolet rays are and why they are dangerous to the skin at the UV Index page by EPA.
- Sun Protection Movie http://www.brainpop.com/health/integumentary/sunprotection/index.weml
- Be Sun Savvy http://www.education-world.com/a_lesson/lesson008.shtml
- Coppertone http://www.coppertone.com/
- Science Under the Sun http://www.scienceunderthesun.com/

- UV Index: Overview http://www.epa.gov/docs/ozone/uvindex/uvover.html

Read Shakespeare's *Midsummer's Night Dream*

The first site is a wonderful hyperlinked text that really helps students understand the text. The second site is about a 5th grade Midsummer Night Dream project.

- Midsummer's Night Dream http://quarles.unbc.ca/midsummer/midsummer1.html
- Pinecrest School http://www.pinecrestschools.com/thousandoaks/middle/midsummer/midsummer.htm
- Listen to *Midsummer's Night Dream* by Mendelssohn http://www.musickit.com/resources/Composerofmon.html This site is by the Virtual Music Classroom and has suggestions for listening.
- Illustrated Midsummer's Night Dream http://www.emory.edu/ENGLISH/classes/Shakespeare_Illustrated/MidsummerPaintings.html

Odds and ends to use throughout the summer

- Summer Fun http://www.beritsbest.com/HolidaysSeasons/Summer/index.shtml
- It's Summer Time http://www.cfc-efc.ca/docs/00001177.htm

Summer Music

- Summer Place http://jadierose.com/midicollection.html
- In the Good Old Summer Time http://tinchicken.com/songs/old/insummer.htm
- Summertime http://perso.wanadoo.fr/jarod.russell/home/s.htm
- Summer Nights http://orion.spaceports.com/~mmp/letras/SummerNights.html
- Tour British Columbia while listening to Lazy, Hazy, Crazy Days of Summer http://members.vavo.com/arch23/Okanagan.html

Dragon Boat Festival
5th day of the fifth moon of the lunar calendar

The Dragon Boat Festival commemorates the death of a Chinese poet and statesman named Chu Yuan. It is one of the three most important Chinese festivals. Read a short biography about Chu Yuan and be sure to one of his poems, *The Mountain Spirit*. The Dragon Boat Festival offers a hyperlinked version of the story that explains many customs associated with the holiday.

- Qu Yuan http://www.chinapage.com/quyuan5.html
  - The Mountain Spirit http://www.chinapage.com/eng1.html#QY
- Dragon Boat Festival http://www.gio.gov.tw/info/festival_c/dragon_e/dragon.htm

According to Paddler Magazine, Dragon Boat racing is the second most popular sport in the world. Take a look at these beautiful dragon boats.

- Dragon Boat Festival http://www.sandiego-online.com/forums/chinese/htmls/dragboat.htm
- Dragon Boat Festival – Boston http://www.bostondragonboat.org/
- International Dragon Boat Racing http://www.dragon-boat.net/

Pentecost (Whitsunday)

Pentecost is known as the Birthday of the Church, the day the Holy Spirit visited the apostles fifty days after the Resurrection of Christ. Pentecost is also a Jewish harvest feast of the first fruits, known as Shavuot, celebrated fifty days after Passover. It is also known as Whitsunday in the UK because of the white garments worn during many ceremonies.

- Pentecost http://www.newadvent.org/cathen/15614b.htm
- Pentecost: Jewish Feast http://www.newadvent.org/cathen/11661a.htm
- Shavuot http://www.holidays.net/shavuot/
- Shavuot/Pentecost http://www.cdn-friends-icej.ca/judeochr/pentcost/pentcost.html

- Seasons of the Church: Sacred Fire http://members.dencity.com/sanctuary/sacredfire.html

Look at how some of the world's greatest artists have depicted Pentecost.

- Art of Pentecost http://www.textweek.com/art/pentecost.htm

Named by James Cook, the Whitsunday Islands off the coast of Queensland, Australia, are best known for the Great Barrier Reef.

- Whitsunday Islands http://www2.tpgi.com.au/users/seaquel/

Special Days

June 2, 1953
Coronation of Queen Elizabeth

Many countries in the United Kingdom celebrate Queen's Day in June. The date may vary, but the celebration is always the same; to pay tribute to the Queen. To learn more about Queen Elizabeth II, read Her Majesty, the Queen.

- Her Majesty, the Queen http://www.royal.gov.uk/family/hmqueen.htm
- Coronation Ceremony http://www.kirkdale113.freeserve.co.uk/queen.htm
- The British Monarchy http://www.royal.gov.uk/index.htm
- Royalty in English History http://www.royalty.nu/Europe/England/index.html

Monarchy vs. Democracy?

What is a monarchy? How does it differ from a democracy? Did you know some people wanted to make George Washington king of the United States? How would that have changed our country? Interesting questions to pose to your students.

- Britannica: Monarchy http://www.britannica.com/eb/article?eu=54642&tocid=0
- Britannica: Democracy http://www.britannica.com/eb/article?eu=30382&tocid=0
- The Papers of George Washington http://www.virginia.edu/gwpapers/project/news/roberts.html

Modern Royal Families

- Belgium http://belgium.fgov.be/monarchie/en00.htm
- Denmark http://www.kongehuset.dk/
- Ethiopian http://www.angelfire.com/ak/sellassie/page8.html
- Japan http://www.geocities.com/jtaliaferro.geo/imphous.html
- Jordan http://www.kingabdullah.jo/
- Nepal http://www.nepalhomepage.com/general/kings/shahkings.html
- Netherlands http://www.koninklijkhuis.nl/UK/
- Saudi Arabia http://www.saudiroyals.com/
- Sweden http://www.royalcourt.se/eng/index.html
- Thailand http://www.escati.com/king_of_thailand.htm
- Yugoslavia http://www.royalfamily.org/

June 5, 1919
Richard Scarry

From an early age, Richard Scarry was interested in art. His first book was published in 1949, but it wasn't until 1963, with the publication of *The Best Word Book Ever*, that his success as a children's author and illustrator was secured. *The Best Word Book Ever* sold seven million copies in twelve years.

- Richard Scarry http://falcon.jmu.edu/~ramseyil/scarry.htm
- Richard Scarry http://www.kirjasto.sci.fi/rscarry.htm
- The Busy World of Richard Scarry Online http://www.krey.org/jumbojet/busyworld/
- BusyTown Traveling Museum http://www.omsi.edu/explore/discovery/busytown/

- Richard Scarry's Birthday
  http://www.smarterkids.com/rescenter/calendar/cal_activity.asp?activity=626 with activities
- Lowly Worm Coloring Page http://www.familychannel.ca/funstuff/printcolor/scarry.htm

Golden Books

Richard Scarry started his career writing and illustrating for Golden Books. For over half a century, these little books have been bringing children and reading together. Golden Books online has wonderful games and activities for children. Enjoy exploring this site with your students.

- Golden Books http://www.goldenbooks.com/
- Collecting Little Golden Books http://www.thesantis.com/home.htm
- Little Golden Books Making A Big Come Back http://www.post-gazette.com/books/20010501corner2.asp

Make a Best _____ Book Ever

Choose a topic and have the students develop a Best _____ Book Ever of their own. For younger children, you might want to choose something like school, but for older children, choose whatever topic they are studying. This is an excellent way to develop vocabulary. The Kid's Domain Icon Center has lots of pictures that are easy to locate. Copy the picture onto a word document or publishing program. Label the picture. This would be a good project to use the stamps on KidPix.

- Kid's Domain Icon Mania http://www.kidsdomain.com/icon/index.html
- KidPix http://www.kidpix.com/

Selected Books by Richard Scarry
Richard Scarry's Best Word Book Ever
Richard Scarry's Best Mother Goose Ever
Busy, Busy World
Is This the House of Mistress Mouse?
Planes
Trains
Cars
Best Storybook Ever
What Do People Do All Day?
Richard Scarry's Lowly Worm Word Book
Richard Scarry's Best Counting Book Ever
Richard Scarry's Busiest People Ever
Richard Scarry's Best Christmas Ever
The Bunny Book
Scarry's Silly Stories
The Cat Family Takes a Trip
Just for Fun
Splish-Splash Sounds
Short and Tall
About Animals
Best Little World Book Ever
Christmas Mice

June 8, 1867
Frank Lloyd Wright

"No house should ever be on any hill or on anything.
It should be of the hill,
belonging to it,
so hill and house could live together
each the happier for the other."

Frank Lloyd Wright

One of the leading architects of the 20th Century, Wright was instrumental in developing the Prairie and Organic styles. He wanted to create something unique to America, not a copy of European style. He made the setting an integral part of the building. Learn more about this man who some say was the greatest American artist of the 20th Century.
- Frank Lloyd Wright http://www.franklloydwright.org/
- Frank Lloyd Wright http://www.pbs.org/flw/
  - Listen to his vision http://www.pbs.org/flw/legacy/reflections.html
  - Locate a Wright Building Near You http://www.pbs.org/flw/locator/index.html

Wright designed everything from homes to gasoline stations to world famous museums. Look at his and other famous buildings. You can download a free demo of the 3D viewer and see many of the buildings in 3D and you will be able to 'walk' through them.
- Great Buildings Online http://www.greatbuildings.com/gbc.html
- Design Workshop Lite http://www.artifice.com/cgi-bin/lite_download_reg.cgi

Design Your Own Dream Space
All of us would like to have a space of our own. The Frank Lloyd Wright Organization sponsors an annual contest for students. Have your students participate in the contest or design a space just for fun. Ask students draw a house plans for their dream house. Look at some house plans at Eplans or Cool House Plans. This is an excellent authentic math activity as it is a natural for applying the concepts for measuring, drawing to scale and finding area.
- Design Your Own Dream Space http://www.franklloydwright.org/08DEV/OUTREACH.html
- Eplans http://www.eplans.com/
- Cool House Plans http://www.coolhouseplans.com/

Odds and Ends
- Whyville http://www.whyville.net/top/index.html build a house online you need to register, but there is no cost.
- Habitat for Humanity http://www.habitat.org/default.html
- This Old House http://www.pbs.org/wgbh/thisoldhouse/home.html
- I Want to Be An Architect http://www.akropolis.net/~zeus/archcareers/
- The Wright Web Guide http://www.cypgrp.com/flw/
- Learn about Structures Around the World http://www.exploratorium.edu/structures/

June 10, 1928
Maurice Sendak

"It's a very good sign if a book feels good,
and smells good, and tastes good.
Because they're love objects."

Maurice Sendak [i]

Read the HomeArts' interview with Maurice Sendak with your students. It is a lovely, in-depth account of his life with illustrations from his favorite books. In this article and others, Sendak credits his father for his love of storytelling. His father never glossed over the bad or scary parts as he addressed children's real fears. Sendak also tells stories that are truthful to the point of being "far too frightening for small children" as some of his critics say. Have your students write a story about what scares them. Use a paint program to illustrate the stories and be sure to put a moon in the pictures. Read the Falcon biography to find out why.

- HomeArt: Maurice Sendak http://homearts.com/depts/relat/sendakf1.htm
- Biography http://falcon.jmu.edu/~ramseyil/sendak.htm
- Maurice Sendak http://www.edupaperback.org/authorbios/Sendak_Maurice.html

Backgrounds

Maurice Sendak began his career by drawing backgrounds for the Mutt and Jeff cartoons. Have the students choose a clip art character from Turtle Through the Ages. Copy the character or characters and paste them on a blank word processor page or PowerPoint page. Print the page and have the students draw a background. This is a good opportunity to talk about setting. Have them print another copy and draw a different background. Discuss how the setting gives meaning to the story.

- Mutt and Jeff Cartoon http://www.adh.brighton.ac.uk/schoolofdesign/MA.COURSE/15/LMJ.html
- Mutt and Jeff http://www.toonopedia.com/muttjeff.htm
- Caricaturtles: Turtles Through the Ages http://www.execpc.com/~strehlow/turtle/Turtle.html

Selected Books by Maurice Sendak
The Sign on Rosie's Door
The Nutshell Library
Where the Wild Things Are, Caldecott medal 1964
Higglety Pigglety Pop!
In the Night Kitchen
Outside Over There
A Hole Is to Dig: A First Book of Definitions
Little Bear
What Do You Say Dear?
What Do You Do Dear?
Little Bear's Visit
The Juniper Tree and Other Tales from Grimm
The Nutcracker
Dear Mili
We Are All in the Dumps with Jack and Guy

"If you're looking for a way to get closer to your kids, there ain't no better way than to grab 'em and read."

Maurice Sendak[ii]

June 11, 1910
Jacques Cousteau

Born in Saint-Andre-de-Dubzac, France, Cousteau always loved the water. Throughout his life, he explored the oceans and educated the public on their conservation and protection. Read Cousteau's biography and view a short clip from the CNN article. Listen to clips about his life by his son.

- Jacques Cousteau bio http://www.incwell.com/Biographies/Cousteau.html
- Earthkeeper Hero: Jacques Cousteau http://www.myhero.com/hero.asp?hero=cousteau
- CNN: Jacques Cousteau http://www.cnn.com/WORLD/9706/25/cousteau.obit/

Learn More About His Expeditions

Jacques Cousteau made many ocean expeditions aboard the Calypso. Have groups of students research a different expedition. Have them map their expedition and tell about the major finds of the journey.

- Cousteau Society http://www.cousteausociety.org/people/people.htm
- Cousteau for Kids: Dophinlog http://www.dolphinlog.org/
- A Sun Remembers Exploring with Jacques Cousteau
  http://magma.nationalgeographic.com/2000/exploration/cousteau/index.cfm

Explore the Oceans

After students have visited the various sites about oceans and ocean plants and animals, have them develop questions for different categories. Arrange the questions from the easiest to the most difficult. Use PowerPoint to develop a Jeopardy-like game. Use the table for the game board and create links to various pages with the questions. Sample categories might include: Ocean Animals, Ocean Plants, Jacques Cousteau, Marine Careers, and Oceans (tides, water, etc.)

Ocean Animals	Ocean Plants	Jacques Cousteau	Marine Careers	Oceans
100	100	100	100	100
200	200	200	200	200
300	300	300	300	300
400	400	400	400	400
500	500	500	500	500

Oceans for $100

- The Pacific, Atlantic, Indian, and Arctic.

?

_____

What are the name of four oceans

- Oceans Alive http://www.mos.org/oceans/
- Explore Oceans http://www.ajkids.com/tours/oceanexploration.asp
- NOAA: Oceans and Coasts http://www.education.noaa.gov/cocean.html
- Visit online aquariums http://now2000.com/kids/zoos.shtml#aquarium
- Ocean Animals http://www.enchantedlearning.com/coloring/oceanlife.shtml
- This Is Jeopardy http://www.spe.sony.com/tv/shows/jeopardy/
- Jeopardy http://www.station.sony.com/jeopardy/ (play online versions)

Odds and Ends

- Dive and Discover http://www.divediscover.whoi.edu/ This is a wonderful site that allows you and your students to join a real ocean expedition to the ocean floor.
- Save the Whales Poster http://www.maryengelbreit.com/Workshop/CB-SaveTheWales.htm
- Ocean/fish coloring http://www.lafishmag.com/clipart.html

- Musical habitats http://www.nero.nmfs.gov/ro/doc/game2.htm
- Sea World and Bush Gardens http://www.seaworld.org/

June 12, 1939
Baseball Hall of Fame

The National Baseball Hall of Fame and Museum was officially dedicated in colorful ceremony on June 12, 1939. Take a tour of this wonderful museum, learn about some of the hall of famers and even listen to rebroadcasts of classic World Series games. Be sure to visit the Games and Activities section. For educators, visit the Primary Sources section for first hand documents about women in baseball, baseball and WWII, the Negro leagues and Jackie Robinson.

- Baseball Hall of Fame http://baseballhalloffame.org/

Visit Other Baseball Halls of Fame

Just like it says, check out these other baseball halls of fame.

- Canadian Baseball Hall of Fame http://www.baseballhof.ca/
- Women's Baseball Hall of Fame http://www.eteamz.com/hallfame/
- Japanese Baseball Hall of Fame http://www.baseball-museum.or.jp/museum_e/index_e.htm

Make Your Own Sports Card

Take a digital picture of students or scan their school pictures. Have them go to PhotoWorkshop at PhotoIsland. *Note: you will probably want to log-on with your password rather than have each student get a log-in identification.* You can create an online album with all of your students' pictures. Then, they can use the pictures again and again without you having to download them each time. Have the students find their picture and go to the trading cards template. Copy the picture and frame into a word processor and key in the student's name. Make a textbox the same size and list the vital information. Print your cards front and back. Printsville by Hewlett Packard has different sports card frames to print.

- PhotoIsland http://www.photoisland.com
- Scottsdale Baseball Cards http://www.scottsdalecards.com/
- Hewlett Packard: Printsville
  http://www.homeandoffice.hp.com/hho/us/eng/baseball_party.html?page_id=6523&role=&preview_date=null&subgroups=baseball_party

Baseball Almanac

The Baseball Almanac is preserving the history of baseball. It has lots of firsts, quotes, stories and history. I am sure your students will enjoy spending time looking at all of the information. To help students learn to locate information and 'skim' when reading, ask each student to find one or two obscure baseball facts; such as 'What was the game George Washington and his soldiers played?' Students will need to record the location and answer. Make a list of all of the questions (without answers) and distribute to the students either individually or in teams. See who can find the correct answers and locations first. Be sure to have the students pair up and try reading Abbott and Costello's famous comedy routine, 'Who's on first?'

- Baseball Almanac http://baseball-almanac.com/
  - Who's on first? http://baseball-almanac.com/humor4.shtml

Check out Little League Week for more baseball related activities.

June 13
Kamehameha Day

King Kamehameha I was Hawaii's first king. He unified the islands in 1810, and then ruled in peace until his death in 1819. Today, Kamehameha Day is celebrated as a state holiday in Hawaii to honor Hawaiian history. For those of us who may never get to the Islands, this is a great opportunity to take a virtual vacation. Start with a virtual tour of the Islands, turn on the music and get ready for a luau.

- Virtually Hawaii http://satftp.soest.hawaii.edu/space/hawaii/
- The Hawaiian Visitor Center http://www.hawaii-hawaii-hawaii.com/virtualtour.html
- While in Hawaii, Do A Little Sightseeing http://www.aloha.net/~ctpa/sublinks/hawaii.html learn you name in Hawaiian, write in the sand, games, web cams
- Hawaiian Web Cams http://www.planet-hawaii.com/gallery/hawaiianeye.html
- Hawaiian Midi http://www.psmaui.com/music.htm
- Kauai Style Midi http://www.hawaiian.net/~kauai/midi.html
- Hawaiian Luau http://www.dltk-kids.com/crafts/luau/index.html

Learn a Little More About King Kamehameha
- Brief History of Kamehameha Day http://www.dailycelebrations.com/061199.htm
- Bishop Museum: King Kamehameha
  http://www.bishopmuseum.org/bishop/specialdays/kamehameha.html

Retell a Hawaiian Folktale
Like most cultures, Hawaiians have many folktales and legends about history, origins and animals. Have the students read some of the Hawaiian folktales and choose one they would like to learn and retell. Retelling stories helps students develop vocabulary, sequencing, and attention to detail and oral interpretation. As folktales were originally from the oral tradition, they lend themselves very well to storytelling.

- The Birth of Hawai'I http://gamma.mhpcc.edu/t3/cnagamine/hawaii.htm
- Mo'olelo (legend)
  http://tqjunior.thinkquest.org/5410/island_formation_web_page/MooleloStudent_Retellings/moolelo_frameset.html
- The Kohola and the Kolea
  http://sustainableseas.noaa.gov/missions/hawaii1/background/hawaiian_culture.html#folktale

Explore the Islands
For a brief introduction to the Islands, go to the Infoplease site. To travel with ocean explorers as they learn about the Islands go to the Sustainable Seas site. To explore on your own, go to the Hawaii ThinkQuest. However you choose to explore the Islands, have the students share their knowledge by making a fishbone-mapping organizer. Substitute person, place or thing for *cause* and Hawaii for *result*. Make a bulletin board display combining the organizers and pictures of Hawaii printed from the Internet.

- Information About Hawaii http://www.infoplease.com/ipa/A0108204.html
- Sustainable Seas: Hawaiian Islands
  http://sustainableseas.noaa.gov/missions/hawaii1/hawaii1.html
- Hawaii ThinkQuest
  http://tqjunior.thinkquest.org/5410/island_formation_web_page/html_folder/enter2.html
- Fishbone Mapping Organizer http://www.sdcoe.k12.ca.us/score/actbank/sfish.htm

June 14
Flag Day

"Shoot, if you must, this old gray head,
But spare your country's flag," she said.
Barbara Frietchie by John Greenleaf Whittier[iii]

It is believed that B.J. Cigrand, a teacher, was the first person to observe June 14 as a day to celebrate and honor the flag as Flag Birthday. Although many cities and states followed with their own celebrations, it wasn't until 1949 that President Truman signed an Act of Congress designating June 14th as National Flag Day.

- U. S. Flag http://www.usflag.org/
- Flag Day Festival http://www.flagday.com

From a very early age, we learn to say the Pledge of Allegiance, but do our students or we know what it means? Both of these sites give easy to understand explanations. After discussing the meaning of the flag salute, order a new flag for your classroom. For about $10.00 you can order a flag that has been flown over the Capitol.

- U.S. Capitol Flag Order Form http://www.usflag.org/capitol.flag.order.html

Flag Etiquette
- The Flag Code http://www.legion.org/flagcode.htm
- Our Grand Old Flag http://www.umkc.edu/imc/flag.htm
- United States Code for Displaying the Flag http://www.azstarnet.com/~rgrogan/flaglaw.htm

The Rest of the Story
Who really designed the 1st flag? After reading the following accounts of the design of the 1st United States flag, have the students combine the information to write a play showing 'the rest of the story.'

- Betsy Ross http://www.ushistory.org/betsy/
- Another View Betsy Ross http://www.icss.com/usflag/about.betsy.ross.html

Design a Flag
If Puerto Rico becomes a state, the United States will add another star to the flag. Challenge the students to design a flag that includes 51 stars. Look at how the flag has changed over the years.

- Flag Pictures http://www.ushistory.org/betsy/flagpics.html
- How to Cut a 5 Pointed Star (with one snip)
  http://www.flagday.com/history/star_in_one_cut/flagstar.shtml

Editorial: Flag Burning – A Matter of Opinion
The 1st amendment states that '*Congress shall make no law abridging freedom of speech.*' Because of that simple statement, congress has been hesitant to pass an amendment that would forbid burning the flag. This issue continues to stir passions on both sides. Have your students research the information for and against this amendment. Encourage them to talk to their parents and others in the community including veterans. Have them write their opinion in the form of a newspaper editorial.

- The Flag Burning Page http://www.esquilax.com/flag/
- Voter's Guide http://www.aclu.org/vote-guide/Senate_SJRes31.html
- Flag Burning http://internet.ggu.edu/university_library/if/burnflag.html
- Editorial Rubric http://www.sdcoe.k12.ca.us/score/actbank/editorialrub.html

Odds and Ends
- Why do we have an American flag?
  http://www.nationalgeographic.com/xpeditions/lessons/13/gk2/eurounion.html this is a lesson plan about national alliances.
- Pledge of Allegiance http://www.lessonplanspage.com/SSPledgeAllegiance5.htm
- Red Skelton's Comentary of on the Pledge of Allegiance http://www.otrsite.com/memoriam/
- Barbara Frietchie http://www.sos.state.md.us/sos/kids/html/poem.html (poem and story plus brief biography of John Greenleaf Whittier
- State Flags http://www.lessonplanspage.com/SS50StateGeography23.htm

- Flag Clip Art http://w3f.com/gifs/flag/old-usa/index.html (including international and animated flags)
- Peter Max http://www.petermax.com/ (U.S.Flag Posters)
- Flag Days of the World http://www.qnet.com/~moonbase/fdjun.htm
- Flag Tag http://www.un.org/Pubs/CyberSchoolBus/flagtag/index.html (recognize international flags)
- Flag Coloring Page http://www.dltk-kids.com/usa/images/bpostersillyflag.gif
- Flag Day http://www.theholidayspot.com/flagday/index.htm (crafts and activities)
- Unofficial Flag Page http://www.azstarnet.com/~rgrogan/flag.htm (lots of links to pictures, writings and patriotic music)
- The Star Spangled Banner http://www.150.si.edu/chap3/flag.htm
  - Photos http://photo2.si.edu/different/dif_banner.html
- The Star Spangled Banner http://www.geocities.com/Heartland/Ranch/9198/war1812/w1812d.htm
- 14 Essays about America's National Symbols: Flags http://www.va.gov/pubaff/celebAm/CAIndex.htm

Flag of America
Red, white and blue,
Flag of America
A salute I give to you!

unknown

June 16
Juggling Day
You know what to do!
- Juggling Information Service http://www.juggling.org/
- Learn2 Juggle http://www.learn2.com/04/0418/0418.asp
- Learn to Juggle http://kids.discovery.com/KIDS/adv13.html
- Instant Jugglers Manual http://yoyoguy.com/info/ball/index2.html
- Learn to Juggle http://blackdog4kids.com/holiday/summer/do/juggle/index.html
- Learning How to Juggle (poem) http://www.nesbitt.com/poetry/juggle.html

June 18, 1949
Chris Van Allsburg
In Van Allsburg's interview with Stephanie Loer, he describes his writing process as first seeing the pictures of the story in his mind. Many students also see the pictures first. Have your students draw a picture; it could be a person, a place or thing. Then, have them ask themselves the questions Chris Van Allsburg asks himself. Encourage the students to draw the answers to the questions. Finally, arrange the pictures in sequence and write the text. Scan the illustrated text and pictures. Put the stories on your web page.
- Chris Van Allsburg http://www.eduplace.com/rdg/author/cva/index.html

Learn More About Multiple Intelligence
Have your students take the Online MI Test. Students need to understand how they learn so they can maximize their strengths and compensate for their weaknesses. Help them understand their learning style.
- Interactive MI Test http://www.ldpride.net/learningstyles.MI.htm
- Multiple Intelligence Key http://www.athena.ivv.nasa.gov/curric/weather/adptcty/multint.html (print this chart out to hang in your classroom)

- The Theory of Multiple Intelligence http://edweb.gsn.org/edref.mi.intro.html

For lots more information about Chris Van Allsburg, including lesson plans to use with his books, refer to these sites:

- Teacher Resource File http://falcon.jmu.edu/~ramseyil/allsburg.htm
- The World of Chris Van Allsburg http://www.houghtonmifflinbooks.com/vanallsburg/
- K-12 Teaching and Learning Center: Chris Van Allsburg http://tlc.ai.org/vanallsb.htm
- Chris Van Allsburg Biography
  http://teacher.scholastic.com/authorsandbooks/authors/van_allsburg/bio.htm

Books by Chris Van Allsburg
Jumanji – Caldecott Award
The Polar Express – Caldecott Award
The Sweetest Fig
The Mysteries of Harris Burdick
Two Bad Ants
Just a Dream
The Z Was Zapped: A Play in Twenty-Six Acts
The Wretched Stone
The Widow's Broom
Ben's Dream
The Wreck of the Zephyr
Bad Day at Riverbend
The Garden of Abdul Gasazi

June 19, 1865
Juneteenth – Texas

On this date, Major General Gordon Granger, of the Union, officially proclaimed freedom for the slaves of Texas, as they had not heard about President Lincoln's Emancipation Proclamation, signed two years before. Thus it is on this day, that African Americans celebrate the Emancipation Proclamation. To help your students understand the significance of Juneteenth, watch the slide show on slavery found at Juneteenth World Wide. Then, together, read more about the historical significance and customs associated with the holiday at the Nation Juneteenth Museum and the Electronic Village. Finally, listen to real accounts of slaves at the Juneteenth in Texas site.

- Juneteenth World Wide http://www.juneteenth.com/
- The National Juneteenth Museum http://hosting.xigroup.com/juneteenth//info.html
- Electronic Village: Juneteenth http://www.elecvillage.com/juneteen.htm
- Juneteenth in Texas http://www.americanvisions.com/juneteenth.htm

Read the Emancipation Proclamation and listen to a former slave discuss life and work after the Emancipation Proclamation.

- Emancipation Proclamation http://www.nara.gov/exhall/featured-document/eman/emanproc.html

Finally, read the acrostic poem about Juneteenth and write your own acrostics using the word freedom or other words meaning freedom. Listen to a little gospel music while you write.

- The Black Church and Juneteenth http://www.actom.com/njclchistory.htm
- Thesaurus http://www.thesaurus.com/
- Acrostic Poetry Form
  http://www.geocities.com/EnchantedForest/5165/pages/poetry_samples.html#acrostic
- Medley of Spirituals http://free.ntv.it/midi_music/midifile/spiritual/Spiritual_main.htm
- Spirituals http://www.laurasmidiheaven.com/Spiritual.shtml

For an in-depth resource for Black History, refer to the following link:

- The Best of Black History on the Internet http://blackhistorypages.com/

June 25, 1929
Eric Carle
Eric Carle is one of children's favorite author/illustrators. He is probably best known for The Very Hungry Caterpillar and Brown Bear, Brown Bear, What Do You See, written by Bill Martin Jr. Eric Carle has, however written over seventy books. His unique artistic style is built on handmade paper collages. Begin with a visit to the Eric Carle Homepage to read his biography. Read teacher's ideas for many of his books and/or submit your own at the Caterpillar Exchange.

- Eric Carle http://www.eric-carle.com/

Make A Book
Have the students open up a paint program and use the fill feature to create a background. Then, use the different paintbrushes and effects to create an interesting paper. When they are happy with their paper, have them cut out shapes to make an animal and paste them on another page. Use drawing tools to add details. Have the students give their animal a name and write a description. Print out your pictures and put them into a class book of animals based on *Brown Bear, Brown Bear What Do You See?* If you want to get fancy, go to FlipAlbum and download a demo copy. Insert the student's pages into the flipbook. WOW!

- Flip Album http://www.flipalbum.com

Books by Eric Carle
Brown Bear, Brown Bear What Do You See?
The Very Hungry Caterpillar
1, 2, 3 to the Zoo
Pancakes, Pancakes
The Tiny Seed
Do You Want to Be My Friend
Rooster's Off to See the World
Walter the Baker
Have you Seen My Cat?
I See A Song
The Grouchy Ladybug
The Very Busy Spider
Papa, Please Get the Moon for Me
A House for Hermit Crab
Animals, Animals
The Very Quiet Cricket
Polar Bear, Polar Bear, What Do You Hear?
Today Is Monday
The Very Lonely Firefly
Little Cloud
The Art of Eric Carle
Hello, Red Fox
The Very Clumsy Click Beetle
Does A Kangaroo Have A Mother, Too?
Dream Snow

June 25, 1876
Battle of the Little Bighorn
Early in 1876, Federal authorities ordered the Lakota chiefs to report to their reservations. Angered by the perceived braking of the 1868 Treaty by the white soldiers, Sitting Bull, Crazy Horse and others refuse. This clash of two wills comes together on June 27th when George Armstrong Custer discovers Sitting Bull's encampment on the Little Bighorn River. When Custer charges the village he discovers that he is outnumbered four-to-one. Hundreds of Lakota warriors overwhelm his troops, killing them to the last man, in a battle later called Custer's Last Stand. The Indians were eventually forced back to their reservations, except Sitting Bull, who escaped with his followers to Canada.
Read more about the Battle of the Little Bighorn and the 1868 Treaty
- Battle of the Little Bighorn http://www.curtis-collection.com/tribe%20data/custer.html
- Custer's Last Battle http://www.custerbattle.com/sub_pages/history_sub/battle.htm
- The Treaty of 1868 and the Battle of Little Bighorn http://www.geocities.com/RainForest/9637/treaty.htm
- The 1868 Fort Laramie Treaty http://www.nara.gov/exhall/originals/sioux.html

This event clearly illustrates the old adage "there are two sides to every story." After reading these accounts, ask the students to prepare a case to be argued before the Supreme Court. With half of the students representing the Native Americans and the other half representing the Custer and the army.

Artist's View of the Battle of the Little Bighorn
Lakota warrior and chief, Kicking Bear, painted his representation of the battle he participated in some twenty years earlier. ArtsEdNet offers lesson plans for elementary, middle school and high school students based on this famous painting.
- Battle of the Little Bighorn http://www.artsednet.getty.edu/ArtsEdNet/Resources/Maps/battle.html

June 27, 1880
Helen Keller's Birthday

> *"I am glad to say I still have a vivid curiosity about the world I live in*
> *...it is as natural for me to believe that the richest harvest*
> *of happiness comes with age*
> *as to believe that true sight and hearing are within, not without..."*
>
> –Helen Keller[iv]

As a young child, Helen Keller was suddenly stricken with a mysterious fever that left her blind and deaf. With the help of her teacher, Annie Sullivan, she learned to communicate and became an inspiration to us all. "She proved how language could liberate the blind and the deaf."[v] To learn more about Helen Keller, read about her amazing life. Use Tom Snyder's Timeliner to create a time line of her life. Illustrate it with pictures and quotes from Helen Keller. You can also use adding machine tape to make timelines. Just tear off a long strip for each student. Print out pictures and paste them (literally paste them) on the strip.
- Helen Keller http://www.afb.org/info_documents.asp?collectionid=1
- Quick Bio and Timeline http://www.graceproducts.com/keller/life.html
- Timeliner: Free Demo http://www.tomsnyder.com/index.shtml

What's In A Name?
Have the students learn to sign their names and write them in Braille by using the following sites. You can also download the Braille font to your computer.

- Hand Speak http://www.handspeak.com
- ASL Alphabet http://www.masterstech-home.com/The_Library/ASL_Dictionary_Project/ASL_Tables/Alphabet.html
- The Braille Alphabet http://www.nbp.org/alph.html
- Sample Braille http://www.hotbraille.com/samplebraille.asp
- Download Braille and ASL Specialty Fonts http://www.tsbvi.edu/Education/fonts.html
- Interactive Finger Spelling and Braille Guide http://www.disserv.stu.umn.edu/AltForm/

Additional Links
- Helen Keller International http://www.hki.org/
- Helen Keller National Center for Deaf – Blind Youths and Adults http://www.helenkeller.org/national/other2.htm

June 27
Decide to be Married Day

Married in White, you have chosen right,
Married in Blue, your love will always be true,
Married in Pearl, you will live in a whirl,
Married in Brown, you will live in town,
Married in Red, you will wish yourself dead,
Married in Yellow, ashamed of your fellow,
Married in Green, ashamed to be seen,
Married in Pink, your spirit will sink,
Married in Grey, you will go far away,
Married in Black, you will wish yourself back.[vi]

For centuries, June has been associated with weddings. It is said that this came about because, during May, observances were made for "the unhappy dead," and was considered unlucky for marriages, so weddings usually were postponed until June, and the custom continues. Learn more about the history of weddings at the following sites.
- Wedding History and Traditions http://www.bridalzine.com/culturehistory.html
- History of Weddings http://mfadt.parsons.edu/~ddavid/wedding/why/3history/3history3.htm
- Genius in June http://sln.fi.edu/qa99/musing6/musing6.html

Because June is known for weddings, you might want to use these activities throughout the month and just conclude these activities with a wedding show on June 27th.

Traditions

Weddings worldwide are an occasion for celebrations and therefore, associated with many different customs and traditions. Start with a KWL chart you have copied into a word processor. With the students, record what the students know about wedding customs and list what they want to know. Assign each student or small group a country to research. After they research their country, have them write a paragraph about the wedding traditions they found, print it out and pin it to a world map. Complete the class KWL chart and post it by the map.
- TeacherVision: KWL Chart 2 http://www.teachervision.com/lesson-plans/lesson-4314.html
- Wedding Traditions http://members.theglobe.com/rockotbello/history.htm?nfhp=993418728&rld=798001562
- Wedding Customs from Around the World http://www.rice.edu/projects/topics/internatl/weddings/wedding-customs.htm
- Hawaiian Wedding Customs http://www.hawaiibride.com/customs.html
- Wedding Customs Around the Muslim World http://www.zawaj.com/weddingways_main.html

- Weddings Around the World http://www.ourmarriage.com/html/around_the_world.html (put on world map)
- Ethnic Wedding Customs http://members.aol.com/Mjkarl/ethnic.htm

Plan a Wedding Budget

The Wedding Channel offers an online budget planner. Have the students predict which cities will be the most expensive and the least expensive. Submit the required information and the city where the wedding will take place. Have the students keep the information the same except for the city and record the results on a spreadsheet. After checking a number of cities in various parts of the United States, have them assess their predictions. What conclusions can they draw from the results they found?

- Plan a Budget http://www.weddingchannel.com/cgi-bin/gx.cgi/AppLogic+com.wc.Utility.NavBarForStaticHTML?frmSection=left&location=http://emerald2.weddingchannel.com/WC2/Budget

Musical Gallery of Wedding Art

Both artists and musicians have commemorated the wedding. Have the students prepare a gallery of wedding art by copying the artwork into PowerPoint or another presentation program. Encourage them to use transitions between paintings. Choose a piece of wedding music for the background. This would be a good time to the students to use the timer feature of the program so that the slides and music will end at the same time.

Art Work
- Peasants at a Wedding http://gallery.euroweb.hu/html/h/hals/harmen/peasants.html by Hals
- Boyar Wedding Feast http://stores.yahoo.com/museumshop/hilpo0074.html by Makovskii
- The Wedding Feast of Cana http://home-3.worldonline.nl/~sb059543/Wed.html by Veronese (see the size http://www.dzre.com/paristrip/louvre.htm)
- Peasant Wedding http://www.gchs.com/teachers/mccall/newweb2/peasant.htm by Bruegel
- Beatrice Meeting Dante at a Wedding Feast http://www.artmagick.com/paintings/painting2037.asp by Rossetti

Music
- Bridal Chorus from *Lohengrin* by Wagner http://www.laurasmidiheaven.com/Classmidi-wagner.htm
- Wedding March from *Midsummer's Night Dream* by Mendelssohn http://www.geocities.com/Paris/3486/mendfi.html
- Lots of wedding music http://home.ici.net/customers/bswindel/music.htm
- And more… http://www.tvkmusic.com/songlist/ceremony.htm

Wedding Photography

One of the most important features of the wedding is the pictures and the stories that go with them. Ask the students to interview their parents about their weddings and to look at their wedding albums. Follow this activity by having the students look at the wedding pictures at Storytellers Photography. To practice voice, have the students develop a character. Ask them to choose a picture, copy it to a word processor and write about the person or one of the people in the picture. Encourage them to write about what the person is thinking, what the person likes, dislikes, his or her favorite saying, movie, food, color, etc. Print your character sketches and place them in a class wedding album.

- Storytellers Photography http://www.storytellersphotography.com/
- 6+1 Writing Traits Overview http://www.nwrel.org/eval/writing/
- 6+1 Writing Traits: Voice http://the-english-room.tripod.com/writing/writing_traits_voice.htm
- Personality Sketch: Puppetools http://www.puppetools.com/

June 27, 1859
Mildred J. Hill
Teacher, Mildred Hill, with her sister, originally wrote the melody to Happy Birthday as a greeting song for her young students. It is one of the best-known melodies in the world. Sing Happy Birthday to Mildred.

Happy Birthday to You
- Fun Facts about Happy Birthday http://www.ibiblio.org/team/fun/birthday/
- Burt Wolf: Birthdays All Over
  http://www.salon.com/travel/food/col/wolf/2000/03/09/birthday/print.html

Challenge your students to write other songs, perhaps about other events in June, using this familiar melody.[2]

---

[i] HomeArts: Maurice Sendak http://homearts.com/depts/relat/sendakb3.htm June 26, 2001
[ii] HomeArts: Maurice Sendak http://homearts.com/depts/relat/sendakbb.htm June 26, 2001
[iii] *Barbara Frietchie*, by John Greenleaf Whittier http://users.erols.com/kfraser/union/homefront/frietchie.html June 24, 2001
[iv] The Life of Helen Keller http://www.graceproducts.com/keller/life.html June 18, 2001
[v] Time 100 *The Miracle of Helen Keller* by Diane Schuur and David Jackson http://www.time.com/time/time100/heroes/profile/keller01.html June 20, 2001
[vi] Wedding Customs and Superstitions http://www.weddings.co.uk/info/tradsupe.htm#dresscolour June 17, 2001

5/7/2002

---

[2] *Take me out of the bathtub*, by Alan Katz, Margaret McElderry; ISBN: 0689829035, has lots of new songs sung to familiar melodies.

July

We hold these truths to be self-evident, that all men are created equal, that they are endowed by their Creator with certain unalienable Rights, that among these are Life, Liberty and the pursuit of Happiness.

Thomas Jefferson - *Declaration of Independence*

Month

Picnic Month
July is Hot Dog Month, Baked Beans Month and Ice Cream Month; sounds like Picnic Month to me! The picnic is one of our oldest traditions. In fact, ladies brought hampers of food with them when they watched the Battle of Bull Run, one of the first battles of the Civil War. Perhaps, we should plan a picnic in a park instead of a battlefield.

The Park
To help students understand that a map represents real places, make a map of your local park. First, draw an outline map of your local park identifying street boundaries. Then, take your students and digital camera on a field trip to the park. Take pictures of the students on the playground, by the picnic tables, on the basketball court, under the biggest tree, on a bench, etc. When you get back to the classroom, print your pictures and place them on the map in the proper location. Have the students enhance the map by drawing additional trees, flowers and the compass rose.

The Food
Besides hot dogs, baked beans and ice cream, what else should we have? Check out these picnic recipes. Recipes offer many different authentic math activities. You can double or half the recipes, learn measurements, figure the cost of the ingredients and many more with the added plus factor that you get to eat the results. What will work best in your classroom?
- Winnie the Pooh's Picnic Cookbook http://100-acrewood.virtualave.net/picnic/pic.html
- Plan a Picnic http://www.recipeamerica.com/picnic.htm
- Lemonade http://www.acplace.com/Special/Lpicnic.htm#lemonade
- Backyard Summer Fruit Smoothie http://www.recipe.com/whatcook/recipes/picnicsmoothie.htm

It Always Seem to Rain
You will want to check on the weather. Challenge the students to find a place where it is raining, the sun is shining, it's over 90 degrees, it's less than 60 degrees. Ask questions such as "Where would you need an umbrella?"
- Weather.com http://www.weather.com/

And for some theme and lesson plans.....
- Picnic http://www.blackdog4kids.com/holiday/summer/go/picnic/index.html
- Picnic Theme http://childfun.com/themes/picnic.shtml
- Picnic Activities http://www.perpetualpreschool.com/picnic/picnic.htm

Teddy Bears Picnic

Top off your month of picnic studies with a Teddy Bear Picnic. About.com has a very nice site to begin with. It has links to crafts and coloring pages and more. Put on the Teddy Bear's Picnic midi while you work.

- Teddy Bear Picnic http://www.dltk-kids.com/crafts/teddy/index.html
- Teddy Bear's Picnic midi and lyrics http://www.niehs.nih.gov/kids/lyrics/teddy.htm

And, more Teddy Bear Sites

- Teddy Bear Fun http://www.geocities.com/~chicky-ma-ma/teddy.html
- Marilee's Teddy Bear and Real Bear Activities and Links http://www.ameritech.net/users/macler/bears.html

Odds and Ends

Cathy's Picnic doesn't have much to do with a picnic, but it does have really neat interactive activities for kids.

- Cathy's Picnic http://www.geocities.com/Heartland/7134/

Think safety first when you're talking about picnic foods.

- Picnic Food Safety http://www.allsands.com/Health/Advice/picnicfoodsafe_wud_gn.htm

Improve listening skills for all of your students. Ask them to listen to this conversation about planning a picnic. Then answer the questions. This is a scenario for older students, but you could record a similar conversation for younger students.

- The Picnic http://www.esl-lab.com/picnic/picrd1.htm#pre

The Lemonade Stand is not really a picnic related site, but is an excellent, online simulation that teaches the basics of supply and demand in a kid-friendly way.

- The Lemonade Stand http://www.littlejason.com/lemonade/

Hot Dogs

Did you know that Americans consume 7 billion hot dogs between Memorial Day and Labor Day? Or, that the Hot Dog Council estimates Americans will consume more than 2 billion hot dogs during National Hot Dog Month this July?[i] To learn other interesting things about hot dogs, go to the National Hot Dog and Sausage Council Homepage. It also has great recipes!

- National Hot Dog and Sausage Council http://www.hot-dog.org/
  - How the hot dog got its name http://www.hot-dog.org/TheHFiles.htm

Hop Aboard the Wienermobile

Oh, I wish I were an Oscar Mayer….
You know the rest.

Oscar Mayer has some fun online activities for you to enjoy. And in honor of Foreign Language Month, you can even learn the jingle in Spanish.

- Oscartown http://www.kraftfoods.com/oscar-mayer/om_index.html?B=1&L=4
- Hot Dog Construction Zone http://www.kraftfoods.com/html/features/hotdog/index.html?B=1&L=4
- The Wienermobile http://www.kraftfoods.com/oscar-mayer/wmobile/index.html
- Oacar Mayer Jingle Jukebox http://www.kraftfoods.com/oscar-mayer/fun/jingles.htm

While you're at the Kraft Foods site, visit Oh Yeah? KoolAid. This site also has cool games and stuff, too. There is even a recipe for making KoolAid play dough to make those picnic ants.

- KoolAid http://www.kraftfoods.com/kool-aid/ka_index.html?B=1&L=4

Hot Dog Stands
Some say the first hot dogs came from the famous Coney Island. Some say they got their name from a dog show. Whatever story you believe, you will enjoy looking at these colorful hot dog stands.
- Coney Island http://www.pbs.org/wgbh/amex/coney/
- A Hot Dog Program http://www.wqed.org/tv/natl/hotdogs/
- Hot dog stands http://www.dinercity.com/driveIn/driveIns.html

And if you think there are hot dog stands just in America, think again.
- Danish Hot Dog Stands http://www.steff.dk/engelsk/Customers/Export/Catering/Polsevognskoncept/polsevognskoncept.html

Baked Beans

"Beans, beans, the musical fruit..."
Maybe you don't want to go there!

The people of Boston began baking beans in colonial times when Boston was one angle of the triangle slavery trade – molasses, slaves, rum. On a lighter note, go to Deb's Fun Page *(you may want to preview this in the privacy of your own home.)*
- Why is Boston called Beantown? http://www.boston-online.com/faq.html#beantown
- Deb's Fun Page http://www.debsfunpages.com/beansp.htm

Recipes
One of the oldest baked bean companies in America is B&M Baked Beans. They've been baking beans and canning them since 1867. Check out their history and enjoy one of their new recipes. How about cheesy bean dip? You could do this one in the classroom.
- B& M Baked Beans http://www.bmbeans.com/
- Root Beer Baked Beans http://www.dianaskitchen.com/page/beans/beerbean.htm (just thought you might like this unusual recipe)

History Cooks
One of the staples of the cowboy and pioneer food was beans...baked, stewed and in soup. Learn a little more about the history of beans and the history of your other favorite foods.
- Westward Ho! Frontier Life and Exploration http://www.lib.ucdavis.edu/exhibits/food/panel3.html
- History Cooks http://www.historycooks.com
- K-12 Food History Lesson Resources http://www.gti.net/mocolib1/kid/food2.html
  - Food Timeline http://www.gti.net/mocolib1/kid/food.html

Odds and Ends
You might as well join them. I know you want to know. What does make gas?
- Yucky.com http://yucky.kids.discovery.com/flash/body/yuckystuff/belch/js.index.html

Nutritionists tell us that we should be eating more legumes. But, what are they? There is some really great information for kids about the food pyramid at the last site. It is presented in an interesting and entertaining manner. Let the kids explore.
- What Are Legumes? http://www.general.uwa.edu.au/u/climaweb/legumes.htm
- FYI: Nutrition and Childhood Lead Poisoning http://www.ag.ohio-state.edu/~ohioline/hyg-fact/5000/5536.html
- The Food Pyramid http://kidshealth.org/kid/stay_healthy/food/pyramid.html

Ice Cream

"I scream, you scream,
we all scream for ice cream!"

- Traditional

What's your favorite?

Vanilla, chocolate, strawberry or cookie dough? Whatever it is, your students will enjoy playing at Ben and Jerry's. Ben and Jerry are always on the lookout for a new flavor. Have your students make up a flavor that is destined to become the next Chunky Monkey! Have them write two description paragraphs of their new flavor of the month. Discuss objective and subjective writing. Use the column feature on your word processor. On one column, key *objective* and on the other, key *subjective*. Brainstorm a list of descriptive words for the ice cream putting the word in either the objective column (95% butter fat) or the subjective column (delicious). When the students have a good list of descriptive words, write two paragraphs. Using the words from the objective column, write one paragraph and using the words from the subjective column, write a subjective paragraph. Which one do you think best describes the new flavor of ice cream? Which one sounds more appealing? Which one is going to sell the idea to Ben and Jerry? I don't know if you are adventurous enough to try one of the new flavors, but just plain vanilla coffee can ice cream is great!

- Ben and Jerry's http://www.benjerry.com/
- How to make with coffee can http://www.kidsdomain.com/holiday/july4/canicecream.html

Odds and Ends

I was surprised to read that Alexander the Great enjoyed honey flavored snow, an early version of ice cream. The International Dairy Foods Association has a very nice history of ice cream.

- From the Cow to the Cone http://www.idfa.org/news/icmonth/page6.htm
- The History of Ice Cream http://www.idfa.org/news/icmonth/page7.htm
- The Cone http://www.idfa.org/news/icmonth/page8.htm

This is a nice little thematic unit that focuses on ice cream.

- Ice Cream Theme http://childfun.com/themes/icecream.shtml

Foreign Language Month

As we celebrate two of the major holiday celebrations this month, Canada Day and Bastille Day, we recognize the need to understand and speak a foreign language. Also, as we look at the World Population Day data, we see that Spanish is the second most spoken language in America. I hope you take this opportunity to learn a little bit more about foreign languages in our schools and to speak a few words and phrases.

- ERIC: K-12 Foreign Language Education
  http://www.accesseric.org:81/resources/ericreview/vol6no1/
- Standards for Foreign Language Learning
  http://www.accesseric.org/resources/ericreview/vol6no1/standard.html

Learn to Count

One of the easy things for children to learn in a foreign language is how to count. Using a publishing program or even a word processor, have the students make a number chart for your room. Give each student a different number. Have them find a clip art picture and then the number word in English, French and Spanish. Use the Babel Fish translator at AltaVista. You might want to use a common theme, like "I'm going on a trip and I'm going to bring….one suitcase, two sweaters, etc.

- Translate with Babel Fish http://world.altavista.com/

ONE	UNO	UN

Where's the bathroom?

At Foreign Languages for Travelers, you can find simple phrases in just about any language. Use a world map for a background for your bulletin board. With the students, decide what phrase or phrases you think would be important for a traveler to know. Have students look up the phrase in different languages, print them out and with map tacks, attach them to the appropriate country. Of course, when we travel, we also need to know what time it is and how much our money's worth. Add this information to your map.

- Travel Languages http://www.travlang.com/languages/
- World Map http://www.lib.utexas.edu/maps/world.html
- World Time Zones http://www.worldtimezone.com/
- Currency Converter http://www.virtualtourist.com/cgi-bin/currency.vtc?s=J

Common Courtesies

Learn to say common phrases such as good morning, please, thank you, etc. Use them throughout the month. The BBC offers a Quick Fix for French and Spanish as well as other languages. This is a great way to learn some helpful phrases. It is also important to learn local customs. This site will guide you.

- Languages http://www.bbc.co.uk/education/languages/index.shtml

Classroom Labels

Have the students make labels for the objects in the classroom such as pencil sharpener, sink, books, etc. These sites should help them find the correct word.

For some short online courses in French, refer to these sites:

- Say it in French: A ...online course http://culturel.org/ALF/
- Fast and Friendly French for Fun
  http://www.thinkquest.org/library/lib/site_sum_outside.html?tname=12447&url=12447/
- French Alphabet http://library.thinkquest.org/12447/lecon1.html#letr

And, for some online courses in Spanish, refer to these sites:

- Spanish http://eleaston.com/spanish.html
- Spanish Course for Beginners http://www.sispain.org/english/course/calgary/index.html
- Learn Spanish Online http://www.studyspanish.com/

Some Cool Links

Tennessee Bob's Globe Gate Project has links to sites about culture, literature and language.

- Globe Gate Project http://globegate.utm.edu/french/globe.html
  - Spanish http://globegate.utm.edu/spanish/span.html
  - French http://www.utm.edu/departments/french/french.html

Little Explorers Picture Dictionary

Not only for little kids, this is fun for everyone. It is a picture dictionary in five different languages with links to various entries.

- Little Explorers Picture Dictionary http://www.enchantedlearning.com/Dictionary.html

Special Week

1ˢᵗ Week
Space Week
Space Week is celebrated in July to commemorate the space firsts that happened in July. Of course, Neil Armstrong's 1ˢᵗ step on the moon, but also the Mars Pathfinder landed on Mars, July 4, 1997, Japan launched its 1ˢᵗ space mission to Mars, July 4, 1998, Telstar, the 1ˢᵗ privately owned satellite and the 1ˢᵗ to relay live TV pictures across the Atlantic was launched July 10, 1962, and Apollo-Soyuz linkup marking the 1ˢᵗ joint USA and USSR space mission, July 17, 1975. It was also in July that the 1ˢᵗ woman walked in space, Cosmonaut Swetlana Savitskaya and the 1ˢᵗ female commander, Colonel Eileen Collins, led a shuttle mission.

World Space Week is celebrated in October, however, there are excellent resources available at the web site that can be used anytime. Download the teacher's manual for ideas and projects. The Space Day site also has resources, projects and lesson plans, plus many interactive and multimedia features for students. These would be excellent resources to use for planning your Space Week celebrations.

- World Space Week http://www.spaceweek.org/
- Space Day http://www.spaceday.com/

Field Trip
It's the next best thing to being there. We don't know how many of our students will ever have the opportunity to travel in outer space, but we all can take a virtual field trip to any planet. There is a really great tour at Space.com. *Note: Space.com is an online magazine about space, with many current articles; it also has marvelous pictures. However, it is not designed just for students, so pick and choose what you think is appropriate.*

- Space.com http://www.space.com
  - Virtual Planet Tour http://www.space.com/php/reference/virtualspacetour

Comparative Study
Have the students do a research project that compares and contrasts Earth and another planet. Prepare a list of topics to research, such as distance from the sun, number of moons, etc. Write the questions on the top of the Venn diagram. Place the answers inside the circles. Using a word processor, write a report comparing and contrasting the two planets. When the report is complete, have the students use the rubric for peer evaluation. Give the students an opportunity to use the evaluation to make changes if necessary before handing in their final project.

- Virtual Solar System http://www.nationalgeographic.com/solarsystem/index.html
- Welcome to the Planets http://pds.jpl.nasa.gov/planets/welcome.htm
- 9 Planets Multimedia Tour http://seds.lpl.arizona.edu/billa/tnp/
- Venn Diagram
  http://curry.edschool.virginia.edu/go/edis771/notes/graphicorganizers/graphic/index.htm
- Comparative Study Rubric http://edweb.sdsu.edu/triton/SDBiarritz/rubric.html

Curriculum Connections
Besides the obvious science and technology connections, the study of space offers opportunities for interdisciplinary studies. The Getty Museum has an excellent site that studies space art. I've found a couple of sites that have to do with math and space lends itself to dreaming, so what better way to express that dream and wonder than through poetry.

- Space Art Through the Ages
- http://www.getty.edu/artsednet/resources/Space/index.html

- Spacey Math http://www.learningplanet.com/sam/sm/spaceymath.htm
- Planet Finder http://www.lightandmatter.com/area2planet.shtml
- Bino Sky http://www.lightandmatter.com/binosky/binosky.html

When You Wish Upon A Star

How many nights have we looked for that first star and made a wish - sometimes for something great, like world peace and sometimes for something very personal like that new pony. Have your students express their wishes using the Never-ending poetry format. String all of your poems together. You might need to use the hallway!

- Never-ending I Wish Poem
  http://www.geocities.com/EnchantedForest/5165/pages/poetry_samples.html#neverending

What's In the Night's Sky?

Check out what is visible in the sky this week. Make a sky map of what you could see using a paint program. Fill the page with black and make the stars in white. Print out the star map and use a hole puncher to punch out the stars. Turn out your lights, and turn on your overhead projector. Project your star map on the ceiling. Wow!

- The Sky This Week http://www.usno.navy.mil/pao/sky/sky_week.shtml
- Earth and Sky Radio http://www.earthsky.com/
- Hubble Space Telescope http://www.stsci.edu/
- Summer Constellations
  http://www.geocities.com/EnchantedForest/Meadow/5115/astro/sucon.htm

Odds and Ends

The National Park Service offers an online theme study of historic landmarks related to our space program.

- Man in Space http://www.cr.nps.gov/history/online_books/butowsky4/

Looking for some great sites for kids? Sites that are full of information, games and interaction? Check these out!

- NASA Kids http://kids.msfc.nasa.gov/
- Space! http://www.uri.edu/ce/faceit/astronomy/

How about some unexplored space – right here on earth!

- Unexplored Space http://magma.nationalgeographic.com/2000/biodiversity/biomes/index.cfm

Resources for Teachers

These are some interesting lesson plans and resources to get your creative juices flowing.

- Educator's Resources http://observe.ivv.nasa.gov/nasa/education/edu_index.shtml.html
- Positive and Negative Space Art Project
  http://www.dickblick.com/lessonplans/positivenegativespace/
- Shuttle Off To Space http://www.teachnet.org/booktour/shawplan.htm
- Space Settlement Lesson Plan
  http://www.belmont.k12.ca.us/ralston/programs/itech/spsetlesson.html
- NYT Lesson Plan: NASA's Frontier
  http://www.nytimes.com/learning/teachers/lessons/981013tuesday_print.html
- Personal Space http://www.teachervision.com/lesson-plans/lesson-2154.html

Date Varies

Nadaam

Nadaam festival is a large community festival in Mongolia. The word Nadaam refers to the three manly sports: horse racing, archery and wrestling. The festival is held to honor various mountain gods. After the students read about Nadaam, have them write an article describing the festival and events. Because there are a number of terms that might be unfamiliar to the students or need further explanation, have them create pages that explain or define the term or event. In their report, create hyperlinks to the explanations or definitions.

- Nadaam http://www.csen.org/Mongol.Nadaam/Mongol.text.html
- The Alternative Olympics http://www.gluckman.com/Naadam.html
- Nadaam Festival http://www.babylontravel.net/english/travelyarns/e-frame_mongolia.htm

Learn More About Mongolia

Where is Mongolia? What are the people like? What is the environment like?
- United Nations in Mongolia http://www.un-mongolia.mn/mongolia/
- National Geographic Map Machine: Mongolia
  http://plasma.nationalgeographic.com/mapmachine/plates.html

Marco Polo

Retrace the steps of famous explorer, Marco Polo. In 1271, young Marco Polo with his father and uncle left his home in Venice, Italy to explore the lands to the East. He was to be gone twenty-four years. Follow his adventures as he meets Mongol emperor, Kublai Khan, with this National Geographic Expeditions. The second Marco Polo site is not really about the explorer, Marco Polo, but is a fantastic Internet resource for educators. Set aside some time to review this resource and plan for how you can use it in your curriculum. *Note: There is online as well as other free training available. Show this site to your colleagues and arrange for faculty inservice.*

- Marco Polo http://www.nationalgeographic.com/ngm/0105/feature1/index.html
- Marco Polo Internet Content for the Classroom http://marcopolo.worldcom.com/

Special Days

July 1
Canada Day

Canada Day celebrates the events that occurred on July 1, 1867, when the British North America Act created the Canadian federal government. Through the years, the day has had other names, such a Dominion Day. It was officially changed to Canada Day in 1982. Learn how Canadians celebrate their Independence Day.

- Canada Day http://www.southam.com/nmc/ohcanada/news/origin.html
- Canada Day http://kidexchange.about.com/library/weekly/aa062798.htm

Canadian Symbols

We are celebrating three countries' Independence Day this month; Canada, the United States and France. Begin a table that will eventually be completed with information about all three countries. It could be set up something like this. Of course you will add or subtract categories to fit your needs.

Country	Canada	United States	France
Flag			
National Anthem	O Canada	Star Spangled Banner	Marseillaise
Date of Independence	July 1, 1867	July 4, 1776	July 14, 1789
Language	English / French	English	French

- About Canada http://canada.gc.ca/main_e.html
- Kids Canada http://www.cio-bic.gc.ca/kc_e.html
- Ceremonial and Canadian Symbols http://www.pch.gc.ca/ceremonial-symb/english/index.html
- Canada National Anthem http://www.pch.gc.ca/ceremonial-symb/english/emb_anthem.html

Odds and Ends
Be inspired by the awesome sight of the Canadian Mounties.
- Royal Canadian Mounted Police http://www.rcmp-grc.gc.ca/index_e.htm
Play some games, color some pictures and get your maps of Canada.
- Canadian Games http://www.pch.gc.ca/ceremonial-symb/english/emb_anthem.html
Learn Canada crafts
- Canadian Crafts http://www.kidsdomain.com/craft/_canada.html
Get to know some famous Canadians.
- Canadian, eh? http://www.southam.com/nmc/ohcanada/canadianeh.html
Hungry? This mom will teach you about Canadian Cooking
- Mom's Cooking http://www.momscooking.com/Canmain.htm
Help your students learn the correct Canadian spelling.
- Canadian English http://www.cornerstoneword.com/misc/cdneng/cdneng.htm

July 1, 1874
1st U.S. Zoo
The first public zoo in the United States opened in Philadelphia, PA, July 1, 1874. Take a virtual field trip of this historic zoo.
- Philadelphia Zoo http://www.philadelphiazoo.org/
- The Philadelphia Zoo http://www.panix.com/~teej/zoo/
Want to visit some other zoos? How about the famous San Diego Zoo, or a zoo in Sweden or Alaska? Zoos.com will help you find it. You won't want to miss the National Zoo in Washington D.C.
- Zoo.com http://www.zoos.com
- National Zoo http://natzoo.si.edu/

Virtual Zoo
Make your own class virtual zoo. Have the students decide what areas or themes you want to have in your zoo. For instance, you might have a zoo of animals native to your state, or animals from the tropics, or a petting zoo. Then, give each student an animal to research. They will need to find a picture of the animals, perhaps the sound the animal makes, the natural habitat of the animal, etc. Using either HyperStudio or PowerPoint, have the students make a slide for their animal. Combine all of the slides for your virtual zoo. You could also have the students print out the shape of their animal and copy the information to make a Zoo Book.

Virtual Zoo
South Dakota

BUFFALO   HONEY BEE
        DEER
COYOTE   RACCOON
        EAGLE
PHEASANT   WALLEYE

"buffalosd.jpg"

http://pics.tech4learning.com

The mature male weighs 1,980 pounds and stands 6 1/2 feet.

American Bison

This magnificent animal is commonly known as the buffalo. It is native to North America. It once roamed the plains by the thousands. The buffalo was the main source of food, shelter, clothing, and tools for the Native Americans.

Encyclopedia Britanica "Bison"
http://www.britanica.com/eb/article?eu=82455&tocid=0&query=american%20bison
August 7, 2001

- Pics4Learning http://pics.tech4learning.com/ (copyright free images)
- Encyclopedia Britannica http://www.britannica.com/
- Animal Sounds http://netvet.wustl.edu/sounds.htm
- Animal Shape Books http://www.abcteach.com/Animals/AnimalShapeMenu.htm

Odds and Ends

Would you like the Zoomobile to visit your school? It can - or at least a virtual one can.
- Cyber Zoomobile http://www.primenet.com/~brendel/

This ThinkQuest project will keep your students active and involved.
- Virtual Zoo
  http://www.thinkquest.org/library/lib/site_sum_outside.html?tname=11922&url=11922/index.htm

These are a couple of more sites your students will enjoy.
- Zoo Net for Kids http://members.aol.com/zoonetkids/index.htm
- The Electronic Zoo http://netvet.wustl.edu/e-zoo.htm

July 1, 1941
TV Broadcast

No one person is credited with inventing the television or country for that matter. But in 1941, NBC and CBS were issued commercial broadcasting licenses and the modern television era was born. There were 400 black and white television receivers. By 1974 more than 97% of American homes had one or more television sets. Use the Timeline Generator to make a timeline about the development of the television.
- Television Milestones http://www.pbs.org/wgbh/amex/technology/bigdream/milestones.html
- History of Television http://www.rcc.ryerson.ca/schools/rta/brd038/clasmat/class1/tvhist.htm
- Timeline Generator http://www.teach-nology.com/web_tools/materials/bigtimeline/

Take A Field Trip

There are a number of museums you can visit to see early television sets and clips from different TV shows.
- Museum of Television http://www.mztv.com/
- Inventing Television http://www.inventorsmuseum.com/television.htm
- Museum of Radio and Television http://www.mtr.org/
- TV Land http://www.tvland.com/TVL.jhtml

Produce and Direct a Commercial

Commercials influence what we wear, what we eat, what movie we see, what car we drive and just about everything in between. The Power of Image webquest helps students understand the impact commercials have on our lives. After looking at some classic commercials, have the students develop a commercial for a new product. The Chef Boyardee site shows you how to use storyboards to design a commercial. Then, use the storyboard cards to design the commercial. Finally, put the commercial together. Students can use either video camera or a presentation tool for their final product.

- Power of Image: Television Commercial WebQuest http://www.harwich.edu/depts/lmcelm/tvadtchr.htm
- Clio Awards http://www.clioawards.com/html/main.cgi
- Directory of Ads (with audio) http://dmoz.org/Arts/Television/Commercials/
- Advertising Age http://adage.com/news_and_features/special_reports/tv/
- Storyboard Cards http://www.harwich.edu/depts/lmcelm/mlws2.htm
- Chef Boyardee Commercial http://www.chefboy.com/
- You Rule School http://www.youruleschool.com

Make a Pitch

New television shows always begin with a pitch – a story outline. Have the students develop a pitch for a new TV show. They will need to decide on a category, such as sit-com, police, game show, variety, etc. the main characters, the setting, possible story lines. Divide the students into groups. Use the graphic organizer details to get started. Have each group develop their pitch and present it to another class. The other class will vote on which new show will be produced for the up-coming year. Use a presentation tool for this project.

- Library of Graphic Organizers: details http://curry.edschool.virginia.edu/go/edis771/notes/graphicorganizers/graphic/index.htm

What's On?

Use a spreadsheet to develop a primetime wish list. Put students in charge and have them make a schedule of their favorite TV shows so that there will be no conflicts. Have the students use the auto fill feature to complete the Days of the Week and the Time. Format the Time cells for standard time.

My TV Schedule

Time	Sunday	Monday	Tuesday	Wednesday	Thursday	Friday	Saturday
4:00 PM							
4:30 PM							
5:00 PM							
5:30 PM							
6:00 PM							
6:30 PM							
7:00 PM							
7:30 PM							
8:00 PM							
8:30 PM							
9:00 PM							
9:30 PM							
10:00 PM							

Note: Word of caution - these sites are designed for all viewers, not just children.
Television Web Sites
- ABC http://www.abc.com
- CBS http://www.cbs.com

- NBC http://www.nbc.com
- PBS http://www.pbs.org
- Nick http://www.nick.com
- ESPN http://www.espn.com
- Disney http://www.disney.com

What's Your Favorite?

Survey other classes, school personnel, friends and family to find the all time favorite TV show. Use a spreadsheet to record your date. You might want to keep track of age of the participants, type of show, cartoons, dramas, sit-coms, etc.

How much is too much?

The average child watches 3 to 4 hours of television daily. By the age of 12, the child has witnessed 100,000 acts of violence.[ii] How much is too much and does it have a negative effect on children? Help students make positive choices for their lives and give parents a heads-up.

- Children and Watching TV http://www.familyresource.com/parenting/43/187/
- Children and TV Violence http://www.aacap.org/publications/factsfam/violence.htm
- Violence on Television http://www.apa.org/pubinfo/violence.html
- Children and TV Violence http://www.familyresource.com/parenting/43/178/
- Children and TV Violence http://www.parenthoodweb.com/parent_cfmfiles/pros.cfm?n=247

July 2, 1919
Jean Craighead George's Birthday

Jean Craighead George's mother and father, brothers and sisters, aunts and uncles were all naturalists so it was natural for her to develop an interest in wildlife. She began writing when in the 3rd grade and hasn't stopped yet. She has written over 100 books. There are many excellent resources on the Internet about her life, her books and her writing.

- Jean Craighead George: Links http://www.indiana.edu/~eric_rec/ieo/bibs/george.html
- Teacher Resource File: Jean Craighead George http://falcon.jmu.edu/~ramseyil/george.htm

Write – Write – Write

On her web page, Ms George offers suggestions for writing with some 'prods' to get the ideas flowing. Fire up the word processor and have the students follow her plan. While at the Jean Craighead George Homepage, be sure to go to the Sights and Sounds. There are some excellent multimedia segments.

- Jean Craighead George http://www.jeancraigheadgeorge.com/

Story Grammar

Ms George also discusses story grammar. If your students need a refresher course on story grammar, abcteach has a very nice worksheet.

- Story Grammar http://www.abcteach.com/Reading/storygrammar.htm

KidViews

Have your students write a review of one of Ms Geroge's books and submit it to Education Place. They can also read reviews written by other students.

- Write Your Own Review http://www.eduplace.com/kids/rdg/chall.html

Some of Ms George's Books

Julie of the Wolves – Newbery Award

My Side of the Mountain – Newbery Honor

Acorn Pancakes & Dandelion Salad and 38 Other Wild Recipes

Animals Who Have Won Our Hearts

Artic Son

The Big Book for Our Planet

The Case of the Missing Cutthroats: An Ecological Mystery

The Cry of the Crow: A Novel

Dear Rebecca, Winter is Here

The First Thanksgiving

Giraffe Trouble

July 4
Independence Day

5 Quick Things To Do

1. Listen to the songs from the Broadway musical, 1776.
   - 1776 the Musical http://www.geocities.com/musical1776/
   - 1776 Midi http://www.hamienet.com/Broadway_Musical/0-9/1776/
2. Make some great decorations.
   - Great Projects http://www.hp.com/printing_ideas/seasonal_gallery/s_09.html
3. View the Original Declaration of Independence
   - Library of Congress http://www.loc.gov/exhibits/jefferson/jeffdec.html
4. Color a Poster
   - Happy 4th of July http://www.dltk-kids.com/usa/images/uspicture5.gif
5. Unscramble the 4th of July Puzzle http://www.kidsdomain.com/holiday/july4/games/slider2.html

> *"Yet through all the gloom I can see the rays of ravishing light and glory. I can see that the end is worth all the means. This is our day of deliverance. With solemn acts of devotion we ought to commemorate it, with pomp and parade...with shows and games, sports and guns, bells and bonfires and illuminations from one end of the continent to the other...from this time forward and forevermore."*
>
> - John Adams[iii]

John Adams set the standard for our national day of celebration – the 4th of July! Start your day of celebration by watching the movie, *Declaring Independence*. Then, go to the National Archives to learn about the history of the Declaration of Independence and read these famous words, *"When in the course of human events..."*. Visit the Capitol and view John Trumbull's famous painting, the Signing of the Declaration of Independence.

- Declaring Independence http://earlyamerica.com/independence.htm
- History of the Declaration of Independence
  http://www.nara.gov/exhall/charters/declaration/dechist.html
  - Declaration of Independence
    http://www.nara.gov/exhall/charters/declaration/declaration.html
- The Signing of the Declaration of Independence
  http://www.aoc.gov/cc/art/rotunda/declaration_independence.htm

Learn more about the men who were instrumental in writing the Declaration of Independence. Ask small groups of students to prepare presentation about one of the original signers of the Declaration of Independence.

- Adams and Jefferson http://www.pbs.org/ktca/liberty/chronicle/adams-jefferson.html
- John Adams http://www.infoplease.com/ipa/A0760588.html
- John Adams: Unsung Hero of the American Revolution
  http://www.universalway.org/johnadams.html

- Thomas Jefferson http://www.infoplease.com/ipa/A0760627.html
- James Monroe http://www.infoplease.com/ipa/A0760590.html
- Benjamin Franklin http://sln.fi.edu/franklin/rotten.html
- Colonial Hall: A Look at America's Founders http://www.colonialhall.com/index.asp
- Happy Birthday, America http://www.geocities.com/EnchantedForest/Dell/7002/july4.html

For an absolutely tremendous database of information about the 4th of July, including chronologies, speeches, stories and much more, refer to the 4th of July Database of Celebration. It has, for instance information about the first 4th of July celebrations.

> The first "official" state celebration of the Fourth as recognized under resolve of a legislature occurred in Massachusetts in 1781. Boston was the first municipality (city/town) to officially designate July Fourth as a holiday, in 1783. Alexander Martin of North Carolina was the first governor to issue a state order (in 1783) for celebrating Independence Day on the Fourth of July.[iv]

- 4th of July Database of Celebration http://www.american.edu/heintze/fourth.htm

With Pomp and Parade, Shows and Games

The way Americans celebrate Independence Day is a varied as the Americans who are doing the celebrating. Click on these web sites to get some ideas for planning your class celebration. Add to the table begun on Canada Day.

- God Bless America http://www.geocities.com/Athens/Acropolis/1465/july4th.html
  Anne's 4th of July Symbols and Things http://www.annieshomepage.com/fourthsymbols.html
- The Holiday Place: 4th of July http://www.theholidayspot.com/july4/index.htm
- Kids Domain 4th of July Fun http://www.kidsdomain.com/holiday/july4/
- 4th of July http://members.aol.com/Donnpages/USHolidays.html#4th

And Bonfires and Illuminations

Turn out the lights, start the America the Beautiful midi and project on a big screen these great firework displays. Get ready to oooh and ahhh!

- Fireworks Arts
  http://www.lessonplanspage.com/ArtSS4thOfJulyArtProjectFireworksDislplay12.htm
- Watch Fireworks http://www.geocities.com/EnchantedForest/Dell/7002/fireworks.html
- Fireworks http://www.factmonster.com/spot/fireworks1.html
- America the Beautiful midi http://wilstar.com/midi/amerbeau.mid
- The Sky Concert http://home.kscable.com/cyberskyconcert/index.html

July 4, 1895
America the Beautiful
1st appeared in print

Katherine Lee Bates wrote the original lyrics to America the Beautiful in 1893 after she and a group of friends climbed to the top of Pike Peak. As she says, "… *when I saw the view, I felt great joy. All the wonder of America seemed displayed there, with the sea-like expanse."* The final version was written in 1913. Read the original lyrics and compare them to the version we sing today.

- Original Lyrics http://www.fuzzylu.com/falmouth/bates/america.html
  - Katherine Lee Bates http://www.fuzzylu.com/falmouth/bates/klbnotes.html
- America the Beautiful http://www.wellesley.edu/PublicAffairs/Commencement/klbates.html
- America the Beautiful Sing Along http://www.melodylane.net/america.html

Field Trip to Pikes Peak

- Pikes Peak Cam http://www.pikespeakcam.com/
- Pikes Peak Ranger District http://www.fs.fed.us/r2/psicc/pp/

Music Video

Use the midi for America the Beautiful and pictures create a music video. Have different groups of students prepare the various verses. Combine them and have the midi play continuously. Use pictures your students take with the digital camera of your city and neighborhood.

- Midi http://ingeb.org/songs/americat.html
- Pic4Learning http://pics.tech4learning.com/
- America the Beautiful http://www.geocities.com/Athens/Acropolis/1465/america.html

July 11, 1944
Patricia Polacco's Birthday

Acclaimed children's author and illustrator, Patricia Polacco, didn't begin writing children's books until she was 41. She ad always loved stories and reports that some of the best times she had growing up was with her grandparents, listening to family stories. But, as a child, she had a hard time learning to read until one of her teachers discovered that she had dyslexia and got her the help she needed to be successful in school. She calls that teacher one of her heroes. The Patricia Polacco Homepage is wonderful resource. It has pictures, audio and video segments, games and puzzles. Enjoy!

- Patricia Polacco http://www.patriciapolacco.com/newsite/homefs.html
- Biography http://www.scils.rutgers.edu/special/kay/polacco.html
- Patricia Polacco http://coe.west.asu.edu/students/dcorley/authors/Polacco.htm

Telling Stories

Ms Polacco says that because of her dyslexia, reading and writing were very difficult for her, so she became very good at telling stories. Have the students think of a story about some event in their life or someone in their family. It could be about the best or worst Christmas present they ever got, a terrible bike accident, the time their dog ate their homework, etc. Ask them to just jot down a few details on a piece of notepaper under the headings of beginning middle and end. Then have them find a partner and tell the story to their partner. The partner needs to listen carefully not interrupting. At the end of the story, the partner should ask questions to clarify the story, such as 'why were you on that road, were you wearing your helmet?' This will help the storyteller identify the parts of the story that need more explanation. Ask the student to go back to their note card and fill in the answers to the questions. Tell the story again following the same procedure. Then, have the storyteller use a word processor to write the story just as he or she told it. Have the student read the story aloud to his or her partner. This time, ask the partner to ask very specific questions, such as 'what color was the dog, how big was the bike, how many stitches did you get?' This will help the storyteller add descriptive words to make the story more exciting. Go back to the word processor and edit the story for spelling and grammatical errors. Finally, make the final corrections and publish the story. By having the partner always ask questions, he or she is not being judgmental or criticizing the other person's work. Make a class book of Family Stories.

- Student Writing Checklist http://abcteach.com/Writing/checklist.htm

Understanding Dyslexia

Undoubtedly many students in your classroom will identify with Patricia Polacco's problems with learning how to read. For a refresher course about signs and symptoms of children with dyslexia refer to the Dyslexia Teacher. This site has lots of information for parents and teachers. The LD Online site offers information for teachers and parents about all types of learning disabilities. They also have a very good KidZone. Another excellent resource is Child Development Institute. One of the things I find students are always interested in is famous people who have dyslexia.

- Dyslexia Teacher http://www.dyslexia-teacher.com/
- LD Online http://www.ldonline.org/
  - KidZone http://www.ldonline.org/kidzone/kidzone.html

- About Dyslexia and Reading Problems http://www.cdipage.com/dyslexia.htm
  - Famous People with Attention Deficit and Learning Disorders
    http://www.cdipage.com/dyslexia.htm

Odds and Ends

Technology is really making a different for people with all types of disabilities. These sites might be helpful for students with dyslexia.

- Try a demo of text to speech technology @ AT&T
  http://www.naturalvoices.att.com/demos/index.html
- Check out WordQ Writing Aid Software – a word processor that predicts what the students is typing, @ WordQ http://www.wordq.com/
- Learn about technology assistance for people with reading difficulties @ Envision Technology
  http://www.envisiontechnology.org/
- Don Johnson develops software for special needs students. See what might be appropriate for your students @ http://www.donjohnston.com/
- View some of these free reading and writing videos for your students @ Reading and Writing
  http://www.learn-reading-writing.com/
- Lest we forget, 21 reasons why English is difficult to learn @
  http://www.ldresources.com/etext/funny/english_hard.txt
- Go to the mall…EnableMart has links to all the major providers of assistive technology @
  http://www.enablemart.com/store/Welcome

July 11, 1899
E.B. White's Birthday

"I have been writing all my life and see no relief in sight."

– E. B. White[v]

Elwyn Brooks White, called Andy by friends and family, was born in Mount Vernon, New York. After service in the Army during WWI, he graduated from Cornell University in 1921. He says, he began writing as soon as he could spell. Celebrate his birthday with an E. B. White Day.

- Daily Celebrations: E. B. White's Birthday http://www.dailycelebrations.com/071199.htm

Language Arts – Some Writer

White says that he got the idea for writing Charlotte's Web while he was in the barn watching the animals. The reader can the barn must be a very special place when he reads the chapter: The Barn. He uses all of his senses to describe the barn. Have the students think of a special place, such as their bedroom, their Grandmother's house, etc. Put that in the middle of a graphic organizer. Use the circle and boxes organizer. Put the special place in the circle and in each box place a different sense: smell, sight, hearing, touch, taste, with links to things that describe their special place. When the organizer is complete, use it to write a descriptive paragraph describing their special place.

- Library of Graphic Organizers
  http://curry.edschool.virginia.edu/go/edis771/notes/graphicorganizers/graphic/index.htm
- Describing the Real World http://teacher.scholastic.com/lessonrepro/lessonplans/nfict1.htm

Reading

One of White's best-known essays is *Once More To The Lake*. This Internet site provides the text and excellent discussion questions. This might be a little difficult for younger children.

- Once More To The Lake http://www.engl.virginia.edu/courses/enwr101/s97/33/reading/white.htm

Abcteach is an excellent resource for the younger students. They offer many different reading activities.

- Charlotte's Web http://www.abcteach.com/ebwhite/ebwhitetoc.htm

Science

When E. B. White was planning the story for Charlotte's Web, he had the basic storyline about a pig who needed to be saved, but needed a hero. Charlotte, the spider, became one of the most famous heroes in all of children's literature. But, what's the real scoop? This thematic unit plan about spiders is a first-rate resource.

- Spiders http://www.theteachersguide.com/crawlies.html#Spiders

Social Studies

E.B. White died of Alzheimer disease on October 1, 1985. Help your students learn about aging and Alzheimer's disease with this ThinkQuest activity.

- ThinkQuest: Understanding Human Behavior http://library.thinkquest.org/26618/index.html
- Alzheimer's Fact Sheet http://www.alzheimers.org/pubs/adfact.html
- Alzheimer's Association http://www.alz.org/
- How To Care For People with Alzheimer's http://www.connect.ie/users/waf/how.htm

Art

Garth Williams, a co-worker at the New Yorker, illustrated all of White's books plus Wilder's Little House books, books by Margaret Wise Brown and a number of Little Golden Books. He was also the author and illustrator of a delightful, if controversial, children's book called the Rabbit's Wedding where a charming white rabbit marries a dashing black rabbit. Amazon.com offers an opportunity to look at these illustrations. Williams worked very hard to have the illustrations for his books enhance, but not overwhelm the text.

- Garth Williams http://webpages.marshall.edu/~irby1/laura/garth.html
- Garth Williams http://www.winsor.edu/library2/ebgarth.htm

In the Times Book Review, Eudora Welty said Charlotte's Web was about friendship on earth, affection and protection, adventure and miracle, life and death, trust and treachery, pleasure and pain, and the passing of time. Referring to the book as a whole, she added, "*As a piece of work it is just about perfect.*"[vi]

Music

Yes, I know, it may be a little hokey, but you can't go wrong with a couple of lively choruses of Farmer in the Dell sung about the animals in Charlotte's Web.

- Farmer in the Dell http://www.heavenlywebs.net/midis/kidsmidis/index.htm
- Had a Little Rooster http://www.theteachersguide.com/Songs/had_a_little_roosterhad_a_little.htm

Biographical Information

- E. B. White http://www.harperchildrens.com/hch/author/author/white/
- Biographical Information http://www.winsor.edu/library2/ebbiog.htm
- E. B. White http://www.eduplace.com/kids/hmr/mtai/white.html
- E. B. White http://www.kirjasto.sci.fi/ebwhite.htm

Teacher Resources

- E. B. White – Some Writer! http://www.umcs.maine.edu/~orono/collaborative/white.html
- Teacher Resource File: E. B. White http://falcon.jmu.edu/~ramseyil/white.htm
- Life & Times: E. B. White http://www.nytimes.com/books/97/08/03/lifetimes/white.html
- E. B. White Corner From his niece http://www.aardvarkexpress.com/EBWhite.htm
- Letter to Children from E. B. White http://www.teachervision.com/lesson-plans/lesson-1734.html

Odds and Ends
Download a Chapter 1 of Charlotte's Web to your palm pilot.
- Charlotte's Web: Chapter 1 – Before Breakfast
  http://www.harperchildrens.com/catalog/excerpt_xml.asp?isbn=0060263857

Read children's reviews of Charlotte's Web.
- Children's Reviews: Charlotte's Web
  http://www.pbs.org/wgbh/zoom/reviews/charlottesweb.txt.shtml

Listen to Julie Andrews read selections from Stewart Little, Trumpet of the Swan and Charlotte's Web.
- New York Times http://www.nytimes.com/books/97/08/03/lifetimes/white.html

Look at the most recent copy of the New Yorker Magazine.
- The New Yorker http://www.newyorker.com/

July 11
World Population Day
As I sit here writing this book the world population stands at 6,165,976,904. What is it when you are reading it?
- World Pop Clock http://www.census.gov/cgi-bin/ipc/popclockw

Have the students use the World Population site to answer the following questions:
1. How many births are there per second?
2. How many deaths are there per second?
3. Are there more births or deaths per month?
4. Is the average growth rate increasing or decreasing?
5. What to you think caused the big decrease and then increase in population in the early 1960s?
- World Population http://www.census.gov/ipc/www/world.html

Look at the map of the United States and list the 5 most populated states and the 5 least populated states. Then have the students answer the following questions:
1. What is your states population?
2. Are there more males or females in your state?
3. What age bracket has the largest population in your state?

Have the students copy the information about race and paste it in a spreadsheet. Delete the rows and columns with subcategories. Make a chart of the population in your state by major race definition.
- U.S. Census Bureau http://www.census.gov/

The United Nations Cyber School Bus has information about the different countries that belong to the United Nations. The user can get statistical information for up to seven different countries at one time. This is a very easy to use database.
- United Nations Info-Nation Data Base
  http://www.un.org/Pubs/CyberSchoolBus/infonation/e_infonation.htm

July 12, 1960
Etch-A-Sketch
Etch-A-Sketch is one of those all time favorite childhood pastimes. Learn who created this wonderful toy and how it works. Then, play with an online version and see some all time masterpieces.
- Etch-A-Sketch http://www.etch-a-sketch.com/
  - Online Etch-A-Sketch http://www.etch-a-sketch.com/html/onlineetch.htm
- How Stuff Works: Etch-A-Sketch http://www.howstuffworks.com/question317.htm
- Meet Mr. Etch-A-Sketch http://seattlep-i.nwsource.com/lifestyle/etch21.shtml
- Gallery http://www.blarg.net/~redone/etch.html

Online Children's Toys

- Kids Ville: Creative Play http://www.kidsville.net/games/art.htm
- Lego http://www.lego.com
- Hot Wheels http://www.hotwheels.com
- Mattel http://www.mattel.com
- Fisher Price http://www.fisher-price.com/us/default.asp
- Milton Bradley http://www.scrabble.com/
- List of Toy Companies and URL
  http://www.bayinsider.com/partners/ktvu/consumer/2000_toy_companies.html

Create a Toy

What will be the next hula-hoop or Beanie Baby? Maybe the designer is right there in your class. See what your students can come up with. Use a publishing program to draw a blueprint.

Collecting Toys

Do you have toys in the attic that could be valuable? How about that old Barbie? What toys should your students be saving? Check it out at the Antique Road Show.

- Antique Road Show http://www.pbs.org/wgbh/pages/roadshow/
- Antique Road Show Jr. http://www.pbs.org/wgbh/pages/roadshow/series/jrroadshow/index.html
- Toy Collecting http://kidscollecting.about.com/cs/toys1/

July 14
Bastille Day

Bastille Day commemorates the storming of the Bastille on July 14, 1789. It symbolizes liberty, democracy and the struggle against all forms of oppression for the French people. Today, the holiday is celebrated with parades, speeches and fireworks. Read more about the French Independence Day.

- The French Fourth http://www.factmonster.com/spot/99bastilleday.html
- Bastille Day http://www.premier-ministre.gouv.fr/en/p.cfm?ref=6769
  - French National Anthem: Marseillaise http://www.premier-ministre.gouv.fr/en/p.cfm?ref=6773
- Bastille Day http://www.hightowertrail.com/Bastil.htm

Read the Declaration of the Rights of Man and compare it to the American Declaration of Independence.

- Declaration of the Rights of Man -1789 http://www.yale.edu/lawweb/avalon/rightsof.htm
- Declaration of Independence – 1776
  http://www.nara.gov/exhall/charters/declaration/declaration.html

Add Information to the Matrix

Find information about France and add it to the matrix comparing Canada, the United States and France.

- World Fact Book: France http://www.cia.gov/cia/publications/factbook/geos/fr.html
- Embassy of France http://www.info-france-usa.org/
- Just for Kids http://www.info-france-usa.org/kids/index.html

Odds and Ends

- Eiffle Tower Web Cam http://www.lecieldeparis.com/
- French Cooking http://www.momscooking.com/french.htm
- Map of France http://www.factmonster.com/atlas/country/france.html
- E-Pals from France http://www.epals.com/index_en.html

July 19, 1713
John Newbery's Birthday
John Newbery is known as the first children's book publisher and bookseller. He is also the author of
Little Goody Two Shoes – 1st book written for children. The prestigious children's book award, the
Newbery Award, is named in his honor. Read about this pioneer in the field of children's literature.
Some of these links have pictures of his original children's books.
- John Newbery http://www.comptons.com/encyclopedia/ARTICLES/0125/01313024_A.html
- Mr. John Newbery http://www.greenbay.co.uk/books/newbery.html (Little Goody Two Shoes)
- Biography http://www.iupui.edu/~engwft/newbery.htm (copies of original books)
- Short Biography with many links http://www.encyclopedia.com/articles/09147.html

Newbery Award
The first Newbery Award was awarded to Hendrik Willem van Loon for *The Story of Mankind* in 1922.
Since it's inception, the award has stood for excellence in children's literature. The American Library
Association's web site has the history of the award, current winners and lists of previous winners. Go to
their site and print out a copy of the award winners.
- Newbery Award http://www.ala.org/alsc/newbery.html
- Newbery Internet Field Trip http://teacher.scholastic.com/fieldtrp/childlit/newbery.htm

Newbery Display
Go to the library and look for all of the Newbery books. Have the students arrange them in chronological
order. What changes do the students notice? Rearrange the books this time by theme. If they haven't
read all of the, the fly often gives a synopsis of the story.

Attention Grabbers
Many children's author feel that they need to grab the readers attention with the first sentence or at least
with the first page. Have the students read just the first page of the Newbery books and vote on their
favorite. Then, have them write a first sentence. Vote for the best, the scariest, the funniest, the most
dramatic and any other category you can think of.
*Note: If you are looking for a lesson plan for Newbery books, use any search engine and search for: John
Newbery+ lesson plan.*

July 20
Moon Day

> *"That's one small step for a man, one giant leap for mankind."*
>
> Neil Armstrong

Moon Day celebrates July 20, 1969, when after a four day trip, the Apollo astronauts arrived at the Sea of
Tranquility, Moon. At 10:56 p.m. Neil Armstrong became the first human to set foot on the Moon.
Approximately a half a billion people worldwide watched the landing and heard Neil Armstrong say,
"That's one small step for man, one giant leap for mankind." For the complete story of the history
making adventure, refer to the 30th Anniversary of Apollo Internet site.
- 30th Anniversary of Apollo 11, 1969-1999
  http://nssdc.gsfc.nasa.gov/planetary/lunar/apollo_11_30th.html
- The Astronauts
  o Neil Armstrong http://www.astronauts.org/astronauts/armstrong.htm
  o Buzz Aldrin http://www.astronauts.org/astronauts/aldrin.htm
The last man on the moon was astronaut Eugene Cernan. Read about his trip to the moon in his own
words.

- Last Man On The Moon http://www.pbs.org/wgbh/nova/tothemoon/lastman.html
- Eugene Cernan http://www.astronauts.org/astronauts/cernan.htm

View the earth or the moon. See day and night on earth. These are fabulous pictures!
- Earth and Moon Viewer http://www.fourmilab.ch/earthview/vplanet.html
  - Moon View http://www.fourmilab.ch/cgi-bin/uncgi/Earth/action?opt=-m&img=Moon.evif
  - Earth View http://www.fourmilab.ch/cgi-bin/uncgi/Earth/action?opt=-p

Discover the Moon

For an absolutely outstanding web site about the moon, its features, landscape, phases and excellent pictures, go to A.Cidadão's Lunar and Planetary Observation Home Page. This is an excellent place to begin any study of the moon.
- Lunar and Planetary Observation Home Page http://www.astrosurf.com/cidadao/index.htm

Another excellent all-purpose site about the moon is from Nine Planets.
- The Moon http://seds.lpl.arizona.edu/nineplanets/nineplanets/luna.html

The Moon in Folklore and Legend

The moon of course has intrigued man since the beginning of time. From that fascination come a number of common questions about the moon. It is made of cheese? Is there a man in the moon or a rabbit? What is a blue moon? Does the Earth have two moons? Inquiring minds want to know.
- Is the Moon Made of Cheese? http://www.katy.isd.tenet.edu/pathways/resources/sci/moon.htm
- Man In The Moon http://www.crosswinds.net/~pignut/Man_in_moon.html
- Folklore of the Blue Moon http://www.griffithobs.org/IPSBlueMoon.html
- What is a blue moon? http://www.skypub.com/sights/moonplanets/9905bluemoon.html
- Jules Verne - From Earth to the Moon http://www.seds.org/billa/tnp/hypo.html#moon2
- Jules Verne – From Earth to the Moon (full text) http://www.literature.org/authors/verne-jules/earth-to-the-moon/index.html
- Jules Verne - From Earth to the Moon (annotated with hyperlinks) http://authorsdirectory.com/c/moon10a.htm

Odds and Ends

Bad Astronomy offers explanations for two frequently asked questions about the moon.
- Why does the Moon look larger on the horizon than overhead? http://www.badastronomy.com/bad/misc/moonbig.html
- How does the Moon cause tides on the Earth? http://www.badastronomy.com/bad/misc/tides.html

This links provide some interesting crafts and projects.
- Moon Day Crafts and Projects http://familycrafts.about.com/library/spdays/bljuly20th.htm?once=true&
- Coloring http://www.coloring.ws/space.htm

Find out about the Korean Festival, Taeborum.
- Taeborum – 1st Full Moon http://www.clickasia.co.kr/about/h0115.htm

Send someone a Moon Day card.
- Full Moon Day Cards http://www.greetsomeone.com/april/fullmoon.htm

July 23, 1827
1st Swimming School

The American Red Cross says that the best thing anyone can do to stay safe in and around the water is to learn how to swim.[vii] The first swimming school was in Boston, MA. Some of the first students were John Q. Adams and James Audubon. Have the students make posters of the safe swimming tips at the American Red Cross site. Ask if you can display them at your local swimming pool.

- American Red Cross Water Safety
http://www.redcross.org/services/hss/tips/healthtips/safetywater.html

Odds and Ends

Do you have students who are interested in becoming a lifeguard? Lead them to this site information.

- Life Guarding http://www.redcross.org/services/hss/aquatics/lifegard.html

How about USA Swim Team? Check out the different events, athletes and results. For current information, use a search engine like www.google.com and search for: Olympics+swim

- USA Swimming Home http://www.usswim.org/
- Olympic Sports: Swimming http://www.sportsline.com/u/olympics/index.html

One of the most famous swimming challenges in the world is to swim the English Channel. Investigate this demanding sport.

- Channel Swimming Association http://www.channelswimmingassociation.com/
- Swim the English Channel http://www.usms.org/longdist/englishchannel.shtml

July 25
Chincoteague Pony Penning

Different legends explain how the ponies came to live on Chincoteague Island, Virginia. Today, there is a herd of approximately 150 wild ponies. The size of the herd is managed by the annual sale of roughly 80 ponies. The proceeds of the sale go to the Chincoteague Fire Department. For beautiful pictures and more history of the Chincoteague Pony penning and auction, refer to these web sites.

- Chincoteague Pony Penning http://www.chincoteague.com/pony/ponies.html
- The Pony Cam http://www.theponycam.com/
- The Chincoteague Pony http://www.imh.org/imh/bw/chinco.html
- National Chincoteague Pony Association http://www.pony-chincoteague.com/
- Chincoteague Island, VA http://www.chincoteague.com/
- The Chincoteague Pony http://www.ansi.okstate.edu/breeds/HORSES/CHINCOTE/index.htm

Persuasive Letter

Award winning author Marguerite Henry wrote *Misty of Chincoteague* based on a real-life pony from Chincoteague Island. Every child, at some point in his or her life, wishes for a pony. Have the students write a letter to their parents asking to go to the pony auction and purchase a pony. Explain in the letter how they will earn the money to buy it, how they will afford to care for it, where they will keep it, and how they will train. Most importantly, explain why this is so important to them.
Read about the real Misty.

- Hoof Prints in the Sand http://www.sover.net/~eohippus/feral/pen.htm

Have your students participate in the webquest: A Trip to Misty's Home.

- WebQuest http://www.plainfield.k12.in.us/hschool/webq/webq21/misty.htm

Learn more about Marguerite Henry.

- Marguerite Henry http://tlc.ai.org/henry.htm

July 28, 1866
Beatrix Potter's Birthday

> *"Once upon a time there were four little Rabbits, and their names were -*
> *Flopsy, Mopsy, Cottontail, and Peter. They lived with their Mother in a*
> *sand-bank, underneath the root of a very big tree"*
>
> Beatrix Potter - The Tale of Peter Rabbit[viii]

Helen Beatrix Potter grew up in Victorian England. As the daughter of wealthy socialites, she was educated at home. Her governess encouraged her artwork and other lady-like pursuits. Her parents were frequently away and her only brother at school. Therefore, her companions were the household servants and a collection of animals that were kept in the attic. It was years later that she wrote what is now a famous letter to that same governesses son. That letter was to become one of the most popular and beloved children's book of all time – *The Tale of Peter Rabbit*. Beatrix Potter was to become a world-renowned author, illustrator, sheep farmer and the owner of Hill Top Farm, now in trust for the children of the world. Read more about her fascinating life and the characters she developed.

- Beatrix Potter http://homepage.fcgnetworks.net/tortakales/Illustrators/Potter.html
- Beatrix Potter http://www.pitt.edu/~enroom/illustrators/potter.htm
- Beatrix Potter http://www.btinternet.com/~lake.district/bpotter.htm

Author Interview
Interview the author by having the students develop a list of questions they would ask Beatrix Potter if they could. A good way to have students ask interesting questions is to look at Bloom's Taxonomy. Answer the questions using the student / Beatrix Potter format.

- Bloom's Taxonomy Questions http://www.kcmetro.cc.mo.us/longview/ctac/blooms.htm

Enjoy Peter Rabbit and Friends Online
The following sites have books, games and projects related to Peter Rabbit. You can also enjoy many of her illustrations and read a copy of the original Peter Rabbit letter.

- Kids Corner http://www.tcom.ohiou.edu/books/kids.htm
- Official Peter Rabbit Web Site http://www.peterrabbit.co.uk/index.html
- Illustrations http://www.pitt.edu/~enroom/illustrators/potter.htm#letter
- Letter http://www.pitt.edu/~enroom/illustrators/potter.htm#letter

Victorian Lifestyle
Beatrix Potter grew up during the Victorian period. This was the period of time during Queen Victoria's reign. Have the students compare and contrast a Victorian house with their house. View a Victorian house, school and ice-cream parlor at the Samantha's World site. Have students take a picture of their schoolroom or local fast food establishment. Import the picture to a word document or slide. Use text boxes to explain different objects. Draw arrows from the text box to the object.

- Samantha's World http://www.americangirl.com/collection/samantha/sam_world_main.html

Learn more about Victorian England
- Victorian England http://www.britainexpress.com/History/Victorian_index.htm
- Victorian Crafts http://www.geocities.com/allamericankids/victorianpage.html

A Selection of Beatrix's Potters Books
The Tale of Peter Rabbit
The Tailor of Gloucester
The Tale of Squirrel Nutkin
The Tale of Two Bad Mice
 The tale of Benjamin Bunny
The Tale of Mrs. Tiggy-winkle
The Tale of Mr. Jeremy Fisher
The Tale of Tom Kitten
The Tale of Jemima Puddle-Duck
Apply Dapply's Nursery Rhymes

July 31, 1790
U.S. Patent Office
The first patent was granted to Samuel Hopkins for his formula for making soap.[ix] Today, there are literally thousands of patents, trademarks and copyrights issued to inventors and other creative individuals. A patent protects a person's invention or intellectual property. The U. S. Patent Office was established by the constitution "to promote the progress of science and the useful arts by securing for limited times to inventors the exclusive right to their respective discoveries." (Article 1, Section 8 of the United States Constitution). Visit the U. S. Patent Office and tour the Museum. The Kids Pages offer many activities and an easily understood explanation of what the office does and basic terminology.

- U.S. Patent Office http://www.uspto.gov
- Kids Pages http://www.uspto.gov/go/kids/

Trademarks
A trademark is a word, symbol, color or sound that distinguishes goods and services.[x] Research has shown that children as young as two can identify objects by it's trademark. Who doesn't recognize the Golden Arches? Brainstorm a list of trademarks using Inspirations' Rapid Fire feature. Then, have the students search the Internet for the product logo, such as the Niki® swash. Make a matching game showing the logo. If you use a program like PowerPoint, you can make a button that will take you to the correct answer.

The Trademark Game

Fill each square with a logo

Make the square a hyperlink to the page with the correct answer.

Note: You can download a demo copy of Inspiration @ http://www.inspiration.com/

Copyright
Copyrights protect the work of an author, poet, musician, or artist. The copyright lasts for the life of the person plus 70 years. So, J.K. Rowling will hold the copyright to Harry Potter for her whole life plus 70 years after she dies. Have the students learn how to document the sources they use in reports and projects.

- How to Compile a Bibliography http://www.intac.com/~aroldi/biblio.html
- Plagiarism: What it is and how to recognize it and avoid it
  http://www.indiana.edu/~wts/wts/plagiarism.html
- Twas the Night Before Christmas: A Lesson in Authorship and Style
  http://www.nytimes.com/learning/teachers/lessons/001027friday.html

[i] National Hot Dog and Sausage Council: Trivia http://www.hot-dog.org/hd_vitalstats.htm August 14, 2001

[ii] Jonathan Vos Post. Open Questions on the Correlation Between Television and Violence http://www.magicdragon.com/EmeraldCity/Nonfiction/socphil.html August 10, 2001

[iii] The 4th of July, William Edelen http://www.infidels.org/library/modern/william_edelen/the4thofjuly.html July 3, 2001

[iv] James R. Heintze, Fourth of July Celebrations Database http://www.american.edu/heintze/fourth.htm August 13, 2001

[v] Educational Paperback Association. E. B. White http://www.edupaperback.org/authorbios/White_EB.html August 7, 2001

[vi] Mel Gussow. Obituary of Garth Williams *New York Times,* May 10, 1996 http://www.winsor.edu/library2/ebgwobit.htm August 8, 2001

[vii] American Red Cross http://www.redcross.org/services/hss/tips/healthtips/safetywater.html August 13, 2001

[viii] Official Peter Rabbit Web Site http://www.peterrabbit.co.uk/index.html August 9, 2001

[ix] U. S. Patent Office: Kids Pages' Frequently Asked Questions http://www.uspto.gov/go/kids/kidprimer.html August 9, 2001

[x] U. S. Patent Office: Kids Pages' Frequently Asked Questions http://www.uspto.gov/go/kids/kidprimer.html August 9, 2001

5/7/2002